Transnational Portuguese Studies

Transnational Modern Languages

Transnational Modern Languages promotes a model of Modern Languages not as the inquiry into separate national traditions, but as the study of languages, cultures and their interactions. The series aims to demonstrate the value – practical and commercial, as well as academic and cultural – of modern language study when conceived as transnational cultural enquiry.

The texts in the series are specifically targeted at a student audience. They address how work on the transnational and the transcultural broadens the confines of Modern Languages; opens an extensive range of objects of research to analysis; deploys a complex set of methodologies; and can be accomplished through the exposition of clearly articulated examples.

The series is anchored by *Transnational Modern Languages: A Handbook*, ed. Jenny Burns (Warwick) and Derek Duncan (St. Andrews), which sets out the theoretical and conceptual scope of the series, the type of research on which it is based and the kinds of questions that it asks. Following on from the *Handbook*, the series includes a text for the study of the following Modern Languages:

Transnational French Studies, ed. Charles Forsdick (Liverpool) and Claire Launchbury (Leeds)

Transnational German Studies, ed. Rebecca Braun (Lancaster) and Ben Schofield (KCL)

Transnational Spanish Studies, ed. Catherine Davies (IMLR) and Rory O'Bryen (Cambridge)

Transnational Italian Studies, ed. Charles Burdett (Durham) and Loredana Polezzi (Cardiff)

Transnational Portuguese Studies, ed. Hilary Owen (Manchester/Oxford) and Claire Williams (Oxford)

Transnational Russian Studies, ed. Andy Byford (Durham), Connor Doak (Bristol) and Stephen Hutchings (Manchester)

Transnational Portuguese Studies

edited by
Hilary Owen and Claire Williams

LIVERPOOL UNIVERSITY PRESS

First published 2020 by
Liverpool University Press
4 Cambridge Street
Liverpool
L69 7ZU

Copyright © 2020 Liverpool University Press

The right of Hilary Owen and Claire Williams to be identified as the editors of this work has been asserted by them in accordance with the Copyright, Designs and Patents Act 1988.

All rights reserved. No part of this book may be reproduced, stored in a retrieval system, or transmitted, in any form or by any means, electronic, mechanical, photocopying, recording, or otherwise, without the prior written permission of the publisher.

British Library Cataloguing-in-Publication data
A British Library CIP record is available

ISBN 978-1-78962-139-6 (HB)
ISBN 978-1-78962-140-2 (PB)

Typeset by Carnegie Book Production, Lancaster
Printed in the UK by CPI Group (UK) Ltd, Croydon CR0 4YY

In memory of Fernando Arenas,
a brilliant inspiration, a great colleague and a warm friend.

Contents

Illustrations and Table xi
Acknowledgements xv
Contributors xvii

Introduction: Transnationalizing Portuguese Studies 1
Hilary Owen and Claire Williams

Part I. Spatiality

1. Global Navigations and the Challenge of World-Making: Introducing the Study of Spatiality in the Portuguese Empire 23
   Zoltán Biedermann

2. Translational Travails of Lusotropicalism 43
   Anna M. Klobucka

3. English Pirates in Brazil: Early Anglo-Portuguese Relations in the New World 57
   Vivien Kogut Lessa de Sá and Sheila Moura Hue

4. Soundtracks of the Lusophone and Creolophone Spheres: 'Tanto' by Aline Frazão (Angola), 'Kreol' by Mário Lúcio (Cape Verde) and 'N na nega bedju' by José Carlos Schwarz (Guinea-Bissau) 71
   Fernando Arenas

viii   *Transnational Portuguese Studies*

5. Transnational, Palimpsestic Journeys in the Art of Bartolomeu
   Cid dos Santos   91
   Maria Luísa Coelho

6. 'Becoming Portuguese': New Europes for Old in Miguel
   Gomes's *Arabian Nights*   109
   Hilary Owen

Part II.   Language

7. Lusotopian or Lusophone Atlantics? The Relevance of
   Transnational African Diasporas to the Question of Language
   and Culture   129
   Toby Green and José Lingna Nafafé

8. Portuguese as a Transnational Language   149
   Susana Afonso

9. Beyond Comprehension: Language, Identity and the
   Transnational in Gil Vicente's Theatre   167
   Simon Park

10. Dialects in Translation: Travelling in Space and Time in the
    Portuguese-Speaking World with *Pygmalion* and *My Fair Lady*   183
    Sara Ramos Pinto

11. The Duality and Ambiguity of Mega-Events in Rio de Janeiro:
    Local and Transnational Dimensions of Urban Transformations
    in the Webdocumentary *Domínio Público*   201
    Tori Holmes

Part III.   Temporality

12. Mining Memory's Archive: Two Portuguese Documentaries
    about the Second World War   221
    Ellen W. Sapega

13. Disjunctive Temporalities of Migration in Photobooks
    from Brazil   233
    Edward King

14. The National and the Transnational in Brazilian
    Postdictatorship Cinema   249
    Tatiana Heise

15. Remembering *New Portuguese Letters* Transnationally: Memory, Emotion, Mobility 267
    Ana Margarida Dias Martins

Part IV. Subjectivity

16. 'Publish and be Damned': *Memórias da Minha Vida* and the Politics of Exclusion in Nineteenth-Century Portugal 285
    Cláudia Pazos Alonso

17. Transnational Pessoa 299
    Paulo de Medeiros

18. Sound Travel: Fadocore in California 317
    Kimberly DaCosta Holton

19. 'Can't We All Just Be Queer?' On Imagining Shared Translational Space 337
    Christopher Larkosh

20. International Departures and Transnational Texts in Contemporary Brazilian Literature: The 'Amores Expressos' Series 353
    Claire Williams

Index 367

Illustrations and Table

Figure 1.1.   The Indian Ocean region in the Miller Atlas attributed to Lopo Homem, Pedro Reinel, Jorge Reinel and António de Holanda, Lisbon, 1519. Image by kind permission of Bibliothèque nationale de France, Paris, Cartes et Plans, GE DD-683 (RES).   28

Figure 1.2.   View of Macau by Pedro Barreto de Resende, in António Bocarro's *Livro das plantas das fortalezas*, c. 1635. Image by kind permission of Biblioteca Pública de Évora, Évora, Reservados 091 Liv.   31

Figure 5.1.   Detail of stone panel by Bartolomeu Cid dos Santos, Entrecampos metro station, Lisbon. Photograph by Maria Luísa Coelho. Image by kind permission of Fernanda Paixão dos Santos.   92

Figure 5.2.   Detail of stone panel by Bartolomeu Cid dos Santos, Entrecampos metro station, Lisbon. Photograph by Maria Luísa Coelho. Image by kind permission of Fernanda Paixão dos Santos.   94

Figure 5.3.   Detail of stone panel by Bartolomeu Cid dos Santos, Entrecampos metro station, Lisbon. Photograph by Maria Luísa Coelho. Image by kind permission of Fernanda Paixão dos Santos.   101

Figure 5.4.	Bartolomeu Cid dos Santos, *Homenagem a Cesário* [*Homage to Cesário*], 1985, etching and aquatint, 106 x 75 cm. Photograph by Paulo Costa. Image by kind permission of Fernanda Paixão dos Santos and the Museu Calouste Gulbenkian – Fundação Calouste Gulbenkian, Lisbon.	102
Figure 5.5.	Bartolomeu Cid dos Santos, *Africa Discovered*, 1981, mixed media, 60 x 51 cm. Image by kind permission of Fernanda Paixão dos Santos.	105
Figure 6.1.	The EU Troika and members of the Portuguese government. Still from *Arabian Nights. Vol. 1. The Restless One.* Directed by Miguel Gomes. © O Som e a Fúria, Shellac Sud, Komplizen Films, Box Productions, Agat Films, ARTE France Cinéma and ZDF/ARTE. 2015.	118
Figure 6.2.	Parliament Steps Invasion. Still from *Arabian Nights. Vol. 3. The Enchanted One.* Directed by Miguel Gomes. © O Som e a Fúria, Shellac Sud, Komplizen Films, Box Productions, Agat Films, ARTE France Cinéma and ZDF/ARTE. 2015.	122
Table 8.1.	Estimated population of Brazil, 1538–1890. Reproduced from Alberto Mussa, 'O papel das línguas africanas na história do português do Brasil', unpublished master's thesis submitted to the Universidade Federal do Rio de Janeiro (1991), p. 163, cited in John Holm, *Languages in Contact: The Partial Restructuring of Vernaculars* (Cambridge: Cambridge University Press, 2004), p. 50.	155
Figure 11.1.	Activist graffiti on a promotional hoarding for construction work relating to the Rio Olympics. Still from *Domínio Público* crowdfunding video, 2012. Producer: Paêbirú Realizações Coletivas. Directed by Fausto Mota, Raoni Vidal and Henrique Ligeiro.	213
Figure 12.1.	Still from *Sob céus estranhos*. Directed by Daniel Blaufuks. © Lx Filmes. 2002.	226
Figure 12.2.	Still from *Fantasia Lusitana*. Directed by João Canijo. © Periferia Filmes. 2010.	229

Illustrations and Table   xiii

Figure 13.1. Photograph of bloodied hands in *Tcharafna*.
Image by kind permission of Gui Mohallem.   240

Figure 13.2. Photograph of family home in Fakiha.
Image by kind permission of Gui Mohallem.   243

Figure 13.3. Still from 'reading video' embedded in Gui Mohallem's website. Image by kind permission of Gui Mohallem.   247

Figure 14.1. The political prisoners released in exchange for US Ambassador to Brazil Charles Burke Elbrick (1969–70) before boarding the flight to Mexico at the Rio de Janeiro International Airport on 7 September 1969. Nine of the surviving prisoners are interviewed in *Hércules 56*. Still from *Dia que Durou 21 Anos*. Directed by Camilo Tavares. © Pequi Filmes and TV Brasil. 2012. Image by kind permission of Camilo Tavares.   254

Figure 14.2. US Ambassador to Brazil Lincoln Gordon (1961–66) and Brazilian President João Goulart (1961–64). Still from *Dia que Durou 21 Anos*. Directed by Camilo Tavares. © Pequi Filmes and TV Brasil. 2012. Image by kind permission of Camilo Tavares.   259

Figure 17.1. Illustration from *Eu, Fernando Pessoa em quadrinhos*, by Susana Ventura and Eloar Guazzelli. Image by kind permission of Susana Ventura and Eloar Guazzelli, and Editora Peirópolis.   311

Figure 17.2. Illustration from *A Vida Oculta de Fernando Pessoa*, written by André F. Morgado and illustrated by Alexandre Leoni. Image by kind permission of André F. Morgado and Alexandre Leoni.   312

Figure 18.1. *Judith and Holofernes* cover art, 2003. Image by kind permission of Chris da Rosa.   329

Figure 18.2. *Judith and Holofernes* cover art, 2005. Image by kind permission of Chris da Rosa.   330

Figure 18.3. *Judith and Holofernes* cover art, 2006. Image by kind permission of Chris da Rosa.   331

Acknowledgements

First and foremost, we are heavily indebted to our excellent contributors for their long-term commitment to this project. It was particularly gratifying to see so many of us presenting versions of our chapters at the ABIL (Association of British and Irish Lusitanists) Conference at Edinburgh University, in September 2019. We are also very much indebted to the series editors – Charles Burdett, Jenny Burns, Derek Duncan and Loredana Polezzi – for their always valuable and supportive guidance and insight. The project and the teamwork with other Transnational Modern Languages series editors have been an absolute pleasure. We also thank Chloe Johnson and Sarah Warren and their respective teams at Liverpool University Press for their unfailing patience and expertise.

We would like to thank the colleagues with whom we have discussed ideas presented in the introduction, to ensure it speaks to different constituencies within our very expansive field: linguists, early modernists and those studying the many and varied Lusophone countries. We extend our particular gratitude to Ellen Sapega, Anna M. Klobucka, Zoltán Biedermann and Lúcia Sá for their specific critical contributions. The anonymous reviewers of the whole volume raised very pertinent and constructive points, which we very much appreciate.

Thanks are due to all those who have authorized the use of images and quotations in this volume, and those who helped us locate and contact the copyright holders. In particular, we acknowledge the generosity of:

Teresa Schwarz and family, and Yannick Jame of Rossio Music, for permission to use lyrics by José Carlos Schwarz in Chapter 4.

Mário Lúcio and Clémence Bianconi and François Post at Africa Nostra for permission to use lyrics by Mário Lúcio, also in Chapter 4.

Thank you to our students, past, present and future, for their enthusiasm for the languages and cultures of the Portuguese-speaking world, which reminds us why we chose to study them in the first place and why we are committed to passing them on.

Hilary would also like to thank Claire for her wonderful partnership in this endeavour and for providing both the cover photo for this volume and the memorable academic visit to Macau University in 2007, which occasioned it. And finally, Hilary most warmly thanks Marlo, Maya and, most especially, as always, Till, for his assistance with the cover design and the index, and his unstinting help and support in countless other ways.

Claire thanks Hilary for being such a generous and dynamic co-editor and colleague. She is grateful to all the friends she has made on her travels round the Lusophone world and especially to Giles and Emily for sharing adventures at home and abroad.

Contributors

Susana Afonso is Senior Lecturer in Portuguese in the Department of Modern Languages at the University of Exeter. Her research interests focus on non-standard and vernacular varieties of Portuguese around the world. She was a member of a Leverhulme Trust international network on 'Shifting Sociolinguistic realities in the nation of East Timor and its diasporas' and has published on the Portuguese spoken in East Timor as well as on the East Timorese diaspora in Portugal. More recently, she has collaborated on a project that aims to measure the distance between the two major national varieties of Portuguese (Brazilian and European) from a cognitive sociolinguistics perspective.

Cláudia Pazos Alonso is Professor of Portuguese and Gender Studies, Wadham College, University of Oxford. Her research interests range widely across modern Lusophone literature. Book publications include *Imagens do Eu na Poesia de Florbela Espanca* (Lisbon: IN-CM, 1996); *Antigone's Daughters? Gender, Genealogy, and the Politics of Authorship in 20th-Century Portuguese Women's Writing* (Lewisburg, PA: Bucknell University Press, 2011, with Hilary Owen); the co-edited volumes *Closer to the Wild Heart: Essays on Clarice Lispector* (Oxford: Legenda, 2002, with Claire Williams), *A Companion to Portuguese Literature* (Woodbridge: Tamesis, 2009, with Stephen Parkinson and T. F. Earle), *Reading Literature in Portuguese: Commentaries in Honour of Tom Earle* (Oxford: Legenda, 2013, with Stephen Parkinson); and new editions of the works of Florbela Espanca and Judith Teixeira (with Fabio Mario da Silva). She is currently Vice-President of the International Association of Lusitanists. Her most recent monograph is entitled, *Francisca Wood and Nineteenth-Century Periodical Culture: Pressing for Change* (Oxford: Legenda, 2020).

Fernando Arenas was a full professor at the University of Michigan-Ann Arbor, in the field of Portuguese, with an emphasis on film, literature and popular music, which he studied through an interdisciplinary and theoretical prism centring on the triad of postcolonialism, migrations and globalization. He received his PhD at the University of California, Berkeley in 1994 and taught for 16 years in the Department of Spanish and Portuguese Studies at the University of Minnesota. In 2005–06, he was awarded a Guggenheim Fellowship for the completion of *Lusophone Africa: Beyond Independence* (Minneapolis, MN: University of Minnesota Press, 2011), a revised and expanded version of which was published in 2019 in Portuguese translation: *África lusófona: além da independência* (São Paulo: Edusp, 2019). He also authored *Utopias of Otherness: Nationhood and Subjectivity in Portugal and Brazil* (Minneapolis, MN: University of Minnesota Press, 2003) and co-edited, with Susan Canty Quinlan, *Lusosex: Gender and Sexuality in the Portuguese-Speaking World* (Minneapolis, MN: University of Minnesota Press, 2002). At the time of his death in October 2019, Fernando Arenas was working on migratory flows in the Portuguese-speaking world and issues related to interculturality, community and citizenship.

Zoltán Biedermann is Professor of Early Modern History in the School of European Languages, Cultures and Society, University College London (UCL). He has helped to create the Portuguese and Brazilian Studies programme at UCL. His research on the early modern Portuguese Empire in Asia focuses on diplomacy, imperial literature, cartography, visual culture and the politics of space. He is the author of *(Dis)connected Empires: Imperial Portugal, Sri Lankan Diplomacy, and the Making of a Habsburg Conquest in Asia* (Oxford: Oxford University Press, 2018), *The Portuguese in Sri Lanka and South India* (Wiesbaden: Harrassowitz, 2014), *The Historical Atlas of the Persian Gulf* (Turnhout: Brepols, 2006) and *Soqotra: Geschichte einer christlichen Insel im Indischen Ozean* (Wiesbaden: Harrassowitz, 2006). He has also co-edited *Global Gifts: The Material Culture of Diplomacy in Early Modern Eurasia* (New York: Cambridge University Press, 2018, with Anne Gerritsen and Giorgio Riello), *Sri Lanka at the Crossroads of History* (London: UCL Press, 2017, with Alan Strathern) and *From the Supernatural to the Uncanny* (Newcastle: Cambridge Scholars, 2017, with Stephen M. Hart).

Maria Luísa Coelho is a post-doctoral fellow at the University of Oxford and Universidade do Minho, where she is developing a project entitled *Portuguese Artists and Writers in Britain (1950–1986): Cultural Networks and Identities in Transit* (Fundação para a Ciência e a Tecnologia grant: reference SFRH/BPD/112293/2015). She holds a PhD in Comparative Literature; her thesis focused on representations of the female body and women's experiences by Portuguese and English women writers and artists. Luísa's recent publications include 'Woman-Body-Paint: Helena Almeida and the Visual Inscription of Sexual Difference' (in *Luso-Brazilian Review*) and 'On Appropriation and Craft: Considering the Feminist Problem of De-politicization' (in *n.paradoxa*). She co-edited with Cláudia Pazos Alonso, a special issue of *Portuguese Studies*, 35.2 (2019) on 'Transnational Portuguese Women Writers' and curated the exhibition 'Identities in Transit: Portuguese Women Artists since 1950' at the University of Oxford in 2017.

Toby Green is Senior Lecturer in Lusophone African History and Culture at King's College London. He is the author of *The Rise of the Trans-Atlantic Slave Trade in Western Africa, 1300–1589* (Cambridge: Cambridge University Press, 2012); and *A Fistful of Shells: West Africa From the Rise of the Slave Trade to the Age of Revolution* (London and Chicago, IL: Allen Lane/Chicago University Press, 2019). He is Chair of the UK Fontes Historiae Africanae Committee and Treasurer of the UK African Studies Association.

Tatiana Heise is Lecturer in Hispanic Studies at the University of Glasgow's School of Modern Languages and Cultures. She is Principal Investigator of the Leverhulme-funded project 'Memories of the Dictatorship', which examines the role of cinema in reconstructing collective memories of traumatic sociopolitical events in Brazil, Chile and Argentina. Heise has authored a monograph, *Remaking Brazil: Contested National Identities in Contemporary Brazilian Cinema* (Cardiff: University of Wales Press, 2012) and numerous articles on political cinema, documentary activism and the sociology of cinema. Her teaching experience includes Latin American Culture, Film Studies and Comparative Literature. Prior to her academic career she worked as Education Manager for an environmental and animal welfare agency in the Amazon region of Brazil.

Tori Holmes is Lecturer in Brazilian Studies at Queen's University Belfast. Her main research interests are digital culture and the texts and practices of urban representation in Brazil, particularly relating to the *favelas* of Rio de Janeiro. She has worked on blogging by *favela* residents and webdocumentaries relating to urban change in Rio during the city's preparations to host the World Cup and Olympics, and her current research focuses on data activism relating to public security in Rio. Dr Holmes also has broader interests in Brazilian documentary and audiovisual production, as well as digital ethnography and ethical and methodological issues in interdisciplinary research. Her publications include articles in *Journal of Latin American Cultural Studies, Journal of Urban Cultural Studies,* and *Journal of Iberian and Latin American Studies.* She is one of the founders of REBRAC (European Network of Brazilianists working in Cultural Analysis).

Kimberly DaCosta Holton is Chair and Associate Professor in the Department of Spanish and Portuguese Studies at Rutgers University, Newark. She researches expressive culture in the Portuguese-speaking world, focusing particularly on the intersections between politics, performance and migration. She is the author of *Performing Folklore: Ranchos Folclóricos from Lisbon to Newark* (Bloomington, IL: Indiana University Press, 2005) and co-editor with Andrea Klimt of *Community, Culture and the Makings of Identity: Portuguese-Americans Along the Eastern Seaboard* (Amherst, MA: University of Massachusetts Press, 2009). She has received fellowships from the Ford Foundation, the Social Science Research Council and the Institute for Research on Women. Her scholarly articles and translations have appeared in numerous academic journals and edited volumes. Holton is the founder and director of the Ironbound Oral History Project and is currently at work on a book about *fado* performance in the USA.

Sheila Moura Hue is Senior Lecturer in the Department of Languages and Literature at the Universidade do Estado do Rio de Janeiro (UERJ). She has published widely on early modern Portuguese literature, book history and colonial Brazil, and edited a number of early modern Portuguese documents, most notably early Jesuit letters, *Primeiras Cartas do Brasil* (Rio de Janeiro: Zahar, 2006) and a collection of dialogues: *Diálogos em defesa e louvor da língua portuguesa* (Rio de Janeiro: 7Letras, 2007). She has coordinated the cataloguing of the manuscript collection of the Real Gabinete Português de Leitura in Rio de Janeiro. Her most recent publication is an annotated edition of a selection of Camões's sonnets: *20 sonetos* (Campinas, SP: Editora da Unicamp, 2018). Dr Hue is a member of the Brazilian group working on the critical edition of *Os Lusíadas*, a project led by the Centro Interuniversitário de Estudos Camonianos da Universidade de Coimbra.

Edward King is Senior Lecturer in the School of Modern Languages, University of Bristol. His research examines interconnections between culture and technology in Latin America, focusing on cultural practices that explore the shifting power dynamics of the digital age. He has published two monographs, *Science Fiction and Digital Technologies in Argentine and Brazilian Culture* (New York: Palgrave Macmillan, 2013) and *Virtual Orientalism in Brazilian Culture* (New York: Palgrave Macmillan, 2015), and a book co-authored with Joanne Page: *Posthumanism and the Graphic Novel in Latin America* (London: University College London Press, 2017).

Anna M. Klobucka is Professor of Portuguese and Women's and Gender Studies at the University of Massachusetts Dartmouth. She is the author of *The Portuguese Nun: Formation of a National Myth* (Lewisburg, PA: Bucknell University Press, 2000); Portuguese translation (Lisbon: IN-CM, 2006), *O Formato Mulher: A Emergência da Autoria Feminina na Poesia Portuguesa* (Coimbra: Angelus Novus, 2009) and *O Mundo Gay de António Botto* (Lisbon: Sistema Solar, 2018). She has also co-edited *After the Revolution: Twenty Years of Portuguese Literature 1974–1994* (Lewisburg, PA: Bucknell University Press, 1997, with Helena Kaufman), *Embodying Pessoa: Corporeality, Gender, Sexuality* (Toronto: University of Toronto Press, 2007, with Mark Sabine); Portuguese edition (Lisbon: Assírio e Alvim, 2010) and *Gender, Empire and Postcolony: Luso-Afro-Brazilian Intersections* (New York: Palgrave Macmillan 2014, with Hilary Owen). She is the editor of the Portuguese Language Textbook Series and co-editor of the journal *Portuguese Literary and Cultural Studies*, both published by Tagus Press/Center for Portuguese Studies and Culture at UMass Dartmouth.

Christopher Larkosh is Associate Professor of Portuguese at the University of Massachusetts Dartmouth. He has published and lectured around the world in a number of global languages, not only in relation to Portuguese-speaking, colonial and diasporic cultures, but also others including Quebec, Argentina, Italy, France, Germany, Turkey, south and east Asia, as well as on the transnational, cross-cultural and gendered interactions between them. He is the author of numerous articles in academic journals such as *Social Dynamics, TOPIA, TTR, The Translator,* and *Transgender Studies Quarterly*, as well as the Routledge/Taylor & Francis journal *Translation Studies*, for which he was reviews editor 2012–14. He is the editor of *Re-Engendering Translation: Transcultural Practice, Gender/Sexuality and the Politics of Alterity* (London and New York: St Jerome/Routledge, 2011) and has co-edited two volumes in transcultural studies: *Writing Spaces*, compiled in collaboration with colleagues in Taiwan (Kaohsiung: NSYSU Press, 2013), and *KulturConfusão: German-Brazilian Interculturalities* (Berlin: De Gruyter, 2015), with Anke Finger and Gabi Kathofer.

Ana Margarida Dias Martins is Senior Lecturer in Portuguese Studies at the University of Exeter, where she helped establish the BA in Portuguese Studies. She is the co-founder of EXCELAS, the Exeter Centre of Latin American Studies. She acts as web liaison for the Lusophone pages of the Centre for the Study of Contemporary Women's Writing (CCWW) at the Institute of Modern Languages Research, University of London. She is the recipient of an AHRC Early Career Leadership Fellows grant (start date: February 2018) with a project entitled: 'Women of the Brown Atlantic: Real and Imaginary Passages in Portuguese, 1711–2011'. She is the author of *Magic Stones and Flying Snakes: Gender and the Postcolonial Exotic in the Work of Paulina Chiziane and Lídia Jorge* (Oxford: Peter Lang, 2012), co-editor, with Hilary Owen, Carmen Ramos Villar and Sheila Khan, of *The Luso-Tropical Tempest: Postcolonial Debates in Portuguese* (Bristol: HiPLAS, 2012), and co-author, with Emma-Jayne Abbots, Rocio Carvajal, Anna Charalambidou, Elaine Forde, Hazel Thomas, and Deborah Toner of *Authentic Recipes from Around the World* (Ceredigion: HAT events, 2015).

Paulo de Medeiros is Professor of English and Comparative Literary Studies at the University of Warwick, with a focus on Modern and Contemporary World Literatures. He was Associate Professor at Bryant College (USA) and Professor at Utrecht University before moving to Warwick. In 2011–12 he was Keeley Fellow at Wadham College, Oxford, and in 2013–14 president of the American Portuguese Studies Association (APSA). Most recently he has published *Pessoa's Geometry of the Abyss: Modernity and the Book of Disquiet* (Oxford: Legenda, 2013). His *O silêncio das Sereias: Ensaio sobre o Livro do Desassossego* (Lisbon: Tinta da China, 2015) was awarded the PEN Portugal Prize for best book of essays in 2016. Current projects include a study on post-imperial Europe.

José Lingna Nafafé is Lecturer in Portuguese and Lusophone Studies and Programme Director of the MA in Black Humanities at the University of Bristol, which he joined in 2014 from the University of Nottingham. He completed his PhD at the University of Birmingham (2001), where he subsequently lectured in various departments: Political Science, International Studies and Portuguese Studies. He was awarded a British Academy Small Grant on the integration and social mobility of African migrants in Europe in 2013. In 2016, he was awarded a Leverhulme Research Fellowship to undertake archival research in Brazil, Portugal, Spain and Italy for a project entitled 'Freedom and Lusophone African Diaspora in the Atlantic'. He is currently Senior Researcher for an ERC Standard Grant at the University of Bristol on 'Modern Marronage? The Pursuit and Practice of Freedom in the Contemporary World'. He has completed the first draft of his second monograph: *Lusophone Black Atlantic Abolition: Mendonça's Freedom Discourse, Brazil, Africa and Europe, 1626–1750*.

Hilary Owen is Professor Emerita of Portuguese and Luso-African Studies at the University of Manchester and Research Fellow in the Sub-Faculty of Portuguese at the University of Oxford. She is the author of *Mother Africa,*

Father Marx. Women's Writing of Mozambique, 1948–1992 (Lewisburg, PA: Bucknell University Press, 2007), co-author with Cláudia Pazos Alonso of *Antigone's Daughters? Gender, Genealogy and the Politics of Authorship in 20th-Century Portuguese Women's Writing* (Lewisburg, PA: Bucknell University Press, 2011), co-editor with Anna M. Klobucka of *Gender, Empire and Postcolony. Luso-Afro-Brazilian Intersections* (New York: Palgrave Macmillan, 2014) and co-editor with Mariana Liz of *Women's Cinema in Contemporary Portugal* (New York: Bloomsbury Press, 2020). She has published extensively on feminism, gender and postcolonial theory in Portuguese and Lusophone African literatures and film.

Simon Park is Associate Professor in Medieval and Renaissance Portuguese at the University of Oxford and Tutorial Fellow at St Anne's College, Oxford. He is co-editor, with Fernando Beleza, of *Mário de Sá-Carneiro, a Cosmopolitan Modernist* (Oxford: Legenda, 2016), and his work on early modern Portuguese literature has appeared in *MLQ*, *Portuguese Studies*, and *Veredas*. He is currently working on a book, provisionally entitled *From Paper to Gold: Poets, Patrons, and Printers in Sixteenth-Century Portugal*, that brings back to life the struggles poets faced in getting powerful people to recognize their work as valuable (both in abstract and financial terms).

Sara Ramos Pinto is Associate Professor in Translation Studies at the University of Leeds, where she was also Director of Translation Studies from 2014 to 2017. Before her current appointment, she was a Marie Curie ITN postdoctoral fellow (University of Turku, 2011–13), and held teaching positions at the University of Manchester (2009–11) and the University of Kent (2008–09). She holds a PhD in Translation Studies (University of Lisbon, 2010). She was a visiting research fellow at University College London (2006–09) and currently collaborates with the Centre for Comparative Studies (University of Lisbon). Parallel to her academic work, she is an experienced translator. Her research focuses on audiovisual and theatre translation, as she is interested in investigating the translation of multimodal products and the impact of specific translation strategies on audience interpretation and perception. She maintains a continued interest in linguistic variation and the challenges it brings to translation.

Vivien Kogut Lessa de Sá is Teaching Associate in Portuguese Studies at the University of Cambridge. Her main interests are comparative studies in Brazilian, Portuguese and English literatures, and early modern travel writing, especially in connection with the Americas. Her book *The Admirable Adventures and Strange Fortunes of Anthony Knivet: an English Pirate in*

Brazil (Cambridge: Cambridge University Press, 2015) is the first critical edition of one of the earliest descriptions of Brazil written by an Englishman. She has published articles on early modern travel to Brazil and has translated and co-edited, with Sheila Moura Hue, *Ingleses no Brasil – Relatos de viagem: 1526–1608* (Campinas, SP: Chão Editora, 2020), a collection of 12 English travel accounts, many hitherto untranslated into Portuguese or unpublished. Her most recent research focuses on the interactions between Jesuits, Indians and pirates in sixteenth-century Brazil.

Ellen W. Sapega is Professor in the Department of Spanish and Portuguese at the University of Wisconsin-Madison. Her publications include articles and book chapters on Portuguese modernism, memory, visual culture and commemoration since the late nineteenth century, and the contemporary Portuguese novel. She has published two monographs: *Ficções Modernistas* (Lisbon: ICALP, 1992) and *Consensus and Debate in Salazar's Portugal 1933–1948* (Philadelphia, PA: Pennsylvania State University Press, 2008) and is currently working on a book on visual and literary representations of Lisbon, Portugal, during the late twentieth and early twenty-first centuries.

Claire Williams is Associate Professor in Brazilian Literature and Culture at the University of Oxford and a Fellow of St Peter's College. She has published widely on contemporary women's writing, minority writing and life writing from the Lusophone world. Selected publications include *The Encounter Between Opposites in the Works of Clarice Lispector* (Bristol: HiPLA, 2006), *Feminine Singular: Women Growing up Through Life Writing* (Oxford: Peter Lang, 2017), with Maria José Blanco, and the forthcoming *After Clarice: Reading Lispector's Legacy in the Twenty-first Century*, with Adriana X. Jacobs (Oxford: Legenda, 2021). She is a member of the Grupo de Estudos em Literatura Brasileira Contemporânea research group based in Brasília and represents Portuguese on the Steering Committee of the Centre for the Study of Contemporary Women's Writing (CCWW), University of London. She sits on the editorial boards of journals such as *Portuguese Studies*, the *Journal of Lusophone Studies* and the *Bulletin of Contemporary Hispanic Studies*.

Introduction

Transnationalizing Portuguese Studies

Hilary Owen and Claire Williams

I caught the morning train to the place which I had always been told was the centre of the universe: the railway junction at Entroncamento. There all the trains on earth met and crossed, carrying men of different races, from the north and the south, crusaders and Muhammadans. These were the fantasies I had carried with me through time, on my peregrinations through the missionary schools. [...] We were in an empty station, full of hot metal tracks that burned beneath the train, which slept on the line like a dead boa constrictor. I asked where all the other trains were and all the different people who should be there, shouting, weeping, embracing, loving, killing and dying. It should have been the place where, for better or worse, men revealed what they were capable of. In the name of God and all His symbols. But it was like a desert, a silent, abandoned place where the remnants of empire were slowly dribbling away.[1]

Luís Cardoso, *The Crossing. A Story of East Timor*

In his autobiographical memoir, *The Crossing*, the East Timorese writer Luís Cardoso records a sense of comic bewilderment when he arrives at the train station in Entroncamento, a small railway town (whose name literally means 'junction') located 60 miles north of Portugal's capital city, Lisbon. A critical and recalcitrant offspring of empire, Cardoso takes a decidedly

---

[1] Luís Cardoso, *The Crossing. A Story of East Timor*, trans. Margaret Jull Costa (London: Granta, 2000), p. 113.

1

unflattering view of the Portuguese-speaking 'homeland' in Europe, which he has been taught, since his childhood in the Asian colony of East Timor, to think of as the metropolitan hub of his cognitive universe. In this, he speaks eloquently to a centripetal fantasy of the languages, histories, and cultural influences that we have named as 'Portuguese' over the centuries. The railway tracks may promise, like the discoverers' ships, to connect different worlds, 'carrying men of different races, from the north and the south, crusaders and Muhammadans' but the sated body of the train, like that of the dead boa constrictor to which Cardoso compares it, has ingested all it can take.[2]

Cardoso describes his disappointment when he does not find in Entroncamento some divine manifestation of the 'worlds' that Portugal legendarily gave to the world. This assertion that Portugal's 'braço vencedor / Deu mundos novos ao Mundo' ['all-conquering arm / Gave new worlds to the World'] originally comes from Luís Vaz de Camões's epic maritime expansion poem of 1572, *Os Lusíadas* [*The Lusiads*], but it was also famously reprised in Henrique Lopes Mendonça's patriotic poem of 1890, 'A Portuguesa', which became the Portuguese national anthem.[3] In common with Camões and Mendonça, although obviously to different ends, Cardoso imagines Portugal here as the heart of a Ptolemaic, geocentric system of the universe, with the earth at its hub orbited by a circling sun and the other celestial bodies, as represented in the concentric, moving ring models of the Portuguese armillary sphere or the spherical astrolabe. This world view was fast becoming scientifically discredited in the sixteenth century by Copernicus, and later by Galileo, as they endorsed what came to be known as the Copernican system, the heliocentric view of a sun-bound universe and a moving earth. The Ptolemaic system was famously, anachronistically resurrected, however, in

---

[2] Phillip Rothwell similarly uses the phrase 'mapa anabolizado' [artificially overgrown map] to refer to Henrique Galvão's 1934 imperialist map of Portugal in which the African and Asian colonies appear in red, superimposed over major European nations, under the heading 'Portugal is Not a Small Country'. See 'Camões ainda conta. Cópias à Procura de Originais', *Colóquio/Letras*, 189 (2015), 7–23 (p. 13), separata with introduction by T. F. Earle.

[3] Luís Vaz de Camões, *The Lusiads*, trans. Landeg White (Oxford: Oxford University Press, 2008), II, 45. Mendonça's 1890 poem, evoking the sixteenth-century Discoveries, was written as a rebellious response to the Ultimatum crisis with Great Britain, following their territorial conflicts with Portugal in Africa. Set to music by Alfredo Keil, and using the first verse and chorus only, the poem went on to become the Portuguese national anthem. See *National Anthems of the World*, eds William Reed and M. J. Bristow (London: Weidenfeld and Nicolson, 2006), pp. 449–50.

Canto IX of Camões's *The Lusiads*, by way of rhetorically reinstating Portugal as epicentre of the world.[4] The anachronism of this Ptolemaic vision is taken to an absurdist extreme from Cardoso's late twentieth-century, post-imperial perspective, when he imagines the centre of the universe not in metropolitan Lisbon but in provincial, landlocked Entroncamento. Yet, for all that the remnants of Camões's Ptolemaically-enhanced Luso-centric universe may appear to be 'dribbling away' into history, the very fact that Cardoso eloquently records their passing attests to their powerful continuity, in many forms, into the twenty-first century. And there are very many ways in which a Portuguese-speaking frame of reference continues to manifest itself across the modern world.

The study of modern-day 'Portuguese', especially when allied to the geopolitically flexible term 'Studies', embracing over 240 million first-language speakers across eight countries and four different continents, scarcely allows for a stable or predictable mapping of space and language, even without taking into account its many manifestations as Creoles or when spoken as a second, 'heritage' language in diaspora.[5] Languages such as Nheengatu, or Língua Geral Amazônica, from the Tupi-Guarani family, continue to exist as minority indigenous languages in Brazil. Portuguese also cohabits with significant, widely spoken indigenous languages such as Macua, Sena and Tsonga in Mozambique or Kimbundu and Umbundu in Angola, which have national status but are not co-official with Portuguese. At least 19 indigenous languages are recorded in the small space of East Timor alone, and Tetum enjoys co-official status there with Portuguese, as does Cantonese in Macau. The very term 'Portuguese-speaking' becomes necessarily polysemous as we ask which language contexts Portuguese has historically displaced, downgraded or mixed with and what it is that 240 million or more contemporary speakers of Portuguese are, in fact, speaking now.[6]

---

[4] Camões, *The Lusiads*. For further interesting discussion, see Ayesha Ramachandran, *The Worldmakers: Global Imagining in Early Modern Europe* (Chicago, IL: Chicago University Press, 2015). Our thanks are due to Zoltán Biedermann for drawing our attention to this work.

[5] Portuguese is the official language in Portugal, Brazil, Angola, Mozambique, Cape Verde, Guinea-Bissau and São Tomé e Príncipe and has co-official status in Macau and East Timor.

[6] The Acordo Ortográfico, a treaty that standardizes spelling in the countries where Portuguese is an official language, was signed in 1990 and finally enacted in Portugal in 2015 and in Brazil in 2016. The Ciberdúvidas website created in 1997 is an interesting example of an online space for comparing, resolving and debating multiple linguistic differences arising from contemporary Portuguese-language spaces. <https://ciberduvidas.iscte-iul.pt/> [accessed 20 February 2019].

Viewed purely in terms of its linguistic history, the Portuguese language possesses a readily discernible genealogy, emerging from the vulgarization of Latin brought by the Roman invaders of the Iberian Peninsula, coalescing around 1200 into Galaico-Portuguese, as a thriving language of poetry and becoming the language of the nascent Portuguese state.[7] Over the centuries, the assertion of a Portuguese territory and nation brought the country into various forms of contact with other peoples and linguistic influences: Germanic tribes and Celt-Iberians from the east, and Islamic Moorish armies from Africa, who gave the Algarve its name (from *al-gharb* [the west]).[8] The Portuguese national narrative is undeniably structured around ethnic and religious violence: the expulsion of the Jews, the defeating of the Moors, the defence of its boundaries with Spain, before reaching the 'glorious era' of expansion. As the Portuguese empire grew around the world, its history became one of shifting and competing centres as controversial explorers and entrepreneurs such as Vasco da Gama went in search of 'Christians and spices'. At different moments in history, political power was centred on metropolitan Lisbon, Old Goa in India as a hub of trade and Catholicism in Asia, and Rio de Janeiro in Brazil, the capital of the empire for 13 years after the Portuguese court transferred there in 1808 following the Napoleonic invasion of the Iberian Peninsula.[9] The court remained in Brazil through the military regency of William Beresford until the king, Dom João VI, felt forced to return to Portugal in 1821, in response to liberal revolutions erupting in both Portugal and Spain, and Brazilian independence was declared in 1822. The Portuguese-speaking world has also undergone dramatic change in more recent times: long periods of dictatorship in Brazil (1964–85) and Portugal (1926–74) in the twentieth century, wars of independence in Portugal's former African colonies (1961–74/75) followed by civil wars in Angola and Mozambique, the Indonesian occupation of East Timor (finally independent in 2002), Goa's union with India (1961) and the handover of Macau to China in 1999. The cultural diversity and patterns of migration and diaspora associated with these events feed powerfully into the variants of Portuguese language and artistic expression that are represented in this book.

---

[7] On early Galaico-Portuguese poetry, see Rip Cohen and Stephen Parkinson, 'The Medieval Galician-Portuguese Lyric', in *A Companion to Portuguese Literature*, eds Stephen Parkinson, Cláudia Pazos Alonso and T. F. Earle (Woodbridge: Tamesis, 2009).

[8] For more on the development of the language, see ch. 1 of Milton Azevedo, *Portuguese: A Linguistic Introduction* (Cambridge: Cambridge University Press, 2005).

[9] For a brief history of the Iberian Peninsula, focusing primarily on Spain, see the introduction to *Transnational Spanish Studies*, eds Catherine Davies and Rory O'Bryen (Liverpool: Liverpool University Press, 2020).

Introduction: Transnationalizing Portuguese Studies   5

The rationale for the present project is, therefore, to open our conceptualization of Portuguese-language cultures in the world onto new and dynamic ways of engaging with the 'transnational' as a means of thinking beyond the disciplinary frames of the 'nation-state', itself a political construct that invites accusations of anachronism when retrospectively applied in narrow terms, before the late eighteenth and early nineteenth centuries. We aim instead to highlight flows of mobility, transcultural points of contact and the dialogues created by the intersectional.[10] Our book aligns itself, in this respect, with the other volumes of the current Transnational Modern Languages (TML) series, all of which participate in reframing 'the disciplinary framework of Modern Languages, arguing that it should be seen as an expert mode of enquiry whose founding research question is how languages and cultures operate and interact across diverse axes of connection'.[11] The volumes in this series find various ways of challenging the simple conflation of language, territory and identity through which Modern Languages as a discipline has tended traditionally to cultivate its sense of purpose. The limitations of this conflation have most obviously, although not only, been called into question by the contemporary phenomenon of global mass migration and, while the transnational turn in Modern Languages is partly a response to demographic and cultural movement, it is not simply a reflection of it. It is fundamental to this project that the transnational be seen as a critical optic or methodology, rather than a bold statement of fact. The transnational is not only a social descriptor, but a transformative means of rethinking both Modern Languages and the Modern Linguist.

Our own contribution to the series aims to equip undergraduate and postgraduate students of Portuguese Studies with a range of methodologically-informed case studies enabling exploration of what is meant by the 'nation' in any given context, and how 'the nation' is always simultaneously in contact with, and shaped by other transnational and transcultural influences, movements and ideas. *Transnational Portuguese Studies* is therefore designed to be read in conjunction with *Transnational Modern Languages*. A

---

[10] The 'transnational turn' as a modern critical concept manifested itself somewhat earlier in other areas of the Humanities, dating back to the 1970s in the Social Sciences. Among the vast literature available here, see Patricia Clavin, 'Defining Transnationalism', *Contemporary European History*, 14.4 (November 2005), 421–39 for a foundational essay on transnational approaches in History research, and for an important differentiation of 'world history' from 'global history', p. 436. See also, *The Transnational Studies Reader*, eds Sanjeev Khagram and Peggy Levitt (New York and Abingdon: Routledge, 2008).

[11] *Transnational Modern Languages. A Handbook*, eds Jenny Burns and Derek Duncan (Liverpool: Liverpool University Press, forthcoming).

Handbook, edited by Jenny Burns and Derek Duncan. *The Handbook* brings together more than 30 short essays, each of which focuses on a key, specific term in cultural criticism, not to provide a definition, but to suggest possible ways in which transnational Modern Languages study and research might usefully be undertaken. Inevitably, given their shared Iberian roots and early global reach, a further important point of cross-reference for the Portuguese volume is, as noted above, the *Transnational Spanish Studies* volume, edited by Catherine Davies and Rory O'Bryen. Portuguese, like Spanish, was a language that crossed territories, spaces and contact zones, centuries before the modern usage of the term 'nationhood' came into being and, as the foregoing will discuss, it offers a series of powerful and engaging possibilities for reconceiving the study of Modern Languages as transnational cultural enquiry.

A central reference point, both for the series as a whole and for our volume specifically, is the seminal essay by Andreas Wimmer and Nina Glick Schiller, 'Methodological Nationalism and Beyond: Nation-state Building, Migration and the Social Sciences'. Wimmer and Glick Schiller take issue with 'the territorialisation of the social science imaginary and the reduction of the analytical focus to the boundaries of the nation-state' in the structuring of research investigation according to the categories of 'container' societies, unthinkingly bound by the borders of the modern nation-state.[12] In the universities of the Anglophone world, Portuguese is most frequently taught alongside Spanish and often as a part of, or in conjunction with, degree programmes that foreground Spain, the Spanish language and Spanish-speaking Latin America – hence the historically existential need of Portuguese Studies in universities to maintain a sufficiently defining differentiation from Spanish. This makes the question of methodological nationalism a particularly interesting and, at times, vexed one because Portuguese so frequently experiences a double 'container' factor, framed by two different 'national' language contexts, which may or may not be in transnational dialogue. Portuguese, as traditionally taught in a Modern Languages disciplinary context, thus remains institutionally bound to Spanish, at the same time as it must clearly assert a multitude of linguistic, historical, geopolitical and cultural differences, and it is often underpinned by the support of distinctly national external bodies such as the Instituto Camões in Portugal and the Ministério das Relações Exteriores in Brazil.

The frequently used (if now a little dated) disciplinary designation, Hispanic Studies, has traditionally tended to erase the name of Portugal and

---

[12] Andreas Wimmer and Nina Glick Schiller, 'Methodological Nationalism and Beyond: Nation-state Building, Migration and the Social Sciences', *Global Networks*, 2.4 (2002), 301–34 (p. 307).

the Portuguese language even if the term 'Hispania' may be cited correctly, in a purely etymological sense, as being the old Roman geographical name for the whole of the Iberian Peninsula. Iberian and Ibero-American, in contrast, clearly do cover both Hispanophone and Lusophone spaces but are rarely used to name academic disciplines.[13] Rather, the assertion of Portuguese difference invests a great deal in those words that derive from the Latin term 'Lusitania', the ancient Roman province that formed the western part of Hispania and was named after the Lusitanian people or 'Lusitani'. From this come the terms 'Lusophone' and 'Lusitanist'. The emphasis this gives to peninsular Portugal, however, tends to occlude Brazil unless it is hyphenated to Luso-Brazilian, as in the name of North America's oldest Portuguese Studies journal, *Luso-Brazilian Review* (University of Wisconsin-Madison) dating back to 1964.[14] Nor are the histories, societies and cultures of Brazil taught only and self-evidently within the Modern Languages remit. Brazil exerts a powerful presence across disciplines, including Area Studies, Social Anthropology and Cultural Studies (particularly with regard to cinema and music). As Piers Armstrong comments, Brazilianists frequently cross what he calls 'the substantial psychological borders between the Social Sciences and the Humanities'.[15] As more and more Modern Language-based programmes also attempt to include Portuguese-language cultural production in Africa and Asia, our terms expand and hyphenate even further into formulations such as Luso-Afro-Brazilian Studies or Luso-Asio-Afro-Brazilian Studies (the term used by a University of Massachusetts Dartmouth publication series to describe its field). In practice, it is often precisely the emphasis on Portuguese as always already requiring a multiply hyphenated 'transcultural' and 'transnational' methodology that enables 'Portuguese Studies' to gain traction as a university subject, while at the same time claiming a sufficiently 'national-looking' language base to demarcate it in relation to Spanish, Spanish American and Hispanophone disciplinary containers.

An important governing principle of the TML series is, as noted above, Wimmer and Glick Schiller's transnational turn away from 'methodological

[13] See the introduction to *Transnational Spanish Studies*, eds Catherine Davies and Rory O'Bryen, for further discussion of the term 'Hispanic'.

[14] *Luso-Brazilian Review* is a biannual, interdisciplinary journal dedicated to research on the Portuguese-speaking world. It was founded by Alberto Machado da Rosa and is published by the University of Wisconsin Press.

[15] Piers Armstrong, 'The Brazilianists' Brazil: Interdisciplinary Portraits of Brazilian Society and Culture', *Latin American Research Review*, 35.1 (2000), 227–42 (p. 227). See also Piers Armstrong, 'Pragmatic, Dynamic, Subjective: Mutual Influences between the Social Sciences and the Humanities in the Brazilianist Field', *Luso-Brazilian Review*, 40.2 (2003), 51–71.

nationalism', but how do we mark this clearly as being, in itself, a necessary and politically-informed methodological turn, when Portuguese Studies is always already so profoundly imbricated in those interpretations of transnationalism that align it more closely with the history of globalization? Portugal continues in myriad ways to historically claim for itself the originary 'worlding' credit for 'inventing' globalization as the hyperbole of an all-encompassing national and world foundational discourse, legendarily captured in Mendonça's designation of a Portugal that 'gave new worlds to the World'.[16] It is no accident that both Brazil and Portugal still feature symbolic forms of the globe on their national flags.[17] How then do we demarcate 'our' contemporary 'transnational' idea, with its transcultural, cross-border emphases and its denaturalization of rigid 'national' formations, from the forces of 'globalization', seen as a more unidirectional process with a tendency to homogenize difference and to channel (neo)imperialism. Powerful myths, materialities and practices of 'globalism' and 'world-making' already infuse the dominant foundational narratives of Portuguese nationhood as imperial, most notoriously those that were rehabilitated by the Estado Novo [New State] dictatorship in the twentieth century.

As the foregoing essays will show, some powerfully naturalized forms of 'methodological *trans*nationalism as imperialism' remain at work in certain specific Portuguese-language epistemologies. The body of twentieth-century sociological and linguistic thought labelled 'Lusotropicalism' is certainly one such. However, probably the most ubiquitous and problematic of these 'methodological *trans*nationalisms', and the most important to deauthorize, from the perspective of Portuguese second-language dissemination in higher education, has been the formal designation *Lusofonia* to refer to the contemporary Portuguese-speaking world. As Ana Paula Ferreira aptly notes in her article 'Specificity Without Exceptionalism', the term is:

> Virtually synonymous with the agreement of mutual support made by the Portuguese-speaking countries under the auspices of the Comunidade de Países de Língua Oficial Portuguesa (CPLP) institutionalized in 1996. If, in practical terms, its main objective would be

---

[16] Camões, *Lusiads*, II, 45.

[17] In the Portuguese flag, the Manueline armillary sphere of the navigational expansion remains a central emblem as part of the national coat of arms: <https://fotw.info/flags/pt.html> [accessed 21 February 2019]. In the Brazilian case, the armillary sphere from the Portuguese coat of arms had featured on the old imperial flag first used in 1815 by the United Kingdom of Portugal, Brazil and the Algarves. Redesigned under the Brazilian Republic of 1889, the sphere evolved into the more abstractly discoid, blue celestial globe, bisected by Auguste Comte's Positivist motto, 'Order and Progress': <https://www.fotw.info/flags/br.html> [accessed 21 February 2019].

to keep the Portuguese language alive in the face of the increasing world domination of English and, more specifically, to fend off the influence of both English and French as dominant languages in Africa and Spanish in South America, Lusofonia was effectively interpreted by many along the lines of neo-colonialism and imperialist fantasy.[18]

If the concept of a Portuguese language-based study of transnationalism is to find purchase in our Modern Language teaching and research methodologies, beyond the post-imperial hall of mirrors but with a genuinely self-reflective practice, then clearly this must be of a more mobile, dialogic nature, involving plural centres and the analysis of power.[19] How then do we reinvent both 'Portuguese Studies' and 'Transnationalism' as reciprocally enlightening and simultaneously mutually contesting terms? As a new domain of knowledge production, this requires, as an obvious first step, a constant deconstructing of the historical boundary work that delimits 'things Portuguese' in naturalized cultural, symbolic, ethnic, racial, religious or linguistic terms. A number of works making explicit use of transnational optics in their approach to key topics in the Portuguese-speaking world have

---

[18] Ana Paula Ferreira, 'Specificity Without Exceptionalism: Towards a Critical Lusophone Postcoloniality', in *Postcolonial Theory and Lusophone Literatures*, ed. Paulo de Medeiros (Utrecht: Portuguese Studies Centre, University of Utrecht, 2007), pp. 21–40 (p. 28). Ferreira's principal interlocutor in this piece is Boaventura de Sousa Santos, the author of the influential and foundational essay for Portuguese postcolonial theory, 'Between Prospero and Caliban. Colonialism, Postcolonialism and Inter-identity', *Luso-Brazilian Review*, 39.2 (2002), 9–43. Here, Ferreira points out that an unquestioned, naturalized language-world of *Lusofonia* underpins Sousa Santos's concept of the 'time-space of official Portuguese language' (16) across a 'vast multi-secular contact zone involving the Portuguese people and other peoples of America, Asia, and Africa' (9), a telescoping of perspective that derives partly from Sousa Santos's indebtedness to world systems theory in this essay.

[19] Vítor Lopes's documentary, *Língua – Vidas em Portugues* (Cor, 2003), exploring variations of the Portuguese language in Mozambique, Japan, France, Portugal, Brazil and Goa is a powerful example of the Utopian post-imperial rehabilitation of *Lusofonia*, authorized by José Saramago's statement, 'não há uma língua portuguesa, há línguas em português' [there is no Portuguese language, there are languages in Portuguese]. For an excellent critique of this Utopian quest to map a 'diverse' *Lusofonia* for the post-imperial age, see Luís Madureira, 'Lusofonia: From Infancy to Necrology, or the Peregrinations of a Floating Signifier', *Portuguese Literary and Cultural Studies*, 25 (August 2013), 66–81. Here, Madureira takes issue with Eduardo Lourenço's too easy invocation of 'plurality' and 'difference' in the latter's works, *A Nau de Ícaro seguido de Imagem e miragem da Lusofonia* (Lisbon: Gradiva, 1999).

already begun this task and we aim to further those initiatives.[20] However, from the perspective of how we think and teach as modern linguists in higher education, one of the most influential and paradigm-shifting turns concerns the language textbook *Ponto de Encontro. Portuguese as a World Language*, first published in 2007.[21] This has become a modern classic among the language-learners' manuals for Portuguese on both sides of the Atlantic, not least in so far as the age-old wisdom of teaching a single European or Brazilian language-standard to absolute beginners is overturned. Rather, the textbook offers European and Brazilian Portuguese variants equally and in parallel throughout, while drawing its dossier of cultural material from across the various Portuguese-speaking countries of the world. Its insistence on a dual focus at the very root of this fundamental pedagogical exercise initiates a multiply reproducible fissure that prevents the fixing of 'Portuguese Studies'

---

[20] A small selection of excellent examples in which transnational methodologies are explicitly deployed in relation to the Portuguese-speaking world would certainly include: *Beyond Slavery: The Multilayered Legacy of Africans in Latin America and the Caribbean*, ed. Darién J. Davis (Lanham and Plymouth: Rowman and Littlefield, 2007); Stefan Helgesson, *Transnationalism in Southern African Literature. Modernists, Realists and the Inequality of Print Culture* (New York and London: Routledge, 2009); José Luís Jobim, *Literatura e cultura: do nacional ao transnacional* (Rio de Janeiro: EDUERJ, 2013); *Portuguese Literary and Cultural Studies*, 25 (August 2013), Special Issue on 'Lusofonia and Its Futures', ed. João Cezar de Castro Rocha; *Portuguese Literary and Cultural Studies*, 30/31 (2017), Special Issue on 'Transnational Africas. Visual, Material and Sonic Cultures of Lusophone Africa', eds Christopher Larkosh, Mario Pereira and Memory Holloway; *Transnacionalidades: Arte e Cultura no Brasil Contemporâneo*, ed. Cimara Valim de Melo (Porto Alegre: Metamorfose, 2017); Lisa Shaw, *Tropical Travels. Brazilian Popular Performance, Transnational Encounters and the Construction of Race* (Austin: University of Texas, 2018); Emanuelle Santos, 'National Representation in the Age of Transnational Film: A Lusophone Story', *Portuguese Studies*, 34.2 (2018), 167–80; *Interdisciplinary Journal of Portuguese Diaspora Studies*, 7 (2018), Special Issue on 'Goans on the Move', eds Cielo G. Festino, Hélder Garmes, Paul Melo e Castro and Robert Newman; *Journal of Lusophone Studies*, 4.1 (May 2019), Special Issue on 'Transnational and Counternational Queer Agencies in Lusophone Cultures', eds Anna M. Klobucka and César Braga-Pinto; *Portuguese Studies*, 35.2 (Autumn 2019), Special Issue on 'Transnational Portuguese Women Writers', eds Cláudia Pazos Alonso and Maria Luísa Coelho; Paulo de Medeiros, 'Lusophone Cinemas in Transnational Perspective', in *Postcolonial Nation and Narrative III: Literature and Cinema. Cape Verde, Guinea-Bissau and São Tomé e Príncipe*, eds Ana Mafalda Leite, Hilary Owen, Ellen W. Sapega and Carmen Tindó Secco (Oxford: Peter Lang, 2019), pp. 21–33.

[21] Clémence M. C. Jouët-Pastré, Anna M. Klobucka, Patrícia Isabel Santos Sobral, Maria Luci De Biaji Moreira and Amélia P. Hutchinson, *Ponto de Encontro. Portuguese as a World Language*, 2nd edn (Boston, MA: Pearson Education Inc., 2013 [2007]).

as based on any single monolithic 'worlding' of the language. Attaching the contextual study of different Lusophone cultures to a dual-focus language model, it enables Portuguese to be pragmatically taught in a way that holds cultural and historical mobility in play.

Self-evidently our own current response to this challenge can in no way be fully comprehensive regarding the endless possible directions that transnational modes of study could pursue in relation to Portuguese-language spaces and contact zones. Nor does it make any such claim. Transnationalism is likely to continue provoking particularly dynamic debate, within the academic field that we contingently call, for our purposes here, Portuguese Studies. The various case histories with which we begin this task, range from the early modern period to the twenty-first century and come from all four continents on which Portuguese has official language status. The case histories will demonstrate how analysing representations of various cultural and linguistic phenomena can provide a powerful lens through which to view contemporary and historical transcultural processes at work. The 20 chapters that follow are sub-divided into four parts: Spatiality, Language, Temporality and Subjectivity, in line with the design of the TML series.

The first section on 'Spatiality' allows a focus on territoriality and its relationship to identity, the translation and transmission of spatial concepts, the construction of memory spaces, the strategic invention of 'utopias' and 'heterotopias', and the many forms of transcultural encounter across spaces in which contact with Portuguese has occurred. Language contact zones, and the transformation and negotiation of power relations, remain central to our section dedicated to 'Language'. Here we will emphasize practices of translingualism, multilingualism, communication blockages, and the limits and possibilities of cultural translation. In the section on 'Temporality' a strong emphasis rests on memory studies. Transnational frames of references are shown here working, with varying degrees of success, to unearth nationally and individually repressed memory sites and images, where monumental forms of national time have appropriated or refused both personal and collective forms of expression. The section on 'Subjectivity' explores the ways in which personhood, identity and political agency may be shaped at the intersection of national and transnational influences and possibilities. It discusses the ways in which race, gender and sexual orientation and their expressive and translational capabilities are shaped by and across borders.

The first chapter on 'Spatiality' by Zoltán Biedermann deals with the relationship between mapping, naming and the exercise of power. If the global spread of Portuguese culture, power and language is conventionally historically associated with the maritime expansion of the fifteenth- and sixteenth-century spice voyages to the East, epitomized by Vasco da Gama, Biedermann tellingly reminds us in the opening chapter to this volume that few scholars today use the term 'Discovery' without qualification. To this end, he cautions the reader against the unthinking reproduction of 'unquestioned and sometime anachronistic spatial notions' such as 'territory', 'nation', 'region', 'continent' and 'globe' (24). The forms of knowledge production that shape the historical mapping of land and sea routes become a multidirectional, centrifugal and centripetal project, with Portugal undergoing major influences from Chinese, Persian and Arabic sources, alerting us also to the tensions that may surface between the local and the global, and calling our attention to the politics of the translocal.

Anna M. Klobucka's chapter analyses the work of Gilberto Freyre, the foundational and controversial Brazilian theorist of 'Lusotropicalism', which posited the Portuguese themselves as an inherently transculturally-constituted people, 'existing indeterminately between Europe and Africa' (43) who enjoyed exceptional integration in the tropics and uniquely good relations with native lands and women. Drawing on two key works from 1953, Klobucka treats Lusotropicalism as a kind of 'embodied theorizing of the transnational and translational Lusophone space' (45) as she focuses on the various asymmetrical power distributions freighting the cross-cultural translatability of his ideas. She also highlights the powerful role that Freyre envisions not for Portugal but for Brazil, already independent by the twentieth century, as transnational mediator in the 'global realignment of post-imperial Lusophone status quo' (54).

Focusing on the late sixteenth century, Vivien Kogut Lessa de Sá and Sheila Moura Hue's account details evolving transnational relationships between Europe and the Americas, through English voyages to, exchange with, and raids on, Brazil. The east coast of Brazil (under the Spanish monarchy, as was Portugal, from 1580) became the object of pirate expeditions that led not only to the plundering of material goods and wealth but also to the capture of manuscripts and texts. Where Portuguese was the international language of the eastern maritime routes, an 'Atlantic circulation of Portuguese papers aboard English ships' becomes discernible in this period, showing the 'permeability of the very notion of cultural identity, even as nations were anxious to assert it' (69).

A resistant counter-appropriation of Lusotropicalism and its contemporary legacies is discernible in the linguistic and racial creolization, identity affirmation and successful transnational marketing that are richly explored in Fernando Arenas's piece. Arenas explores African song within and beyond the variously transcultural spaces and cultural transmission networks of contemporary Angola, Cape Verde and Guinea-Bissau. Here Arenas shows how the

'Creole languages [...] set the limits to, or "interrupt" the signifier "luso"' (72), enjoying predominance over Portuguese in the music industry and everyday life in Cape Verde and Guinea-Bissau, in contrast to the continued centrality of Portuguese in the urban popular music of Angola.

If Arenas captures Luso-Afro-Brazilian transitions and multiple home spaces in the language of song lyrics and instrumentalization choices, Maria Luísa Coelho's piece shifts the terrain to the artwork of the Portuguese anti-Estado Novo artist Bartolomeu Cid dos Santos, exiled to London in the 1950s. His paintings, tile design and print-making focus heavily on the subjective memory experiences triggered by travel and movement, as well as capturing shifting national identifications in relation to Portugal's empire in Africa, its aftermath and loss. Coelho shows how his different visual and artistic correlatives for displacement and transit reproduce concepts of self and home that are never fixed or stable, rather permitting a visible layering effect that foregrounds the palimpsestic co-existence of different places and transitive cultural memories.

The centrifugal history of transit comes home to roost in Hilary Owen's chapter on Miguel Gomes's three-part film project *Arabian Nights* from 2015, protesting the effects of EU austerity on a trapped and static Portugal. Owen shows how Gomes uses his transnational funding from various European nations and the EU itself, not only to critique the effects of EU-driven austerity on his nation's wellbeing but also to delegitimize nostalgic nationalism. To this end, his characters' tales present a specificity of experience, grounded in class and poverty (standing in place of the nation as collective), and the structure of multiply embedded narratives afforded by the original *Tales from the Arabian Nights* creates a series of heterotopic spaces on screen that position Portuguese space as an alternative 'Europe from below'.

Where the previous section deploys various selected cultural histories from Portugal, Brazil and Africa to ask how the global, local and glocal have played out from the sixteenth to the twenty-first centuries, the section on 'Language' opens with the chapter by Toby Green and José Lingna Nafafé. Their study affords a bridge from our focus on the centrality of space to 'the place of language in early [seventeenth-century] colonial power' (145). Offering a pertinent historical critique of the convenient catch-all term for the Portuguese-speaking world, *Lusofonia*, they recall its Euro- and Christocentric historical roots in foundational civilizing missions, such as those of the Jesuit Padre António Vieira in the seventeenth century. *Lusofonia* has frequently served as a Eurocentric, imperial 'one-way street', revived in official twentieth- and twenty-first-century Portuguese cultural policy-making and its formal consolidation in the contemporary CPLP (Comunidade dos Países de Lingua

Portuguesa).[22] Yet as the authors point out, the focus on one single centripetal and centrifugal centre (Lisbon) fails to account for the pull of alternative, competing centres, including those generated by the importance of African languages, historically influencing both European and Brazilian Portuguese in their turn. They go on to provide a reminder of how African cultures and the history of enslaved and Christianized Africans also impacted Portuguese language, religion, spheres of influence and linguistic theories of creolization, in scenarios where language was crucially instrumentalized by empire in both its early seventeenth-century iterations and their twentieth-century successors under the New State dictatorship of 1933–74. They conclude that, 'it shows why the notion of *Lusofonia* must be viewed as transnationalism in reverse. *Lusofonia* was not a culture emerging from the metropole and its language, and spreading itself outwards, through some kind of pure imperial projection. It has to travel to a meeting point with others' (133).

Susana Afonso pays precise sociolinguistic attention to these phenomena in her study of how these contact zones are shaped through their social histories. She works both diachronically on the historical emergence of multiple varieties of Portuguese, specifically in Afro-Brazilian and Luso-Asian social networks (including here Mozambique) and synchronically on the particular implications and importance of this history for the formation of new language varieties produced by 'members of social networks' working as 'agents of change' (152) as they form new identities in transnational and diaspora settings.

Translanguaging alternations and codeswitching are central to Simon Park's historical chapter discussing works by Portugal's founding father of national theatre, the bilingual playwright Gil Vicente, whose characters speak a mix of vernacular and erudite Portuguese, alongside Castilian, French, Italian, Latin and German, as well as using some 'pidgin' Africanized words, demonstrating the 'close connection between language and collective character' (181). He shows how their failure to achieve the desired intelligibility across multiple languages is a mainstay of many of Vicente's dialogues, underpinning not only their humour and double entendre, but also their marking (or scrambling) of identity in negotiations of race and colour difference that are socially indicative.

Class-based registers of language and colloquial Portuguese continue to cause communication problems in modern and contemporary translation settings crossing Portugal, Brazil and the English language, as Sara Ramos

---

[22] Sometimes known as the Lusophone Commonwealth, the CPLP was founded in 1996 and currently has nine members: Angola, Brazil, Cape Verde, East Timor, Equatorial Guinea, Guinea-Bissau, Mozambique, Portugal and São Tomé and Príncipe. <https://www.cplp.org> [accessed 22 February 2019].

Pinto shows. In her chapter, she explores how transnational practices of translation, here seven different Portuguese and Brazilian versions of Bernard Shaw's *Pygmalion* and the corresponding musical, *My Fair Lady*, contributed to refashioning existing literary norms and accepted standards, specifically in this case, in response to the problems of translating 'working-class' and regional dialects. The solutions that had to be found, she argues, pushed Portuguese and Brazilian literatures towards wider transnational trends of variety and away from literary discourses wedded to a single language standard.

The limits to transnational cultural and linguistic flow across borders are explored by Tori Holmes in relation to the virtual environment and mega-events such as the FIFA World Cup (2014) and the Olympic Games (2016) in Rio. Her case history analyses a particular webdocumentary project, *Domínio Público* (2014), dedicated to investigating the urban changes forced by mega-events, in terms of remediation between the transnational and the 'local'. Indicative in this regard is the way in which the documentary, and the paratextual elements surrounding it, provide translation and subtitling for international audiences only on a selective basis, such that a complex interplay between local and international forms of knowledge, both 'facilitated and frustrated a transnational gaze' (204), effectively complicating non-local comprehension.

Where Holmes's chapter shows local concerns in urban Rio being refractory to and partly protected from full international dissemination as a necessary long-term political strategy, the section on 'Temporality' begins with Ellen W. Sapega's chapter also focusing on the documentary genre. Sapega looks at the revelatory and potentially liberating impact of transnational perspectives for specific moments of collective national amnesia and silencing of the Second World War, as evidenced in two Portuguese documentaries. *Sob Céus Estranhos* (2002) is Daniel Blaufuks's film of his Jewish grandparents' experience, and João Canijo's *Fantasia Lusitana* (2010) recalls Lisbon as a clearing port and international crossroads for foreign war refugees and exiles most notably the writers Alfred Döblin, Erika Mann and Antoine de Saint-Exupéry. The French and German voiceovers from these writers, accompanying an ironic montage of official Salazarist Portuguese film from 1940, mediate a collective past by using public and archive images and shared narratives in line with Astrid Erll's dynamics of 'travelling memory', inserting Portugal into 'stories of transnational dimensions' (225), such as the Holocaust. In this, Sapega demonstrates particularly well Patricia Clavin's contention, in her seminal history essay 'Defining Transnationalism', that 'transnationalism enables history to break free from the nationally determined timescales that dominate the historiographical landscape'.[23]

---

[23] Clavin, 'Defining Transnationalism', p. 429.

Edward King's chapter also deals with a bringing back from invisibility, this time in terms of migrant experiences diverging from the homogeneities of traditional core Brazilian national identifications, such as Sérgio Buarque de Holanda's 'homem cordial' [cordial man].[24] King reads the multiple temporalities of an autobiographical photobook by Gui Mohallem, a second generation Lebanese migrant to Brazil, following a journey to his parent's home in eastern Lebanon in a meditation on his family's migration history. King explores how it exemplifies Chiara De Cesari and Ann Rigney's insistence on the 'non-linear trajectories and complex temporalities' of transnationalism, in the photographer's 'attempt to construct a vision and a temporality of a transnational future' (238).

Tatiana Heise's chapter reads three Brazilian films about a 1969 kidnapping that was an act of resistance against the Brazilian dictatorship. Her readings work at the interface of emerging memory studies and the transnational turn in film studies to inform her discussion of how far specific, nationally-embedded memories may be conveyed through transnational film media, and what happens when they are. She asks 'what aspects of the past are more appropriately addressed in films that utilize a distinctively national framework for remembering? [...] What new elements are brought to light in films that widen the focus to locate the past within a transnational or global context?' (250), as national memories travel beyond borders. She also observes, in her critical evaluation of transnational cinematic distribution practices, counter to Sapega's example in Portugal, that while some mediated memories can travel transnationally and acquire new emancipatory dimensions that dislodge national regimes of memory and invoke transnational frames of solidarity, other travelling memories may reinforce stereotypes and create an enhanced climate for collective amnesia.

Travelling memories are also central to Ana Margarida Dias Martins's reading of the feminist text, the Three Marias' *New Portuguese Letters* of 1972, which afforded the first ever case of international solidarity for women's movements worldwide. Going beyond the retrospective tendency to cast the Three Marias in an ideological hierarchizing of memories, according to the competitive, binary frame of the universal versus the particular, Martins focuses on their contemporary transnational remembrance through recent interviews and re-enactments with British and US supporters of the campaign. Taking memory as 'multidirectional', she deconstructs the implications of the historical national 'container approach' to ask how memory of the Three Marias as iconic entities has 'broken the frame of the nation-state' to

---

[24] Sérgio Buarque de Holanda, *Raízes do Brasil* (São Paulo: Companhia das Letras, 2014 [1936]).

Introduction: Transnationalizing Portuguese Studies 17

exemplify the 'transportable logic of mnemonic practices' (272) and demonstrate the 'border-crossing itineraries [...] of [...] flows of memory' (280).

The section on 'Subjectivity' begins with the chapter by Cláudia Pazos Alonso as she takes Portuguese feminist debate back to the nineteenth century, through the little-known memoir of the French-educated Portuguese woman writer and thinker, Josephina Neuville, to show how pre-1900 women in Portugal cannot be 'understood as transnational subjects in the same way as men of letters' (286). Showing how Neuville's acquisition of French cultural capital enabled her 'to articulate and memorialize her own embodied subjectivity' (286), she reveals a Portuguese woman leveraging new forms of identity politics from her various travel experiences, arguing for the importance of reading Portugal's nineteenth-century *estrangeiradas* or 'foreignerized women' as actively transnational in their various quests to articulate protofeminist positions. In this chapter, and the next by Paulo de Medeiros, the use of a 'transnational lens' allows us to see 'retrospectively some of the paths not taken in the formation of dominant national narratives, and so re-open archives and reactivate the potential of certain icons and narratives'.[25]

Paulo de Medeiros angles the 'transnational lens' from several different viewpoints, including Brazilian graphic novels, to undertake a strategic 'displacement' of Portugal's best-known Modernist poet and celebrated export, Fernando Pessoa, productively releasing him from various straitjacketed forms of national iconicity. Although he was an Anglo- and Lusophone bilingual poet, Pessoa has long been held as emblematic of Portugal, associated with the phrase 'my fatherland is the Portuguese language'. Unweaving these assumptions, de Medeiros argues that Pessoa's famous heteronymic project, 'feel[ing] for and as another' (304), as Pessoa forges different poetic forms and identities under alternative names and signatures, blurs the boundary between self and other, effectively aligning him with 'transnationalism as a refusal to establish solid borders between nations' (304). The result is an 'estrangement of the self from itself that [...] is the mark of the transnational at the individual level' (305).

Transatlantic fusions, in the form of migrant cultural syncretism, are central to Kimberly DaCosta Holton's chapter on Judith and Holofernes, a Portuguese-American 'fadocore' band from Manteca, California. They were founded by Azorean-descended Chris da Rosa, who has blended traditional Portuguese *fado* music with contemporary Gothic and postpunk modes as a hybridized expression of mourning for two deceased former band members.

---

[25] Chiara De Cesari and Ann Rigney, 'Beyond methodological nationalism', in *Transnational Memory: Circulation, Articulation, Scales*, eds Chiara De Cesari and Ann Rigney (Berlin: De Gruyter, 2014), pp. 1–25 (p. 7).

Holton shows how da Rosa's physical journeying back to Portuguese *fado* roots in Lisbon has taken him 'along vectors of transnational as well as local migrations' (326), permitting an expression of new diasporic identities as responses to various traumatic forms of personal and collective loss, departure, mourning and death.

Working at the intersections of Lusophone Studies, queer theory and Translation Studies, mourning and loss also profoundly mark Christopher Larkosh's chapter, as he explores transnational and translational communications across borders, arguing for the importance of autobiographical self-referentiality, as a necessary mediation of actively politicized academic discourse. As a result of this, 'queer theory, or any literary theory, for that matter, can only be considered such when it takes on these uncommonly personal ways of thinking and imagining literary texts, whether those firmly centred within the Portuguese language or, as is perhaps more common, in translational dialogue with an ever-expanding set of texts, lived experiences, and cultural materialities in other languages' (339). His own experiences in translating famous queer Brazilian writers such as Caio Fernando Abreu, João Gilberto Noll and Wilson Bueno, are shown to be powerfully underpinned by their early deaths in tragic circumstances and particularly by Larkosh's personal meeting with Bueno, as he notes that a 'queerness of shared translational space' (351) calls for social, discursive and political practices that are also adequate to the task.

Our final chapter, by Claire Williams, is a timely reflection on our first by Zoltán Biedermann. Biedermann tells us in Chapter 1 that 'connectedness does not inevitably produce a detachment from the local, nor can the cosmopolitanism resulting from contacts be reduced to a single, frictionless vehicle of mutual understandings' (39). This is nowhere more evident than in Williams's analysis of the Brazilian 'Amores Expressos' writers' project, a collaboration begun in 2007 between a film producer, a writer and a major Brazilian publishing house, which dispersed 17 Brazilian novelists across major cities around the globe, acting as citizens of the world as well as Brazilians, and required to write a love story based on their experiences. Here, as Williams notes, vestiges of the 'homem cordial' or 'cordial man' image as well as Lusotropical mediation fantasies re-emerge in the idea of a specifically Brazilian 'way of doing global citizenship, underpinned by a twenty-first-century cosmopolitanism' (354). Tracing the different ways in which they negotiate internal and external perceptions of Brazilianness abroad, Williams explores the various degrees of difficulty the project encounters in making Brazilianness a clear mediatory force. Those novels that make least reference to Brazilian essentialisms and go beyond exoticist local colour in their self-projections are those aspiring most closely to a cosmopolitan aesthetics.

Introduction: Transnationalizing Portuguese Studies 19

As this collection of essays endeavours to demonstrate, our response to the reductive and relativistic frameworks associated with globalization demands dialogue with new methodologies and critiques drawn from the broader, more open concept of the 'transnational'. At the same time, it requires a simultaneous questioning of the ways in which certain trans- (if ultimately pre-) nationally-informed epistemologies such as *Lusofonia* and the Maritime Expansion, have become embedded in Portuguese Studies, projecting a naturalized, originary symbolic force equivalent to that which emanates from the blinkered perspectives of 'methodological nationalism'. It has been our objective to ask how contemporary epistemic reframings of the 'transnational', in a dynamic and unbounding sense, enable us to re-evaluate and resituate Portuguese Studies as such, as well as exploring conversely how the history of Portuguese Studies impacts on our evolving definition of the transnational in the Humanities. The study of Modern Languages has much to gain from being conceived in terms of transnational cultural enquiries and communications, revealing the silo of the 'nation-state' to be, itself, historically contingent and always enmeshed in alternative networks and movements. And Portuguese Studies, in this twenty-first-century context, has a vital part to play in the broader project of realigning Modern Languages with the future trajectory of the Humanities in a changing world order. However, it is worth remembering, lest the term become a talisman, that transnational approaches may often follow paradoxical rather than unidirectional pathways. As we hope to have shown, and as Clavin notes, the border crossings and encounters that result from transnational mobility may operate in terms of 'repulsion' as well as 'attraction', they are not 'consistently progressive and cooperative in character' and, in specific instances, such as post-war European integration, the transnational may also reinforce nation-states in such a way as to work against globalization.[26] We believe that, far from territorializing a newly inflexible all-encompassing term or closing off a field of transnationally-informed studies for Portuguese, the 20 essays in this volume offer a wide range of different transnational methodologies. When read in conjunction, they interrogate and expand one another. As Clavin claims, 'the value of transnationalism lies in its openness as an historical concept.'[27] It is this value of 'openness', both reflecting upon and reaching beyond the borders of the nation-state, that provides the watchword for

---

[26] Clavin, 'Defining Transnationalism', pp. 423–24. On the European integration case, Clavin refers on p. 431 to the foundational research of international historian Alan Milward, *The European Rescue of the Nation-State*, 2nd edn (London: Routledge, 2000).

[27] Clavin, 'Defining Transnationalism', p. 438.

our collection, challenging the inevitability of resurgent nationalisms in the twenty-first century, and reaffirming the centrality of translingual and transcultural communication to the ways in which we study and conceptualize transnational communities and people(s).

Part I

Spatiality

1

Global Navigations and the Challenge of World-Making

Introducing the Study of Spatiality in the Portuguese Empire

Zoltán Biedermann
University College London

The more familiar the historical categories that we operate with and tell stories about, the greater the danger of fundamental misunderstandings. Take 'presence' (*presença*), a keyword with spatial implications frequently used by historians and literary historians as they describe Portuguese activities across the globe. It has the neutral qualities necessary to fit a great variety of situations, and yet this very neutrality also sits rather awkwardly with the violence that empire-building involved. There is, to be sure, no lack of evidence suggesting that Portuguese individuals and power structures moved into many different parts of the globe after the conquest of Ceuta in 1415, establishing new 'presences'.[1] But there is clearly a debate to be had about how a nation that still sees its global reach with considerable (and, to some extent, legitimate) appreciation may also need to confront the ghosts of a deeply violent imperial past.[2] Rather than censoring words, it is urgent to bring to

---

[1] On the Portuguese case, see Sanjay Subrahmanyam, *The Portuguese Empire in Asia* (London: Longman, 1993); *Portuguese Oceanic Expansion*, eds Francisco Bethencourt and Diogo Ramada Curto (Cambridge: Cambridge University Press, 2007); *A History of Portugal and the Portuguese Empire*, ed. Anthony Disney, 2 vols (Cambridge: Cambridge University Press, 2009); Jorge Flores, 'The Iberian Empires, 1400–1800', in *The Cambridge World History VI. The Construction of a Global World, 1400–1800 CE*, part I, eds Jerry H. Bentley, Sanjay Subrahmanyam and Merry E. Wiesner-Hanks (Cambridge: Cambridge University Press, 2015), pp. 271–96. All translations are mine.

[2] See Diogo Ramada Curto, 'Portuguese Navigations. The Pitfalls of National Histories', in *Encompassing the Globe. Portugal and the World in the 16th and 17th Centuries*, ed. Jay Levenson, 1 (Washington DC: Smithsonian, 2007), pp. 36–43.

everyone's conscience their deep political implications. This amounts to a difficult exercise, but not an impossible one. 'Discovery', for example, has gone through such a process in the context of New World historiography, and few scholars use it today without qualification.

There is also a deeper level at which words with spatial implications – for example, 'expansion', 'conquest' or 'territory' – call for a debate, and here we are in largely uncharted terrain. Much of what has been written about Portuguese imperial and sub-imperial processes in the early modern period has been built around unquestioned and sometimes anachronistic spatial notions. To gain access to this hidden dimension of history, questions need to be asked about words including 'territory', 'nation', 'region', 'continent' (the most recent of these categories to have been explored as a myth) and indeed 'globe' (a challenge now on the table).[3] Historicizing the concepts behind those words does not mean hollowing them out, but seeking meanings somewhere else than traditionally expected. Some of the most promising fields of new research into the political, economic, literary, artistic and scientific production of early modern Lusophone societies involve a gesture describable as an 'archaeology' of imperial space. It is significant that, both in the Castilian grammarian Antonio de Nebrija's famous dictum and in the less widely known thinking of his Portuguese counterpart João de Barros, language was the vehicle not of nations, but of empires. Empires, in their turn, are complicated political constructs that are about more than just one nation conquering others.[4] Most artefacts considered as 'Portuguese' by historians – from texts through maps to entire cities or provinces – were expressions of the complex global interactions that, while carrying intensely hierarchical traits, cannot be reduced to a simple project of extending national hegemony. In fact, many were composite expressions involving a variety of voices from diverse societies in constant dialogue with external and internal 'Others'. Maps attributed to Portuguese cartographers

---

[3] See Stuart Elden, *The Birth of Territory* (Chicago, IL: University of Chicago Press, 2013); Benedict Anderson, *Imagined Communities* (London and New York: Verso, 1991); R. Bin Wong, 'Regions and global history', in *Writing the History of the Global. Challenges for the 21st century*, ed. Maxine Berg (Oxford: Oxford University Press, 2013), pp. 83–105; Martin W. Lewis and Kären Wigen, *The Myth of Continents. A Critique of Metageography* (Berkeley and Los Angeles, CA: University of California Press, 1997). Ayesha Ramachandran, *The Worldmakers. Global Imagining in Early Modern Europe* (Chicago, IL and London: University of Chicago Press, 2015) engages with the category 'globe', but fails to consider Lusophone materials.

[4] See John H. Elliott, 'A Europe of Composite Monarchies', *Past and Present*, 137 (1992), 48–71; Jeremy Adelman and Stephen Aron, 'From Borderlands to Borders: Empires, Nation-States, and the Peoples in Between in North American History', *American Historical Review*, 104 (1999), 814–41.

were often based on information received from Asian pilots or other agents on the ground, whose voices were then silenced in the finished cartographical artefacts we possess. And, of course, many were produced by cartographers born in Portugal but serving in other countries such as Spain, France, or England – or indeed, at times, men born in Goa, Macau or Brazil.[5] Chronicles and geographical works such as João de Barros's *Décadas da Ásia* were full of information gleaned in texts and maps originally written in Chinese, or Persian, or Arabic.[6] Many other authors, especially of travelogues and linguistic works (grammars, vocabularies), but also some chronicles such as Fernão de Queiroz's *Conquista Temporal e Espirital de Ceilão*, relied heavily on less erudite, often oral sources of information that were not Portuguese. Last, but not least, letters written in Portuguese by Asian and African individuals engaging in diplomatic exchanges with Goa and Lisbon were often deeply rooted in their own cultures. They are Asian and African artefacts written in Portuguese.[7] Even places nominally subjected to Portuguese rule were in general complex battlegrounds of conflicting or complementary identities involving *reinóis* (people born in Portugal), the local families into which most of them married, the successive generations resulting from such miscegenation, and certain societal groups that resisted the mingling and maintained a clearer distance.[8]

One could of course contend that people of different backgrounds may still have identified in some way with Portugal as a distant territorial mother state, or other places around the globe as 'Portuguese territories', thus following an inclusive logic where 'place' set the agenda rather than 'race'. However, the very notion of the state as a construct grounded in territoriality is itself historically contingent. The drawing of clear lines around realms is a key characteristic of the making of territories in the emerging political system

---

[5] See for example, Neil Safier, *Measuring the New World. Enlightenment Science and South America* (Chicago, IL and London: Chicago University Press, 2008); *Atlas historique du golfe Persique/Historical Atlas of the Persian Gulf*, ed. Zoltán Biedermann (Turnhout: Brepols, 2006).

[6] On Barros in general, see Charles Ralph Boxer, *João de Barros. Portuguese Humanist and Historian of Asia*, Xavier Centre of Historical Research Series, 1 (New Delhi: Concept Publishing, 1981).

[7] One of the most spectacular corpuses, from Sri Lanka, is in Georg Schurhammer and Ernst August Voretzsch, *Ceylon zur Zeit des Königs Bhuvaneka Bahu und Franz Xavers 1539–1552. Quellen zur Geschichte der Portugiesen, sowie der Franziskaner- und Jesuitenmission auf Ceylon, im Urtext herausgegeben und erklärt*, 2 vols (Leipzig: Verlag der Asia Major, 1928).

[8] A good overview on the social and cultural processes involved is in A. J. R. Russell-Wood, *The Portuguese Empire. 1415–1808: A World on the Move* (Baltimore, MD and London: Johns Hopkins University Press, 1998).

of seventeenth-century Europe, but it was very much an incipient reality during the sixteenth century.[9] Although Portugal had a very old and stable border, this did not function as a strict dividing line until the 1520s. The mapping of Portugal, to fixate and politicize its exact outlines, seems to have begun precisely at that time, and yielded a first printed map of the kingdom in 1561.[10] Even then, however, the territory apparently unified through cartography remained a poorly integrated, heterogeneous patchwork of distinct jurisdictions.[11] When it comes to territoriality overseas, things are further complicated. While colonies (in the sense of settlements of groups of people originally coming from or through Portugal) were established in a variety of places from Madeira to Japan, i.e. 'terrestrially', only some of these became territories in the stricter sense of the word, and no single impulse has been identified so far to explain the various instances of 'territorialization'.

Examples abound. About three decades after the Portuguese conquest of the city of Goa in 1510, the local elite decided to take control of the surrounding villages and lands subsequently known as the 'Old Conquests' of Bardez and Salcete (as opposed to the 'New Conquests' of the 1700s, which make up the rest of today's state).[12] Very little is known about the exact motivations, decision-making processes, and intellectual perceptions of space at play. Further north, in the region of Mumbai, agricultural villages passed under Portuguese control in the 1530s as part of a deal with the Sultanate of Gujarat, under circumstances that remain poorly understood.[13] In Sri Lanka, it took almost a century of interactions before the Portuguese authorities embraced the project of territory-building through conquest in the 1590s.[14] Once the decision to conquer was

---

[9] See Michael Biggs, 'Putting the State on the Map: Cartography, Territory, and European State Formation', *Comparative Studies in Society and History*, 41.2 (1999), 374–405.

[10] Suzanne Daveau, *Um mapa corográfico de Portugal (c. 1525). Reconstituição a partir do Códice de Hamburgo* (Lisbon: Centro de Estudos Geográficos, 2010); Joaquim Romero de Magalhães, 'As descrições geográficas de Portugal: 1500–1650', *Revista de História Económica e Social*, 5 (1980), 15–56.

[11] António Manuel Hespanha, *As Vésperas do Leviathan. Instituições e poder político, Portugal – séc. XVII* (Coimbra: Livraria Almedina, 1994).

[12] Ângela Barreto Xavier, *A invenção de Goa: poder imperial e conversões culturais nos séculos XVI e XVII* (Lisbon: ICS, 2008).

[13] Luís Frederico Antunes, 'Algumas considerações sobre os prazos de Baçaim e Damão', *Anais de História de Além-Mar*, 3 (2002), 231–57. For an attempt at sketching a wider panorama of territorialization, see Sanjay Subrahmanyam, 'Holding the World in Balance: The Connected Histories of the Iberian Empires, 1500–1640', *American Historical Review*, 112.5 (2007), 1379–81.

[14] Zoltán Biedermann, *(Dis)connected Empires. Imperial Portugal, Sri Lankan*

taken, several decades of warfare ensued, ending in the takeover of all official possessions by the Dutch East India Company, the VOC. In countless ports from Ceuta to Macau, no conquests were made beyond the city walls at all (and indeed many of these ports were themselves not the result of conquest, but concession).[15] In some Atlantic islands, geologically delimited spaces were only very gradually made into economically and politically viable and meaningful territories. Across much of Africa, diseases hindered the establishment of Portuguese colonies in the interior up to the late nineteenth century. And in South America, it took centuries to build, through a succession of different strategies ranging from trade and diplomacy through interloping and conquest to missionary, administrative and cartographic reinvention, what eventually became Brazil.[16] In each of these instances, identities necessarily played out differently in relationship to the space in which society-building occurred. The question is not whether there was a territorial turn across the empire at some point in the sixteenth or early seventeenth century, but what forms of territoriality emerged, under what local circumstances, with what implications.

The very act of mapping, through which new spatial realities could be visually represented, underwent profound changes during the late medieval and early modern period. Much of the technology used to change the image of the world was closely connected to navigation and the collecting of observational data from ships to increase the safety and viability of travelling on ships. The outlines of continents and islands emerged negatively, as it were, as the result of the charting of the seas. The technology was firmly anchored in a Medieval charting practice (known to specialists as 'portolan'-style charting) originally coming from the Mediterranean. Portolan charts were made by putting together a large number of relational data gathered on ships about travel directions and times.[17] This was only adapted gradually,

---

Diplomacy, and the Making of a Habsburg Conquest in Asia (Oxford: Oxford University Press, 2018).

[15] On the legal mechanisms of incorporation, see António Vasconcelos de Saldanha, *Iustum Imperium. Dos tratados como fundamento do império dos portugueses no Oriente. Estudo de história do direito internacional e do direito português* (Lisbon and Macau: Fundação Oriente/Instituto Português do Oriente, 1997).

[16] Excellent overview chapters on these different areas can be found in Disney, *A History of Portugal and the Portuguese Empire*.

[17] The standard reference works on cartographical history in the medieval and early modern period are *Cartography in Prehistoric, Ancient and Medieval Europe and the Mediterranean. The History of Cartography* I, eds David Woodward and J. B. Harley (Chicago, IL and London: University of Chicago Press, 1987); and *Cartography in the European Renaissance. The History of Cartography III*, ed. David Woodward (Chicago, IL and London: University of Chicago Press, 1987).

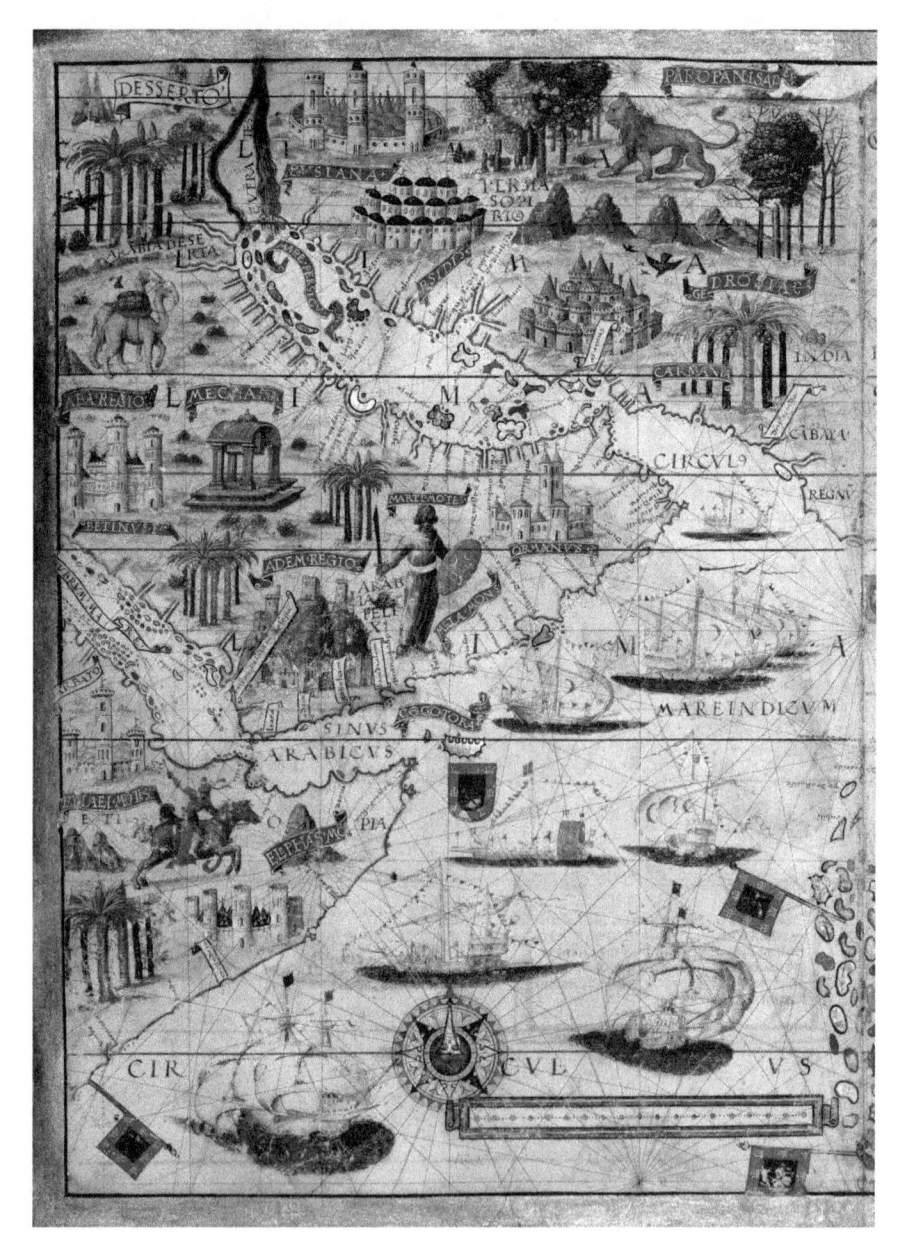

Figure 1.1. The Indian Ocean region in the Miller Atlas attributed to Lopo Homem, Pedro Reinel, Jorge Reinel and António de Holanda, Lisbon, 1519.

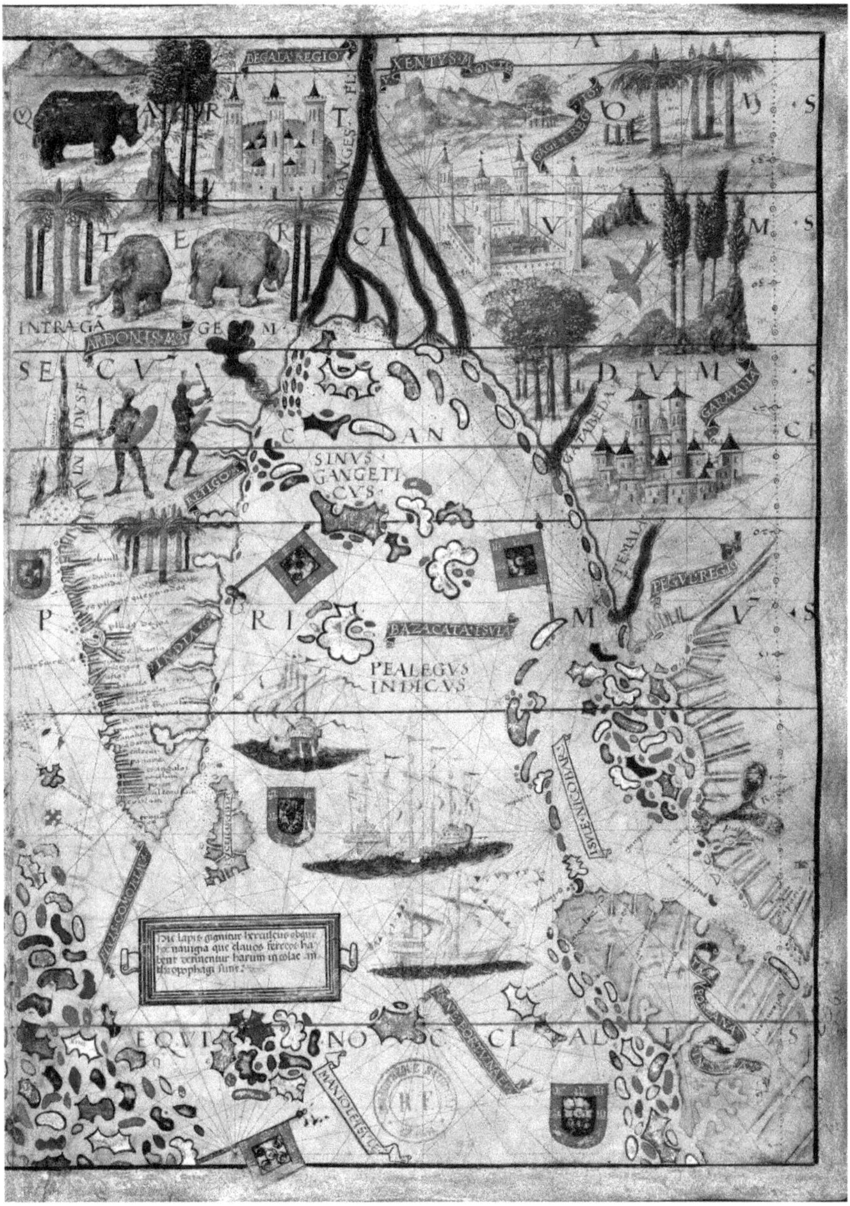
BEGALA REGIO
SINVS GANGETICVS
PEALEGVS INDICVS
BAZACATA ISVL
PEGV REGIO

as the Portuguese sailed the larger expanses of the Atlantic, to include measurements of latitude and, to some extent, longitude.[18] By the time the Portuguese (and soon others) produced charts of the Indian Ocean – as can be seen in a richly illustrated example included in the so-called Miller Atlas made in Lisbon in 1519 (Figure 1.1) – these often included both the web of rhumb lines (lines indicating up to 32 fixed directions, sometimes associated with winds) subjacent to traditional 'portolan' charts and the lines and scales of latitude and longitude (a much more abstract, mathematically conceived, graticule or grid) characteristic of the new era.[19]

Upon the freshly drawn coastlines reflecting what the navigators experienced as they hugged new shores, ports could be placed, but by default maritime cartographers refrained from going further inland with their mapping efforts. Occasionally, trophy maps such as the ones in the Miller Atlas (probably a diplomatic gift) would be richly decorated, but the inland areas remained a domain that maritime charting techniques could not cover (instead, an artist like António de Holanda might be hired to decorate them). Only gradually did terrestrial maps appear and, even then, they were not necessarily territorial in the narrow, historically congruent sense of the word extolled above. For example, the first 'Portuguese' map of Sri Lanka (made in Goa in 1568, but probably following a sketch from the 1540s), offered a representation of inland areas punctuated by various capital cities giving a sense of a power constellation, but no territories with clear borders. A map construing such a sense of territoriality only emerged a few decades later, around 1600, at the same time as the idea of military conquest took hold.[20]

The most expressive pictorial tradition to have engaged with and thus created 'place' (as opposed to a more abstract notion of 'space'), consisted of plans and views of individual cities (Figure 1.2).[21] In a genre that flourished during the seventeenth century in particular, much in line with the fashion of city views that had emerged across Europe in the sixteenth century, incipient

---

[18] Joaquim Alves Gaspar, 'From the Portolan Chart to the Latitude Chart: The Silent Cartographic Revolution', *Cartes & Géomatique. Revue du Comité Français de Cartographie*, 216 (2013), 67–77.

[19] Most 'Portuguese' charts are published in Armando Cortesão and Avelino Teixeira da Mota, *Portugaliae Monumenta Cartographica*, 5 vols (Lisbon: PMC, 1960).

[20] Zoltán Biedermann, 'Imagining Space before Conquest: Two Contrasting Maps of Sri Lanka, 1568–1606', in *The Portuguese in Sri Lanka and South India. Studies in the History of Diplomacy, Empire and Trade* (Wiesbaden: Harrassowitz, 2014), pp. 73–86.

[21] For an introduction to the distinction between space and place, see Yi-Fu Tuan, *Space and Place. The Perspective of Experience*, rev. edn (Minneapolis, MN: University of Minnesota Press, 2001).

Figure 1.2. View of Macau by Pedro Barreto de Resende, in António Bocarro's *Livro das plantas das fortalezas*, c. 1635.

city maps implying a zenithal (vertical) viewpoint or vistas giving a bird's eye view (the two subtypes cannot always be clearly separated) offered an interesting combination of references to the local and the supra-local. On the one hand, they conveyed a sense of specific place: in that, for example, Bassein (now Vasai, north of Mumbai) looked different from Colombo; or Cannanore (today Kannur in Kerala) was set on a lush peninsula and Hormuz on an arid island; or Salvador da Bahia on a hilltop and São Paulo de Luanda in a bay. These were, in other words, *portraits* of individual cities with an ambition to realism, as they had been appearing across Europe from the late 1400s. On the other hand, such collections of city views also visualized a more overarching connectedness to the larger common framework: the empire manifested itself in the same institutions everywhere, including religious orders, royal financial and juridical organs, municipal councils, and some architectural fundamentals such as churches, town halls, customs houses, jails or city walls. The practice itself of producing series of city views, such as the famous series drawn by Pedro Barreto de Resende for António Bocarro's *Livro das plantas das fortalezas da Índia* [*Book of the Plans of the Fortresses of India*] in the 1630s, goes back to the imperial project of Phillip II of Spain and his painter Anton van den Wyngaerde in the 1560s, who produced a large series of vistas of Spanish towns – many of which had been defeated by the Crown during the Revolt of the Comuneros in 1520–21.[22] In this sense, being part of a series of portraits ran counter to the apparent autonomy created by the individual image. The struggle between these two spatial political forms – the empire and the city – is one of the most important aspects of the sixteenth century.

Cities are, in fact, one spatial construct that did rely on the production of unambiguous physical and imaginary boundaries, usually in the form of walls, moats or other dividing features of the landscape. Even then, however, the presence of such structures did not preclude the movement of people, goods and ideas – again, borders could be activated and deactivated following the perceived necessities of each moment.[23] Beyond the fortifications, the

[22] Portuguese collections of maps and plans can be found in Luís Silveira, *Ensaio de Iconografia das cidades portuguesas do Ultramar*, 4 vols (Lisbon: Junta de Investigates do Ultramar, n.d.); and José Manuel Garcia, *Cidades e fortalezas do Estado da Índia. Séculos XVI e XVII* (Lisbon: QuidNovi, 2009). On Wyngaerde, see *Spanish Cities of the Golden Age: The Views of Anton van den Wyngaerde*, ed. Richard Kagan (Berkeley and Los Angeles, CA: University of California Press, 1989).

[23] On the fortresses of the *Estado da Índia* until 1521, see André Teixeira, *Fortalezas. Estado Português da Índia. A arquitectura militar na construção do império de D. Manuel I* (Lisbon: Tribuna da História, 2008). On Portuguese urban heritage in general, see Walter Rossa, *Indo-Portuguese Cities: A Contribution to the Study*

surrounding hinterlands, sometimes provided with a sacred landscape of churches and other religious structures, had few to no defences. Some maps were produced of such areas mostly from the seventeenth century onwards, but only gradually did a clear sense emerge of where one ruler's authority ended and the other's began.

Travelogues rarely describe acts of border-crossing, though they do naturally explore the impressions caused by leaving a reasonably familiar city and arriving somewhere else, in a stranger and more daunting environment.[24] Even here, there is often a spectrum of possibilities, rather than a simple contrast between the familiar and the unfamiliar. It has been shown how in a space as confined as the Catholic mission at Madurai, in south India, missionaries could opt either for a confrontational attitude emphasizing cultural difference, or an accommodational attitude seeking to highlight shared values and features of culture.[25] Exposure to Asian, African and Native American cultures often produced complex reactions. In many instances the authors of travelogues written in Portuguese deployed a remarkably dry and matter-of-fact, descriptive style suggestive of a certain normality as traveller, text and reader roam across culturally diverse regions.[26] Then, for example in the descriptions of the south Indian imperial capital of Vijayanagara produced by Domingos Pais and Fernão Nunes around 1520–30, awe-inspiring passages about the beauty of architecture and artwork alternate with judgemental references to specific mores such as the 'Juggernaut' festival.[27]

---

of Portuguese Urbanism in the Western Hindustan (Lisbon: CNCDP, 1997); and Portuguese Heritage Around the World: Architecture and Urbanism: Asia and Oceania, eds Walter Rossa and José Mattoso (Lisbon: Fundação Calouste Gulbenkian, 2010).

[24] A good monograph on regional travelogues is Joan-Pau Rubiès, Travel and Ethnology in the Renaissance. South India through European Eyes, 1250–1625 (Cambridge: Cambridge University Press, 2000).

[25] Ines G. Županov, 'Aristocratic Analogies and Demotic Descriptions in the Seventeenth-Century Madurai Mission', Representations, 41 (1993), 123–48.

[26] Onésimo T. Almeida, 'Experiência a madre das cousas – experience, the mother of things – on the "revolution of experience" in 16th-century Portuguese maritime discoveries and its foundational role in the emergence of the scientific worldview', in Portuguese Humanism and the Republic of Letters, eds M. Berbara and K. Enenkel (Leiden: Brill, 2011), pp. 375–94.

[27] Zoltán Biedermann, 'Imagining Asia from the Margins: Early Portuguese Mappings of the Continent's Architecture and Space', in Architecturalized Asia. Mapping the Continent through Architecture and Geography, eds V. Rujivacharakul, H. H. Hahn, K. T. Oshima and P. Christensen (Hong Kong: Hong Kong University Press, 2013), pp. 35–51. See also Partha Mitter, Much Maligned Monsters. A History of European Reactions to Indian Art, 2nd edn (Chicago, IL and London: University of Chicago Press, 1992).

Large amounts of texts and images were indeed produced by more or less free-floating missionaries, traders, diplomatic envoys and spies especially in the more distant corners of Asia and Africa. They often felt the attraction of Asian or African political and cultural centres, such as the Mughal court, the shifting seats of the Ethiopian and Persian monarchs, royal capitals in west Africa, the imperial court at Beijing, or the strongholds of feudal warlords in Japan.[28] Read in the past as testimonies to the resourcefulness of Portuguese travellers, and essentially as materials for a Portuguese cultural history, these texts are better understood as profoundly transnational, at times hybrid artefacts negotiating complex, cross-cultural images of the world in the interstices of an increasingly interconnected global economy. Some of the most remarkable achievements in terms of writing to understand other cultures from within ('emically', as modern anthropologists would have it) emerge from the most distant places visited by Lusophone travellers, where Portuguese political authority was at its thinnest: the towering text in this regard is João Rodrigues Tçuzu's description of Japan, containing highly accomplished cultural translations of the workings of poetry, painting, architecture and the consumption of tea.[29]

It may be important at this stage to point out how language reflected and acted upon spatial realities and perceptions not only at the level of literature (ranging from poetry through epistles to travelogues and geographical treatises), but also more fundamentally at the level of words. The naming of places is an interesting matter rarely explored.[30] The early modern period produced place names of many kinds. Some were self-referential, pointing to Portuguese culture even in the remotest of places (*Cabo da Boa Esperança* (Cape of Good Hope) for a cape formerly un-navigated; *Ilha de São Lourenço* for Madagascar because the island was 'discovered' on St Lawrence's Day); some revived classical Greco-Roman concepts (*India aquém do Ganges*, that is, 'India this side of the Ganges', for Cis-Gangetic India; *Etiópia* for Africa, or parts of Africa); some resulted from phonetic adaptations of local names (*Socotorá* for Soqotra; *Ceitavaca* for Sītāvaka); others were local names taken over without adaptation (*Guanabara*; *Luanda*). The most intriguing

[28] On the 'Shadow Empire', see Sanjay Subrahmanyam, *The Portuguese Empire in Asia*.

[29] João Rodrigues Tçuzu, *João Rodrigues's Account of Sixteenth-Century Japan*, ed. Michael Cooper (London: The Hakluyt Society, 2001).

[30] There is no work specifically on names of places and things, but many appear in Sir Henry Yule, *Hobson-Jobson: A Glossary of Colloquial Anglo-Indian Words and Phrases, and of Kindred Terms, Etymological, Historical, Geographical and Discursive*, new edn by William Crooke (London: J. Murray, 1903).

new question to ask though is what exactly names were given to. The study of metageography, the categories through which humans have historically ordered the word surrounding them, is in its infancy for the early modern period. What *category* of place deserved or required a new name? For example, on what grounds did Portuguese observers consider the 'kingdom of Malindi' to be a valid and meaningful geo-political entity? On what grounds were designations such as 'king', 'sultan', 'sheikh', 'lord' or 'emperor' deployed? Words including *sultão, xeque,* or *Grão-Mogor* adopt African and Asian vocabulary, while others such as *rei, senhor,* or *imperador* often serve to translate non-Portuguese concepts such as *rāja* or *cakravarti* into more familiar categories. In both cases, however, the Portuguese language worked with the notional and sometimes the verbal currency of African and Asian political cultures. Through the communicational channels of diplomacy and trade, the local political lore entered the Portuguese language. Even the use of a western vernacular word with a Latin root, such as *rei* (from *rex*), indicates dialogue and apprenticeship rather than monologue and obliterative imposition.[31] By translating a foreign term into a familiar one, travellers, diplomats and other writers were of course projecting aspects of European spatiality into the wider world; but they did so precisely to come closer to what political authority meant to other societies. The resulting tension between local original and Portuguese rendering points to the wider problem of cultural translation, which still haunts anthropologists, geographers and historians today.

Border-crossings in the language pertaining to space and place were frequent in the context of the specific cities that Portuguese groups visited, conquered, settled in, and later lost. While we are limited in our sources regarding pre-colonial street names, for example, a denomination such as *'rua dos mercadores'* ('Merchants' Street') constitutes, most probably, a translation of an existing reality – a street with many shops – into Portuguese. In Goa, the old summer palace of Yusuf Adil Shah or Khan (called 'Idalcão' in Portuguese sources), remained known as 'Palace of Idalcão' despite the fact that it came to be used by the Portuguese viceroys. An engagement with Asian toponyms and ethnonyms could also result in misunderstandings: the Sinhalese people of Sri Lanka – *'chingalas'* – carried this name, one author argued erroneously, because they were *'chins de Galle'*, descendants of 'Chinese people who had settled in the town of Galle'.[32]

---

[31] Biedermann, *(Dis)connected Empires*, pp. 12–36.
[32] João de Barros, *Ásia de João de Barros, Dos feitos que os Portugueses fizeram no descobrimento e conquista dos mares e terras do Oriente*, eds António Baião and Luís F. Lindley Sintra, reprint, 4 vols (Lisbon: IN-CM, 1988–2001), III, book ii, chapter 1.

Beyond the realm of place names, there is much work to be done on how spatial relations were described in early modern Portuguese texts: in other words, how language supported and reflected spatial perceptions, and how texts functioned cartographically.[33] One widespread approach consisted in describing space by narrating human movement through it. A passage from the *Book of Francisco Rodrigues*, an early sixteenth-century compilation of nautical information, describes the Red Sea by telling the following 'story':

> This was the way we came when we left the island of *ceybam* [Jebel Teir Island, 45 miles W/NW of Kamaran Island] for *Dalaca* [Dalak] [...] fifteen or sixteen leagues West of *ceybam* we encountered shallows that are about three or four leagues long and about two thirds of a league wide, running northwest to southeast, and at its most shallow point there are four *braças* of water depth, and down to one and a half *braças* of depth, these shallows are of stone and sand [...] and [as we journeyed on] we encountered another sandbank, which is half a league long [...] and the first island is distinguished by a wood [made up] of trees about as large as a carrack and apart from the trees there is a bay [for anchorage] such as that at *camaram* [...] and if one goes along it and around [the island] towards the northwest there are two rocky hills, as we were told by the Moorish *Robā* whom we had with us [...] From there we made our way to the northwest [...] and anchored that night in water fifteen *braças* deep as we were left without wind. And the next day we saw ourselves surrounded by islands and many shallows and reefs.[34]

Such spatial narratives, engaging with a certain area of the globe by following a navigational logic and revealing geographical space as if mediated by a travelling pair of eyes, were the lifeblood of so-called '*roteiros*' or 'rutter books'. They were often meant to accompany navigational charts of the above-mentioned, portolan type, and part of a wider universe of texts that, following the Portuguese cultural historian Luís Filipe Barreto, we may describe as 'hyper-mimetic'.[35] Their expressed purpose was to offer nothing but verifiable

---

[33] An interesting overview can be found in Neil Safier and Ilda Mendes dos Santos, 'Mapping Maritime Triumph and the Enchantment of Empire: Portuguese Literature of the Renaissance', in *The History of Cartography III*, ed. Woodward, pp. 461–68.

[34] Tomé Pires, *A Suma Oriental de Tomé Pires e o Livro de Francisco Rodrigues*, ed. Armando Cortesão (Coimbra: Imprensa da Universidade, 1978), p. 106.

[35] Luís Filipe Barreto, *Descobrimentos e Renascimento. Formas de ser e pensar nos séculos XV e XVI* (Lisbon: IN-CM, 1983), p. 129.

data, creating texts as if they were simple mirrors of geographical reality and what could be seen by walking or navigating through space. We may add that, while the space here created is de facto homogenous (although no scale is displayed, portolan charts are built upon an assumption that every inch on the surface of the map stands for a fixed distance in reality), it also enshrines the very concrete movements of human bodies and eyes, and the subjective verbal exchange of information with, for example, a Muslim pilot. The space of such texts and maps is thus abstract and embodied at the same time. A high point in this tradition – and one that demonstrates how we are not talking about a specifically 'Portuguese' habit, but about a certain way of writing running through both Iberian empires – is the diary of Don García de Silva y Figueroa, a Castilian-born ambassador (with Portuguese ancestry) sent by Philipp III through Lisbon and Goa to the court of the Persian Shah in 1614, at the time of the Iberian Union of Crowns. The following passage describes in minute detail the inner entrails of the fort of Masqat in Arabia:

> On the 19th [...] late in the day we got an easterly wind and travelled west-northwest, and could see already the rocky mountains of Masqat appearing, and hence we sailed until the night fell. [...] On the 20th the ambassador wished to set foot on the land and hear mass, and this he did at seven in the morning 200 steps [*pasos*] from where we had anchored, on a small beach less than 40 *pasos* wide, between two very high rocks, and there was no other entrance. And from here those rugged rocks gradually receded, leaving some ground between them, and where [this opening] is at its widest, the town is placed, and it is 200 by 5 to 600 *pasos* wide [...] From the captain's house one goes up ten or twelve steps to the highest point of the fort, where there is a little *placeta* about 13 or 14 *pasos* in diameter, under which there is a wide and deep cistern that can provide water to 300 men for two years. From here one goes up another three or four steps to where a little chapel stands with its bell tower.[36]

The minuteness of the description goes beyond that of any maps or plans made at the time. Such textual strategies, offering the reader a down-to-earth, literally pedestrian, embodied prose on space, are in dramatic contrast

---

[36] Don García de Silva y Figueroa, *Comentarios de la Embaxada al Rey Xa Abbas de Persia (1614–1624)*, ed. Rui Manuel Loureiro, 4 vols (Lisbon: CHAM, 2011). An English translation is now available: *The Commentaries of D. García de Silva y Figueroa on His Embassy to Shah 'Abbas I of Persia on Behalf of Philip III, King of Spain*, trans. and ed. Jeffrey Scott Turley and George Bryan Souza (Leiden: Brill, 2017).

with another strand of writing, a prime exponent of which is the armchair geographer João de Barros, active at the court of João III in the mid-1500s. The Great Wall of China, described by other authors, for example Fernão Mendes Pinto in the third quarter of the sixteenth century, as an object approached by walking on the ground, touchable and overwhelming in its physical reality to the actual traveller, takes a very different shape in the writing of Barros.[37] Firstly, the geographer tells us about a map he received from China. He then proceeds ekphrastically to describe how *on that map* there is a long, sinuous line running west to east. He does explain that this represents a wall, but the reader sees the edifice as an abstracted geometrical form from far above, as if anticipating the modern notion that the Great Wall can be seen from space. Something similar happens with the city of *Cantão* (Guangzhou), the walls of which the chronicler Fernão Lopes de Castanheda had described as experienced from a ship sailing up the river. This structure was, again, rewritten by Barros to appear as a cartographical abstraction seen from above, a mere geometrical form rendered through words devoid of a haptic dimension.[38]

Generally speaking, Barros's approach does not seem to reflect a dominant episteme in the Portuguese context. Much Lusophone writing about space and place in the early modern period seems – such is the current understanding – to have followed a more embodied perspective often explicitly linked to the travails of whoever originally witnessed the described realities. Logically, the porosity of the language and its exposure to Asian, African and American cultural realities and spatial experiences may then have been even more significant than in the armchair approach of humanists such as Barros. At both levels, the penetration of the 'Portuguese' text by other linguistic and cultural realities is remarkable and deserving of further scrutiny.

Given the abundance of movement, the lack of territorial stability, and the porosity of the language used to engage with space, one might feel compelled to conclude that no significant prospects exist for scholarly explorations of practices producing a clear, reliable sense of location and of belonging in the early modern Lusophone archive, other than one referring to the globe as a whole. It would be incorrect to do so, however, because a critique of old

---

[37] The standard English translation is Fernão Mendes Pinto, *The Travels of Mendes Pinto*, trans. and ed. Rebecca Catz (Chicago, IL and London: University of Chicago Press, 1989). The best annotated edition, serving as a gateway into the cultural and literary world of Luso-Asian encounters, is Fernão Mendes Pinto, *Peregrinação*, ed. Jorge Santos Alves, 4 vols (Lisbon: Fundação Oriente, 2010).

[38] Zoltán Biedermann, 'Imperial Reflections: China, Rome and the Logics of Global History in the *Décadas da Ásia* of João de Barros', in *Empires on the Move. Empires en marche*, eds François Lachaud and Dejanirah Couto (Paris: EFEO, 2017), pp. 23–47.

spatial categories does not necessarily entail discarding them altogether. In a delightful inversion of the logics of historical research, we may now seek out the 'local' in the interstices of texts and images apparently dominated by the supra-local. It is precisely here that the notion of 'translocality' (or, with a pinch of salt to alert us to the potential anachronism, 'transnationality') becomes central. Even historians of early globalization may wish to invoke the possibility of a specific sense of belonging, to anchor texts in local contexts, and to consider boundaries. Connectedness does not inevitably produce a detachment from the local, nor can the cosmopolitanism resulting from contacts be reduced to a single, frictionless vehicle of mutual understandings.[39] It has been shown how Goan authors engaging in the writing of global histories during the seventeenth and eighteenth centuries did so precisely to address local issues. These pertained to caste identity – a matter with wider pan-Indian implications – entwined with a profound, specifically Goan, sense of place.[40] The practice of localist encomiastic writing, i.e. singing the praise of one particular city over all others, was widespread in the European Renaissance and saw comparable expressions – sometimes in dialogue with Asian or African discourses – in places such as Hormuz (the 'precious stone' set into the 'ring' that was 'the world')[41] or Macau (a centre of learning, painting and devotion acting as a gateway to the highly sophisticated but pagan realms of China, Korea and Japan).[42]

Overall it may be advantageous to draw more attention than has been the case so far to complex, centripetal *and* centrifugal forces, where Lusophone texts became interwoven with other narratives – for example about the quasi-miraculous abundance and fertility of lands like the blessed *Laṅkā* (the island of Sri Lanka or Ceylon, associated in Pāli and Sinhala poetry with quasi-wondrous qualities), or the *Aurea Chersoneso* (an imagined southeast Asian realm abounding in gold), or the mysterious realms of the priestly kings of Ethiopia and Tibet.[43] As we gradually break free from the Eurocentric

---

[39] See *Sri Lanka at the Crossroads of History*, eds Zoltán Biedermann and Alan Strathern (London: UCL Press, 2017).

[40] Xavier, *A Invenção de Goa*.

[41] Barros, *Ásia*, II, book ii, chapter 2.

[42] On Macau as a central place, see Rui Manuel Loureiro, 'Macao: Frontier City and Maritime Trading Center', in *Encompassing the Globe. Portugal and the World in the 16th and 17th Centuries*, ed. Jay Levenson, II (Washington DC: Smithsonian, 2007), pp. 213–21.

[43] On Lanka, see Biedermann, *(Dis)connected Empires*; on the *Aurea Chersoneso*, see Manuel Godinho de Erédia, *Informação da Aurea Chersoneso ou Península, e das Ilhas Auríferas, Carbúnculas e Aromáticas*, ed. Rui Manuel Loureiro (Lisbon: CCCM, 2008).

perspective, the 'centrifugal' logics of the previous sentence then gradually assume the inverse, 'centripetal' character of a world where Lusophone travellers were not so much agents of 'expansion', as free-floating subjects attracted by powerful, prosperous and self-confident Asian, African, and to some extent American cultural centres in their own right. It was often after having been sucked into such a context that Portuguese individuals became disruptive agents of empire.

It is precisely in the latter sense of a process involving exposure, across the globe, to numerous local and regional forces, rather than in the sense of a linear process of diffusionist-cum-universalist power-building, that the historical process traditionally described as 'Portuguese expansion' gains significance for an understanding of the making of the early modern world. While it would be unwise to ignore the imperial logics of the process as it unfolded from the point of view of Lisbon and other European cities, the most challenging perspective today is clearly the one that opens up the panorama to include other foci and points of view (while *also* remaining alert, naturally, to expansionist, historically Eurocentric, impulses developing throughout the sixteenth and seventeenth centuries). If there is one lesson to be learnt from a rereading of the *Peregrinação* [*Peregrination*] of Fernão Mendes Pinto, for example, then it is this: while this key text of early modern Portuguese travel literature, one of the greatest travelogues ever written in any language, is deeply fascinating as a product of the European transition from Renaissance to Baroque, participating as it does in key discourses about the Portuguese monarchy, public mores and religious identity – it also does many other things.[44] Paramount among these is how Pinto opens up his 800-page account to distant voices from India, Burma, Siam, China, the Malay world and Japan. These are, then, not best described as entirely 'distant' anymore, but also as remarkably proximate. Like the porosity of borders in space and the porosity of language in time, the porosity of narrative traditions created a universe that was more than the sum of its parts. It is from its sustained and profound engagement with a whole series of different cultural and political centres far beyond Portuguese imperial reach that the *Peregrinação* draws its own power of attraction.

While the spatial logics of 'Portuguese expansion' have received some scholarly attention on the surface, the most interesting challenges today involve a questioning of the deeper layers of spatial (and, attached to that,

---

[44] The most authoritative exploration of this complexity can be found in Catarina Fouto, 'Revisiting Baroque Poetics in Fernão Mendes Pinto's *Peregrinação*: The Hermeneutics of Worldview', *ellipsis – Journal of the American Portuguese Studies Association*, 12 (2014), 65–89.

cultural) representation. New insights may be gained by submitting materials traditionally understood to be purely political to methods taken from cultural history. Even more may be obtained, inversely, from repoliticizing the analysis of cultural artefacts. The act of world-making cannot, after all, be seen as anything but a deeply political gesture when it comes to a period that saw such dramatic change on a global scale. The politics of space are deeply steeped in the politics of spatial representation, and vice versa. This interdependence, moreover, should not be studied in isolation from the profound impact that Asian, African and American cultures had on the so-called Portuguese sphere. The topics flagged up in this brief, exploratory overview are the tip of the iceberg, and there is reason to expect significant further developments once the spatial turn and the transnational turn begin to cross-pollinate in the realm of early modern Lusophone studies.

2

Translational Travails of Lusotropicalism

Anna M. Klobucka
University of Massachusetts Dartmouth

The relevance of Gilberto Freyre's voluminous intellectual output to modern and postmodern conceptualizations of transnational Lusophone space can hardly be overestimated. Regarded by many as 'the most famous intellectual of twentieth-century Brazil',[1] he was also among the most comparatively minded thinkers of the Portuguese-speaking world, his voracious but often vexingly undisciplined and self-indulgent mind moving restlessly across national and imperial boundaries in its search for defining constants of the global formation (not quite a system) Freyre came to assemble under the label of Lusotropicalism. With its basic outlines developed already in his first major work, which remains his most famous, *Casa-Grande & Senzala* [*The Masters and the Slaves*], published in 1933, Lusotropicalism received its resonant name and was fleshed out extensively by Freyre, over the following decades, as a doctrine of Portuguese colonial and postcolonial exceptionalism. Briefly, Freyre's reasoning proceeded from the foundational premise of the always already transcultural makeup of the Portuguese as 'the people existing indeterminately between Europe and Africa'.[2] This claim of constitutive cultural and ethnic hybridity in turn served to explain what Freyre described as the exceedingly successful integration of Portuguese colonizers in 'the tropics', integration manifest in a wide range of exhibits from the realm of material culture and immaterial sociocultural practices, but both driven and epitomized by the allegedly exceptional propensity of Portuguese men

---

[1] Peter Burke and Maria Lúcia G. Pallares-Burke, *Gilberto Freyre: Social Theory in the Tropics* (Oxford: Peter Lang, 2008), p. 15.

[2] Gilberto Freyre, *The Masters and the Slaves*, trans. Samuel Putnam, rev. edn (New York: Alfred A. Knopf, 1971), p. 4.

to engage in sexual relations with women of colour, leading to widespread miscegenation across the Portuguese empire.[3]

Freyre's Lusotropicalist writings consistently address the transnational, whether probing contrasts between imperial aspirations and practices of western European nation-states or commenting on postcolonial interplays among established and emergent nationalisms, for example. At the same time, they were themselves the product of a learning process that derived much of its substantive impetus from the cosmopolitan trajectory of Freyre's journeys from 1918 to the early 1950s. At the age of 18, he was sent from his native Recife to Baylor University in Texas, where he took his undergraduate degree, followed by a master's degree at Columbia University in New York.[4] In the interim, he travelled for the first time to Europe, spending a few 'so brief and so intense' days in Oxford, before visiting France, Germany, Belgium, Spain and Portugal.[5] Having returned to Brazil in 1923, he left again, in the wake of the 1930 revolution, for an extended period of travel and residence first in Portugal and later at Stanford University in California, where he held a visiting professorship. Having concluded his teaching duties at Stanford, he travelled across the US South and went on to spend some research time in Germany – all before coming back to Brazil to conclude and publish *Casa-Grande & Senzala*.

In later years, Freyre's most momentous international travels were propelled by invitations to present his increasingly influential work, as well as to encourage the expansion of his insights on the formation of Brazil onto the contemporary ground of late Portuguese empire. This was the case of his late-1930s lecture tour in Portugal and the UK and of the extended journey through Portugal and the Portuguese colonies in Africa and Asia, which he undertook between August 1951 and February 1952 at the invitation of Salazar's Estado Novo regime. The resulting publications

---

[3] For a succinct summary of the main features and chronological development of Freyre's Lusotropicalist doctrine, see Anna M. Klobucka, 'Lusotropicalism, Race and Ethnicity', in *A Historical Companion to Postcolonial Literatures: Continental Europe and Its Empires*, eds Prem Poddar, Rajeev S. Patke and Lars Jensen (Edinburgh: Edinburgh University Press, 2008), pp. 471–76.

[4] Jeffrey Needell offers a thorough account of Freyre's formative years in 'Identity, Race, Gender, and Modernity in the Origins of Gilberto Freyre's Oeuvre', *American Historical Review*, 100.1 (1995), 51–77. Alfredo Cesar Melo stresses the importance of Freyre's apprenticeship of US culture as the 'force structuring the worldview of the author of *Casa-Grande & Senzala*' in 'A outra América de Gilberto Freyre', *Revista USP*, 112 (2017), 55–66 (p. 58). Unless otherwise referenced, all translations are mine.

[5] As characterized in his diary, quoted by Maria Lúcia Garcia Pallares-Burke in *Gilberto Freyre: Um vitoriano dos trópicos* (São Paulo: Editora UNESP, 2005), p. 115.

– in particular, *O Mundo que o Português Criou* [*The World the Portuguese Created*] (1940) and *Aventura e Rotina* [*Adventure and Routine*] (1953) – testified to the shift of Freyre's intellectual direction from a thinker of the historical formation of Brazil into a doctrinaire of Luso-flavoured globalization and, crucially, of Brazil's future place in the evolving planetary order.[6] If the Freyre of *Casa-Grande & Senzala* was, in many respects, the product of its author's North American apprenticeship (with anthropologist Franz Boas, at Columbia, pointed to as the book's 'patron saint'),[7] the mid-century transatlantic and global Freyre was forged most clearly in the course of the grand tour he described in *Aventura e Rotina*, a diary of the voyage. The other book that resulted from the experience, *Um Brasileiro em Terras Portuguesas* [*A Brazilian in Portuguese Lands*], also published in 1953, gathered the lectures Freyre gave in the course of his tour, in which Lusotropicalism was for the first time explicitly named and conceptualized as such.[8] The latter, however, as Cristiana Bastos observes, was 'an academic volume along the lines of many others', while the more improvisational *Aventura e Rotina* displayed a 'contrapuntal fluidity, an ongoing flux of thought and reflection transcribed in the form of diary entries'.[9]

In the following pages, I will draw primarily on *Aventura e Rotina* and *Um Brasileiro em Terras Portuguesas* to consider Freyre's Lusotropicalism as a form of embodied theorizing of the transnational and translational Lusophone space, forged in the process of continuous refashioning of his ideas in response to spatial displacement and relational engagement with the human actors he encountered on his travels. This refashioning, on the one hand, bears out the essential adaptability and malleability of Freyre's thought (so that the author himself becomes a true counterpart of the mobile and flexible Portuguese subject of his doctrine), while on the other hand it reveals what could be named, echoing the subtitle of *Aventura e Rotina*, as 'the Freyrean constants of character and action'. One such constant is Freyre's recourse to filtering his thought processes and conclusions through an impressionistic and gendered prism of sensory perception, explicitly

---

[6] *O Mundo que o Português Criou* (Rio de Janeiro: José Olympio, 1940); *Aventura e Rotina. Sugestões de uma viagem à procura das constantes portuguesas de caráter e ação* (Rio de Janeiro: José Olympio, 1953). Henceforth, references to this volume will appear in the body of the text.

[7] Needell, 'Identity, Race, Gender, and Modernity in the Origins of Gilberto Freyre's Oeuvre', p. 67.

[8] *Um Brasileiro em Terras Portuguesas* (Lisbon: Livros do Brasil, n.d. [1953]).

[9] Cristiana Bastos, '*Aventura e Rotina*. Um livro de meio de percurso revisitado', in *Gilberto Freyre. Novas Leituras do Outro Lado do Atlântico*, eds Marcos Cardão and Cláudia Castelo (São Paulo: EDUSP, 2015), p. 35.

subjective perspective, and embodied affect. Another is his representation of the imperial and post-imperial Lusophone continuum as a space of ongoing intercultural translation, in which Freyre takes up the position of the interpreter in both senses of the word: as a person who interprets, i.e. explicates the meaning of the matter at hand; and as a person who performs simultaneous, *in situ* translation between (cultural) subjects who lack the means to communicate directly. I will identify some intersections of these two dimensions of Freyre's intellectual agency in the works that mark his transition from 'Freyre the interpreter of Brazil' to 'the Freyre who expands the sphere of his analysis from the Brazilian Northeast to the ensemble of connections and exchanges that will become known as [...] the "Lusotropical" universe'.[10] It is also in these works that the travelling Freyre may be said to reincarnate as an updated version of the hero of his doctrine, the male Portuguese subject of the colonial conquest and settlement, whose affective engagement with the welcoming woman/land of the tropics defines and distinguishes the Lusophone imperial and post-imperial experience.

Lusotropicalism as embodied translation

Translation has been an important, structuring concept in modern cultural anthropology, particularly since the 1950s, when the recognition of the centrality of language in the processes of historical continuity and social learning came to dominate the perspective of social anthropologists. Concomitantly, the notion of culture, earlier understood (to quote E. B. Tylor's famous definition) as 'that complex whole which includes knowledge, belief, art, morals, law, custom, and any other capabilities and habits acquired by man as a member of society', was transformed 'into the notion of a *text* – that is, into something resembling an inscribed discourse', while the phrase 'the translation of cultures' has become, in the words of Talal Asad, 'an almost banal description of the distinctive task of social anthropology'.[11] Freyre's Lusotropicalist writings, although rooted conceptually in a view of culture more akin to Tylor's broadly ethnographic perspective than to the contemporary anthropological mindset diagnosed by Asad, rely to a considerable degree on the notion of cultural translatability. Their author did not, of course, ascribe to the notions of language and discourse the kind of

---

[10] Bastos, '*Aventura e Rotina*. Um livro de meio de percurso revisitado', p. 36.

[11] Talal Asad, 'The Concept of Cultural Translation in British Social Anthropology', in *Writing Culture: The Poetics and Politics of Ethnography*, eds James Clifford and George E. Marcus (Berkeley, CA: University of California Press, 1986), p. 141. Original emphasis.

theoretical centrality that has become commonplace in much of the more recent anthropological writing, in the aftermath of what came to be termed the 'literary turn' in cultural anthropology.[12] On the other hand, however, Freyre's insistent emphasis on forms of cultural hybridity and the processes of what we would now call transculturation[13] makes reading his texts a strangely asynchronic experience, which Miguel Vale de Almeida has diagnosed aptly by referring to Freyre's 'premature postcolonial discourse'.[14]

Freyre's propensity toward translational modes of thought and imagination lies at the very root of his Lusotropicalist enterprise. As already noted, the basic premise of his doctrine was the 'singular disposition of the Portuguese to the hybrid, slave-exploiting colonization of the tropics' explicable by 'the ethnic or, better, the cultural past of the people existing indeterminately between Europe and Africa'.[15] This identitarian construct became then the pivotal point in Freyre's translation (in its original etymological sense of 'carrying over') of Brazilian miscegenation ideology onto the ground of the Portuguese colonies in Africa and Asia. To reiterate, it is the 'always already' translated character of the Portuguese – Africans in Europe, Europeans in Africa – that makes them, in Freyre's estimation, such successful colonizers of Brazil; and it is the central place occupied by their translational fluency in Freyre's Brazilian historical narrative that makes this narrative, in turn, such a highly translatable one – translatable not so much *back* into its 'original' Luso-African idiom as *forward* into what Freyre would eventually describe and label as the lingua franca of Lusotropicalism.

Freyre's tour of Portugal and most of its colonies – specifically, Portuguese Guinea (now Guinea-Bissau), Cape Verde, São Tomé, Angola, Mozambique

---

[12] As exemplified, for instance, by Clifford and Marcus's influential collection *Writing Culture* (see note 11 above).

[13] The term 'transculturation' was coined in 1947 by Cuban anthropologist Fernando Ortiz in opposition to the then common concept of 'acculturation', which referred to the assimilation of indigenous and other subaltern groups to the dominant culture. As Robert J. C. Young elaborates, transculturation 'does not describe cultural contact as such, nor the cultural synthesis that may be its eventual product, but the moment of passage from one culture to another in which different heterogeneous cultures collide and ferment [...] [and which] also enables the reinvention and reinscription of cultural materials that may have been transmitted by a culturally dominant group', Robert J. C. Young, *Postcolonialism: An Historical Introduction* (Oxford: Blackwell, 2001), p. 202.

[14] Miguel Vale de Almeida, 'The Brown Atlantic', Colloquium *Race, Culture, Nation: Arguments across the Portuguese-Speaking World* (unpublished talk presented at the Watson Institute for International Relations, Brown University, 6 April 2001).

[15] Freyre, *The Masters and the Slaves*, p. 4.

and Goa – in the early 1950s was a decisive event in the process of gradual cooptation of his ideas by Salazar's propagandists, chronicled by Cláudia Castelo in her comprehensive historical account.[16] As Castelo documents, the initial reception of Freyre's claims by the regime in the 1930s and 1940s had been largely negative, given that the forms of Portuguese colonial ideology dominant at the time appeared incompatible with Freyre's attribution of positive value to reciprocal exchanges leading toward generalized racial and cultural hybridity. The Estado Novo's ideologues promoted, by contrast, the colonial policy of a one-sided dissemination of Western civilizational principles, with the colonizers remaining unaffected at their core by the cultures of the colonized. This divergence between the two approaches to the processes of cultural translation occurring in the colonial context may be viewed in terms of the contrastive binary discussed in Friedrich Schleiermacher's foundational lecture, 'On the Different Methods of Translating' (1813). In this text, Schleiermacher famously identified two courses available to a translator: 'Either the translator leaves the author in peace [...] and moves the reader towards him; or he leaves the reader in peace [...] and moves the author toward him.'[17] In Lawrence Venuti's rephrasing of Schleiermacher's terminology, the translator's choice lies 'between the domesticating method, an ethnocentric reduction of the foreign text to target-language cultural values [...] and a foreignizing method, an ethnodeviant pressure on those values to register the linguistic and cultural difference of the foreign text [...]'.[18] Freyre's theory of intercultural translation appeared to offer a strong endorsement of the foreignizing approach to the transmission of values and forms of existence – the Portuguese becoming thoroughly 'tropicalized' even as they busied themselves with lusifying the tropics – while the colonial ideology of the Portuguese regime in the 1930s and 1940s favoured the domesticating mode of uncompromising acculturation of the colonial other, with no reciprocal effect on the colonizing agents themselves.

Of course, what made Freyre's doctrine particularly objectionable in the early stages of its dissemination in Portugal was the Brazilian author's positive emphasis on racial miscegenation: that is, on a foreignizing translation not just of cultural realities but of actual human bodies. It is instructive to note,

---

[16] Cláudia Castelo, *O modo português de estar no mundo'. O luso-tropicalismo e a ideologia colonial portuguesa (1933–1961)* (Porto: Afrontamento, 1998).

[17] Friedrich Schleiermacher, 'On the Different Methods of Translating', in *Translating Literature: The German Tradition from Luther to Rozenzweig*, trans. and ed. André Lefevere (Assen: Van Gorcum, 1977), p. 74.

[18] Lawrence Venuti, *The Translator's Invisibility: A History of Translation* (New York: Routledge, 1995), p. 20.

in this context, that Schleiermacher's ambivalent meditation expresses its strongest criticism of the foreignizing method through the metaphor of illegitimate reproduction. As he asks rhetorically, 'Who would not like to permit his mother tongue to stand forth everywhere in the most universally appealing beauty each genre is capable of? Who would not rather sire children who are their parents' pure effigy, and not bastards?'[19] Gilberto Freyre, that is who, by way of the Portuguese protagonists of his narrative:

> The Portuguese man's body nearly always belonged more to the Overseas colonies than to Europe. [...] No matter how much his soul remained that of a Christian from Minho or Trás-os-Montes [...], his vigorous male body multiplied, in the Orient, in the Africas, and in America, into brown, red, yellow, tawny bodies; and to these bodies he communicated his Portuguese character.[20]

Freyre's apparently wholehearted embrace of the foreignizing direction in intercultural translation is most clearly articulated in his comments on the Portuguese language and the transformations it has undergone in colonial contact zones, becoming marked, as a result, 'by a quality of exuberance, crossbreeding, contradiction'.[21] While (male) Portuguese bodies propagated themselves like texts through genetic channels of communication, Portuguese words behaved, in Freyre's imagination, as extraordinarily mobile and flexible travellers who, 'having gone to the Orient [...] or to the Overseas colonies [...] returned to Europe transformed. Some rounded, others elongated. All augmented by the addition of a new meaning or a new flavour.'[22] In this process, the role of the most adventurous and successful of facilitators is attributed to Luís de Camões, the words of whose epic poem 'appear [...] in positions and relationships so new to Portuguese eyes and ears, and so adventurous to European intelligence and sensibility, that *Os Lusíadas*, [as] linguistic creation and literary work, [...] must have had something [sic] the same impact on its first XVIth century readers in Europe as James Joyce's *Ulysses* on modern readers'.[23]

---

[19] Schleiermacher, 'On the Different Methods of Translating', p. 79.
[20] Freyre, *Um Brasileiro*, p. 21.
[21] Freyre, *Um Brasileiro*, p. 17.
[22] Freyre, *Um Brasileiro*, p. 18.
[23] Freyre, *The Portuguese and the Tropics*, trans. Helen M. D'O. Matthew and F. de Mello Moser (Lisbon: Executive Committee for the Commemoration of the Fifth Centenary of the Death of Prince Henry the Navigator, 1961), p. 114. This English translation was published by the Estado Novo government concurrently with the

The new 'positions and relationships' that Camões's proto-Lusotropical genius forced upon the Portuguese language recall, once again, Schleiermacher's ambivalent wrestling with the potential disadvantages of the foreignizing method (which nonetheless he ends up advocating). Here he is, once again, rhetorically questioning its profoundly 'unnatural' and counterintuitive tendencies: 'Who would put up with being considered clumsy, by trying to keep as close to the foreign language as his own language allows? Who would suffer being accused, like those parents who abandon their children to acrobats, of bending his mother tongue to foreign and unnatural dislocations instead of skillfully exercising it in its own natural gymnastics?'[24]

Freyre's enthusiasm for the sort of transcultural transformation of linguistic (and other) matter that from a more orthodox viewpoint of cultural nationalism has tended to be denounced in terms akin to Schleiermacher's 'foreign and unnatural dislocations' would appear to make him an ideal precursor of the postcolonial and multicultural trends in contemporary translation theory. Venuti's explicitly political endorsement of the foreignizing method (in the Anglophone context) illustrates this point well: as a check on 'the ethnocentric violence of translation', it becomes 'a strategic cultural intervention [...] pitched against the hegemonic English-language nations and the unequal cultural exchanges in which they engage their global others [...] a form of resistance against ethnocentrism and racism, cultural narcissism and imperialism, in the interest of democratic geopolitical relations'.[25]

However, potential cooptation of Freyre's translational imagination into the political orbit sketched out by Venuti falters on at least one substantial stumbling block, contained in the account of his encounter with Cape Verde in *Aventura e Rotina*. Freyre's visit to the archipelago was highly anticipated, given that, in the 1930s and 1940s, his perspectives on racial miscegenation and interpenetration of cultures in the Brazilian context proved very attractive to Cape Verdean intellectuals of the *Claridade* movement.[26] For example, Baltasar Lopes's essay, 'Uma experiência românica nos trópicos' ['A Romance Experience in the Tropics'] (published in *Claridade* in 1947), discussed Cape

Portuguese original, *O Luso e o Trópico*, in which the Lusotropicalist doctrine assumed its definitive form. A French translation also appeared at the same time.

[24] Schleiermacher, 'On the Different Methods of Translating', p. 79.

[25] Venuti, *The Translator's Invisibility*, p. 20.

[26] *Claridade* was a literary and cultural magazine published in Mindelo, on the island of São Vicente, between 1936 and 1960, whose editors dedicated themselves to examining and expressing Cape Verde's cultural specificity. For a focused overview of *Claridade*'s intellectual and political project, see Ellen W. Sapega, 'Notes on the Historical Context of *Claridade*', *Portuguese Literary and Cultural Studies*, 8 (2002), 159–70.

Verdean Creole in a Freyrean framework as a particularly successful product of Lusotropical transculturation.

It therefore came as a painful surprise to his Cape Verdean readers that in the pages of *Aventura e Rotina* devoted to the islands, Freyre nearly denounces Cape Verde as unworthy of belonging to the Lusotropical continuum.[27] In lieu of the near-replica of the Brazilian northeast that he was led to believe he would encounter in the archipelago, to his eyes, its population and material culture resemble instead more closely the Caribbean islands, an 'Afro-Portuguese' Martinique or Trinidad (291). Paradoxically, Freyre points to the generalized use of the Creole 'dialect' – 'which no Portuguese or Brazilian can comprehend unless he has been initiated into its secrets' (291) – as one of two main reasons for Cape Verde's 'indefinition of cultural character', the other being the alleged absence of culturally hybrid popular arts (304). The same Freyre who a month later will write that his dominant impression of Goa is 'that I am not in an exotic land but [...] in Brazil' (319) now uses the same vocabulary to describe 'the first exotic impression Cape Verde produces in any Brazilian': 'We are accustomed to an immense Brazil in which only Portuguese is spoken, better or worse, in some areas influenced by Italians or Germans, in others by Africans or Amerindians. But always Portuguese' (291). The excessive foreignization at work in the interpenetration of cultures that has produced Cape Verdean Creole is contrasted by Freyre with the Brazilian transculturation of the Portuguese language: 'At the same time that I am repulsed by the Cape Verdean dialect, I enjoy hearing Cape Verdean people speak Portuguese in their own way, which is a tropical, Brazilian way' (301). Even then, however, the Cape Verdean modality of the prospective Lusotropical utopia stands as a borderline case. Some Portuguese words become more expressive, richer, when spoken by Cape Verdeans, but others, 'instead of gaining in expressiveness, appear to lose it [...] dissolv[ing] into [...] words so mushy that they seem to only be of use to mothers speaking to small children, old maids to their lapdogs, and girls to their dolls' (301). And the conclusion of this passage is unambiguously censorious, as well as quite uncharacteristic in the context of Freyre's usual, broadly promiscuous,

---

[27] For comprehensive accounts of Freyre's Cape Verdean sojourn and its consequences, see Osvaldo Manuel Silvestre, 'A aventura Crioula revisitada: versões do Atlântico negro em Gilberto Freyre, Baltasar Lopes e Manuel Ferreira', in *ACT 6: Literatura e Viagens Pós-Coloniais*, eds Helena C. Buescu and Manuela Ribeiro Sanches (Lisbon: Centro de Estudos Comparatistas/Edições Colibri, 2002), pp. 63–103; and Fernando Arenas, 'Reverberações lusotropicais: Gilberto Freyre em África', in *Gilberto Freyre e os Estudos Latino-Americanos*, eds Joshua Lund and Malcolm McNee (Pittsburgh, PA: Instituto Internacional de Literatura Iberoamericana, 2006), pp. 123–45.

view of cultural miscegenation: 'The tropics act upon the words and the men who arrive from Europe in a way that needs to have its limits set in order to be healthy' (301).

It is worth observing that Freyre's gendered criticism of Cape Verdean linguistic transculturation resonates with other rhetorical figures of personification scattered throughout *Aventura e Rotina*, in which cultural products – ranging from language sounds to cities – are ideologized by way of their inscription into the gender binary. Here is Freyre on nasal diphtongs, for instance: 'But the "ãos" of the Portuguese language [...]. What other language has sounds as virile as that spoken by the mariners who first ventured out into "seas never before sailed" by Europeans?' (166).[28] The essentialized masculine and 'virile' quality, metonymically shared by the Portuguese conquerors and their language, is the necessary complement of the metaphorical convergence, recurrently expressed by Freyre, between the conquerable land and the penetrable female body, which in turn becomes the core premise of the Lusotropicalist worldview. Praising the action of the so-called 'lançados' (early land explorers and settlers) in West Africa, Freyre describes them as leading agents of the 'penetration' of Guinea by the Portuguese: 'Penetration of the black women's flesh, of the bowels of black lands, of indigenous cultures filled with darkness to the eyes of blind Europeans' (267). In the twentieth-century reality Freyre observes in Portuguese Guinea, the metaphor remains valid, although it is rephrased in more politically correct Lusotropicalist terms: the land now begins to be 'loved and not merely deflowered', and several Portuguese Freyre spoke to are attached to Guinea 'by love and not by the Don Juanism of a brutal conqueror of exotic lands' (279).

The apparently free-wheeling enterprise of intercultural translation, as laid out by Freyre in his 'transatlantic' mid-century texts, reveals therefore at least two categorical and unsurpassable internal limits. One arises in opposition to linguistic and cultural creolization, which is claimed to have moved beyond the tipping point in Cape Verde, into a sphere of incommensurability and hence incommunicability in the European idiom of colonization; to attempt to communicate with Cape Verdeans on their own, creolized and thus decolonial terms appears as an impossibility to Freyre.[29] The other

---

[28] 'Seas never before sailed' is Camões's famous expression in the first stanza of *Os Lusíadas* [*The Lusiads*]. Freyre is responding here to the commonplace characterization of the Portuguese language as a 'softer' version of Spanish, 'a Hispanic language so spineless as to be some kind of women's idiom when compared to Spanish, always so hard and macho' (166).

[29] For further discussion of this issue, and in particular of Cape Verdean oppositional appropriation (by Gabriel Mariano) of Freyre's ideas on hybridity, which

limit, which remains a constant throughout his writings, is the naturalized maleness of Lusotropicalist agency. If, as Jessica Berman has claimed, any truly consequential transnationalist epistemology 'must intersect with discursive categories surrounding not only the nation/state but also the sex/gender and other normative systems that undergird it' and must give full due to 'the challenges [global texts] can pose to normative regimes of embodiment and subjectivity', then Freyre's gender ideology becomes exposed as one of the leading paradoxes of his work: his global and transcultural thinking remains firmly rooted in normative and indeed deeply conservative models of gendered embodiment and relationality.[30]

Freyre's post-imperial spatiality

Commenting, in *Aventura e Rotina*, on his meeting with the Portuguese Minister of the Overseas,[31] Freyre conveys (and appears to endorse) the official's view that the country's 'overseas provinces', formerly known as colonies, 'all form one single Portugal, ever more conscious of its unity, which encompasses the audacity of diversity' (383). What we might diagnose as a centripetal consolidation of global Portugueseness – in the wake of poorly regulated scattering of the national substance throughout the history of Portuguese colonialism – pervades Freyre's travel narrative in idiosyncratic but generally well-aligned conformity with official Estado Novo ideology. This consolidation may be contrasted with the contrary rhetorical and spatial movement patent in *Aventura e Rotina*, which places Brazil on a centrifugal trajectory of global propagation that mimics discursively the centuries-old impetus of the Portuguese 'Discoveries'. Although in his preface Freyre juxtaposes the plural 'various Portugals dispersed throughout the world' (9) with the singular Brazil, it is Freyre's homeland, as evoked recurrently in *Aventura e Rotina*, that plays the role of a dynamically multiplying and advancing signifier of present and future global Lusophone networking. As Bastos notes,

---

manages to 'highlight in positive terms what Freyre had diagnosed as negative', see Alfredo Cesar Melo, 'Hibridismos (in)domáveis: Possíveis contribuições da obra de Gilberto Freyre para uma teoria pós-colonial lusófona', *Luso-Brazilian Review*, 51.1 (2014), 68–92 (p. 83).

[30] Jessica Berman, 'Is the Trans in Transnational the Trans in Transgender?', *Modernism/Modernity*, 2.2 (2017) <https://modernismmodernity.org/articles/trans-transnational> [accessed 13 September 2017].

[31] The Ministério do Ultramar [Overseas Ministry] was created in August 1950, replacing the Ministry of the Colonies; the change reflected the constitutional revision according to which Portuguese colonies were rebranded as 'overseas provinces'. At the time of Freyre's journey, the post was held by Manuel Sarmento Rodrigues.

'*Aventura* is not a book about Brazil, but it is a book that carries Brazil with it in its pocket, its soul, its vision, and its heart.'[32] I will highlight here some examples of Freyre's nationalist sentiment that make it possible to read his travelogue as an aspirational narrative of Brazil claiming for itself – two decades ahead of the ultimate demise of the Portuguese empire – the global leadership role in the prospective evolution of the Lusotropical cultural and political sphere.

At one point in *Aventura e Rotina*, Freyre narrates a conversation with an 'Angolan separatist' who asked him whether the moment had come for Angola to detach itself from Portugal, as Brazil had done in 1822, to which Freyre answers: 'No, I think the moment has come for Brazil to reconnect with Portugal' (493). This conversation illustrates, first of all, the place occupied by Brazil as a role model in the anticolonial and nationalist imagination of African intellectuals, as 'an example of a culturally autonomous country that had succeeded in affirming its difference with respect to its former colonizer'.[33] But Freyre's coyly indirect answer encourages a multiplicity of possible readings. On the one hand, it provides a cover for any suspicion, potentially attributable to his Estado Novo sponsors, of Freyre's intention to grant Angola an actual or prospective status superior to that of Portugal's 'overseas province': the 'Portugal' of his answer can be read as the transcontinental nation-state stretching 'from Minho to Timor', as the imperial regime's official slogan had it, in which Angola can have no political subjecthood of its own.[34] But by implying that any answer to Angola's aspirations passes through Brazil's international agency, Freyre at once reinforces his country's status as the only autonomous Lusophone state player on an equal footing with Portugal and floats the possibility of a potentially independent Brazilian–Angolan alliance across the South Atlantic. In any case, the active movement of 'reconnecting with Portugal' is Brazil's to make or withhold, emphasizing the former colony's centrality to any global realignment of post-imperial Lusophone status quo.

Writing about the medieval and postmedieval genealogy of the notion of translatability of cultures, Karlheinz Stierle explores the interplay of the concepts of *translatio sapientiae* or *studii* (translation of knowledge) and *translatio imperii* (translation of power), which organized such cultural and political transfers as the vertical 'act of translation' of the Roman Empire

---

[32] Bastos, '*Aventura e Rotina*. Um livro de meio de percurso revisitado', p. 41.

[33] Melo, 'A outra América de Gilberto Freyre', p. 86.

[34] On the mapping of Portuguese imperial spatiality in Estado Novo propaganda, see Heriberto Cairo, '"Portugal Is Not a Small Country": Maps and Propaganda in the Salazar Regime', *Geopolitics*, 11 (2006), 367–95.

from Byzantium to Franconia (with the crowning of Charlemagne in Rome in 800) and the successive horizontal displacements of the European centre of learning and culture, from Greece to Rome, then to France (or England), and finally (in Dante's estimation) to Italy.[35] An analogous intersection of the translation of (imperial) power and the translation of (Lusotropical) knowledges is a useful prism through which to observe Freyre's participatory survey of the Portuguese empire. In the course of his travels, he acts as a symbolic cartographer who maps Brazilian realities onto his perception of the Portuguese colonies in Africa and Asia, with his impressionistically embodied vision deploying intuitive recognition as a tool that enables a *translatio sapientiae* whose implied (and sometimes near-explicit) telos is a *translatio imperii*.

This process of mapping obeys distinct, site-specific logics as Freyre progresses on his journey. In Guinea, the focus is historical: as he visits indigenous villages, the traveller comments on his 'impression that I am seeing the very African beginnings of Brazil'; their inhabitants are 'my old acquaintances from drawings by Rugendas and Debret, from books by Koster and Maria Graham' (263). The black Guineans appear to Freyre 'as if frozen in time [...] in the same state as those from 1500 and 1600', who 'left here to enter the history, and the life and culture, of Brazil' (268). Guinea is the past of Brazil, but Brazil can also be its future, since that is where its allegedly static, unevolving inhabitants were originally able to 'enter history' through their enslavement and removal across the Atlantic; and since the developmental challenges Guinea presents to its imperial masters are modeled by Freyre on those of Brazil's own incompletely colonized territories: it is 'as if Guinea were to Portugal what the interior of Amazonas or Mato Grosso is to Brazil' (277). Angola exists, for Freyre, on the same historical continuum, but occupying a more advanced place on the trajectory of Lusotropical progress, like a Brazil 'already matured into a hybrid society, with an already sizeable mixed-race population' (397). At any rate, the flash of recognition is unmistakable – 'Even in his speech, a Portuguese born in Angola [...] seems more Brazilian than Portuguese' – and Brazil-as-aspiration remains firmly in play: the example Freyre gives of an Angolan who 'has a lot more in common with a Brazilian than with a Portuguese from Europe' is a talented journalist 'who dreams day and night about Brazil: about going to Rio or São Paulo' (394).

Goa, however, epitomizes more than any other location on Freyre's itinerary the intuitively sensed convergence with Brazil. His impression of

---

[35] Karlheinz Stierle, '*Translatio Studii* and Renaissance: From Vertical to Horizontal Translation', in *The Translatability of Cultures: Figuration of the Space in Between*, eds Sanford Budick and Wolfgang Iser (Stanford, CA: Stanford University Press, 1996), pp. 55–67 (p. 56).

the capital Panaji (Pangim in Portuguese) is that of a small colonial city in the Brazilian north, and the lens of exoticism and estrangement is conclusively rejected: 'both the landscape and the population appear to a Brazilian as landscapes and populations already seen and already known, and not Oriental to the point of being exotic' (319). In Goa, Freyre's claims of recognition become insistent and redundant as he shares the impression of finding himself 'completely' in Brazil: 'It is not only the similarities between people in form and colour. [...] Not just all the more conspicuous outward features. But also the subtler ones' (323). This absolute identification stands in contrast to the prospective relationship between Goa and the recently proclaimed Republic of India: should Goa cease to belong to Portugal, Freyre declares, it 'would remain so Luso-Indian in its culture that its situation within the Union of India might be, if not that of an alien body, that of a supremely alien soul. A lost soul' (333).[36] And this geopolitical pivot continues with the encouragement for Brazil to take advantage of the economic opportunities Goa presents, 'facilitating for Portuguese-speaking and technically trained Luso-Indians integration into Brazilian life and activities' (335). Decades before any mention of the BRIC bloc, Freyre effectively assumes the role of a bilateral negotiator between emerging economic and political powers of the southern hemisphere, diverting away from the Soviet Union and toward the 'restlessly revolutionary' nation of Brazil the hopeful vision of a young Marxist he encounters in Goa (377). In his vision, as expressed in *Aventura e Rotina*, Brazil's place in relation to the (still virtual) post-imperial Lusophone sphere remains politically ambivalent: once the jewel in the crown of the Portuguese empire, twentieth-century Brazil figures simultaneously as the emancipated and emancipating model of anti-imperial struggle, and as the prospective future metropolis of the reimagined, or translated, Lusotropical *imperium*.

---

[36] India became independent from British rule in August 1947; the constitution of the Republic of India came into effect in January 1950.

3

English Pirates in Brazil

Early Anglo-Portuguese Relations in the New World

Vivien Kogut Lessa de Sá and Sheila Moura Hue

University of Cambridge and
Universidade do Estado do Rio de Janeiro

England and Brazil in the sixteenth century

The maritime expansion begun by Portugal in the fifteenth century ushered in a period of widespread cultural exchange, which took on new dimensions when Columbus first arrived in the Caribbean in 1492, touching a hitherto unknown continent. The encounter with this 'New World' led not only to refashionings of the world map but, most importantly, to a reassessment of existing knowledge and beliefs as Europeans came into contact with cultures vastly different from their own. The first century following Columbus's momentous landfall saw ideas of national identity and cultural prerogative being radically challenged as European powers fought over political and economic hegemony of the newfound lands. Portugal and Spain tried to assert their alleged territorial ownership over the Americas only to see France, the Netherlands and England challenging their claims on land and at sea. One palpable result of the political, cultural and epistemological impact of the discovery of America and the many voyages that ensued was the vast body of texts produced by European voyagers, missionaries, merchants, cosmographers and settlers. Their attempt to record and reflect on early encounters with the new lands and people offers a good representation of the various perspectives and aims involved in maritime enterprises in the New World. It also brings into focus the complexity of transnational relationships evolving during the early modern period between Europe and the Americas.

One of the most interesting and yet little studied parts of this *corpus* relates to English voyages to Brazil in the sixteenth century. Throughout the first century after its discovery in 1500, Brazil was intermittently visited by English travellers bent on varying endeavours: from replenishing their ships to trading with locals, from exploring unknown parts of Iberian possessions to amassing for themselves at least a portion of their riches. The extant records of such voyages, which begin with Sebastian Cabot's in 1526, form a fascinating testament to the changing commercial, religious and political relations between England and the Iberian colonies, most specifically the one Portuguese colony in the New World. Many of these texts – travelogues, letters, relations and depositions – were compiled and published by the English cosmographer Richard Hakluyt between 1598 and 1600 in his renowned three-volume collection, *The Principal Navigations*.[1] Though the collection covered voyages of exploration across the world, Hakluyt's excitement about the New World is palpable in volume 3. It manifested itself not only in his personal involvement with the Virginia colony project in North America, but also in his proposal for a permanent English outpost located on the southern coast of Brazil, to aid English expeditions heading for the Pacific.[2]

Even though a permanent English settlement in Brazil was never established, since the early decades of the sixteenth century the Brazilian coast was frequented by English ships looking for trade. Such voyages also involved gaining a better knowledge of the new Portuguese dominions and the riches they could yield.[3] Hakluyt suggests it was the navigator William Hawkins who pioneered these voyages in the early 1530s and who was so bold as to bring back to England a native Brazilian chief to be displayed at Henry VIII's court.[4] At the time, Hawkins boasted about the ease with which the English dealt with the indigenous people, setting the tone for many later accounts of such encounters, as will be seen below in Thomas Cavendish's attack on Santos. Still, according to Hakluyt, in the 1540s a number of English merchants engaged in the 'commodious and gainefull voyage to Brasil', which involved bartering with Brazilian coastal tribes for 'commodities of the country'.[5] This informal coastal trade had been exploited by the French since the first years

---

[1] *The Principall Navigations, Voyages, Traffiques and Discovery of the English Nation*, ed. Richard Hakluyt (London: Bishop Newberie and Barker, 1598–1600).

[2] *The Original Writings and Correspondence of the Two Richard Hakluyts*, ed. E. G. R. Taylor, 2 vols (London: The Hakluyt Society, 1935), I, p. 146.

[3] For a comprehensive survey of English accounts of voyages to Brazil in the sixteenth and early seventeenth centuries, see Sheila Hue, 'Ingleses no Brasil: relatos de viagem 1526–1608', *Anais da Biblioteca Nacional*, 126 (2009), 7–68.

[4] 'A brief relation of two sundry voyages made by the worshipful M. William Hawkins…', in Hakluyt, *Principall Navigations* [1600], p. 700.

[5] 'An ancient voyage of M. Robert Reniger and M. Thomas Borey to Brasil in the yeere of our Lord 1540', in Hakluyt, *Principall Navigations* [1600], p. 701.

after the discovery of Brazil in 1500, and became so intense as to prompt Portuguese action in the 1530s in the form of coastguard expeditions and, later, as systematic settlement.

French, English and later Dutch intrusions on the coast of Brazil were largely the result of territorial disputes over the New World, which, from the mid-sixteenth century, began being played out at sea. For England, privateering voyages were a way of countering Spain's and Portugal's claim to territory in the Americas. Still, until the mid-1570s Brazil managed to stay largely free of corsair attacks, such as those of Francis Drake on the Spanish possessions in the New World. At the time, Brazil represented merely a convenient waystation to the mineral-rich Spanish territories. But a number of factors conspired to change this. On the one hand, news of recently discovered mines near São Vicente in southeast Brazil fed into already existing English ambitions in the New World. On the other, relations between England and Spain degenerated into open war in 1585, following the union of the Iberian crowns under Spain. Brazil, now a Spanish possession, automatically became the focus of systematic corsair attacks. A number of privateering expeditions funded by nobles, merchants and 'adventurers' and often bearing the royal seal of approval sailed the Atlantic with dubious intentions: to fulfil high material ambitions but also, and very importantly, to assert and extend national hegemonies while stoking patriotic fervour.

The extant accounts of English voyages to Brazil in the late sixteenth century attest to changing political relations between England and Portugal. From 1580, with the Spanish king taking over the Portuguese crown,[6] encounters became increasingly tense on the coast of Brazil, and peaceful trade often deteriorated into mutual suspicion and, occasionally, into hostile confrontation. In the same decade the first all-out siege would take place in Salvador da Bahia by the Earl of Cumberland's men.[7] The outcome of such incursions involved not just material loss or gain but intense cultural interactions that would outlive these encounters. The documents emerging from two other attacks on the coast of Brazil in the late sixteenth century are perhaps exemplary of such transnational negotiations.

---

[6] The Iberian crowns were united under the Spanish king for 60 years, between 1580 and 1640.

[7] See John Sarracol, 'The voiage set out by the right honorable the Earl of Cumberland...', in *Principall Navigations* [1600], ed. Hakluyt, pp. 793–803.

Thomas Cavendish and the 1591 attack on Santos

When Thomas Cavendish landed in Santos, in December 1591, he already enjoyed a solid reputation for great maritime exploits. He had successfully circumnavigated the world three years earlier (1586–88), when he made a brief stop in Brazil at an uninhabited island. His main aim then had been to plunder Spanish shipping both in the Atlantic and the Pacific while asserting English maritime hegemony, following the example of Drake's circumnavigation (1577–80). His arrival back in England, after seizing a phenomenal Spanish cargo in the Pacific, coincided with the defeat of the Spanish Armada in the English Channel and fed into the patriotic frenzy that ensued.[8] Famously, Queen Elizabeth I, upon seeing such wealth being brought to her kingdom straight from the hands of the loathed Spaniards, was reported to have said: 'The king of Spain barks a good deal but he does not bite. We care nothing for Spaniards, their ships loaded with gold and silver from the Indies come hither after all.'[9] The voyage's far-reaching echoes of nationalistic enthusiasm could be seen not only in ballads composed at the time but also in the various translations and editions of Cavendish's letter of triumph which began circulating in Europe shortly after his return.[10]

On the 1591 voyage, the plan was to bank on the knowledge previously obtained in order to destabilize Iberian hegemony in both the Atlantic and the Pacific and to make sizable financial gains. In July, Cavendish set sail for the Pacific via the Straits of Magellan, but this time the planned stopover in Brazil would include an attack on Santos, a coastal settlement in the southeast where rumours of mineral riches were beginning to emerge. Cavendish attacked the village late in December and besieged it for two months. Ironically, this long siege may have led to the failure of the whole enterprise: the fleet never managed to cross the Straits of Magellan and only a third of its men managed to return to England (Cavendish himself not being one of them).

Luckily for us, there are three extant accounts of the voyage: a letter written by Cavendish, an account given by John Jane, travelling aboard

---

[8] In 1588 the conflict between England and Spain came to a head when the mighty Spanish fleet, also known as the 'Invincible Armada', attempted, and failed, to invade England via the English Channel.

[9] Letter dated November 1588 written by D. Bernardino de Mendoza, Spanish Ambassador to England, in *Calendar of State Papers, Spanish, IV, 1587–1603* (London: Longman, 1899), p. 481.

[10] For details on the use of Cavendish's circumnavigation for English nationalistic propaganda, see David B. Quinn and David R. Ransome, 'Economic and Political Profit-Taking in the Aftermath of Thomas Cavendish's Circumnavigation of the Globe, 1588–89', *Terrae Incognitae*, 29.1 (1997), 22–34.

the ship *Desire*, and the account of Anthony Knivet, a young soldier on Cavendish's ship. Each of these narrators had very different agendas in describing the events taking place in Santos late in 1591.[11] Cavendish's letter was written shortly before he died at sea and is infused with hatred. His main aim was to lay the blame for the failure of the whole enterprise on John Davis, a renowned sea captain in charge of the *Desire*. Jane prepared his account upon returning to England in 1593 deliberately to clear the name of Davis, on whose ship he travelled. Our third informant, Knivet, was left behind in Brazil in 1592 to die at the hands of the Portuguese. Nine years later he managed to return to England and left us a remarkable description of early colonial Brazil.[12] He also provides some interesting details of the English incursion in Santos.

Knivet reports how the English seized the village on Christmas Eve, taking advantage of the fact that almost all the inhabitants of Santos were 'in the middle of their Masse, and at that instant the Friar was holding up the Bread of Sacrament before the people to worship it' (48). His remark evokes the burning religious rift ravaging Europe at the time that often extended to New World territorial disputes. It had become commonplace for English travellers in Brazil to mock and ridicule Catholic practices, while the Portuguese invariably referred to the English as 'heretics'. Knivet's use of the possessive pronoun 'their' clearly marks these religious boundaries by exoticizing the Catholic mass at Santos. Anyway, the timing was all on the Englishmen's side: Cavendish's men took advantage of the element of surprise and duly took hostages from among the people in the church before moving on to seize the town, and loot and burn the surrounding sugar mills. During the siege the English officers made their lodgings at the Jesuit College, where, according to Knivet, one night

> two Savages being abused by the Portugals ran away, and [...] came [...] to the Generals bed-side, and brought with them Turkeys and Hennes: The Generall being awaked by them cryed out for helpe. One of them that speake Portugall, fell downe on his knees, and said, that hee came to crave his favour, and not to offend him. (48–49)

[11] For an annotated modern edition containing extracts of all three accounts, see 'The Last Voyage of Thomas Cavendish, 1591–1593', in *Last Voyages: Cavendish, Hudson and Ralegh*, ed. Philip Edwards (Oxford: Clarendon Press, 1988), pp. 19–122.

[12] Anthony Knivet, *The Admirable Adventures and Strange Fortunes of Master Anthony Knivet*, ed. Vivien Kogut Lessa de Sá (Cambridge: Cambridge University Press, 2015). Henceforth, page numbers from this volume will appear in the body of the text.

These 'savages' then led Cavendish to hidden treasures and grazing cattle, doing their best to please the invaders. The scenes evoke several similar ones mentioned in English accounts of Brazil whereby the ruling Portuguese or Spanish feature as brutal and inept settlers, something that would justify English incursions in these foreign territories. The tale of exploited indigenous peoples – far from untrue – fed into anti-Iberian propaganda that was rife in England. Knivet duly replicates the usual view of bloodthirsty Iberian settlers and their exploited subjects in his account of the siege of Santos: 'In the time that we were there many Canibals came unto us, desiring the General that he would destroy the Portugals, and keepe the Countrie to himselfe, protesting to bee all on his side.' Cavendish, however, 'thanked them for their kindesse, and told them that at that time he had a farther pretence' (49). His aim had not been to establish a colony, but to make a profit from finding precious metals, trading with the east and plundering at sea. This was not to be, as we have seen.

Still, the voyage yielded not only the three accounts mentioned above, but an unexpected historical token as well. During the siege of Santos, Cavendish and his men took lodgings at the Jesuit College, which they promptly ransacked. But one man on the expedition had something else in mind. This was the poet and playwright Thomas Lodge, best known for his poem 'Rosalynde', one of the sources for Shakespeare's *As You Like It*. Lodge had joined the South Sea voyage in search of fortune and adventure. A few years after his return, in 1596, he would publish the prose romance *A Margarite of America*, a work he claimed was a direct result of his time in Brazil. In the preface, he wrote: 'some four years since being at sea with M. Candish [...] it was my chance in the library of the Jesuits in Sanctum to find this history in the Spanish tongue, which as I read delighted me, and delighting me won me, and winning me made me write it'.[13] Though the 'Spanish history' has never been identified, we have reason to believe that this was not an isolated occurrence. Lodge must have taken other books and/or manuscripts from the library and brought them to England, for he later donated a Jesuit manuscript to the Bodleian Library which bears the following *ex-libris*: 'Previously owned by Thomas Lodge, from Oxford University, who with his own hand removed it from Brazil.'[14]

The manuscript that has been preserved in Oxford is a Christian doctrine written mostly in Tupi, the indigenous coastal dialect spoken in Brazil at the time, though there are also sections in Portuguese and in Latin. It was

---

[13] Thomas Lodge, 'Preface', in *A Margarite of America* (London: Printed for John Busby, 1596).

[14] Our literal translation from the Latin, *MS Bodl. 617*.

prepared and used by the Jesuits who, since they first arrived in Brazil in 1549, had made it their mission to convert the indigenous people. This missionary work soon entailed the production of a grammar that reduced the varieties of Tupi to one dialect, the 'Língua Geral', or general language. This grammar was first published in 1595 in Portugal while the first Christian doctrine in the 'Língua Geral' only came out in print in 1618.[15] This suggests that the Santos manuscript is possibly one of the oldest known extant catechisms in Tupi.

Though short lived and not always successful, the English corsair attacks on the Brazilian coast in the late sixteenth century resulted in unexpected cultural interactions whose impact can still be seen in written records. While the Cavendish voyage may not have yielded any financial gain, the array of texts linked to it is an invaluable source for understanding the dynamics of transnational negotiations on the shores of Brazil (between the English, the Portuguese, the indigenous people and the Brazilian settlers). While the voyage accounts reveal the English fears, ambitions and anxieties about Brazil, the stolen manuscript carries, in its own ironic tale of survival, the unexpected cultural and religious crossings typical of early maritime exploration. But it is James Lancaster's attack on Recife and its accompanying reports and ballads that point most clearly to Portuguese literary resonances in Elizabethan England.

James Lancaster and the 1595 attack on Recife

The voyage of James Lancaster to Brazil was registered in two different documents, apparently deriving from the same source: an anonymous account published by Richard Hakluyt in 1600[16] and a pamphlet by the popular writer Henry Roberts published in 1595,[17] the very year Lancaster returned to London. The piratical enterprise, financed by eminent London merchants, concentrated its efforts on the port of Recife, in the captaincy of Pernambuco in northeast Brazil. After a successful one-month siege, Lancaster's men

---

[15] Respectively, José de Anchieta, *Arte de Grammatica da Lingua Mais Usada na Costa do Brasil* (Coimbra: Antonio de Mariz, 1595); and Antonio de Araújo, *Catecismo na Lingoa Brasilica no qual se contem a summa da doctrina christã* (Lisbon: Pedro Craesbeek, 1618).

[16] 'The well governed and prosperous voyage of M. James Lancaster', in Hakluyt, *Principall Navigations* [1600], pp. 708–15.

[17] Henry Roberts, *Lancaster His Allarums, Honourable Assaultes, and Suprising of the Block-houses and Store-houses Belonging to Fernand Bucke in Brasill* (London: Abel Jeffes for William Barley, 1595). Reprinted in *The Voyages of James Lancaster*, ed. William Foster (London: Hakluyt Society, 1940). All further references will be to this edition and will appear in parentheses in the text.

loaded their ships with an impressive amount of oriental and tropical products seized from the warehouses at the harbour. The loot that arrived in London, compared with that brought back by Francis Drake or Thomas Cavendish, was considered astonishing and the news rapidly reached the continent. In June 1595, just after Lancaster's return, the Venetian ambassador to Madrid wrote a letter to the Doge remarking, amazed, that 'the booty amounts to seven thousand cases of sugar, six thousand hundred weight of pepper, and other goods to the value of about two millions in gold'.[18]

Rather than objective reports of the expedition, both narratives of Lancaster's voyage to Brazil – Hakluyt's account and Roberts's pamphlet[19] – are literary representations of the piratical or commercial actions, which portray them as a heroic enterprise undertaken by a group of brave knights, 'Champions of our Queene' (71). The war between England and Spain was being fought out not only at sea but also in printed papers, in the form of nationalistic propaganda, such as Hakluyt's *Principall Navigations* and the ballads written by the sailor-poet Roberts in praise of Drake, Cavendish, Lancaster and other maritime protagonists. Elizabethan geopolitical policies, in the context of the Anglo-Spanish war, found an effective counterpart in editorial initiatives. The patriotism represented in those narratives can thus be seen as linked to a process of legitimating an emerging empire and building a new national identity.

Nevertheless, reports of Lancaster's venture present a peculiar characteristic when compared to other narratives of English voyages to Brazil, as they emphasize not the voyage itself and its exploits, or the encounters with the native people, but the battles and the military clashes, portraying those concerned with commercial enterprise as 'Cavallers' – to use Roberts's word, echoing the Spanish 'caballeros' and the Portuguese 'cavaleiros' – turning mariners and soldiers into chivalric heroes, who fought not only for profit, but mainly for 'their countreys honor and princes benefit' against the 'cowardly Portugales' and 'our enemies the Spaniards' (53, 57–58).

Before his profitable experience in Brazil, Lancaster, a native of Basingstoke, 'by birth of gentility', according to one of the accounts of his voyage, had been the only English captain who had managed to return from an English voyage to the East Indies (1591–94). On that troubled voyage, also financed by London magnates, he captained the *Edward Bonaventure*, the same vessel he had led

---

[18] 'Venice: June 1595', *Calendar of State Papers*, Venice, IX: 1592–1603 (London: n.pub., 1897), pp. 161–62.

[19] The pamphlet comprises one ballad in praise of Lancaster, a narrative account written in the first person and a final ballad in tribute to Barker and Cotton who died in Pernambuco.

against the Spanish Armada in 1588. His pioneering enterprise on the India Run routes,[20] in spite of being a complete financial failure, certainly helped establish Lancaster's reputation as a navigator. William Foster observes, in his edition of Lancaster's voyages, that he had been appointed for that eastbound journey 'especially in view of Lancaster's experience and his thorough acquaintance with the Portuguese language'.[21] Later, in 1601, he commanded the first East India Company voyage, when he founded the earliest English trading post in the region, in Java, opening the spice trade to England along maritime routes that until then had been exclusively navigated by Spain and Portugal. In 1602, he was knighted by King James I – the climax to his successful career as a navigator and a privateer.

Lancaster was no stranger to Portuguese commercial maritime routes to the East, or to the Portuguese language, as he had lived in Portugal as a young man. Like many of the English merchants who had settled there, he probably left Lisbon in 1585, when the open war between Spain and England forced them to abandon Portugal, leaving behind their property and wealth which had been confiscated by Philip II, king of Portugal and Spain. In Hakluyt's account of the Pernambuco attack, we hear Lancaster distilling bitter resentment of his former hosts, the Portuguese, and summarizing his Iberian experience: 'I have bene brought up among this people: I have lived among them as a gentleman, served with them as a soldier, and lived among them as a merchant; [...] and I know, when they cannot prevaile with the sword by force, then they deale with their deceiveable tongues; for faith and trueth they have none.'[22]

Lancaster was probably familiar with Lisbon's custom house, warehouses and with vessels coming from Pernambuco, the richest sugar-producing province in the Portuguese colony. Crews aboard ships departing from England to Brazil commonly included mariners, pilots and merchants who had previously taken part in similar enterprises and who spoke Portuguese, the international language of the eastern maritime routes. There was also an Atlantic circulation of Portuguese papers aboard English ships, such as the stolen treatise about Brazil written by the Jesuit Fernão Cardim, first published in Samuel Purchas's collection of voyages in 1625,[23] and the report

[20] Also known as *Carreira da Índia*, these were routes established by the Portuguese connecting the Atlantic and Indian Ocean around the Cape of Good Hope.
[21] Introduction, *The Voyages of James Lancaster*, ed. Foster, p. XIV.
[22] *The Voyages of James Lancaster*, ed. Foster, p. 43.
[23] 'A treatise of Brazil, written by a Portugal which had long lived there', in *Hakluythus Porthumus*, ed. Samuel Purchas (London: William Stansby for Henrie Fetherstone, 1625), pp. 1289–320.

of a Portuguese called Lopez Vaz, whose manuscript was also stolen from an Iberian ship by Cumberland's men in 1587, and printed two years later by Hakluyt. Lopez Vaz wrote about Pernambuco and its main town, Olinda: 'it is the greatest towne in all that coast, and hath above three thousand houses in it, with seventie Ingenios for sugar, and great stores of Brasill-wood and abundance of cotton'.[24]

In 1595, the capture and plunder of Recife, at the time a small port with a lively and busy harbour near Olinda, was marked by resolute and direct action. The Portuguese settlers could not resist the attack from the English, who were much better armed than them. Lancaster's company, with method and efficiency, began to transfer to their ships the 'wonderful great riches'[25] stocked in Recife's warehouses, resulting in 14 shiploads of plunder. The English were helped by Captain John Venner, who had joined the fleet at the Cape Verde Islands. Dutch cargo ships and a French fleet commanded by Jean Lenoir (an old acquaintance of Lancaster's) were also at the Recife harbour supporting the English action. The profits of this international joint venture were a superb shipment of sugar, a highly valued commodity, and, through sheer luck, the treasures taken from an East India carrack (one of the much-coveted *Indiamen*) that had been shipwrecked near the coast of Pernambuco. Thus, unexpectedly, the warehouses were filled with the East Indies' richest goods, alongside their habitual tropical commodities of sugar and Brazilwood.

In addition to their competent ship loading, Lancaster's company staged two significant military raids against the Portuguese settlers, among whom were members of the most prominent families of the colonial elite. The first took place upon their arrival, when Lancaster attacked a stronghold at the entrance to the harbour, which enabled the English to take Recife with very little opposition. According to Hakluyt's account there were 80 English against 600 Portuguese settlers. Henry Roberts's pamphlet, in his encomiastic and amplified tone, claims numbers of 80 versus a thousand from Olinda, in an invasion led by Lancaster with great dynamism.

The second skirmish was the closing act of their stay there and triggered their hasty escape. In this last clash, also reported in two different versions – Hakluyt's account and Roberts's pamphlet – the Portuguese of Olinda organized a large group of men, made up of settlers and Indians, to ambush a much smaller group of English and French. The two accounts of Lancaster's voyage stress that the invaders were strongly outnumbered by the settlers. A military company of 275 plunderers against 5,000 Portuguese and Indians, according to Roberts, met near Recife, and three of the principal commanders were killed, two of them

---

[24] *Principall Navigations* [1600], ed. Hakluyt, pp. 778–802.
[25] *The Voyages of James Lancaster*, ed. Foster, p. XXII.

close to Lancaster. In Hakluyt's account, Lancaster was not fighting in the battle, and in Roberts's he was leading the English troops.

Compared to the other pamphlets Roberts had written celebrating maritime enterprises, in *Lancaster his Allarums* there is a noticeable difference in tone and in the focus on the protagonist. He apparently abandons what he called his 'rustic pen' and starts to emulate epic formulae. Furthermore, Lancaster takes centre stage. His acts, 'whose manhood dooth excell', and his Pernambuco attack, 'an act of more resolve hath not / beene complisht at the sea' (54–55), are represented in a more elevated tone than the one used for Francis Drake, John Hawkins and William Grafton[26] in Roberts's encomiastic pamphlets. *Lancaster his Allarums*, in addition, presents a woodcut depicting Lancaster in Brazil, crowned with laurel leaves in the centre of the scene, surrounded by his troops, like a Roman general (fl. 1585–1616). It must be noted that Roberts's propagandistic pamphlet was probably printed under Lancaster's patronage. One year later, on his way up the maritime ranks, Lancaster was portrayed in an oil painting – an ennobling event – with his right hand resting on a globe.[27]

Some of Roberts's epic claims resemble those used by Luís de Camões's *Os Lusíadas* [*The Lusiads*], the most distinguished and best known Portuguese epic poem, and the first verses of his ballad on Lancaster are a parody of the overture of *La Araucana*, D. Alonso de Ercilla's epic about Spain's conquest of Chile. Neither Camoes's nor Ercilla's poems had been translated into English at the time, but this did not mean that they were unknown in learned circles or on the Atlantic maritime routes.[28] It is revealing that the contemporary poet Barnabe Googe wrote poems that are near translations of lines from Jorge de Montemayor's *La Diana*, many years before its translation into English. Similarly, Sir George Carew undertook the translation of 16 cantos of *La Araucana* in 1599, which remained in manuscript form.[29] Printed books were not the unique means through which poems and ideas

---

[26] *Ours Ladys Retorne to England, Accompannied with Saint Frances and the Good Jesus of Viana in Portugall, Who Coming from Brasell, Arived at Clavelly in Devonshire, the Third of June 1592* (London: Abel Jeffes, 1592).

[27] Sir James Lancaster, 1554/5–1618 (BHC2828), National Maritime Museum, Greenwich: <http://collections.rmg.co.uk/collections/objects/14301.html> [accessed 21 November 2018].

[28] In 1595, there had been three Portuguese editions of *Os Lusíadas*, and three Spanish translations. The poem was therefore widely known in Spain and on the Atlantic routes.

[29] On the relations between early modern England and Spain, see Barbara Fuchs, *The Poetics of Piracy: Emulating Spain in English Literature* (Philadelphia: University of Pennsylvania Press, 2013).

circulated, and Roberts's use of some of Camões's emblematic images and Ercilla's initial stanza does not mean he had actually read those lengthy and complex epic poems. Roberts's encomium of a former Lisbon merchant and his own experience with Portuguese and Brazilian ships connected him with the routes where Portuguese commodities and ideas circulated.[30]

One of the emblematic images of *Os Lusíadas* is the opposition between *fábulas sonhadas* (dreamed fables) and *puras verdades* (pure truths),[31] which is to say between the tales told by epic poems and the true Portuguese acts narrated by Camões. When Henry Roberts parodies *La Araucana*[32] in the opening lines of his ballad – 'No tale of Robinhood I sing, / Ne olde wives stories write; / Nor idle toyes to mervaile at, / Vaine people to delight. / But woorkes of woorth most rare and true/ To you I do present' (54) – he proclaims that he will not sing tales of Robin Hood, nor fairy tales, nor mention the Trojan Horse (idle toy). Roberts imitates the series of denials that characterize the opening verses of *La Araucana*, but his denial does not refer to the refutation of the erotic theme, which is what Ercilla did as a contrast to the first verses of Ariosto's *Orlando Furioso*,[33] but states, like Camões, that rather than fictional or literary events, he will instead tell the true story of Lancaster's acts in Brazil.[34] This claim of telling the truth instead of fiction is not present in the other maritime ballads written by Roberts.

There are other resonances of emblematic images of *Os Lusíadas* that can be traced in *Lancaster his Allarums*. These echoes of a Portuguese epic poem in a popular English ballad praising privateers in Brazil suggest there is still much to be explored, beyond national boundaries, in the literary and cultural exchanges between early modern England and Portugal.

---

[30] In 1592, Roberts was in Clovelly, Devonshire, where he personally received two Portuguese ships captured by Captain William Grafton, one of which, the *Jesus of Viana*, had travelled from Pernambuco.

[31] *Os Lusíadas*, V, stanzas 89 and 23 respectively.

[32] Alonso de Ercilla, *La Araucana* (Madrid: Pierres Cosin, 1578), fl. 1r; 'I sing not love of ladies, nor of fights/ devised for gentle dames by courteous knights/ nor feasts, nor tourneys, nor that tender care', trans. William Hayley, in *Poems and Plays in six volumes* (London: T. Cadell, 1785), IV, 94.

[33] 'Of loves and ladies, knights and arms, I sing', L. Ariosto, *Orlando Furioso*, trans. William Stewart Rose (London, John Murray, 1823). All these opening lines are, of course, emulations of the famous opening line of Virgil's *Aeneid*: 'Arms, and the man I sing, who, forc'ed by fate/[...]', trans. John Dryden (New York: P. F. Collier and Son, 1909).

[34] Roberts's insistence on declaring his intention to write the truth can be verified in another excerpt: 'Recorde may wee his worthines, / And write but what is true' (54).

Treasures and texts: piracy and its transnational legacy

As we have seen, early encounters between the English and the Portuguese on the shores of Brazil offer a telling example of the complex power dynamics at play in the first century after the discovery of the new lands. The English piratical incursions into late sixteenth-century Brazil may have had mixed financial gains, but their real 'booty' is yet to be assessed. As the incursions by Cavendish and Lancaster attest, these hostile encounters triggered a far deeper cultural exchange, whose consequences can be seen in the various texts resulting, directly or indirectly, from each voyage. Henry Roberts's ballads, Thomas Lodge's romance and Anthony Knivet's travel account suggest the permeability of the very notion of cultural identity, even as nations were anxious to assert it. The Jesuit catechism stolen by an English poet and preserved in the Bodleian Library (founded by a devout Calvinist), adds just another layer to the complexity of these commercial, political, religious and literary exchanges. Instead of pointing to irreconcilable cultural differences, these clashes reveal rich transnational negotiations.

4

Soundtracks of the Lusophone and Creolophone Spheres

'Tanto' by Aline Frazão (Angola), 'Kreol' by Mário Lúcio (Cape Verde) and 'N na nega bedju' by José Carlos Schwarz (Guinea-Bissau)

Fernando Arenas
University of Michigan

This essay offers a critical exploration of contemporary urban popular music from Angola, Cape Verde, and Guinea-Bissau through a series of close readings of paradigmatic song-texts focusing on the analysis of lyrics, sound (music) and image (music video).[1] It argues for the importance of studying popular music as a rich interdisciplinary platform in order to discuss larger, transnational cultural questions, while mobilizing key concepts for understanding the countries in question, the Lusophone (or Portuguese-speaking) and Creolophone (or Creole-speaking) worlds at large.[2] The featured song-texts are: 'Kreol' by Mário Lúcio (Cape Verde, 2010); 'N na nega bedju' ['I refuse to grow old'] by José Carlos Schwarz (Guinea-Bissau, 1975) performed by Schwarz himself, Terezinha Araújo (Cape Verde, 2003) and Karyna Gomes (Guinea-Bissau, 2014); and 'Tanto' ['So much'] by Aline Frazão (Angola,

---

[1] I would like to warmly thank Charlie Sugnet, Marlyse Baptista and the volume editors for their invaluable ideas and suggestions for this essay.

[2] Creole languages typically emerge in a multilingual setting in which speakers of distinct native languages come in contact with each other and ultimately create a new language for the purpose of communication. See Marlyse Baptista, 'Competition and Selection in Creole Genesis: How 'Minimalist' Languages Yield Maximal Output', *Journal of Pidgin and Creole Languages*, 32.1 (2017), 138–58.

2013). The chosen song-texts fit thematically within a 'coloniality continuum' involving the traumatic scene of European conquest over and enslavement of Africans ('Kreol'), the African struggles against European colonialism, as well as the euphoria of postcolonial nation-building ('N na nega bedju'), and the critique of pervasive socioeconomic inequality in Angola – one of the wealthiest countries in Africa – almost 50 years after independence ('Tanto').

All three songs are composed and performed by important figures from their individual countries: a founding figure (Schwarz), cultural pioneers (Terezinha Araújo, Mário Lúcio), a political leader (Mário Lúcio), and members of a new generation raising their critical voices (Aline Frazão and Karyna Gomes). While 'Tanto' is sung in Portuguese, the other two are sung in the Creole languages of Guinea-Bissau and Cape Verde respectively. Portuguese-based Creoles are the dominant languages of these two West African nations. While the Creole languages exist within a larger Lusophone sphere, they also set the limits to, or 'interrupt' the signifier 'luso' as markers of national and cultural distinctiveness, not only vis-à-vis Portugal and Brazil, but also within a globalized field of cultural production such as the world music market.[3] One could make a similar case regarding the Portuguese spoken and sung in Angola, where it is not only the official language, but also the lingua franca within a multilingual nation-state. In Angola, music is sung in multiple languages, including Portuguese, Kimbundu, Kikongo and Umbundu, while the Portuguese that is spoken or sung is inflected by the various national or vernacular languages in terms of its cadence, syntax and lexicon.

This essay posits the Lusophone and Creolophone spheres as simultaneously differentiated and overlapping linguistic and cultural domains on account of the legacy of the Atlantic slave trade and colonialism in both Cape Verde and Guinea-Bissau and the choice of Portuguese as the official language in these postcolonial states.[4] Not only are the Creoles the overwhelmingly dominant languages in the field of music within these two nations, but they are also the primary mode of communication in everyday life; in the intimate, domestic and public spheres, as well as in the realm of affect; all

---

[3] Derek Pardue, *Cape Verde Let's Go: Creole Rappers and Citizenship in Portugal* (Urbana, Chicago and Springfield, IL: University of Illinois Press, 2015), p. 83.

[4] Currently, Portuguese is the only official language of both Cape Verde and Guinea-Bissau, while the Creole languages are considered 'national languages'. In practice, Cape Verdean Creole, in its multiple island variants, is the most widely spoken language when we compare these countries. In the case of Guinea-Bissau, Creole is the lingua franca and the most widely spoken language in a multilingual country. There have been efforts at the political level, especially in Cape Verde, to declare Creole the country's co-official language, but these have yet to bear fruit.

key articulating principles[5] with regard to music. In the case of Angola, the Portuguese language is becoming increasingly common in the realm of urban popular music, particularly across genres such as *semba*, *kizomba* and *kuduro*.

The field of Afro-Luso-Brazilian Studies has historically focused on the study of language and literature. More recently, the field has opened itself to the study of cinema, television and popular music, especially in the case of Brazil, but to a far lesser degree in the cases of Portugal or Lusophone Africa. Hence, this essay argues for the centrality of popular music for the study of Angola, Cape Verde and Guinea-Bissau in order to gain a broader understanding of the societies in question, whether through song-texts and/or musical performance, and music consumption in Portuguese or in the vernacular/national languages (including the Portuguese-based Creole languages).[6] Further, it highlights the intrinsic interdisciplinarity of popular music in its various dimensions, whether musicological, lyrical, visual, performative, historical, sociopolitical, linguistic, philosophical, and so forth.

* * *

Cape Verdean Mário Lúcio, who wrote the song 'Kreol', was born in Tarrafal (Santiago island), studied in Cuba on a scholarship, and has been a musician and writer from a very young age. Today, he is the foremost cultural figure in Cape Verde: a singer, songwriter, musician, composer, producer and arranger, as well as an acclaimed writer of poetry, fiction and theatre, in addition to being a painter and a politician. Lúcio served as the archipelago's Minister of Culture between 2011 and 2016, and he has played a key role as a cultural mediator and promoter. For instance, he co-founded and directed the Kriol Jazz Festival in addition to the Atlantic Music Expo, which have been held yearly since 2009 and 2013 respectively. He is the founder and director of Quintal da Música, which is one the most important live music venues in the capital city, Praia, and a composer for Raiz di Polon, Cape Verde's major dance company. Lúcio was also behind the internationally acclaimed Simentera group, whose music highlighted the African roots of Cape Verdean culture,[7]

---

[5] A term used by Richard Middleton in *Studying Popular Music* (Buckingham: Open University Press, 1990), p. 11.

[6] One of the most trenchant historical studies on the power of musical expression and consumption in the rise of national consciousness in late colonial Angola is Marissa Moorman's *Intonations: A Social History of Music and Nation in Luanda, Angola, from 1945 to Recent Times* (Athens: Ohio University Press, 2008).

[7] This information is taken from programme notes from a concert on the *Kreol* tour, which I attended in Lisbon on 10 October 2012, Mário Lúcio, *Kreol* (Lisbon: Fundação Calouste Gulbenkian, 2012).

and which featured in its line-up some of the country's most talented musicians and singers including Terezinha Araújo, Tete Alhinho, Lela Violão and Lúcio himself.[8] The group released four albums,[9] touring extensively at a time when Cape Verdean music was emerging on the global stage, thanks to Cesária Évora, one of the world's most successful and beloved female African artists.[10]

In his solo career, Mário Lúcio is a prolific composer whose songs have been performed by Cesária Évora and most major young Cape Verdean artists (including Lura and Mayra Andrade). He has released five albums,[11] while collaborating with numerous major artists from Africa, Latin America, and beyond, among them: Gilberto Gil and Milton Nascimento (Brazil), Harry Belafonte (USA), Manu Dibango (Cameroon), Pablo Milanés (Cuba), Maria João and Teresa Salgueiro (Portugal), Toumani Diabaté and Zoumana Tereta (Mali) and Oliver Mtukudzi (Zimbabwe).[12]

Kreol is a concept album that took Mário Lúcio in multiple directions across Africa and its diaspora, mapping out nodal points and routes of a Creole Atlantic, including the roots of his native Cape Verde. The album was recorded and mixed in Praia, Rio de Janeiro, Dakar, Bamako, Havana, Paris, Lisbon and New York. Lúcio wrote all the songs, which are sung in multiple languages and dialects (Brazilian Portuguese, European Portuguese, Cape Verdean Creole, French, Bambara and English) showcasing an array of musical styles in an electroacoustic format including Cape Verdean musical genres such as *funaná*, *tabanka* and *morna*.[13] The concept behind the album is Lúcio's notion that Cape Verde was the world's first Creole society as a

[8] Biographical information on Mário Lúcio is taken from his website <http://www.mariolucio.com/> and his Wikipedia entry: <https://en.wikipedia.org/wiki/M%C3%A1rio_L%C3%BAcio_(singer)> [both accessed 16 September 2017].

[9] *Raiz* (Paris: Lusafrica, 1992); *Barro e voz* (Paris: Mélodie, 1997); *Cabo Verde em serenata* (Berlin: Piranha Musik, 2000); *Tr'Adictional* (Paris: Mélodie, 2003).

[10] For more on Cesária Évora and the globalization of Cape Verdean music, see Fernando Arenas, *Lusophone Africa: Beyond Independence* (Minneapolis: University of Minnesota Press, 2011); or its translated and updated version in Portuguese, *África lusófona, além da independência*, trans. Cristiano Mazzei (São Paulo: Edusp, 2019). Also, see Carla Martin, 'Sounding Creole: The Politics of Cape Verdean Language, Music and Diaspora' (unpublished doctoral dissertation, Harvard University, 2012).

[11] *Mar e luz* (Rooster Blues, 2004); *Ao vivo e aos outros* (2006); *Badyo* (Paris and Praia: Lusafrica/Harmonia, 2007); *Kreol* (Paris and Praia: Lusafrica/Harmonia, 2010); *Funanight* (Maremúsica, 2017).

[12] Several of these artists participated on the album *Kreol*.

[13] *Kreol* inspired an eponymous documentary directed by Frédéric Menant in 2010 (Zaradoc films).

result of the forced contact dating from 1460 between European colonizers and African slaves on the previously uninhabited islands.[14] In this reading, Cape Verde emerges as an archetype and microcosm of world history centred in the Atlantic. *Kreol* is simultaneously African and diasporic while located across a broad Atlantic spectrum where Cape Verde would occupy a nodal position.[15]

One of the many highlights of the album is the song 'Planet', sung in English, in which Lúcio pays tribute to Harry Belafonte and his role as a tireless Pan-Africanist campaigner. The song is a paean to the contribution of Pan-Africanist figures to the history of the modern world that is both pantheistic and humanistic in its core values. With soaring polyphonic choral voices punctuated by a steady triple metre mid-tempo percussive beat, 'Planet' effectively conveys the gravitas that the subject matter warrants. The centrepiece entails excerpts from a speech by Belafonte when he received the Amílcar Cabral International Award from Howard University, the historically black college located in Washington DC. In the excerpt from his speech, Belafonte celebrates the struggles of black activists against Apartheid who later on undertook the task of building the new South Africa (among them Oliver Tambo, Walter and Albertina Sisulu, Winnie Mandela and Desmond Tutu). He expresses deep-felt pride for those African nationalists who fought for or contributed to independence from colonialism such as Jomo Kenyatta, Léopold Senghor, Sekou Touré, Habib Bourguiba, Amílcar Cabral and Miriam Makeba.

History undergoes a process of poetic and musical transfiguration in the eponymous song-text 'Kreol' as it evokes the 'primal scene' of the emergence of Cape Verdean society. In a fast tempo 2/4 off-beat *funaná* rhythm, undergirded by a deep bass, where the opening melodic contour is sung by wailing in a series of vocables,[16] the listener is dramatically thrust into the whirlwind of history. At the same time, a sense of solemnity regarding the subject matter is conveyed by the dissonant harmonic structure that prevails throughout the

---

[14] Mário Lúcio gave me this information during an interview in July 2009 in Praia, Cape Verde.

[15] While Robert Stam and Ella Shohat speak of the cultural politics of the Enlightenment mapped out across a 'broad Black Atlantic spectrum' when considering the Haitian Revolution, Lúcio locates Cape Verde's nodal location across a 'broad Atlantic spectrum' that includes Africa, its diaspora and also Europe, from a historical and cultural point of view; Stam and Shohat, *Race in Translation: Culture Wars Around the Postcolonial Atlantic* (New York and London: New York University Press, 2012), p. 19.

[16] According to the Merriam Webster dictionary, 'vocable' is a word composed of sounds without regard to meaning. It is used extensively in music.

song. 'Kreol' features rich layers of polyphonic vocals, in addition to acoustic and electric guitars, *cavaquinho*,[17] percussion, bass guitar and drums.[18]

The content is organized in an elliptical and fragmentary fashion where historical causes and effects underlying the concept of 'Kreol' are implied:

Branko bai, preto ben	[White men are gone, Black men have arrived
Branku bem, preto bai	White men have arrived, Black men are gone
Nós nu ka staba li nem pa tadja	We Creoles weren't here to prevent it
Nem pa fla ma nu ka odja	Or to say we didn't see anything
Pai fidjo Spritu Santo	In the name of the Father, the Son, and the Holy Spirit
Na fundu'l barco bu ta obiba so lamento	But, in the holds of the ships the only prayer you heard was
Ess ta fla: 'oh nha mae, oh nha mae'	'Oh mother, Oh mother'][19]

The first half of the opening verse is structured in the form of a conceptual chiasmus or inverted parallelism describing the voluntary and forced migratory movements of Europeans and Africans in the Atlantic. While there is structural symmetry in the ebb and flow of these populations, there is also an inherent asymmetry in the power relations between them in the settlement of the previously uninhabited islands. The second half of the first verse draws attention to a collective subject in the present ('We Creoles') that emerged from the migration and intermixing of Africans and Europeans. Yet the verse alludes to the lack of historical agency or responsibility among contemporary Creoles as regards their origins. The second verse is framed by the Christian prayer invocation of 'In the Name of the Father, the Son, and the Holy Spirit', which is subsequently contrasted by the tragic image of slaves at the bottom of the ship with their own prayer ('Oh mother, Oh mother').

---

[17] The *cavaquinho* is a small four-stringed instrument of four metallic or gut strings of Portuguese origin with different tuning patterns that is used extensively in Brazil (in *choro* and *samba*), Cape Verde (in *morna* and *coladera*) and in folk music across northern and central Portugal. It is believed to be the forerunner of the ukulele.

[18] Lúcio himself performed all the vocals on the track and played most of the instruments.

[19] 'Kreol', lyrics and music: Mário Lúcio © 2009 Africa Nostra.

This prayer is sung in the form of a lament that lasts throughout several bars. The verse itself reproduces the power structure of colonialism and slavery through the 'chronotopic' figure of the slave ship, with Catholicism located on the upper deck, imposed by conquering Europeans, reflected in the prayer blessing, while African slaves are imprisoned in the hull.[20] 'Kreol' alludes elliptically to the forced conversion of Africans and the use of religion as a justification for European conquest and African enslavement. Not only did Cape Verde manage to emerge successfully from this traumatic experience but, during the early decades of the Atlantic slave trade, the archipelago operated as a strategic entrepôt between the Guinea coast and Europe, the Caribbean and Brazil.[21]

The Bissau-Guinean song-text 'N na nega bedju' (literally 'I deny old age' or 'I refuse to grow old'), written by legendary figure José Carlos Schwarz and sung in the country's Kriol language, is a quintessential message about deferred hopes and dreams deferred in the context of the liberation struggle against Portuguese colonialism, and the task of nation-building after independence. Schwarz died tragically in a 1977 plane crash in Cuba when he was only 27 years old. As a result, his life and artistic contribution have acquired a mythical status in Guinea-Bissau. 'N na nega bedju' is a mellifluous anthem-like song rooted in the history of the country's liberation struggle. Written in 1975, it expresses an unwavering commitment to building an independent and egalitarian society as well as a deep love for both Guinea-Bissau and Cape Verde, which became a binational state after independence in 1975 until 1980, following the dream of the countries' founding father, Amílcar Cabral. Today, the utopian vision projected by 'N na nega bedju' resonates in an achingly nostalgic manner for Guinea-Bissau, at a time in the early twenty-first century when the country has been described by scholars and the world media as a 'failed state' or even a 'narco-state'.[22] In this tragic scenario the vows expressed by the song have been given a poignant new life by younger artists.

---

[20] In his classic study of the black Atlantic, Paul Gilroy refers to the 'chronotope' of the slave ship moving across spaces and time as a central organizing symbol, 'a living micro-cultural system in motion': *The Black Atlantic: Modernity and Double Consciousness* (Cambridge, MA: Harvard University Press, 1993), p. 6.

[21] See Antonio Carreira, *The People of the Cape Verde Islands: Exploitation and Emigration*, trans. Christopher Fyfe (London: C. Hurst & Co, 1982), pp. 7–8; António Correia e Silva, *Histórias de um Sahel insular* (Praia: Spleen Edições, 1995), pp. 20–24.

[22] For some of the most lucid and exhaustive accounts on Guinea-Bissau, see Joshua B. Forrest, 'Anatomy of State Fragility: The Case of Guinea-Bissau', in *Security and Development: Searching for Critical Connections*, eds Neclâ Tschirgi, Michael S. Lund and Francesco Mancini (Boulder, CO and London: Lynne Rienner Publishers, 2010), pp. 171–210; and the volume of essays edited by Patrick Chabal and Toby Green,

One of Guinea-Bissau's most fascinating cultural figures, José Carlos Schwarz, was a poet, musician, composer and revolutionary. He participated in the urban resistance movement against Portuguese colonialism alongside the national liberation movement, PAIGC,[23] for which he was imprisoned in Bissau and on Galinhas island between 1972 and 1974. Along with the group Cobiana Djazz, which he co-founded shortly before independence in 1971, Schwarz is considered a seminal figure in modern Bissau-Guinean urban music, according to academics Ibrahima Diallo and Moema Parente Augel.[24] After starting his musical career playing covers of Anglo-American and Brazilian songs, he became inspired not only to play local music genres such as *ngumbé*, but also to sing in Guinean Kriol.[25] In fact, Schwarz became a defender of Kriol as the lingua franca of Guinea-Bissau and a tool for the dissemination of urban popular music. His championing of Kriol became an act of cultural resistance that was seen as subversive by the colonial authorities.[26]

During the final years of the national liberation struggle in Guinea-Bissau, Cobiana Djazz became a mouthpiece for the PAIGC to reach the population using coded metaphors in their lyrics in Kriol in order to elude the colonial authorities. After independence, Cobiana Djazz was elevated to the status of national orchestra, like Bembeya Jazz National in Francophone Guinea. Schwarz recorded two albums with Cobiana Djazz[27] and was discovered by Miriam Makeba, then residing in Conakry.[28] They developed a great friendship

Guinea-Bissau: From Micro-State to 'Narco-State' (London: C. Hurst & Co, 2016). For a detailed analysis of the drug trafficking situation in Guinea-Bissau and West Africa, see Davin O'Regan, Center for Security Studies, 'The Evolving Drug Trade in Guinea-Bissau and West Africa' (2014) <http://www.css.ethz.ch/content/specialinterest/gess/cis/center-for-securities- studies/en/services/digital-library/articles/article.html/182200)> [accessed 20 August 2016].

[23] African Party for the Independence of Guinea-Bissau and Cape Verde.

[24] Based on a statement broadcast on Rádio Sol Mansi (29 May 2017) and Moema Parente Augel, *Ora di kanta tchiga: José Carlos Schwarz e o Cobiana Djazz* (Bissau: INEP, 1997).

[25] Most of Schwarz's biographical information is based on the seminal 1997 study by Augel, mentioned above.

[26] Augel, *Ora di kanta tchiga*, pp. 13, 336, and James H. Kennedy, 'José Carlos Schwarz: Bard of Popular Mobilization in Guinea-Bissau', *Présence Africaine*, 137/138 (1986), 91–101.

[27] *José Carlos et le Cobiana Jazz*, vols I and II (France: Sonafric, 1978).

[28] After residing in the USA for almost a decade and marrying civil rights activist and Black Panther leader Stokely Carmichael, Makeba suffered harassment from the US government to the point of being banned from returning to the country after a tour in 1968. She then moved to Guinea where she lived for 15 years under the

based on mutual admiration.[29] Eventually, Makeba sponsored him to record an album in New York under the *nom d'artiste* José Carlos.[30] Beyond the personal dimension of their friendship, there was also a powerful symbolic Pan-African bond linking the anti-Apartheid movement with the war against Portuguese colonialism. The liberation war in Guinea-Bissau under the leadership of Amílcar Cabral is considered a success story in the history of African struggles against European colonialisms. Furthermore, there is the pivotal socialist internationalism that linked Guinea-Bissau to Cuba, where Schwarz became the *chargé d'affaires* before his untimely death.[31] Years before his Cuban experience, he was appointed to various posts in the area of culture and the arts in his home country.

According to Augel, most of Schwarz's literary-musical production took place between 1970 and 1977. She divides it into four phases: anti-colonial, prison, post-independence euphoria and postcolonial disillusionment.[32] The subject matter of his song-poems reveals a profound humanistic ethos, alongside a sense of sacrifice for a larger cause, solidarity towards working people, and particular empathy towards mothers and children. The dominant themes range from the intimate sphere of emotions and family relations to the collective sphere of the struggle against colonialism, including the liberation war with its male and female heroes, a call for national unity across ethnic groups (one of Cabral's key concerns), a critique of those who betrayed the values of PAIGC, and a keen awareness of the struggles beyond independence.

'N na nega bedju' ['I refuse to grow old'] is arguably Guinea-Bissau's most emblematic song. It makes a categorical statement expressed by the lyrical

---

auspices of Sékou Touré. See 'Miriam Makeba', *South African History Online* (2011) <http://www.sahistory.org.za/people/miriam-makeba)> [accessed 16 September 2017].

[29] Several interviewees in Augel's study who knew Schwarz and/or followed his musical career mention his close friendship with Miriam Makeba (Antonio Oscar Barbosa, Huco Monteiro, Ibraima Djallo and Serifo Banora), *Ora di kanta tchiga*, pp. 330, 339, 363, 367.

[30] *Djiu di Galinha* [*Galinhas Island*] (Bissau: Departamento de Edição-Difusão do Livro e do Disco, 1978). On the front cover of the LP José Carlos appears with Miriam Makeba, who also wrote the notes on the back of the album. *Djiu di Galinha* is available on YouTube and was digitally rereleased on ITunes in 2017 under a new title, *Udjus ke odja* [*Eyes that See*] (Lisbon: Sons d'África, 2017).

[31] In the documentary *José Carlos Schwarz, a voz do povo*, dir. Adulai Jamanca (Lx Filmes, 2006), Teresa Loft Fernandes, Schwarz's widow, describes her husband's appointment in Cuba as a conscious strategy on the part of PAIGC to keep him away from Bissau since he had become an outspoken critic of the party in the years following independence.

[32] Augel, *A nova literatura da Guiné-Bissau*, pp. 224–25.

subject that is projected onto the collective national subject, vowing to remain physically young and strong in order to continue the task of nation-building after independence. The desire 'not to grow old' in the title is repeated at the beginning of each stanza and in the final chorus, while the rest of the song offers examples of the rationale behind such a desire, couched in a metaphorical language related to mind and body and the ability to exercise physical strength and intellectual discernment throughout the long and arduous process of reconstruction:

N na nega bedju	[I refuse to grow old
Ka djudju bin pirgisa	My knees mustn't wear out
Kaminhu lundju inda di ianda	for the road ahead is still long
N na nega bedju	I refuse to grow old
Ka udjus bin sukuru	My eyes mustn't lose sight
N misti mati bardadi di tudu dia	for I wish to witness everyday reality
N na nega bedju	I refuse to grow old
Ka mon bin moli	My hands mustn't lose strength
pa tempu di kumpu tera, ka fika-n	for I may not be able to stay in order to rebuild.][33]

The final stanzas shift the focus towards the expression of love of country, in this case both Guinea-Bissau and Cape Verde, echoing Amílcar Cabral's briefly fulfilled dream of an integrated binational state emerging from the liberation war 'N na nega bedju / Pa kerensa ku N ten na bo, Guiné [...] Pa kerensa ku N ten na bo' ['I refuse to grow old / For the love I have for you Guinea [...] For the love I have for you Cape Verde'].[34] As mentioned earlier, there is a utopian thrust at the heart of this poem-song which is the collective dream of a just and democratic society that reverberates at a time when Guinea-Bissau's viability as a nation-state has been questioned due to its perennially weak and unstable political structures as well as its stagnant

[33] 'N na nega bedju', lyrics and music: José Carlos Schwarz © 2019 Rossio Music Publishing. The translation from Kriol to English is my own, partly inspired by the Portuguese translation by Augel in *Ora di kanta tchiga*, p. 112.

[34] Amílcar Cabral was the main proponent of a unified state for Cape Verde and Guinea-Bissau under the aegis of PAIGC. See Patrick Chabal's biography, *Amilcar Cabral: Revolutionary Leadership and People's War* (London: C. Hurst & Co, 2002), p. 138; and António Tomás's, *O fazedor de utopias: uma biografia de Amílcar Cabral* (Lisbon: Tinta da China, 2007), pp. 297–301, for an analysis of the practical dimensions of this unified state and the possible reasons behind its collapse.

economy. This dream retains a powerful galvanizing force that is highlighted in the documentary *José Carlos Schwarz, a voz do povo* [*José Carlos Schwarz, The Voice of the People*], directed by Adulai Jamanca in 2006.

Every year, on the anniversary of Schwarz's death, there is a procession through the streets of Bissau leading to the cemetery where he is buried in order to celebrate his life and contribution to the culture of Guinea-Bissau. Dozens of people, of all ages, sing Schwarz's songs as they renew the vows expressed in 'N na nega bedju', which are also inscribed upon his tombstone. Through this yearly ritual in Guinea-Bissau, we see an example of Simon Frith's conceptualization of music text as not only 'reflecting' popular values, but also (re)producing them through performance.[35]

Musically speaking, 'N na nega bedju' is a syncopated waltz played with a fast to mid- to slow tempo in accordance with each of the three versions considered here: the original by Schwarz and covers by Terezinha Araújo and Karyna Gomes. The 11-syllable metre drives the variable tempo, while the rich alliteration enhances the sense of rhythm: 'Kaminhu lundju inda di ianda', 'N misti mati bardadi di tudu dia', or 'pa tempu di kumpu tera'. Schwarz's version is the fastest. It includes acoustic guitars, percussion, electric bass, electric keyboards, drums and backing vocals by Miriam Makeba, in addition to a saxophone, which plays a jazz improvisational interlude in the middle of the song and accompaniment towards the end, punctuated by the repeated chorus 'N na nega bedju'. Schwarz's raw baritone intonation conveys a sense of buoyancy that inspires listeners with its message.

From a Cape Verdean and Angolan background, Terezinha Araújo is a near contemporary of José Carlos Schwarz. She studied at the Escola-Piloto (or PAIGC Elementary Boarding School) supported by the Pan-African leader of Guinea, Sékou Touré, in Conakry, where her parents lived in exile, like many other Bissau-Guinean and Cape Verdean nationalists during late Portuguese colonialism.[36] At a performance at the Palais du Peuple in Conakry, Araújo was discovered by Miriam Makeba, who took an interest in her musical education as a senior fellow artist and Pan-Africanist, much as she had done with Schwarz. Araújo later on attended boarding school and college in the

---

[35] Simon Frith, *Performing Rites: On the Value of Popular Music* (Cambridge, MA: Harvard University Press, 1996), p. 270.

[36] The Escola-Piloto in Conakry was created in 1964 by PAIGC and played a key role in the history of the liberation struggle against Portuguese colonialism and the founding of the newly independent nations. It was a highly competitive elite school that opened doors for promising students to attend universities in Dakar and Conakry, as well as gaining access to scholarships to study in Cuba and other socialist countries in eastern Europe. Celebrated film directors Flora Gomes and Sana Na N'Hada were once pupils there and went on to study in Cuba.

USSR, performing widely there. She returned to independent Cape Verde after her college years and worked at the Ministry of Education and Culture.[37] Between 1992 and 2001 she was a member of Simentera, a group that experimented with Cape Verdean folk music traditions in a modern acoustic format. Araújo's only solo album, *Nôs riqueza* [*Our Wealth*] (2003) was recorded in Berlin. It features an acoustic ensemble of Western and African string and wind instruments, in addition to percussion and piano, all revolving around her exquisite soprano voice. The album comprises a repertoire of mostly classics from Cape Verde, Guinea-Bissau and Angola, among them four signature songs by Schwarz (including 'N na nega bedju'). Araújo's mid-tempo version is outstanding, due to the sweet solemnity conveyed by her pristine voice, buttressed by a fine ensemble of musicians playing piano, *balafon*, *kora*,[38] multiple string instruments (including *cavaquinho*) and percussion. The song reaches its climactic moment through the multiple repetitions of the stanza that expresses the love for Guinea-Bissau and Cape Verde described above, further intensified by the rich harmonic and rhythmic interplay among the *kora*, acoustic guitars and percussion.

Karyna Gomes was born in Bissau to a Guinean father and a Cape Verdean mother. Like many other Lusophone African artists who are simultaneously aiming to reach audiences in their home countries as well as in Brazil, Europe and North America, she is currently based in Lisbon, which has become a major cultural node in the postcolonial Lusophone world, especially in the realm of music. Her repertoire is rooted in music performed at courtyard gatherings, typical of many African societies. She started her singing career in a gospel choir in São Paulo, the city where she pursued her college degree in journalism, a profession she has practised in both Guinea-Bissau and Cape Verde. Gomes's musical experience in Brazil exposed her to African-American gospel traditions but, since returning to Guinea-Bissau, she has immersed herself in local musical traditions (including *ngumbé* and *madjuandadi*), while singing in Kriol and other vernacular languages.[39]

---

[37] Biographical information is taken from the CD booklet of Araújo's album *Nôs riqueza* (2003) and the website <https://www.womex.com/virtual/malagueta_music_ltd> [accessed 20 November 2018].

[38] The *kora* is a 21-string harp-lute instrument used extensively in Manding cultures across Senegambia, Mali, Guinea and Burkina Faso, as well as Guinea-Bissau. The *balafon* is another traditional Manding instrument. It is a xylophone with 18–21 keys which, according to the authors of *The Rough Guide* to world music, are cut from rosewood and are 'suspended on a bamboo frame over gourd resonators of graduated sizes': *World Music: The Rough Guide*, eds Simon Broughton, Mark Ellingham, David Muddyman and Richard Trillo (London: Rough Guides, 1994), p. 248.

[39] Biographical information about Gomes is taken from Nuno Pacheco's article,

The invitation to sing with Super Mama Djombo on their comeback album, *Ar puro* [*Clean Air*] (2008), recorded in Iceland, was a turning point in her musical career. Since then, she has shared the stage with major Lusophone and Creolophone African artists such as Bonga, Tito Paris and Boss AC. Her outstanding debut album, *Mindjer* [*Woman*] (2014), has garnered several musical awards.[40] The Portuguese website *Gazeta dos Artistas* describes the album as offering 'a genealogy of Guinea-Bissau's modern music'[41] that features songs by towering figures such as Zé Manel, José Carlos Schwarz, Armando Salvaterra and Adriano Ferreira Atchutchi. Even more importantly, however, *Mindjer* includes five songs written and composed by Gomes herself, signalling the rising contribution of female songwriters to the country's modern music genealogy, including iconic figures such as Dulce Neves, the poet Odete Semedo and Eneida Marta.

Karyna Gomes's version of 'N na nega bedju' is a delicate slow to mid-tempo rendition that prominently features the *kora*, percussion and bass (in addition to subtle accordion flourishes), with extensive vocal arrangements that highlight the richness of her contralto voice. Gomes represents a new wave of artists in Guinea-Bissau who are building upon the legacy of pioneers such as Schwarz himself as well as Cobiana Djazz and the legendary group Super Mama Djombo[42] (the country's most popular group since independence), as well as Zé Manel and Dulce Neves (both former members

'Karyna Gomes: uma voz urbana para a Guiné-Bissau', *Público Online* (7 November 2014) <https://www.publico.pt/2014/11/07/culturaipsilon/noticia/karyna-gomes-uma-voz-urbana-para-a-guinebissau-1675184> [accessed 7 September 2017] and on the Gindungo website <https://gindungo.org/en/artists/karyna-gomes/> [accessed 7 September 2017].

[40] *Mindjer* (Paço de Arcos: Get!Records, 2014). According to the Gindungo website, Gomes was awarded two Best Singer prizes in Guinea-Bissau and was selected for a showcase at the Atlantic Music Expo (in Praia, Cape Verde) <https://gindungo.org/en/artists/karyna-gomes/> [accessed 7 September 2017].

[41] *Gazeta dos Artistas*, 'Karyna Gomes apresenta "Amor Livre" o 1º single de avanço de "Mindjer", o álbum de estreia' (2016) <http://www.gazetadosartistas.pt/?p=37065)> [accessed 7 September 2017].

[42] Super Mama Djombo was founded by Adriano Ferreira Atchutchi in 1973 and followed in the footsteps of Cobiana Djazz by singing in Kriol and playing local/regional music genres. It was politically committed at the same time as it defended a unified pan-ethnic nation. The original group disbanded in 1980 at the same time as the coup d'état that ended the binational state project. The regime that emerged afterwards was not interested in supporting art that was critical of the state. Super Mama Djombo has sporadically re-emerged with varying line-ups. such as in 1992 for the soundtrack of Flora Gomes's film *Udju azul di Yonta* [*The Blue Eyes of Yonta*]; a José Carlos Schwarz tribute album (1999); and in 2008 for the comeback album recorded in

of Super Mama Djombo), the late Bidinte and Manecas Costa,[43] among others, working with roots music in a modern acoustic or electro-acoustic format. Gomes's music privileges a mix of traditional West African instruments of Mandinka origin such as the *kora*, the *balafon* and the *calabash*, in addition to the *bombolom*,[44] along with acoustic guitar, piano, bass, accordion, cello and trumpet. Aside from offering a richer sonic palette, the inclusion of traditional instruments emphasizes Guinea-Bissau's shared musical heritage with neighbouring countries in West Africa, as well as their distinctiveness and authenticity across a broad spectrum of world musics. In contrast, back in the formative 1970s, Cobiana Djazz and Super Mama Djombo's embrace of the modernity embodied by instruments such as the electric guitar reflected not only the influence of Anglo-American musical styles in vogue, but also a gesture of cultural appropriation and musical hybridization.

The song-text 'Tanto' from the album *Movimento* by Angolan Aline Frazão offers a critical distillation of Angolan contemporary society and its deep socio-economic fault lines. Frazão is a singer-songwriter, composer, musician and producer. Born to Cape Verdean and Angolan parents and raised in the capital city of Luanda, she now resides in Lisbon. Frazão has also worked as a journalist for the alternative digital media platform, Rede Angola. She considers herself an heir to the Angolan musical 'legacy' (or *matriz musical angolana*), which includes the seminal group Ngola Ritmos (the most popular band during the final decades of Portuguese colonialism), featuring pioneering women vocalists Lourdes van Dunem and Belita Palma (as Marissa Moorman reminds us),[45] in addition to Bonga (arguably the world's best-known Angolan artist), Waldemar Bastos and Paulo Flores (the immensely talented defender and innovator of the country's musical traditions). All these artists have cultivated primarily acoustic or electroacoustic sounds based on Angolan roots music including genres such as *semba*,

---

Iceland, *Ar Puro*. This information is taken from the sleeve notes of the album *Super Mama Djombo* (1980, 2003).

[43] Zé Manel, Dulce Neves and Manecas Costa have been part of Super Mama Djombo at different junctures.

[44] The *bombolom* is a percussive instrument typical of Guinea-Bissau that consists of a large hollow tree trunk with an opening at the top played horizontally with sticks.

[45] See Marissa Moorman, 'Introducing: Angolan Singer Aline Frazão', *Africa Is a Country* (13 February 2012) <https://africasacountry.com/2012/02/clave-bantu> [accessed 23 December 2018]; Katrin Wilke, 'Die Inselschönheit nützt nichts, wenn du sie nicht teilst' ['The beauty of the island is of no use if you do not share it'], *Deutschland Kultur* (20 April 2016) <http://www.deutschlandfunkkultur.de/aline-frazao-insular-die-inselschoenheit-nuetzt-nichts-wenn.2177.de.html?dram:article_id=352003> [accessed 7 September 2017].

rebita, kilapanda, merengue and/or *kizomba*. Yet, contrary to most Angolan urban popular music, Frazão's music is decidedly non-danceable. In fact, one could consider her music as the antithesis to the wildly popular Angolan electronic dance music genre of *kuduro* that became mainstream after the late 1990s. Her musical project is more authorial and 'art-oriented', rather than 'pop-commercial'.

As of 2017, Frazão has released three albums with highly positive critical reviews.[46] Her musical territories span the South Atlantic from Angola to Brazil, including jazz, rock, and noise influences. She is a skillful wordsmith, whose songwriting is highly literary and reminiscent of some of the outstanding singer-songwriters from the field of Brazilian popular music from Caetano Veloso to Adriana Calcanhotto. Indeed, critic Katrin Wilke describes her songs as 'song-poems'.[47] Her writing is imbued with a profound sense of social consciousness that stands out in her most musically impressive song, 'Tanto'.

'Tanto' features voice, acoustic guitar, piano, bass and percussion. It favours jazz-inspired chromatic keys undergirded by a syncopated mid-tempo beat. The song structure is based on an oscillating dynamic of tension and release that culminates in a climactic moment that is especially palpable in the music video, as we shall see later on. From a philosophical point of view, through words and image, the song posits a 'phenomenology of seeing/looking' in relationship to Angola, encapsulated metonymically by the city of Luanda. Ricardo Soares de Oliveira describes Luanda as 'a magnetic metropolis pulling in 6 million Angolans and hundreds of thousands of expatriates' that is 'routinely awarded the dubious title of the world's most expensive city'.[48]

Angola has been ruled since independence in 1975 by the triumphant liberation movement-party, MPLA,[49] under the auspices of José Eduardo dos Santos and his family since 1980,[50] with little political opposition beyond its

---

[46] Aline Frazão, *Clave Bantu* (Coast to Coast, 2011); *Movimento* (Portugal: Pontozurca, 2013); *Insular* (Portugal: Norte-Sul, 2015).
[47] See Wilke, 'Die Inselschönheit nützt nichts'.
[48] Ricardo Soares de Oliveira, *Magnificent and Beggar Land: Angola Since the Civil War* (London: C. Hurst & Co, 2015), p. 2.
[49] Popular Movement for the Liberation of Angola.
[50] Elections took place in 2017 in which José Eduardo dos Santos did not run for office. Instead, the former Minister of Defense and MPLA Secretary-General, João Lourenço, triumphed. While the MPLA garnered fewer votes than in past elections, the final results were strongly contested by the opposition, arguing that there were irregularities prior to the voting. Nevertheless, opposition parties obtained at least half of the votes in Luanda province, signalling an important political

former archrival guerrilla movement UNITA,[51] now a steadfast but relatively weak opposition party, and with a near complete MPLA monopoly over the media. Its economy has been almost completely dependent upon oil exports to the point of being labelled an 'oilacracy' by historian Christine Messiant.[52] In 'Tanto', Aline Frazão compels listeners/viewers to calibrate their perception to see through an Angolan reality that has been clouded by appearances. Part of this phenomenological recalibration entails becoming aware of the disenfranchised population in one of the world's most inequitable societies, ruled by one of the world's most corrupt governments.[53] This particular dimension becomes quite prominent in the song's music video.

The lyrics of 'Tanto' are structured around a series of suggested 'commonsensical' cause-and-effect relationships that are destabilized: 'É tanta luz aqui que até parece claridade' ['There is so much light here that there seems to be clarity'], 'É tanto excesso aqui que até parece não há falta' ['There is so much excess here that there seems to be no scarcity'] or 'É tanto muro aqui que até parece que é seguro' ['There are so many walls here that it seems to be safe'].[54] The equivalencies implied by the pairings *tanta luz = claridade, excesso = não há falta, tanto muro = seguro* are destabilized by the hypothesizing clause 'que até parece' ['that there seems to be' or 'it seems to be'] that sows doubt into the pairings. This particular logic and rhetorical structure are maintained over 20 lines with content variations in the pairings. The overall effect is to inject deep scepticism into this state of affairs while calling critical attention to a perception of social reality built upon appearances, where excess obstructs clarity of vision, thus leading to political disempowerment, especially in a country where challenging the government carries a heavy price, since political protests tend to be systematically repressed. There is a play on words in Portuguese in the chorus that says, 'É tanto "tanto faz"/que ninguém sabe quem fez' ['There are so many "who cares" that no one knows

shift for the country. See Johannes Beck, 'Angola's New President in Waiting', *Deutsche Welle* (3 February 2017) <http://www.dw.com/en/angolas-new-president-in-waiting/a-36705629> [accessed 6 September 2017]; and 'Angola Elections: Ruling MPLA Wins Parliamentary Vote', *Al Jazeera* (25 August 2017) <http://www.aljazeera.com/news/2017/08/170825124719728.html> [accessed 6 September 2017].

[51] National Union for the Total Independence of Angola.

[52] Christine Messiant, *L'Angola postcolonial: la guerre et paix sans democratization* (Paris: Karthala, 2008), p. 23.

[53] Transparency International ranked Angola as the 164th most corrupt country in the world out of 176 considered in its Corruption Perceptions Index 2016: <https://www.transparency.org/news/feature/corruption_perceptions_index_2016> [accessed 16 September 2017].

[54] The English translation is my own.

who's behind them']. Frazão simultaneously points to a generalized political indifference and lack of social responsibility, but also to a relationship of alienation on the part of the majority population in regard to the source of political and economic power in Angola.

The ethical implications of the phenomenology of seeing/looking as proposed by Aline Frazão in 'Tanto' as well as the discrepancy between reality and appearances become more palpable in the outstanding music video (directed by Mário Bastos), where a syncretic relationship is built up between song and moving image.[55] In fact, Frazão is physically embedded in the music video, while positioning herself as simultaneously insider and outsider in relation to the world portrayed within it. She appears in the video's first sequence with her back turned towards the audience, thus privileging her perspective over theirs. Through her voice and physical presence, Frazão guides us through many different landscapes of Luanda showing the socioeconomic chasm between the wealthy and the poor/lower middle-class suggested in the song lyrics. We follow her as she moves through multiple urban spaces and social situations observing wealth, luxury, signs of conspicuous consumption, historical monuments, and enclosures (such as walls), in addition to poverty, urban decay, a ship cargo dock, traffic jams, ubiquitous SUVs and street vendors. The song/video's second sequence prominently features average working-class residents of Luanda, women, men and children, at work or play: a cook, a night watchman, a fisherman, a driver, a female money exchanger (known as *kínguila* in Kimbundu), a gardener, a waitress and children playing soccer on an apartment balcony. In between these sequences there is an instrumental jazz piano interlude filmed in black and white and in colour, featuring a young urban hip female dancer on the rooftop of a tall building with debris strewn around, against a background of more high rises; some glistening new glass towers, some semi-decrepit older buildings, and a multitude of satellite dishes.

The third and climatic sequence at the end of the song/video features all the various men, women, and children who appeared earlier, but this time turning their faces towards the camera and looking directly at it. The song's refrain, 'Não olhes se não vês' ['Don't look if you can't see'], is repeated in a crescendo mode, creating a highly dramatic effect. The exhortation calls for an unobstructed vision in order for social awareness and empathy to emerge. As Luanda's poor look back, they are no longer passive objects gazed upon by viewers. The 'others', the excluded and the oppressed of Angola, return the gaze, thus confronting the viewer-listener. Their individualized collective

[55] Mário Bastos, *Tanto*, online video recording, *YouTube* (13 May 2013) <https://www.youtube.com/watch?v=AFDJFzYpBH0> [accessed 16 September 2017].

gaze in a close-up format shatters the 'invisible fourth wall' performance convention, beckoning the viewer's interest. Gilles Deleuze's 'affection-image' exemplified by the close-up, which is at the same time encompassed by the face, is used here to maximum effect in order to call attention to or to question the ways of seeing/looking in a society where what appears has occluded what is.[56] The ethical implications here evoke a key dimension in the philosophical thought of Emmanuel Lévinas, most specifically the structure of responsibility towards the other, whereby the encounter with the other's face plays a central role: 'the epiphany of the face as face, opens humanity'.[57] For the philosopher, it is through the face and through a sense of responsibility towards the other that an 'ethical moment' and a sense of justice may emerge.[58]

These particular insights are most apt when thinking about the power of the close-up and its relevance for understanding the ethical strategy on the part of Aline Frazão and the politics of representation in the 'Tanto' music video. Even though the song-text, as well as the harmonic and rhythmic structure are highly sophisticated in and of themselves, the music video adds complex semiotic layers to the social, philosophical and political issues raised, altogether creating a powerful syncretic and multidisciplinary platform.

* * *

The song-texts and artists from Cape Verde, Guinea-Bissau and Angola featured throughout this essay allow us to map out transnational networks and routes/roots in the histories of the cultures in question. The experiences of Portuguese colonialism, the Atlantic slave trade, the African struggles against European colonialism from the mid- to late twentieth century,

---

[56] Deleuze's 'affection-image' is inspired by Sergei Eisenstein's own conceptualization of the close-up image and its power to convey an 'affective reading' of a film, as well as Henri Bergson's definition of affect. For the latter, it is the moment in which the moving body loses its 'movement of extension' thus becoming a 'movement of expression'. So, affect according to Bergson via Deleuze would be a 'combination of a reflecting, immobile unity and of intensive expressive movements': Gilles Deleuze, *Cinema 1: The Movement Image* (1983), trans. Hugh Tomlinson and Barbara Habberjam (Minneapolis: University of Minnesota Press, 1986), p. 87.

[57] Emmanuel Lévinas, *Le visage de l'autre* (Paris: Éditions du Seuil, 2001), p. 30 (translation mine).

[58] Emmanuel Lévinas, *Entre nous: essais sur le penser-à-l'autre* (Paris: Éditions Grasset & Fasquelle, 1991), pp. 113–14. I would like to warmly thank Charlie Sugnet for our ongoing conversations on cinema, music, politics and Africa, and for reminding me of the continued relevance of Emmanuel Lévinas.

Pan-Africanism, socialist internationalism and 'Third World' solidarity (where Cuba played a key role), are inextricably intertwined in the formative processes of these societies. Furthermore, in this study we are able to witness the flourishing of the Portuguese-based Creole languages of Cape Verde and Guinea-Bissau in the realm of music, in addition to the synergistic role played by postcolonial Lisbon for the production and dissemination of Lusophone and Creolophone African and Afro-diasporic musics. Finally, these song-texts and artists bring to light the potency of expressive culture in the form of popular music for the purposes of social intervention, political mobilization, philosophical reflection and historical remembrance.

5

Transnational, Palimpsestic Journeys in the Art of Bartolomeu Cid dos Santos

Maria Luísa Coelho

Universidade do Minho and University of Oxford

For those visiting Lisbon, the underground network may be an unexpected but frequent place for aesthetic pleasure: witnessing the bustle of commuters and tourists getting in and out of the metro, the stations display mural artwork by some of the most well-known Portuguese contemporary artists, who have worked the stone or, more frequently, the Portuguese tradition of ceramic tiling (*azulejos*), in order to evoke national, local or toponymic history. One of the most outstanding examples of such public art is found at Entrecampos station, situated near the National Library, where, between 1991 and 1993, the artist Bartolomeu Cid dos Santos (1935–2008) created an intricate sequence of stone panels (Figures 5.1–5.3) and summoned the central figures of the poets Luís Vaz de Camões and Fernando Pessoa – the latter here under the heteronymic guise of Álvaro de Campos and in close articulation with the poetry of Cesário Verde – to revisit Portuguese literary history.[1]

[1] Luís Vaz de Camões (1524 or 1525–80) is a central figure of the Portuguese literary canon, famed primarily for his epic poem *Os Lusíadas* [*The Lusiads*] which narrates, at once triumphantly and critically, the first voyage of the Portuguese to India and recounts key moments of Portuguese history. In the nineteenth century, another Portuguese poet – the realist Cesário Verde (1855–86) – recalled the expeditions and discoveries of Portuguese sailors in his masterpiece 'O Sentimento dum Ocidental' ['The Feeling of a Westerner'], originally published in a special issue of *Jornal de Viagens* commemorating the death of Camões. Strongly influenced by Baudelaire and French *flâneurie*, but also foreshadowing Modernist poetry, in this long, descriptive poem Cesário is an acute observer of urban life, revealed in surprising insights and associations of images, while the poet perambulates through and gazes at the streets of Lisbon, the decadent present of which contrasts with the glories of its past. Practically unknown during his lifetime, Cesário was recovered decades later

92   *Maria Luísa Coelho*

Figure 5.1. Detail of stone panel by Bartolomeu Cid dos Santos, Entrecampos metro station, Lisbon. © Maria Luísa Coelho.

Looking in more detail at dos Santos's artistic intervention, it displays two distinct, albeit interrelated, sections: one is located in the atrium, where the artist depicted a library with books chosen according to his personal taste and interests and organized in terms of chronology, themes and movements; the other one is positioned on the two platforms and focuses on Álvaro de Campos and Camões, whose works dialogue with each other across the tracks.[2] Despite their differences, both sections place great emphasis on texts that depict Portuguese encounters with other peoples and places, such as Camões's *Os Lusíadas* [*The Lusiads*] (1572), Fernão Mendes Pinto's *Peregrinação* [*The Travels of Mendes Pinto*] (1614) and the shipwreck narratives known as *História Trágico-Marítima* [*Tragic Story of the Sea*] (compiled by Bernardo Gomes de Brito in the eighteenth century), or imagined journeys, like those longed for by Álvaro de Campos in his 'Ode Marítima' ['Maritime Ode'].[3] Along with the overarching theme of Portuguese literary history or, rather, in close articulation with it, the theme of travel thus traverses dos Santos's panels, particularly when the literary fragments reproduced from 'Ode Marítima' and *Os Lusíadas* become entangled with visual correlatives: images of ancient ships, maps and navigation instruments overlap with mermaids and other magical sea creatures, as well as with exotic plants and animals, and far-off tropical lands. The end-result is a densely layered, fluid, richly textured visual fabric, whose characteristics are further enhanced by the way the stone was corroded and engraved, in a process described by the artist as close to graffiti, which is in itself an urban form of public art.[4] Moreover, not only is the theme fitting to such a transitory place of arrivals and departures, but it is also a

by Fernando Pessoa (1888–1935) and explicitly referred to in poems by Álvaro de Campos, one of Pessoa's literary personae or heteronyms. Through Campos, Pessoa embraced the Futurism of Marinetti and the free verse espoused by Walt Whitman, in odes that enthusiastically celebrate machinery, progress and modern forms of travel. Luís de Camões: *Os Lusíadas*, ed. Alvaro Júlio da Costa Pimpão (Lisbon: Instituto de Cultura e Língua Portuguesa, 1989); Cesário Verde, 'O Sentimento dum Ocidental', in *Obra Completa de Cesário Verde*, ed. Joel Serrão (Lisbon: Portugália Editora, 1964), pp. 103–11; Álvaro de Campos, 'Ode Marítima', in *Orpheu: Números 1 e 2, Provas de Página do Terceiro Número* (Barcelos: Contexto, 1994), pp. 131–52. All translations into English are my own unless otherwise indicated.

[2] There is also a third section of the work on the stairs that connect the platforms to the atrium and that is dedicated to American artist and printmaker Robert Motherwell (1915–91), who had died shortly before the station was decorated.

[3] Fernão Mendes Pinto, *Peregrinação* (Lisbon: Imprensa Nacional-Casa da Moeda, 1983); Bernardo Gomes de Brito, *História Trágico-Marítima* (Lisbon: Editorial SUL, 1955). See also ch. 1, n. 37 in this volume.

[4] See Margarida Botelho and Pina Cabral, *O Novo Interface do Metro de Entrecampos* (Lisbon: Metropolitano de Lisboa, n.d.).

94   *Maria Luísa Coelho*

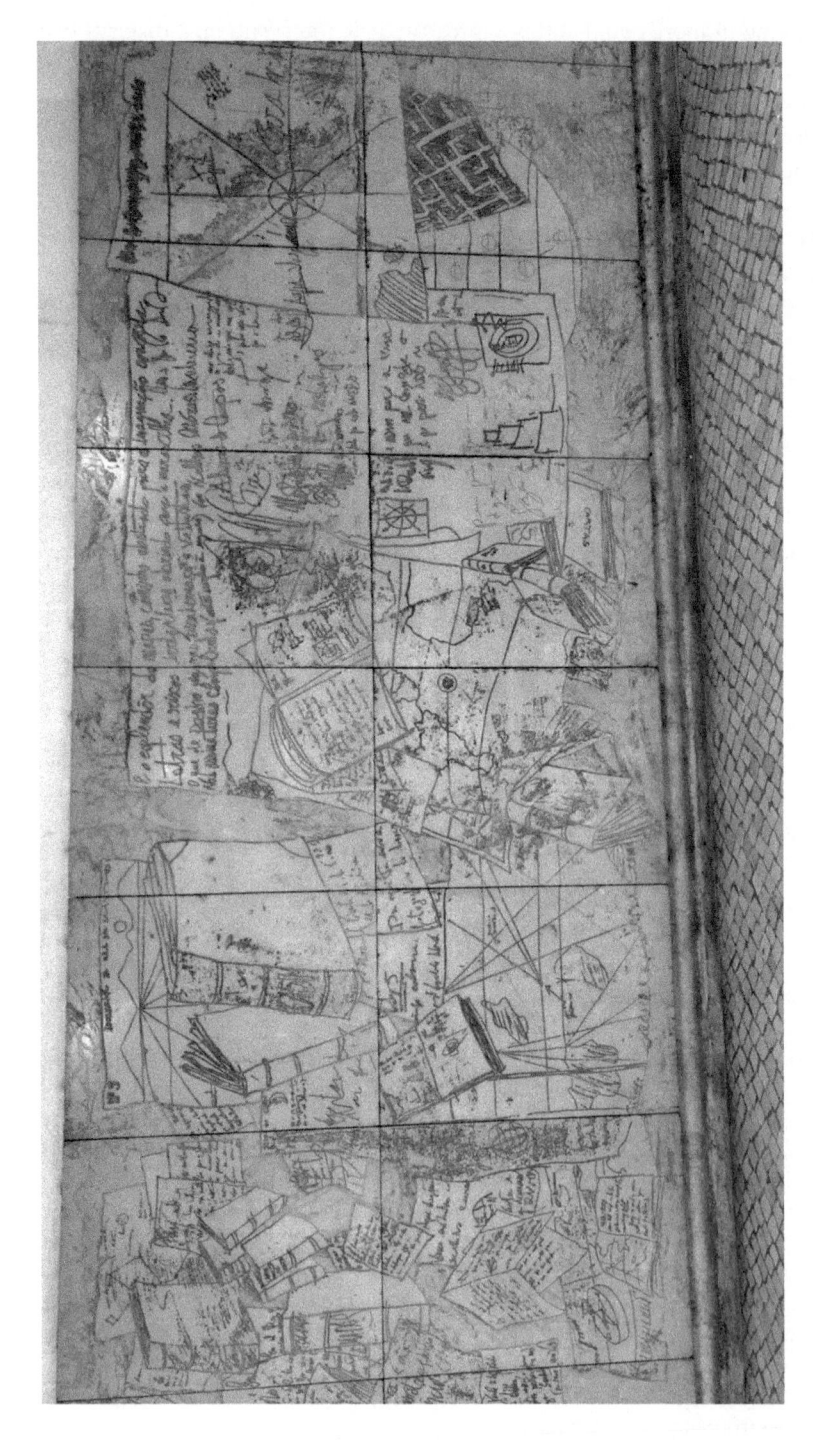

Figure 5.2. Detail of stone panel by Bartolomeu Cid dos Santos, Entrecampos metro station, Lisbon. © Maria Luísa Coelho.

constant one in dos Santos's work and life, since he was born in Lisbon, into a wealthy, educated family used to visiting Europe and whose ancestors could be traced as far as Scotland. As a young adult dos Santos moved to London, where he established himself as a renowned engraver and art professor at the Slade School of Fine Art. While based in London, he held visiting lectureships in other countries and travelled extensively around the world.[5]

Bartolomeu dos Santos's life and work seem to epitomize a contemporary reality in which movement, dislocation and migration have become central. Nevertheless, this 'liquid modernity' does not necessarily entail the mere disappearance of spatial grounding and processes of homing, since forms of detachment or deterritorialization are accompanied by attachments and reterritorializations of various kinds and uprooting and regrounding are constantly enacted in relation to one another. This is so much the case that '[b]eing grounded is not necessarily about being fixed; being mobile is not necessarily about being detached'.[6] As art historians Marion Arnold and Marsha Meskimmon have recently concluded, 'self' and 'home' are processes that are never fixed nor stable, as 'we produce multiple, mutable and transformative identifications – mobile, global homes'.[7] Sheller and Urry similarly talk about a 'new mobilities paradigm' that frames home and migration as interrelated experiences;[8] furthermore, it has contributed to an epistemological shift from nation-based ideas of culture and communities as rigidly bounded, self-contained entities, existing within fixed and stable geographic spaces, to complex cultural and social phenomena through which individuals and communities connect across different times and spaces.

---

[5] See *Bartolomeu Cid dos Santos: Por Terras Devastadas*, dir. Jorge Silva Melo (Midas, 2009) [on DVD].

[6] Zygmunt Bauman, *Liquid Times: Living in an Age of Uncertainty* (Cambridge: Polity Press, 2000); Mimi Sheller and John Urry, 'The New Mobilities Paradigm', *Environment and Planning A*, 36 (2006), 207–26, (p. 210); Sara Ahmed, 'Introduction', in *Uprootings/Regroundings: Questions of Home and Migration*, ed. Sara Ahmed et al (Oxford: Berg, 2003), pp. 1–19 (p. 1). See also *Mobilizing Place, Placing Mobility: The Politics of Representation in a Globalized World*, eds Ginette Verstraete and Tim Cresswell (Amsterdam: Rodopi, 2002).

[7] Marion Arnold and Marsha Meskimmon, 'Making Oneself at Home', *Third Text*, 29.4–5 (2015), 256–65 (p. 259). See also Marsha Meskimmon, 'Chronology through Cartography: Mapping 1970s Feminist Art Globally', in *Wack! Art and the Feminist Revolution*, ed. Cornelia Butler (Cambridge, MA: The MIT Press, 2007), pp. 322–35; Marsha Meskimmon, *Contemporary Art and the Cosmopolitan Imagination* (London: Routledge, 2011); and *Women, the Arts and Globalization*, eds Marsha Meskimmon and Dorothy C. Rowe (Manchester: Manchester University Press, 2013). See also *The Culture of Migration: Politics, Aesthetics and Histories*, eds Sten Pultz Moslund et al (London: I. B. Tauris, 2015).

[8] Sheller and Urry, 'The New Mobilities Paradigm', p. 210.

Framed by this critical position, in this chapter I intend to show the potential of a transnational methodology for generating further revisions of pre-established notions of national identity, culture and art, as well as of fixed and stable subjective identities, by looking at the work of Bartolomeu Cid dos Santos, who belonged to a generation of Portuguese artists who began living in London in the 1950s. With artists such as Paula Rego, João Cutileiro and João Vieira, as well as dos Santos, among its most prominent members, this generation not only made important contributions to what is generally defined as 'Portuguese art', but also disturbed the conceptual stability of the term itself through a series of transcultural practices involving processes of appropriation, negotiation and transformation. The chapter ultimately aims to contribute to a transnational approach to art history, a critical stance that is here akin to the transcultural methodology argued for by Birgit Mersmann when she states that through a transcultural art history '[f]ixed art-historical categorizations, be they national, regional or religious, are problematized and questioned by transculturations as processes of entangled art histories'.[9]

When dos Santos arrived in London, in 1956, Britain was emerging from the ruins of the Second World War, the aftermath of which included the dismantling of the British Empire and the arrival of many former British subjects to Albion's shores. Britain went on to take part in the economic recovery that characterized most of Western Europe, as well as witnessing marked changes of lifestyle and patterns of cultural behaviour that led to the cultural revolution of the 1960s. In contrast, the Portugal that dos Santos had left behind had assumed an officially neutral position during the war and was controlled by a dictatorial regime (known as Estado Novo) that maintained a tight civil, religious and military grip to keep one of the poorest, most underdeveloped and illiterate peoples in Europe firmly subjugated. One of the direct consequences of the repressive, fascist regime that had taken hold of Portugal since 1933 was a wave of migration, which increased even further with the beginning of Portugal's colonial wars in Africa, in 1961. Positioned at the junction of these two contrasting, albeit co-existing, political, social and cultural environments, dos Santos soon became part of a growing community of Portuguese artists living in Britain, particularly in London, where they found an increasingly multicultural and cosmopolitan urban atmosphere and produced a diverse, intensely exploratory body of work. It was an informal group (rather than a coherent movement), united by a common rejection of

---

[9] Birgit Mersmann, 'D/Rifts between Visual Culture and Image Culture: Relocations of the Transnational Study of the Visual', in *The Trans/National Study of Culture: A Translational Perspective*, ed. Doris Bachmann-Medick (Berlin: Walter de Gruyter GmbH, 2014), pp. 237–60 (p. 256).

conservatism, conformity and oppression, and a celebration of experimentation, freedom and friendship, to which the cloak of anonymity brought about by life in a foreign metropolis clearly contributed.

Paula Rego is undoubtedly the most well-known and studied member of this group: one of the first artists of her generation to arrive to London (in 1951), Rego has produced a multidirectional oeuvre characterized by a complex network of references across time and space and, as a result, she is constantly destabilizing traditional discourses on national identity and hampering attempts to frame her work as either Portuguese or British.[10] Nevertheless, she is not alone in her approach, which may also be found in many other migrant Portuguese artists of her generation, effectively becoming symptomatic of a wider and more expressive phenomenon, with an impact on the way we apprehend national and transnational forms of being and representation. Viewed in this context, the work of Bartolomeu dos Santos is particularly significant.

Experiencing a cultured, liberal and cosmopolitan setting from a very early age, dos Santos left for London in order to enrol at the Slade School of Fine Art. It was love at first sight, as confirmed by the aquatint prints of that first year: dreamy, foggy, moonlit images of London where, through a restricted palette of dark, muted tones, the artist explored the *chiaroscuro* effect in order to represent a mysterious, enticing city, revealed in its rooftops, chimneys and neon signs. In their melancholic visions of the city, these first works already disclose the influence of neo-romantic British artists such as Graham Sutherland and John Piper, who dos Santos admired and who were also great printmakers. Nevertheless, cultural differences were also immediately felt by the young Portuguese artist:

> My first months at the Slade were traumatic due to the culture shock I had to face. A different atmosphere, a kind of work and teaching based on critical discussion and analytical observation of the model, created, at the time, serious problems for someone who had recently left a School in which independent thought was not looked upon favourably and intelligent criticism was discouraged.[11]

---

[10] See Ruth Rosengarten, *Contrariar, Esmagar, Amar: A Família e o Estado Novo na Obra de Paula Rego* (Lisbon: Assírio e Alvim, 2009); and Ana Gabriela Macedo, *Paula Rego e o Poder da Visão: A Minha Pintura É como uma História Interior* (Lisbon: Cotovia, 2010).

[11] José Sommer Ribeiro and Bartolomeu Cid dos Santos, *Bartolomeu Cid dos Santos: Exposição Retrospectiva* (Lisbon: Fundação Calouste Gulbenkian, Centro de Arte Moderna, 1989), n.pag.

The *School* mentioned by dos Santos was the Escola de Belas Artes [Fine Arts School] in Lisbon, part of a conservative educational system which, according to Delfim Sardo, was one of the most common reasons for the migration of Portuguese artists in the twentieth century.[12]

Returning to Portugal in 1958, dos Santos immediately felt smothered by the environment found at Belas-Artes and the restrictive existence enforced by the fascist regime and, in 1961, he returned to London, after being offered a position at the Slade, as a teacher of printmaking. From that point onwards, the Slade became for dos Santos the home to which he would always return from his frequent journeys, in what may be regarded as a reterritorialization and a process of regrounding brought about by the artist's migrant movements.[13] The Slade was also a multicultural, dialogic space that mirrored the wider transformations experienced in London at the time and that had a tremendous impact on the direction of dos Santos's work, not least in his decision to become a printmaker. At the Slade, dos Santos developed as an artist (the school was in effect his printing studio) and shared (more than transmitted) knowledge with his students, who he greatly valued: 'At the school where I work [...] many points-of-view are exchanged, because the students come from different countries and so from very different cultures. The work becomes very interesting.'[14] In fact, the way teaching was regarded by dos Santos as a process of exchange and the close relationship he promoted between the role of the artist and the role of the educator would come to dictate the collaborative dimension of a considerable amount of his work, one example of which is the Entrecampos panels, which were created with the active involvement of several of his Slade students.

The contrast, experienced first-hand, between a life of imprisonment and one of freedom soon became a dominant theme in dos Santos's work. Take for example the series of bishops produced in 1961, summarized by Helder Macedo as 'aggressive, phantasmagorical, decadent'.[15] Figuratively very much influenced by Goya, particularly by the bleak scenes depicted in his series of prints *The Disasters of War* (1810–20) and his effective use of light, shadow and shade in that same series, dos Santos's bishops are silent, fossilized or skeletal beings, with a stillness emphasized by their sitting position and the barren landscape. This landscape also evokes one of dos Santos's favourite poems – T. S. Eliot's 'The Waste Land' (1922) – and thence the sterile land left

---

[12] Delfim Sardo, *Obras Primas da Arte Portuguesa: Século XX – Artes Visuais*, (Lisbon: Athena, n.d.), p. 10.

[13] Sheller and Urry, 'The New Mobilities', p. 210; Ahmed, 'Introduction'.

[14] Ribeiro and dos Santos, *Bartolomeu*, n.pag.

[15] Helder Macedo, in *Bartolomeu Cid* (Lisbon: Galeria Gravura, 1967), n.pag.

behind by any war, be it a nineteenth-century conflict in Spain, Eliot's First World War, the Second World War, the spoils of which had been glimpsed by the young Bartolomeu through the windows of his grandfather's car, or even the Portuguese colonial wars, which were just beginning in Africa. Despite their stillness, the bishops' sinister presence and insidious power are incisively suggested by the symbols of their status and position – the mitre, the crozier, and the throne. In some of the prints this is further intimated by the creation of a tightly clustered group of clerical figures as, for example, in *The Confession* (1963), whose allusion to Kafka's *The Trial* (1925) further highlights the political dimension of the work and its condemnation of both the Portuguese authoritarian state and the role played by the Catholic Church in maintaining the Estado Novo and its repressive policies.

In the 1970s, architectonic and geometric landscapes become the dominant setting for dos Santos's prints, but there is still a disquieting atmosphere, in which labyrinths with no escape, barred windows and interiors shaped by sharp corners and thick walls create the claustrophobic, frightening feeling of captivity and enclosure. The historical and political implications of these stifling, confining spaces are made more explicit in works created immediately after the Carnation Revolution of 1974, such as *Homenagem* [*Tribute*] (1975) and *Para Que Não Voltem É Preciso Não Esquecer* [*It Must Not Be Forgotten So That They Don't Return*] (1976), in which the artist explicitly recalls the incarceration and torture of opponents to Salazar's regime.

In contrast to the stiff, decomposing figures and landscapes segmented by bars, walls and restricted views, other works from the 1970s seem to suggest a mythic time, travelling and the liberation and freedom that they provide. In many of these works colossal, overwhelming spheres dominate the visual space. There is a long history of images of spheres in artworks, but dos Santos's may be traced back to visual artists such as M. C. Escher, whose graphic work also explored complex, architectural mazes and impossible spaces, as well as to the surrealist compositions of René Magritte. Nevertheless, the chief influence comes from the sublime, vast, awe-inspiring architectural scenes imagined by visionary French neoclassical architect Étienne-Louis Boullée. For Boullée, as indeed for dos Santos, the sphere represents a perfect celestial body, and thus symbolizes perfection, boundlessness and the sublime. The fact that in some of dos Santos's works a Vitruvian man is discernible within the sphere – as in the series *Aleph* (1978), whose title refers both to Kabbalistic literature and to Jorge Luis Borges's short story addressing the theme of infinity – suggests a humanist belief in the power of the self to reach that higher state. On one level, this may be related to the freedom and democracy that were new to the Portuguese after 1974. However, it also relates to elements that go beyond the national, given that, according to dos Santos, his production of cosmic landscapes was considerably influenced by British director Stanley Kubrick and his *2001: Space Odyssey* (1968), a film that explores future directions for discovery and travel and which dos Santos first saw in 1969, the same year he discovered the writings of Borges.[16] This network of possibilities underlines highly complex interconnections and cultural entanglements that further underline the transnational significance of dos Santos's oeuvre, where the viewer travels across cultures and traditions, overcoming national borders.

From his earliest works onwards, in fact, dos Santos clearly displayed an interest in the imagery of travel, particularly sea travelling, frequently summoned in images of a submerged Atlantis (in prints from the 1960s and 1970s), or in references to ships carrying foolish Portuguese men of war pursuing dreams of wealth (a theme that he also explored in the 1960s) or, more recently, in the combination of elements and figures that evoke modern maritime forms of travelling. In the Entrecampos panels, with which I began this discussion, and in several prints produced in the 1980s, the viewer enters the maze of real and imaginary references to nautical journeys, guided by three Portuguese poets, themselves either experienced or imaginary sea travellers: Camões, Cesário Verde and Pessoa's heteronymic double Álvaro de Campos (the latter a transnational figure who had studied naval engineering in Glasgow and, like dos Santos, worked in London).[17] Dos Santos greatly admired the poetry of Verde and Campos and, in the closing section of this chapter, I will turn my attention to the specific perspective on transnationalism that their relationship with his artwork permits.

Both poets wrote in praise of the Lisbon dos Santos left behind when he moved to London and which he revisited throughout his life and in his artistic practice. But, more importantly, in Verde, dos Santos found the subjective gaze that drew on the Baudelarian movement of the *flâneur* across the city and the mind, to reproduce co-existing fragments of daily life and create the intersection of different planes, crossing past and present, here and there, reality and imagination, to such an extent that in the second stanza of 'O Sentimento dum Ocidental' ['The Feeling of a Westerner'] the poet conflates Lisbon with the other city that was so central to dos Santos's life experience: 'The sky hangs low and seems all hazy; / The gas from the streetlamps makes me queasy; / The tumult of buildings, chimneys and people / Is cloaked in a dullish, Londonish hue.'[18] Dos Santos was clearly

---

[16] Ribeiro and dos Santos, *Bartolomeu*, n.pag.
[17] See note 1 above.
[18] Cesário Verde, 'The Feeling of a Westerner', trans. Richard Zenith, <http://www.poetryinternationalweb.net/pi/site/poem/item/14822/auto/0/Cesario-Verde-O-Sentimento-dum-Ocidental> [accessed 15 October 2017].

Transnational, Palimpsestic Journeys   101

Figure 5.3. Detail of stone panel by Bartolomeu Cid dos Santos, Entrecampos metro station, Lisbon. © Maria Luísa Coelho.

Figure 5.4. Bartolomeu Cid dos Santos, *Homenagem a Cesário* [*Homage to Cesário*], 1985, etching and aquatint, 106 x 75 cm.
© Paulo Costa.

interested in Verde's creation of a fluid and unbounded geographic, literary and subjective space; the above section of 'O Sentimento dum Ocidental', for instance, is reproduced in *Homenagem a Cesário* [*Homage to Cesário*] (1985) (Figure 5.4), along with another stanza that explicitly refers to Lisbon and the river Tagus.

In *Homenagem a Cesário*, as in dos Santos's other visual invocations of Lisbon, the vague feeling of melancholy that was characteristic of his early representations of London is also present, with the Tagus mirroring the Thames in its suggestion of a fleeting reality on top of which the city seems to float. This geographic overlapping and the configuration of transcultural connections leading to a flowing transnational space are shared by the Entrecampos metro station panels, where a predominantly Portuguese literary canon intersects with references to British history and literature – namely to poet Joseph Crabtree (1754–1854) and philosopher and social reformer Jeremy Bentham (1748–1832), both of whom warranted a small shelf of their own in dos Santos's imagined library.[19]

As for Campos, dos Santos was fascinated by his 'Ode Marítima', fragments of which were repeatedly used in his homonymous print series, as well as in *Homenagem a Cesário* and the Entrecampos panels. In 'Ode Marítima' Pessoa's heteronym paid tribute to Verde at the same time as he offered a vision of modern urban life (the cars, the trains, the cargo ships, the cruises and the bustle of harbours and streets) and, more crucially, of imaginary and literary voyages, journeys across space and time through a process of subjective memory and unbounded imagination: 'The surging of the Tagus inundates my senses, / And I begin to dream, to be wrapped by the dream of the waters, / The transmission belts on my soul start turning hard, / And I'm visibly shaken by the flywheel's increasing speed.'[20]

Dos Santos's Entrecampos panels, in which books, letters and drawings fly out of the library and into the world, reiterate Álvaro de Campos's proposition. His 'Ode Marítima' also suggests that travelling, even if in a poem, a library or a flight of imagination, produces cultural exchanges that result in transnational forms of existence. This was understood by Campos, as it subsequently was by dos Santos, not as a process of detachment, but one through which the world becomes a moving, global home, thus exposing the

---

[19] Both Crabtree and Bentham are associated with the foundation of the University of London (UCL), where dos Santos worked. In fact, dos Santos was a member of the Crabtree Foundation at UCL and its president in 1993.

[20] Álvaro de Campos, 'Maritime Ode', in *A Little Larger than the Entire Universe: Selected Poems*, trans. Richard Zenith (New York: Penguin, 2006), pp. 166–96 (pp. 172–73).

fiction of national borders and identities: 'Voyages on the sea, where we're all companions / In a special way, as if a maritime mystery / Brought our souls together and transformed us for a moment / Into transient citizens of the same uncertain country.'[21]

In Campos's poem as in Verde's, the river Tagus and the sea occupy central places and therefore underpin both poets' apologia for travelling. These poems mirror the aquatic element found in so many of dos Santos's prints, in which words, ships or the contours of ancient buildings seem to float over the marks and blotches left by the acid involved in the printing process. As we have seen, this liquid reality corresponds to the crossing of geographic and historical boundaries and to the construction of an intricate, rhizomatic network of juxtaposed references and fragments, in a visual translation of the intersecting strategy developed by the two Portuguese poets.[22]

Occupying a respectable and long-established position in the history of British art, the practice of printmaking was masterfully developed by dos Santos, particularly through the processes of etching and aquatint, which not only allowed him to experiment with a palette of tonal effects, but also to explore intersecting possibilities. These possibilities are not only developed in the works we have been discussing but also in others produced since the 1980s, where multilayered representations evidence the handling and combination of materials that co-exist in the same jam-packed print and reveal the juxtaposition of different media, as well as of multiple times and spaces.

Works such as the series *Stanley* (1980) and *Africa Discovered* (1981) (Figure 5.5) are superlative examples of such processes. The title of *Stanley* refers to the nineteenth-century Welsh-American explorer Henry Morton Stanley (1841–1904), better known for his explorations of Africa in the service of European colonialism, a system to which the Portuguese contribution is more explicitly addressed in *Africa Discovered*. These works were ingeniously developed through the technique of photoengraving, a process similar to that of collage, through which the artist superimposed photographs, shipping documents and nautical and territorial maps, in order to create a visual representation of things that are in themselves representations of something else, as rightly suggested by Joaquim Matos Chaves.[23] Nevertheless, according to Edward Lucie-Smith:

---

[21] Campos, 'Maritime Ode', p. 194.

[22] See Gilles Deleuze and Félix Guattari, *A Thousand Plateaus* (London: Bloomsbury, 2013 [1988]), especially the introduction, for their discussion of the rhizome, a hybrid and non-hierarchical concept.

[23] Joaquim Matos Chaves, 'Uma Obra, uma Profunda Lição', in *Bartolomeu dos Santos* (Braga: Galeria da Universidade, 1987), n.pag.

Figure 5.5. Bartolomeu Cid dos Santos, *Africa Discovered*, 1981, mixed media, 60 x 51 cm.

Dos Santos takes the *idea* of the collage and takes it further. The borrowed images and signs which he incorporates into his prints no longer need to be intruders. They take leave of the original surfaces where the printmaker found them and are completely intermingled on a new surface with other marks and signs. Often they become transparent, so that one looks past – or rather through – one image (a treated photograph, a postmark, a scrap of handwriting) in order to get a glimpse of another.[24]

Lucie-Smith's analysis highlights the fact that the different elements of dos Santos's work do not exclude or intrude upon each other, as in the case of the collage, but rather they co-exist in an exercise of shadow and transparency that lets the viewer look through them. Ana Ruivo and José Luís Porfírio fittingly describe this process as a palimpsest, because the artwork is similar to a manuscript in which earlier writing has been scraped or washed off in order to be replaced by later writing, and yet still bears the visible traces of that older text.[25] The two critics do not develop this connection in any great length, but I think it is an absolutely crucial one for understanding dos Santos's art practice, which often resulted in visual documents built with images upon images; images that may compete with, interrupt or contradict each other; images that originate from myriad sources (linguistic, photographic, cartographic, etc.) and that are then submitted to a process of negotiation, appropriation and transformation.

Going back to *Stanley*, we find here fragments or traces of documents relating to sea voyages and land explorations that point to a time when Europeans crossed the ocean and took possession of the rest of the world, in a movement that transformed pre-colonial space into colonial place through processes of naming and representation, among other consequences. These naming documents find themselves ruthlessly desecrated in a palimpsestic practice that has, on the one hand, partially erased, blotched, disfigured or truncated the original images and, on the other hand, allowed them to resurface and overlap in the final composition. Consequently, many of dos Santos's works, of which *Stanley* is a paradigmatic example, not only invoke a

---

[24] Edward Lucie-Smith, in *Bartolomeu Cid dos Santos: Exposição Retrospectiva*, eds José Sommer Ribeiro and Bartolomeu Cid dos Santos (Lisbon: Fundação Calouste Gulbenkian, Centro de Arte Moderna, 1989), n.pag.

[25] Ana Ruivo, in *Bartolomeu: Sonhos e Pesadelos*, ed. Rui Brito (Lisbon: Gravura, 2004), n.pag.; José Luís Porfírio, 'Uma Viagem com Bartolomeu Cid dos Santos', in *A Biblioteca de Bartolomeu* (Ponta Delgada: Presidência do Governo Regional dos Açores, 2010), pp. 13–19 (p. 17).

melancholy nostalgia for a bygone era (a feeling further enhanced by the sepia tint given to many of the prints) but also seem to contradict a chronological view of time and a concomitant linear approach to space, thus suggesting that the present and the 'here' contain ineffaceable traces of the past and the 'there'. In the case of *Stanley*, as well as in *Africa Discovered*, where the artist conflates the heyday of the colonial era with the throes of its moribund state, the anachronism of these palimpsestic images situates these works within a postcolonial perspective, as it illustrates 'the ways in which pre-colonial culture as well as the experience of colonization are continuing aspects of a postcolonial's society developing cultural identity'.[26]

More importantly for the transnational argument I have been endeavouring to put forward, dos Santos's palimpsestic prints provide a visual commentary on the workings of memory – a subjective library-maze where tenses and worlds co-exist and overlap – and, in particular, of cultural memory.[27] The latter is a concept that in recent years and in the context of transnational studies has been particularly associated with travelling. According to Astrid Erll, 'travel is [...] an expression of the principal logic of memory' and 'memory fundamentally means movement'.[28] Such assumptions prompt Erll to embrace the study of transcultural memory, in as much as we are 'moving away from site-bound, nation-bound, and in a naïve sense, cultures-bound research and displaying an interest in the mnemonic dynamics unfolding across and beyond boundaries'.[29] Ernst van Alphen takes a similar perspective when arguing that, in the case of migrant identity, '[t]he act of imagining homeland identity is always framed by the historical dimensions of that place and of the migration that started from there, but it is also inflected by those acts of imagining that produce the cultural identity in the present'.[30] He therefore corroborates the

---

[26] Bill Ashcroft et al, *Postcolonial Studies: The Key Concepts* (Oxford: Routledge, 2013), p. 190. The notion of the palimpsest has been productively employed in the context of postcolonial studies, since the term is capable of representing the dynamic, hybrid and dialogic nature of postcolonial experience.

[27] Perceptive critics of dos Santos's work were already drawing attention to these implications in the 1980s. See Alexandre Melo's review in *Expresso* (18 January 1986), in which the workings of memory are associated with the printing process followed by dos Santos and its different stages (cited in Ribeiro and dos Santos, *Bartolomeu*, n.pag).

[28] Astrid Erll, 'Travelling Memory', *Parallax*, 17 (2011), 4–18 (pp. 12, 15).

[29] Erll, 'Travelling Memory', p. 15.

[30] Ernst van Alphen, 'Imagined Homelands: Re-Mapping Cultural Identity', in *Mobilizing Place, Placing Mobility: The Politics of Representation in a Globalized World*, eds Ginette Verstraete and Tim Cresswell (Amsterdam: Rodopi, 2002), pp. 53–70 (p. 53).

idea of a continuum intrinsic to a new mobility paradigm and a transnational existence, through which the experience of dislocation and separation may be positively subverted. The notion of a transitive cultural memory and that of a temporal and spatial continuum both afford very useful perspectives on dos Santos's artwork. Take for example the stone panels he created for the Lisbon metro station (Figures 5.1–5.3): the slabs, which spread across different functional spaces within the station, depict boundaries artistically trespassed by the recurrent passing of one form into the other and the interweaving of diverse cultural and historical references, as well as geographic imaginings, giving rise to a joyous, careless freedom that is further conveyed by the childlike style of the engraved images and texts.

When dos Santos died, in 2008, *The Independent*'s obituary also placed the artist within a transcultural continuum and intimated how much he had adopted 'multiple, mutable and transformative identifications'.[31] As Negley Harte then noted, 'Bartolomeu dos Santos was always proudly Portuguese, and he came to be proudly Anglophile too; he made his career in England without losing any of his Portuguese roots.'[32] Moving away from home, dos Santos did not espouse a vague form of existence, devoid of attachments, but rather he developed new forms – artistic, literary, existential – of making himself at home. As such, his art practice is marked not only by the traveller's free spirit, but also by journeys *across*, in other words, journeys that connect present and past, roots and routes, reality and imagination. Stylistically speaking, these journeys are often conveyed through a palimpsestic practice made possible by the processes of printmaking developed by the artist and suggestive of diverse and overlapping historical, cultural and geographic sediments. Dos Santos's oeuvre is thus symptomatic of a transnational experience, which should not be understood merely as a process of deterritorialization, but rather as bringing about the creation of mobile, changeable and multiple homes, unbounded by national callings.

---

[31] Arnold and Meskimmon, 'Making Oneself', p. 259.

[32] Negley Harte, 'Professor Bartolomeu dos Santos: Creative Printmaker and Teacher at the Slade School of Fine Art', *Independent* (3 June 2008) <http://www.independent.co.uk/news/obituaries/professor-bartolomeu-dos-santos-creative-printmaker-and-teacher-at-the-slade-school-of-fine-art-839559.html> [accessed 13 September 2017].

6

'Becoming Portuguese'

New Europes for Old in Miguel Gomes's *Arabian Nights*

Hilary Owen
University of Manchester/University of Oxford

> Portugal offers a powerful rebuke. Europe's left should use the Portuguese experience to reshape the European Union and bring austerity across the eurozone to a halt. [...] Throughout Europe's lost decade, millions of us held that there was indeed an alternative. Now we have the proof.[1]

There is no shortage of rebuke in Miguel Gomes's 2015 film trilogy, *Mil e Uma Noites* [*Arabian Nights*]. Shot in 2013–14, this six-hour three-film epic responds to the worst effects of economic crisis and austerity in Portugal that were triggered by the 2008 banking crash. It was premiered in the Director's Fortnight at Cannes Film Festival in 2015 and it differs markedly from other more reflective, and conventionally realist, film releases on the subject from 2016 and 2017.[2] Offering a mix of overt political satire, documentary and surreal absurdist fantasy, the trilogy hit the screens internationally in May 2015 (and Portugal in August 2015) just before the political tide began to turn

---

[1] Owen Jones, 'No Alternative to Austerity? That Lie Has Now Been Nailed', *The Guardian Online* (24 August 2017) <https://www.theguardian.com/commentisfree/2017/aug/24/austerity-lie-deep-cuts-economy-portugal-socialist> [accessed 14 January 2018].

[2] See Mariana Liz, 'After the Crisis: Europe and Nationhood in Twenty-First-Century Portuguese Cinema', in *Nationalism in Contemporary Western European Cinema*, ed. J. Harvey (New York: Palgrave Macmillan, 2018), pp. 235–56. See also, Mariana Liz, *Euro-Visions. Europe in Contemporary Cinema* (London: Bloomsbury, 2016).

with the November 2015 elections, and the regime change and dismantling of the bailout programme that followed.

Divided into three separate volumes, *O Inquieto* [*The Restless One*], *O Desolado* [*The Desolate One*] and *O Encantado* [*The Enchanted One*], Gomes's contemporary, austerity narratives of depression, suicide and surrealist absurdity are embedded within the frame tale of Scheherazade's storytelling cycle. Scenes depicting her situation in a comically mythical 'old Baghdad' thus provide the overall structuring device whose point of overlap is the logic of crisis, be it the European deficit or King Shariya's impending death sentence on Scheherazade.[3] There are constant switches not only between separate episodes, time zones and cinematic references, but also between different types of film stock, recalling Gomes's famous use of contrasting black and white stocks to mark time periods and memory in his 2012 international success, *Tabu*. In *Arabian Nights*, the consciously exoticized scenes of 'Baghdad' are shot on a clear, at times, highly coloured 35 mm while the Portuguese 'reality' events are filmed on a dull and grainy 16 mm (Gomes terms it 'lo-fi analogue feeling for reality'), elevating by contrast the 'reality effect' of the contemporary austerity sequences.[4]

The very precise period that Gomes highlights here places the spotlight on the actions of the coalition government of the Partido Social Democrata (PSD) led by Prime Minister Pedro Passos Coelho and the CDS-PP, the far-right People's Party, led by Paulo Portas, which had come to power in the June 2011 general elections, with the defeat of the Partido Socialista (PS). The Socialists' 2011 memorandum of understanding between Portugal and the European Union (EU) had laid out the programme of financial assistance to the government to be delivered by the 'Troika' consisting of the European Commission (EC), the International Monetary Fund (IMF) and the European Central Bank (ECB).[5]

---

[3] Gomes derived his real-life episodes from the press and from sending reporters to gather stories about the effects of the crisis, from August 2013 to July 2014. The journalistic sources are archived at: <http://www.as1001noites.com/> [accessed 22 November 2018]. I am indebted to Persis Love for making me aware of this.

[4] On Gomes's choices of film stock, see Mark Peranson, 'Cock and Bull Stories: Miguel Gomes on *Arabian Nights*', *Cinema Scope*, 63, n.d. <http://cinema-scope.com/cinema-scope-magazine/cock-and-bull-stories-miguel-gomes-on-arabian-nights/> [accessed 20 November 2018].

[5] See Guya Accornero and Pedro Ramos Pinto, 'Politics in Austerity: Strategic Interactions between Social Movements and Institutional Actors in Portugal, 2010–2015', in *Political Representation and Citizenship in Portugal – From Crisis to Renewal*, eds Marco Lisi, André Freire and Emmanouil Tsatsanis (London: Lexington Books, 2020), pp. 45–68. My thanks are due to the authors for permission to cite from this manuscript pre-publication.

The effects of this produced the nation's strongest and most intense period of public demonstration and mobilization since the famous protests of the 25 April 1974 Revolution.[6] The Prime Minister José Sócrates resigned and the PS went on to negotiate a bailout package with the IMF, the EC and the ECB, totalling $78 billion. The resulting cuts to salaries, pensions, benefits and public services triggered their election defeat in 2011. As Guya Accornero and Pedro Ramos Pinto have noted, there was, in social protest organizations such as 'Que se Lixe a Troika' (QLT) [Screw the Troika], a strong vein of resentment expressed in terms of 'opposition to the external intervention by the EU–ECB–IMF (the so-called Troika) considered an unacceptable limitation of the country's sovereignty, and responsible for declining standards of living and retrenchment of social rights'.[7] However, as they and most other commentators conclude, Portugal's wave of anti-austerity protests was primarily trade union- and social movement-based and it was directed primarily at the Portuguese nation-state, at least in terms of their calls for action and underlying frameworks for cooperation.[8]

Gomes's cinematic intervention in this situation, however, remains intriguingly indirect and at times ambivalent as regards the calibration of national and transnational responsibilities. The representation of the Portuguese nation somehow refuses to cohere as it falls between the lines drawn by Gomes's ostensibly disjointed episodic organization. The main connecting thread that links all three volumes to each other and to the theme of the EU debt crisis takes the Brechtian form of an explanatory intertitle which prefaces each of the volumes in identical terms with the following wording:

> The stories, characters and places that Scheherazade will tell us about acquired a fictional form from facts that occurred in Portugal between August 2013 and July 2014. During this period the country was held hostage to a program of economic austerity executed by a government apparently devoid of social justice. As a result, almost all Portuguese became more impoverished.

Expressed in the passive voice, these intertitles refer to the country being 'held hostage' to a programme of austerity executed by a government (implicitly Portugal's) such that Gomes obliquely, if unmistakeably, targets Portugal's PSD coalition. Meanwhile, the external supranational forces that

---

[6] See Accornero and Pinto, 'Politics in Austerity', p. 45.

[7] Accornero and Pinto, 'Politics in Austerity', p. 49.

[8] See Accornero and Pinto, 'Politics in Austerity'. See also Britta Baumgarten, 'Geração à Rasca and Beyond: Mobilizations in Portugal after 12 March 2011', *Current Sociology*, 61.4 (2013), 457–73 (p. 469).

are holding the country hostage lurk somewhere behind this 'government apparently devoid of social justice', which is described as merely 'executing' the austerity programme. Notable here is the extent to which Gomes refuses to characterize this beleaguered country in recognizably 'national' symbolic terms. Rather his references to the 'country', the impoverishment of the Portuguese people and the need for social justice operate as stand-ins for the collectivity of the 'nation'. The type of discursive appeal associated with 'nationalism' is thus downplayed and dispersed here into class, economic and social concerns. The 'national' is never cleanly defined in opposition to a 'transnational' other. The cinematic strategies that Gomes uses to maintain his deferral of 'nationhood' and his resistance of nationalism in this discussion of Portuguese austerity afford the principal question that concerns me in the body of this chapter.

Underpinning this question in pragmatic terms, is the paradox that ensues from shooting an EU-critical film constrained by European funding imperatives and target audiences. It is worth noting that by far the highest viewing figures for *Arabian Nights* were in France, not Portugal.[9] As Anne Jäckel has observed, the vast majority of Portugal's current film output relies on European co-production.[10] The very nature of Portuguese film industry financing means that Gomes's aesthetic, linguistic and practical production choices were shaped by the transnational, primarily EU-based, character of Portugal's 'small nation' film industry.[11] Indeed, his *Arabian Nights* acknowledges support from a

---

[9] The trilogy's international release and festival screenings signalled a clear intent to communicate Portugal's travails internationally, although this met with mixed success. According to the European Audiovisual Observatory's Lumière database, the box office figures were much lower than for Gomes's iconic *Tabu* in 2012. They also show a considerable decline from the first volume to the third, totalling 87,618 for volume 1, 39,673 for volume 2 and 25,288 for volume 3. By far the highest box office figure for all three volumes of *Arabian Nights* was in France which provided at least 50 per cent of total admissions. See <http://lumiere.obs.coe.int/web/film_info/?id=64056> [accessed 12 December 2018]. The Lumière database records cinema admissions in Austria, Belgium, Germany, Great Britain, Estonia, France, Iceland, Italy, Luxembourg, the Netherlands, Poland, Portugal, Spain, Switzerland and Slovenia.

[10] Anne Jäckel, 'Changing the Image of Europe? The Role of European Co-Productions, Funds and Film Awards', in *The Europeanness of European Cinema. Identity, Meaning, Globalization*, eds Mary Harrod, Mariana Liz and Alissa Timoshkina (London and New York: I. B. Tauris, 2015), pp. 59–71 (p. 60).

[11] The Lumière European film database lists Portugal, Germany, France and Switzerland as the co-producing countries: <http://lumiere.obs.coe.int/web/search/index.php> [accessed 12 December 2018]. The credits for *Arabian Nights* acknowledge support from ICA (Portugal's Instituto de Cinema e Audiovisual), the CNC (the French Centre national du cinéma et de l'image animée), PACA (Feature film

huge range of EU and non-EU national and regional bodies supporting tv and film, in Portugal, France, Germany, Switzerland and Italy as well as the Council of Europe's own fund, Eurimages.[12] Eurimages was founded in 1989 to support films promoting European identity and values as part of the Council of Europe's cultural programme. For this reason, it specifically evaluates the 'European character' of the films applying for its grants.[13] A reliance on Eurimages monies in particular positions *Arabian Nights* in the realm of what Anne Jäckel terms an 'anti-European European cinema'.[14]

In order to negotiate this dilemma, Gomes deconstructs the ingredients that are characteristic of the pejoratively named 'Euro-pudding' film. The term 'Euro-pudding' was coined by film critics to describe slavish adherence to the conditions of international co-production funding, resulting in the compromising of cinematic quality, innovation and focus.[15] Gomes's treatment of the formula effectively bears out Mariana Liz's contention that the Euro-pudding phenomenon can also itself acquire a political edge in so far as it 'invites reflections on the geo-political affiliations at play in Europe and its cinema'.[16] In a context of crisis and rupture, Gomes reframes Portugal's own national, historical experiences in terms of the power that those particular experiences possess to call forth alternative forms of transnational allegiance.[17] In light of

production fund from Provence-Alpes-Côte-d'Azur) OFC, Cineforum (an Italian funding source), Loterie Romande (the Francophone Swiss lottery), Swiss Films, CML (Câmera Municipal de Lisboa/Lisbon Film Commission), Arte (Franco-German public TV network), ZDF (Zweite Deutsche Fernsehen), RTP (Portuguese TV), SRG SSR (the Swiss Broadcasting Company) and RTS Suisse (Radio-Télévision Suisse).

[12] See Gomes's interview for *Público* on how the funding problems of *Arabian Nights* drove its expedient political urgency. Kathleen Gomes, 'Portugal, este país de maravilhas existe', *Público. Ípsilon* (27 August 2015) <https://www.publico.pt/2015/08/27/culturaipsilon/noticia/o-cinema-ajusta-contas-com-a-troika-1705938> [accessed 14 January 2018].

[13] On Eurimages funding, see Jäckel, 'Changing the Image of Europe?', p. 61.

[14] See Jäckel, 'Changing the Image of Europe?', p. 68.

[15] Mariana Liz, 'From European Co-Productions to the Euro-Pudding', in *The Europeanness of European Cinema. Identity, Meaning, Globalization*, eds Mary Harrod, Mariana Liz and Alissa Timoshkina (London and New York: I. B. Tauris, 2015), pp. 73–85 (pp. 73–74).

[16] Liz, 'From European Co-Productions to the Euro-Pudding', pp. 75, 78.

[17] See Mariana Liz (ed.), *Portugal's Global Cinema. Industry, History and Culture* (London: I. B. Tauris, 2017), p. 2. See also Nick Pinkerton, After the Goldrush', *Sight & Sound*, 26.5 (May 2016), 30–33 (p. 32). In this interview Gomes observes, 'I even imagined in the beginning that this was not a film, but a TV series and we could contact people from the other PIIGS countries. And each one of us would do one episode every week.'

this, I argue in what follows that Gomes constructs his 'Portuguese austerity experience' as a series of Foucauldian heterotopic 'other spaces' in relation to the EU as a locus of crisis. Heterotopia are the spaces that mirror but also distort the hegemonic (in this instance hegemonic EU) spaces around them, echoing Foucault's description of heterotopology as a 'simultaneously mythic and real contestation of the space in which we live'.[18] Gomes's representation of 'Portugal under austerity' is thus posited as a form of 'crisis heterotopia within', a series of simultaneously real and mythic spaces refracting different facets of dysfunctional EU transnationalism, without reinstalling the monolith of 'the nation' in their place. The result is a call for reflective pause issued to, but crucially also from within, the EU.

Gomes's very choice of the *Thousand and One Nights* as his universally recognizable frame tale (a common accessibility strategy with Euro-pudding films) means that his *Arabian Nights* project is built around a careful mirror structure of framing and reframing, of contrast, mirroring and contiguity, which favours heterotopic, and correspondingly also heterochronic, interrelations. His three films thus reconstruct the Chinese box structure of multiply embedded narratives. As a strictly 'pre-national' medieval story derived from various linguistic and cultural traditions, a Euro-centred, indeed originally French-language transmission of a 'pan-Arabian' fantasy, *Arabian Nights* draws its model of 'transnationalism' out of Europe's textual archival past. Gomes also relies heavily on the cinema archives, and on the transnational appeal of cinematic language *per se*, as he ramps up his characteristic cinephile aesthetic in order to reference other European Art cinema and Hollywood traditions. Particularly prominent among these is Pier Paolo Pasolini's *Le Fiore delle Mille e Una Notte* from 1974, (the third part of his *Trilogia de la Vitta* 1971–74, consisting also of Boccaccio's *Decameron* and Chaucer's *Canterbury Tales*).[19] The Italian cinema scholar, Patrick Rumble, refers to Pasolini's reliance on 'the "transnational" and "transclassist" language of film in order to displace nationalistic cultural paradigms, and to engage in a search for a *società futura possibile*: a society glimpsed in the self-generating but also self-destructive structures of his films *da farsi* (a term that translates [...] as "in process")'.[20]

---

[18] Michel Foucault, 'Des Espaces Autres. Hétérotopies', *Architecture, Mouvement, Continuité*, 5 (October 1984), 46–49. This was a lecture originally delivered in 1967 to the Cercle d'études architecturales. The English translation by Jay Miskowiec, 'Of Other Spaces: Utopias and Heterotopias', pp. 1–9 (p. 4) is available on-line at: http://web.mit.edu/allanmc/www/foucault1.pdf [accessed 12 January 2018].

[19] On Pasolini's influence on Gomes, see Hannah McGill, '*Arabian Nights* Volume Three. The Enchanted One', *Sight & Sound*, 26.6 (June 2016), 58–59 (p. 58).

[20] Patrick Rumble, *Allegories of Contamination. Pier Paolo Pasolini's Trilogy of Life* (Toronto: Toronto University Press, 1996), p. 9.

The idea of a productive Euro-ambivalence, a future society that is a kind of 'Europeanness in process' has, of course, long been a constitutive perspective of Portuguese film. As Liz aptly observes, from the 1990s onwards, 'contemporary Portuguese cinema shows not so much a variation in attitudes towards Europe, but more the continuous opposition between the positive realization of effectively being European and the doubtful consciousness of being (at) Europe's periphery, if not outside of Europe altogether – between an interest in, and a rejection of what Europe stands for'.[21] Filming in a context where austerity considerably sharpened the horns of this dilemma, Gomes develops the 'continuous opposition' that Liz describes here as a strategic means of diffusing national identification and holding dogmatic nationalism at bay. Indeed, it is no coincidence that Gomes describes his own favourite parts of the film as 'the transitions, [...] it's how you transport things one to the other that interests me'.[22] This is an interestingly provocative statement from Gomes given that many of his key scenes and episodes have no explicit visual or diegetic transition at all, relying only on his ubiquitous use of textual intertitling to introduce them, such that they are connected to his overall frame structure of austerity but not to each other. The critic Jonathon Kyle Sturgeon, in his article 'The Neutral', sees the potential to read this technique politically. Referencing a 1977 Roland Barthes essay of that name, he reframes the idea of 'the neutral' to describe objects that sit conceptually between 'warring signifiers' and thus '"baffle the paradigm" of accepted meaning'.[23] Tracing the anti-capitalist potential of this idea, Sturgeon locates Miguel Gomes specifically among a young 'upstart' generation of world directors producing, 'hybrid cinema', whose cinema aesthetic he positions in 'the neutral era', representing 'an art born in a period of overlap', an in-between space where the gains of digital cinema are weighed against the loss of their ties with 'the body of the photograph'.[24] For Sturgeon, this Barthesian concept of a 'neutral cinema has begun to archive pockets of space and time situated on the margins of global capitalism' with a particular emphasis precisely on their use of Foucauldian heterotopias to 'hit the pause button on the unrelenting flow of capital'.[25]

Gomes's parallel worlds of 'Portugal in austerity' take the form, precisely, of separate temporal and spatial pockets, multiply layered and juxtaposed at

---

[21] Liz, *Portugal's Global Cinema*, p. 120.

[22] Peranson, 'Cock and Bull Stories'.

[23] See Jonathon Kyle Sturgeon, 'The Neutral', *N + 1* (24 February 2011) <https://nplusonemag.com/online-only/film-review/the-neutral/> [accessed 18 December 2018].

[24] Sturgeon, 'The Neutral'.

[25] Sturgeon, 'The Neutral'.

the margins of global capital. He provides timely reminders of the power that photographic stills possess to halt the relentless flux of capitalist events. He deploys playful heterotopias such as the fairground, the brothel, the magic island of Baghdad, political demonstrations and the spaces of homodiegetic musical performance and gigs, to refuse the hegemonic temporalities and space relations imposed by a supranational EU vision of Portugal's 'otherness' and 'marginality', and to demonstrate alternative imagined forms of ongoing collectivity and community resistance. The court hearing in volume 2 is, significantly, set not in a modern courtroom but in an open-air amphitheatre at dusk, a lucid nightmare vision of pervasive austerity hardship, reconstructed in terms of the crimes it has necessitated, driven by offshore international bankers and Chinese oligarchs, obtaining Portuguese citizenship with the golden visa scheme. In volume 1, the formal summit meeting of the Portuguese government and the Troika descends into the spatial and social logic of the brothel, as will be discussed in greater detail shortly. In 'O Banho dos Magníficos' ['The Swim of the Magnificents'], also in volume 1, the festive ritual of a New Year's Day Atlantic swim restores the dignity of the unemployed men encouraged to take part by their trade union representative.

The possible future society that Gomes sketches in *Arabian Nights* draws on these critical heterotopic scenarios and moments to conjure 'another Portugal' that is never securely emplaced in 'national' terms. Correspondingly, the chronotope, the classic figuration of space–time unity in realist representations of nationhood, also finds itself fractured through the use of heterochronic temporality. Thus we experience discontinuity, anachronism and desynchronization, exemplified at their most blatant by the playful use of split-screen effects, the superimposition of old black and white footage onto modern colour stock, and the splicing in of some 1970s home movie-style Super 8, in volume 3. These heterotopic and heterochronic structures also accompany a refusal to territorialize nation through language.[26] The dialogues and musical soundtracks are multilingual and translingual, even at times including subtitles that interpret animal and plant speech, cockerels, dogs, a papier mâché cow, bees and a talking olive tree. The English song 'Perfídia' (in versions that include Nat King Cole, Phyllis Dillon, Glenn Miller and the Modernaires, and the *Arabian Nights*' own star Crista Alfaiate) affords a multilingual *leitmotif.* Diegetic locations and the languages used in them are frequently mismatched. Indeed, Gomes's actors interact across a range of different languages such that we are exposed to German, French, English and

---

[26] On the construction of place through language, see Yi-Fu Tuan, 'Language and the Making of Place. A Narrative-Descriptive Approach', *Annals of the Association of American Geographers*, 81.4 (1991), 684–96.

Mandarin Chinese as well as various regional accents in European Portuguese and the comic translation of English into Brazilian Portuguese by a Brazilian character, hammed up by the Portuguese actor, Carloto Cotta, in 'Os Homens de Pau Feito' ['The Men with Hard-ons'] in volume 1. The effect is a deterritorializing of Portugal's 'national' language made internationally relevant here only through the global reach of Brazil.

This episode provides a particularly rich satirical example of how heterotopian logic is expressed partly through multi and translingual communication. A high-level international meeting of the Portuguese Prime Minister and his government with the EU Troika is transmuted into the critical 'other space' of a pseudo-primitivized Portugal, that degenerates into a kind of pan-European sex paradise somewhere on the EU's most indeterminate margins. A large male group (with one token woman, the Portuguese Finance Minister) alternates between Portuguese and English, as they haggle about the national deficit and the 4 per cent interest rate. The location is initially signalled as 'Portugal' by the national flag hanging over the bar. The after-lunch site-seeing *passeio*, with the Troika on camels evoking the Three Wise Men, soon drifts into the homosocial 'Latin' logic of the brothel. One Troika official appreciates the scene (which he designates as 'very typical') of a humble desert shack, as he reassures his hosts that the EU actually likes the Portuguese because they are 'quite clean'. The mock exotic setting of Scheherazade's 'desert Arabia' channels Portugal's raced and subalternized status as Europe's neo-colonial other, a performative 'stand in' for capitalism's 'Global South'.

A black, French-speaking wizard emerges from the desert shack to offer a magic viagra-like spray to cure a melancholy Troika official, diagnosed with impotence. The acutely priapic result of his ministrations to the entire male group (except the woman) leaves the Troika more than willing to cancel the financial deficit. This multilingual heterotopian reflection of the EU constructs its European 'unity' around the logic of phallocentric global capitalism, taken to a fantasmatic, absurdist extreme.[27] The allegorical message is obvious. A common metaphor of austerity resistance is here literalized. In the Portugal of a protest movement called 'Que se lixe a Troika' ['Screw the Troika'], the Portuguese people are the ones getting 'lixado', as much by their own complicit national elites under a thinly disguised Passos Coelho, as by the

[27] The specific cuts to police pay and pensions and other austerity measures discussed in this sequence closely reference the various decisions taken in the PSD government's third budget, presented in October 2013, by the Finance Minister, Maria Luís Albuquerque. See João Pedro Pereira, 'Os Orçamentos de Pedro Passos Coelho', *Público* <https://acervo.publico.pt/economia/os-orcamentos-de-pedro-passos-coelho> [accessed 14 January 2018].

118   *Hilary Owen*

it was no use going against fate.

Figure 6.1. The EU Troika and members of the Portuguese government. Still from *Arabian Nights. Vol. 1. The Restless One.* Directed by Miguel Gomes. © O Som e a Fúria, Shellac Sud, Komplizen Films, Box Productions, Agat Films, ARTE France Cinéma and ZDF/ARTE. 2015.

Troika. The cancellation of the deficit is driven by nothing more communal that the universal myth of priapism. Indeed, Gomes slyly alerts us to his inverted heterotopic and heterochronic vision of society here, with a shot from the perspective of the event's official photographer, using an anachronistically old-fashioned camera that inverts the group portrait (Figure 6.1).

Other languages, races and peoples of Europe are also implied, and implicated, in the inverted mirror world that Gomes creates here. The wizard with the magic spray is Francophone African, on one level clearly playing to Gomes's French funders as well as his predominantly French film audiences. The wizard's Senegalese accent typifies the speech of Marseilles, the actual French film location used to connote 'Arabia' throughout the film, as well as channelling the real-life background of Basirou Diallou, the Senegalese-descended actor playing the wizard.[28] The French language, however, finds itself juxtaposed not only with Portuguese but also with the film trilogy's only German-speaking scene. The 'Men with Hard-ons' episode interpolates a short, embedded story unfolding in a German-speaking classroom evoking, albeit obliquely, the perceived culprit of austerity. The foundations of Portugal's current economic subjection have implicitly been laid elsewhere, in Germany,

[28] See note 9 above.

or at least in the German language, in some long distant schoolroom humiliation of a German child, an avatar, perhaps, of the German Finance Minister, Wolfgang Schäuble, excoriated by the Portuguese press during the crisis. And yet, the classroom is at the same time associated with 'Poland', with three huge Polish flags draped at the windows.[29] Germany's historic relations with Poland thus provide a literal 'backdrop' to the scene, emphasized by a disproportionately grandiose German opera soundtrack. However, the potential to read the scene as a definitive chronotope of Germany's role in European history is just as suddenly truncated. The narrative returns abruptly to the Portuguese government, the Troika and the deficit. The men are exhausted by their sexual activity. The wizard is persuaded to reverse the gift of their magic erections, but he charges the original amount of the deficit to do so and warns them about the monstrous capitalist 'toad' that will consume all nations on earth if unchecked. The Portuguese prostitutes who had been rendering their services to the group, finally lead the men away from the scene. The Portuguese Prime Minister carves his name and the date into a log, effectively consecrating the space with a debased form of memorial sanctity.

The Portuguese government does not 'reappear' until volume 3 and, even then, only implicitly and off-screen, as they sit inside the real Portuguese Parliament building while it was being besieged in 2013. On this occasion the Parliament scenes are intercut with the heterotopian spaces of an impoverished Lisbon community captured in 'O Inebriante Canto dos Tentilhões' ['The Inebriating Chorus of Chaffinches']. At this point, an increasingly restless Scheherazade has failed to escape her endless storytelling cycle. However, her father catches up with her and forces her back into the narrating role. Overlooking the heterotopic space *par excellence*, the fairground, they sit together on a giant Ferris wheel, evoking a toy in a hamster cage, a never-ending cycle of stories. It is also, perhaps, a sly cinephile reference to Harry Lime's famous attempt at corrupting Holly Martins by shrinking his moral perspective from the height of the big wheel in Vienna in Carol Reed's 1948 classic, *The Third Man*. The point of the father's lecture here, however, is to restore, rather than remove, a sense of ethical responsibility by sending Scheherazade back to her task. This re-affirmation of purpose is reinforced by Gomes himself making a brief directorial appearance here, as if he has wandered into shot by accident, wearing an Ali Baba costume and smoking a desperate cigarette.

---

[29] Various allegorical readings suggest themselves here. The Polish, but famously Germanophile, President of the EU at the time, Donald Tusk, was born in Gdansk, formerly the German city of Danzig. Anti-German feeling in particular was heightened by austerity.

The final tale Scheherazade tells is rendered in an observational documentary format and concerns a group of humble, working-class men who come from particular Lisbon *bairros*, Boavista and Alta de Lisboa, that were associated with the famous housing occupations following the Carnation Revolution of 25 April 1974.[30] In contrast to the preceding episodes and volumes, a very precise sense of Lisbon location is suddenly made significant. The men who live in the contemporary *bairros*, fighting poverty rather than fascism, cope with their situation by training caged chaffinches to sing competitively, a mental survival tactic first adopted by soldiers in the trenches, when Portugal fought on the allied side in the First World War. Gomes himself, significantly, interprets the arcane habits of these men politically as he remarks, 'even if they are not doing much to change their life conditions, and they are not politically active, that community does have a political aspect to it because it is being offered as an alternative.'[31] The urban locations the men inhabit are heavily overwritten by the utopian pastness of 1974, as Gomes's textual intertitles are at pains to emphasize. An aura of Portuguese revolutionary history is brought strongly and purposefully into play here with some grainy original 1970s archive footage, shot on 8 mm and resembling a home movie. To further reinforce this historic resonance, Gomes also uses shots of Boavista from 2014, showing the 40th anniversary commemorations of the revolution, which served as a rallying point for anti-government protests. Read in this contextual framing, the men's dedication to chaffinch training is as much a political demonstration as the official protests and rallies across the capital, and the two are further connected by the aural motif of birds and people singing in public. These linking sound cues are often heard before their source is visible on screen, as the camera transitions from one location to another using travelling shots that play with distances across urban *bairros* and interlinking woodlands. Indeed, volume 3 intensifies the trilogy's characteristic play of scale and perspective, derived from the use of aerial shooting, and the homodiegetic inclusion of flight motifs, with drones, flying genies, birds, bees and the Ferris wheel, allowing the viewer to dominate artificially miniaturized spaces from a vantage point that is alluringly panoptical but always ultimately unstable and deceptive.

---

[30] The critic Richard Brody aptly describes this scenario as 'a warmly majestic look at a community of bird-catchers whose passionately engaged self-regulation yields an autonomous, populist utopia'. 'Present Tense. The New York Film Festival Displays History on the Wing', *The New Yorker* (8 September 2015) <https://www.newyorker.com/magazine/2015/09/28/present-tense> [accessed 19 November 2018].

[31] See Kathleen Gomes, 'Portugal, este país de maravilhas existe'.

The bird trainers, in contrast to their birds, seem decidedly earthbound and unremarkable in these quasi ethnographic sequences, with only the constant intertitle captions dividing Scheherazade's ongoing narration into successive days and nights, reminding us of the film's fantasy-inspired macro structure. However, Scheherazade's tale is itself interrupted and temporarily silenced by Gomes's sudden switch to real, contemporary footage of anti-austerity demonstrations from 2013 and 2014. There is a rather contrived diegetic connection in the persona of the policeman, nicknamed Catá, who is both a bird trainer and an anti-austerity protester. But the real connection is heterotopian, the revolutionary spatial aura that emanates from Boavista. The film's protest sequences thus afford hegemonically understood national memory sites that combine with the bird training scenes to convert Gomes's 'Lisbon under austerity' into what Foucault describes as 'a kind of effectively enacted utopia in which the real sites, all the other real sites that can be found within the culture, are simultaneously represented, contested and inverted'.[32]

This Foucauldian logic of contestatory spatial inversion is central to Gomes's dramatic climax to volume 3. Just as volume 1 witnessed the exploding 'insides' of a beached whale threatening to become, literally, 'the outside', a corresponding movement of inversion in volume 3 shows an 'outside' about to burst, inappropriately, onto 'the inside', when a mass physical invasion of the Portuguese Parliament building is threatened in the real-life demonstrations of 21 November 2013. These particular protests were mounted by Portugal's various police forces and prison services unions (ASPP-PSP, GNR, ASAE, SEF, Polícia Judiciária, Polícia Marítima, Guarda Prisional, and Polícia Municipal) in Lisbon's largest ever public demonstration, uniting approximately 10,000 members. The incidents came to be collectively dubbed the 'Invasão das Escadarias da Assembléia' or 'the Invasion of the Parliament Steps'. Triggered by the October budget's cuts to police pay and pensions, the demonstrations were ironically policed by the protesters' own on-duty colleagues, who were invited to change sides, and the drama that ensued was captured live on national television by RTP1.[33] Although various news teams did relay the events, Gomes shot his own footage of the battle raging on the Parliament steps, offering powerful visual echoes of the famous Odessa Steps

---

[32] Foucault, 'Of Other Spaces', p. 3.

[33] See Guya Accornero and Pedro Ramos Pinto, '"Mild Mannered?" Protest and Mobilization in Portugal under Austerity, 2010–2013', *West European Politics*, 38.3 (2015), 491–515. 'The historic symbols of protest and democracy are recurrently used by the QLT [Que se Lixe a Troika] as is the case with the song "Grândola Vila Morena" symbolic of the 1974–1975 Revolution', p. 507.

Figure 6.2. Parliament Steps Invasion. Still from *Arabian Nights. Vol. 3. The Enchanted One*. Directed by Miguel Gomes.
© O Som e a Fúria, Shellac Sud, Komplizen Films, Box Productions, Agat Films, ARTE France Cinéma and ZDF/ARTE. 2015.

sequence in Eisenstein's *Battleship Potemkin*.[34] In Gomes's film, however, the direction of physical impetus on the steps reverses Eisenstein's. His focus rests on the police making triumphal surges upwards, in contrast to the Soviet director's famously chaotic defeat, with the protesters being shot at, repelled and progressively driven downwards (Figure 6.2).

Furthermore, in Gomes's revision, this epic scenario finds itself incongruously paired with the soundtrack voiceover of an intimately personal story, affording an alienating perspective, narrated in Mandarin by a Chinese tourist Lin Nuan (nicknamed 'Hot Forest') who has come to Lisbon on an academic prize-winning trip. Not only is she consuming Portugal on the global tourist market, her trip is a freebie. She has been swept up in the Parliament steps demonstration by mistake, leading to a failed relationship with Catá, the protesting (and also married) policeman and bird trainer that we had met previously in Boavista. Where the couple have no common language, the course of globalized romance does not run smooth. There is no question of

---

[34] My thanks are owed to Raquel Freire for making me aware that Miguel Gomes filmed the 'Invasão das Escadarias' in person alongside the news camera crews. Many such protests were cast as the ongoing work of an unfinished 1974 Revolution and the defence of the hard-won, basic rights enshrined in the 1976 constitution. See also Tiago Carvalho and Pedro Ramos Pinto, 'From the "Unfinished Revolution" to the "Defence of the Revolution": Framing the Transition in Austerity-era Portugal', in *Rethinking South European Democratization in Spain, Greece and Portugal: Lost in Transition?*, eds Maria Elena Cavallaro and Kostis Kornetis (New York: Palgrave Macmillan, 2019). My thanks are due to Pedro Ramos Pinto for allowing me access to a pre-publication manuscript version of this article.

Portugal being the one that gets 'screwed' this time, in contrast to the episode of the 'Men with Hard-ons'. In her sad and increasingly absurdist tale, Hot Forest has a hasty abortion and is eventually deported following a catalogue of disasters. The 2013 'Invasão das Escadarias' was actively compared by the police demonstrators at the time with the MFA army coup of 1974 and this longer transversal history is echoed here, albeit faintly in the chanting of 'o povo unido jamais será vencido' ['the people united will never be defeated'] an iconic sound of the 1974 Revolution that is not quite drowned out by the dominant music of 'Perfídia', with its double connotation here of personal and political betrayal. The rendering of iconic national events through a naive tourist's perspective, set against a global music soundtrack, challenges the reduction of Portugal's crisis to the status of a global travel blog or a TripAdvisor post. It also effectively pre-empts the kind of alienating outsider's gaze that a European viewer from the global North might bring to the scene of Portugal's political implosion.

In the subsequent scenes of Boavista's 1974 commemorative rally, however, the mass singing of the 25 April anthem 'Grândola Vila Morena', followed by the Portuguese national anthem 'Heróis do Mar' is loud and clear. With the juxtaposition of these anti-austerity sequences (the bird trainers, the Invasão and the Boavista rally) the contemporary EU and its bitter economic legacy are powerfully heterotopically refracted in the distorting mirror of Portugal's revolutionary past. A profoundly resonant 'national' moment is certainly revisited in these sequences, but only so that it can be strategically put to the service of a new and alternatively transnational left agenda, ironizing and deflecting Hot Forest's naively cosmopolitan consumerism. As the film's closing sequences confirm, Portugal's historical 'marginality' can be positioned as an anti-capitalist cutting edge in relation to an excessively monumentalized European time–space. The final and infinitely minute unit of heterotopic space that we are confronted with in the episode of the chaffinches, is that of a nation-prison that is also a prism, in the form of the cages that contain the birds. The cages are repeatedly paralleled with shots of balconies, rails, wire mesh and netting, reflecting a country in a cage, the fate of an austerity-bound Portuguese community still singing against all odds. Their profound, if temporarily static, imbrication in global politics is further hinted at when their metal balconies and *bairros* are shown in the episode's establishing shots with international airliners such as Aer Lingus in the background taking off from the nearby airport at Alvalade.

The birdsong competition reaches a muted tragic climax when one of the caged chaffinches sings itself to death and falls silent. A travelling shot then pans through the air, like the departed spirit of the bird, away from the competition arenas moving out beyond the urban *bairros* of Lisbon to the open fields and the actions of an old man we have met previously, Chico

124 Hilary Owen

Chapas, here playing himself, a bird trapper and former colonial war veteran who is revered in the Boavista community.[35] As Chico is checking his bird traps in an open field, he comes across a man who is literally, physically trapped in one of his nets. The man claims to be a flying genie, described by the intertitles as 'poor and sick', in common with many of the individuals we have seen throughout the three films. Chico jokingly asks to be paid a ransom of 'Euromillions' to cut the genie free, in mock imitation of EU debt crisis extortion. But he readily releases the genie without payment, turning down even the ten euros that the genie offers him to buy cigarettes. He refuses to be reduced to the nothingness of a gratuity in capitalism's transactional logic.

The film ends with a long travelling shot of Chico Chapas, as he walks along a path across open fields, with a very long take finally ending at sundown and fading into the castle of Baghdad from the Arabian Nights' frame narrative. On one level, Chico clearly channels the heroic grandeur of an epic Western cliché, the lone drifter on the plains.[36] But the path that Chico follows through a tended and cultivated rural scene, also suggests the heterotopic zone of a city's garden spaces. As Sturgeon notes, the 'gardens' that are created by what he had termed 'neutral era' film-makers, such as Miguel Gomes, are characteristically tended by the figure of an 'non-actor-actor, typically a laborer'. This seems indeed to be the role allocated to Chico Chapas who is, precisely, a non-actor playing himself in volume 3, as distinct from the role of Simão sem Tripas that he took in volume 2.[37] And the long take afforded this travelling shot draws the viewer along with Chico, first behind him and then overtaking him, accompanied by the song, 'Calling Occupants of Interplanetary Craft', made famous by the Carpenters' recording of it in 1977 and billed on the Carpenters' subsequent eponymous album as 'the Recognized Anthem of World Contact Day'.[38] This sung appeal to the occupants of interplanetary craft in outer space effectively magnifies Portugal and Chico from the local to the global sphere, through the implied perspective of the object of this appeal, the extraterrestrial, interplanetary craft traveller who might be looking down upon Portugal as a representation of 'our world'.

[35] In volume 2, Chico Chapas plays a character role as Simão sem Tripas, the lone Portuguese bandit on the run, in Western style.
[36] See Matthew R. Turner, 'Cowboys and Comedy: The Simultaneous Deconstruction and Reinforcement of Generic Conventions in the Western Parody', *Film and History: An Interdisciplinary Journal of Film and Television Studies*, 33.2 (2003), 48–54 (pp. 52–53).
[37] Sturgeon, 'The Neutral'.
[38] The song was originally recorded by Klaatu in 1976, at the height of Portuguese post-revolutionary change, and it became an international hit with the Carpenters' cover version of 1977.

The 'Portugal' that Miguel Gomes offers to us in *Arabian Nights* is the austerity experience that cannot and does not exist on its own. The iconic socialist experiences of resistance and revolution that are embedded in Portugal's national memory interrupt and refract hegemonic European memory politics, bringing urgently into focus the need for new forms of communitarian transnationalism. The contribution that Gomes's cinema makes to this debate is his use of heterotopic and heterochronic time–spaces to break up the EU's unacknowledged assumptions about its own internal others. The result is at least a tentative response to Euro-apocalyptic pronouncements such as Étienne Balibar's when he stated in 2010, 'unless it finds the capacity to start again on radically new bases, Europe is a dead political project.'[39]

The testimonies delivered by Gomes's *Arabian Nights* were, themselves, rapidly and tellingly overtaken by Portugal's own political events in November 2015. Five months after the films' international release in May 2015, Passos Coelho's PSD coalition government was brought down. Following the PSD's narrow election win in October 2015, the PS leader António Costa successfully put forward a Socialist-led coalition, eventually dubbed the *geringonça* (the 'contraption', a term recuperated from the originally insulting connotations of 'makeshift', bandied by Paulo Portas) backed in Parliament by the Communist PCP, the Green Party, and the Independent Marxists (Bloco da Esquerda). The 2015 *geringonça* brought with it a refusal of German-style austerity economics that was unique in the EU, with Mário Centeno, as Portugal's Finance Minister, progressively reversing most of the austerity measures necessitated by the bailout, while still remaining in the EU and the Euro zone. Obviously, one major international consequence of this was the debate, invoked by Owen Jones in the epigraph to this chapter, that positions Portugal as evidence of a viable alternative to austerity from within the EU.[40]

Aiming as much at his trans-European audiences and funders as his own countrymen, Gomes's 'Portugal in crisis' is an attempt to suspend and de-articulate the leviathans of a neoliberal capitalist Europe. The Portuguese heterotopian space that he conjures up for this purpose is made sufficiently dynamically 'hetero' in its relation to the hegemonic European 'North' (most obviously through the satirical filter of Portugal's performative 'Arabianness') as to hit Sturgeon's 'pause button on the unrelenting flow of capital' for six reflective hours. During this time, 'Portugal' becomes a flying, floating, falling,

---

[39] Étienne Balibar, 'Europe is a dead political project', *Guardian Online* (25 May 2010) <https://www.theguardian.com/commentisfree/2010/may/25/eu-crisis-catastrophic-consequences> [accessed 18 December 2018].

[40] Jones, 'No alternative to austerity?'.

always mobile symbol of austerity, an outside on the inside of an over-inflated Europe, connoted by the literally 'revolting' belly of Gomes's beached whale in volume 1, running the risk of explosion at the slightest jolt. To invoke the national signifier 'Portuguese' here, in any sense at all, is always ultimately to metonymize the broader, transnational nature of the crisis experience. Who knows, after all, whose beach the exploding whale might wash up on next?

Part II

Language

7

Lusotopian or Lusophone Atlantics?

The Relevance of Transnational African Diasporas to the Question of Language and Culture

Toby Green and José Lingna Nafafé
King's College London and University of Bristol

Introduction: the importance of language in rethinking Portuguese imperialism from the seventeenth century to the present

Understanding the significance of language when it comes to Portugal's historical relationship with Africa from the seventeenth century onwards requires a multiple approach. The concept of *lusofonia* itself is not used until much later, specifically the twentieth century when, since the independence of Portugal's African colonies, it has become a sort of substitute term for the lusotropicalist myth of Portugal's influence in the world. Nevertheless, there are vital proxies that can help to explore how significant the place of language was for both the Portuguese idea of Africa and the expansion of Portuguese political hegemony in the pre-colonial phase.

In the first place it is important to emphasize the significance of the study of language in articulating early African-European relationships. The place of language is vital in understanding cultural exchange and transformation, and in thinking through the terms and human experiences through which commercial exchange took place. And yet historians of the early modern Atlantic world very rarely pay much attention to language. Over time, European languages became the language of knowledge and culture. Learning the language of Africans for historical studies or literature of the period is thus driven into the background, while knowledge of Portuguese is paramount – exemplifying how the framing of pre-colonial African history often takes shape within the paradigm of *lusofonia*.

Sources may be written in the European languages in the case of Lusophone Africa and Brazil. The Portuguese went to Angola in 1483 and the Dutch invaded what was the Portuguese settlement there in 1641. Intriguingly, the Portuguese or the Dutch worldview became dominant in terms of understanding the history of the region, because they offer the 'sources' that must be studied. Their languages and concepts became the yardstick from which to measure African history.

Some examples make the point. The historiography of Portugal, Brazil and the Atlantic world is rich on the 'slave trade'. Yet in Angola, in reality, there is not a person called 'slave' or *pesa*[1] in the Kimbundu language. However, in the language of slave traders in the period post 1580, the words *peças da Índia* became significant for shifting the humanity of the person being enslaved into a thing, hence dehumanizing the person into an object or commercial good.[2] In the Kimbundu language, there is no word that is the equivalent of slave in Western terms. The *kijikos*, meaning a war captive or a right-hand man, does not imply slave as a property to be sold. Yet this vital piece of knowledge, which might change the way in which the history of slavery is written, is rarely discussed.

Emphasis on the importance of acquiring African languages for research in this period has not been forthcoming. The effort of learning African languages for the sake of deciphering the African meanings of the terms used by the slave traders, religious leaders or administrators has been very much left as a task for anthropologists rather than historians. Historians of the Atlantic are quite happy to take lessons in Portuguese, Latin, Spanish or Dutch in order to have access to the documents in the archive about the Portuguese experience in Africa and Brazil, but few would bother to learn an African language, which often is not seen as a carrier of knowledge.

Yet this preconception itself stems from the early expansion of the intertwined model of language and empire. We may, first, look to the seventeenth century, and the works of one of the first embodiments of what would become known as the Lusophone ideal, Father António Vieira. Vieira was a Portuguese Jesuit priest who worked in Maranhão, Brazil, in the seventeenth century. He also served as a Portuguese diplomat, and member of the Royal Council during the reign of Dom João IV, the King of Portugal. The concept of Lusophony or *Lusofonia* is a political and ideological notion as implied in the Portuguese overseas conquest post-1640, after the Portuguese

---

[1] See António de Oliveira Cadornega, *História Geral das Guerras Angolanas*, 1680, ed. José Matias Delgado, 3 vols (Lisboa: Agencia Geral das Colónias, 1972), III.

[2] Stuart Hall, *Representation: Cultural Representations and Signifying Practices* (London: Thousand Oaks: Sage in association with the Open University, 1997).

Restoration from Spain. At least that is a reasonable understanding of the ideas of Vieira, and his development of the idea of *o Quinto Império* [the Fifth Empire]. For Vieira, Portugal was the fifth empire after Assyria, Persia, Greece and Rome, and was to be ruled by the perfect emperor, Dom João IV, who was to be resurrected from the dead and whose rule was to last for 1,000 years.[3]

Vieira may rightly be called the father of *lusofonia*. Having spent time in Cape Verde as well as Brazil, Vieira was aware of the influence of *lusofonia* through the propagation of the Portuguese civilizing mission. For him, the fifth empire or *lusofonia* required one language, one master and one God. This entailed broadly championing it through a Christianizing mission on the one hand; and, on the other, through silencing other emergent resistance voices of the Atlantic, such as the African maroon community in Brazil, where the maroons had challenged the centrality of this *lusofonia* ideological vision by establishing a state of their own, called Palmares.[4] Hence, *lusofonia* as a concept is both a loud opening up (of Portuguese culture) and a silencing (of other cultures and languages); therefore, this is something that contemporary Lusophone Studies needs to remain constantly aware of.

Regarding Palmares, the Portuguese crown decided to negotiate with the leaders of Palmares in 1678.[5] In 1691, Vieira was commissioned by the Portuguese King Dom Pedro II to share his grand and proto-lusophonist vision with the Palmarinos by giving them the blessing of Christ and turning them into good citizens of his fifth empire. However, Vieira rejected the idea, arguing that the Palmarinos must return first to their previous slave masters and accept the civilizing mission of one God, the 'Portuguese God', to use Gil Vicente's term.[6] In effect, therefore, the Portuguese language was seen as a crucial element in the Westernizing of Africa and the New World. Vieira's refusal to negotiate with the Palmarinos until they had accepted subjection

---

[3] See Alfredo Bosi, 'Antônio Vieira, profeta e missionário. Um estudo sobre a pseudomorfose e a contradição', *Estudos Avançados*, 23.65 (2009), 247–75. See also Bart P. Vanspauwen, 'Cultural Struggles in the Lusofonia Arena: Portuguese-Speaking Migrant Musicians in Lisbon', *Afrika Focus*, 26.1 (2013), 67–88; Cristine Gorski Severo, 'Lusofonia, colonialismo e globalização', *Fórum Linguístico*, 13.3 (1 October 2016), 1321–33.

[4] See the forthcoming monograph, José Lingna Nafafé, *Black Atlantic Abolition Movement in the 17th Century: Lourenço da Silva Mendonça, the Vatican, and the Court Case* (Cambridge: Cambridge University Press, 2021).

[5] Arquivo Histórico Ultramarino, hereafter AHU, AHU_ACL_CU_015, Cx. 11, D. 1116, Brasil-Pernambuco, Carta de Aires de Souza de Castro de 22 de junho 1678.

[6] Gil Vicente, *Obras Completas com Prefácio e Notas do Professor Marques Braga*, 6 vols (Lisbon: Livraria Sá da Costa Lisboa, 1971), IV, 187.

to their masters encapsulated this vision: the blessing was reserved for the Lusophone citizens who accepted the Portuguese God, and the hierarchical vision of human order which this deity enshrined.

It must also be noted that the discussion on the theme of the expansion of *lusofonia* appeared earlier in the seventeenth century, during Vieira's mission to the Africans in Cape Verde. In 1652, Father André Fernandes, a powerful bishop probably in Portugal at the time, asked Vieira to remain on the island of São Tiago, Cape Verde, to proselytize his imperial vision and then take it to mainland Africa. Through Fernandes's request to Vieira, we get to perceive the magnitude of *lusofonia* as understood by Vieira. During this stay, Vieira informed Father Fernandes that the Africans were the true speakers of Portuguese and that the only distinction between the Africans and Europeans was their physical appearance, 'they are all Blacks, but only in this accident [colour] are they different from Europeans' or from other members of the Portuguese-speaking world.[7] In Vieira's terms the Africans, 'have great judgement and ability, and in all polity'.[8] He claimed that nature is what sometimes teaches us the separation in terms of those without faith and those who nature made poor. However, he also asserts:

> They [Cape Verdeans] are the most minded among all the Nations of the new conquests, to imprint on them [the mainland Africans] all that they are being taught [...] there are here clergies and canons who are as black as coal, but so minded, very learned, so erudite, great musicians, discreet and well-mannered, that they could make us feel jealous about those we have there [in Portugal and Brazil] in our cathedrals.[9]

For Vieira, these Africans at home were displaying a contribution to the imperial ideal of *lusofonia* beyond his own expectations. However, it is one thing to be a captive and to be forced to contribute, and quite another when one is free and acting through one's own volition. Those enslaved Africans in the Atlantic could not manifest their true potential through the prism of slavery. They needed a space of equal footing to show their ability.

For Vieira, the tool that shaped this Lusophone culture, and transformed it into a global community, was language. This is where the place of language

---

[7] Cartas do Padre António Vieira, *Monumenta Missionaria Africana África Ocidental*, 2.a Série (1651–84) (hereafter *MMA*), VI, 24–26.

[8] Cartas do Padre António Vieira, *MMA*, VI, 24–26. This is in sharp contrast to the infamous sermon he delivered in Brazil where he claimed enslaved Africans had been fortunate to be enslaved and so come to God. All translations are ours.

[9] Cartas do Padre António Vieira, *MMA*, VI, 24–26.

in this first imperial iteration of *lusofonia* becomes apparent. He declared: 'Because [Africa] is very close to Portugal, together they are willing, and as people they are without comparison, they are more capable, and are a lot more numerous, and in these islands they do not have the need to learn [or be taught] the language, because they all speak Portuguese.'[10]

This helps us to explore the origins of *lusofonia* through a new prism. It shows why, in spite of the ideology behind it, the notion of *lusofonia* must be viewed as transnationalism in reverse. *Lusofonia* was not a culture emerging from the metropole and its language, and spreading itself outwards through some kind of pure imperial projection. It had to travel to a meeting point with others. These people, whether they were Africans or Amerindians, also came to offer their culture in the Iberian Peninsula itself and, in so doing, offered a transformation of *lusofonia* itself.

To think of *lusofonia* as a one-way street is to overlook the transnational influences flowing the other way. Several authors were aware of this in the pre-colonial period. The Guinean writer Marques de Barros argued that Africans transnationalized the Iberian Peninsula; that is, they performed the Lusophone equivalent of inversion or turning 'upside down', to use the philosopher K. Anthony Appiah's term.[11] Lipski meanwhile[12] has shown that in the sixteenth century Portuguese literary writers such as Gil Vicente were imitating Afro-Portuguese pidgin in their works. In other words, Africans were influencing Portuguese society.[13]

---

[10] Cartas do Padre António, *MMA*, VI, 24–26.

[11] See, for instance, the seminal work of M. Barros, discussed in José Lingna Nafafé, 'African Orality in Iberian Space: Critique of Barros and Myth of Racial Discourse', *Portuguese Studies*, 28 (2012), 126–42. See also Kwame Anthony Appiah, *In My Father's House: Africa in the Philosophy of Culture* (London: Oxford University Press, 1992), and 'Europe upside down: fallacies of the new Afrocentrism', in *Perspectives on Africa: A Reader in Culture, History, and Representation*, eds Roy Richard Grinker, Stephen C. Lubkemann and Christopher B. Steiner (Cambridge, MA: Blackwell, 1997), pp. 728–31; and José Lingna Nafafe, 'West African Perspectives on Ancient Egypt: African Renaissance', in *Egypt in its African Context*, ed. Karen Exell (Oxford: Oxbow Press, 2011), pp. 80–91.

[12] See John M. Lipski, 'A Historical Perspective of Afro-Portuguese and Afro-Spanish Varieties in the Iberian Peninsula', in *Portuguese-Spanish Interfaces: Diachrony, Synchrony, and Contact (Issues in Hispanic and Lusophone Linguistics)*, eds Patrícia Amaral and Ana Maria Carvalho (Amsterdam and Philadelphia, PA: John Benjamins, 2014), pp. 360–70.

[13] On Vicente's poems, see Paul Teyssier, *La Langue de Gil Vicente* (Paris: Klincksieck, 1959), pp. 229–42. For discussion on Vicente and Africans, see W. Giese, 'Notas sobre a Fala dos Negros em Lisboa no Princípio do Século XVI', *Revista Lusitana*, 33 (1932), 251–57; and Park, ch. 9 in this volume.

This early framework must be borne in mind, and not overshadowed by the second imperial iteration of *lusofonia*, coming in the twentieth century. The unresolved colonial contradictions of *lusofonia* were much fostered in the modern colonial era. *Lusofonia* as a concept assumes that the peoples of the former Portuguese colonies in Africa share a language, a history and a culture rooted in the Iberian Peninsula. It offers ways of describing and explaining 'affective ties, forms of belonging and relationships of mutuality'.[14] However, it is based on fragile relationships and on the myth of harmonious Portuguese colonial rule, and serves as a tool of closure on the reality of Portugal's selective policy overseas.

The myth of *lusofonia* was exposed after the Carnation Revolution of 1974, by the treatment Portuguese *retornados* received when they had to return to Portugal when Portugal's African colonies became independent.[15] The rhetoric of Portuguese exceptionalism was exposed in demonstrating that it was a country incapable of dealing with diversity.[16] *Lusofonia* is thus based on a 'culture of denial', which aims to camouflage problems of inequality, racism and prejudice.[17] The narratives of equality and fraternity that it propagated during the Estado Novo contrasted greatly with the actual status of indigenous peoples in Africa.[18]

We take the view that there is no such thing as a free-floating *lusofonia* that is just 'out there', unprecedented or controlled. More broadly, there is no one core political, ideological value waiting to be embraced by all colonized countries within the sphere of *lusofonia*; rather there are ever-changing values and challenges that stem from the variety of other values to be found in Africa and Brazil. This is the core model of the analysis that follows.

---

[14] Rosa Williams, 'Luso-African Intimacies: Conceptions of National and Transnational Community', in *Imperial Migrations*, eds Eric Morier-Genoud and Michel Cahen (London: Palgrave, 2013), pp. 265–85 (p. 265).

[15] *Retornados* is a Portuguese word meaning 'returnees'. *Retornados* were Portuguese subjects formerly resident or born in a Portuguese colony in Africa and who returned to settle in Portugal after colonial independence, between 1974 and 1975. Afro-Brazilians who returned to Africa after the Malê (Muslim) revolt in Salvador to countries such as Ghana, Nigeria, Benin and Togo from 1835 to 1836 were also called *retornados*.

[16] José Carlos Pina Almeida and David Corkill 'On Being Portuguese: Luso-tropicalism, Migrations and the Politics of Citizenship', in *Creolizing Europe*, eds Encarnación Gutiérrez Rodríguez and Shirley Anne Tate (Liverpool: Liverpool University Press, 2015), pp. 157–74 (p. 168).

[17] Almeida and Corkill, 'On Being Portuguese'.

[18] Bernd Reiter, 'Portugal: National Pride and Imperial Neurosis', *Race & Class*, 47.1 (2005), 79–91 (pp. 80–88).

Traditional colonial approaches in Allada

The significance of the first, i.e. seventeenth-century, iteration of Portuguese colonialism for the purposes of this essay was spelt out in a recent article by Michel Cahen. Cahen related the emergence of a distinctive Lusophone African space to institutional, historical and structural convergences between Lusophone Africa and Latin America. This offers an interesting comparison between the history of formal Portuguese colonialism in Africa and its relationship to earlier proto-colonial dynamics on the one hand, and historical patterns of colonization in Latin America on the other. As Cahen writes, his interest is to show a common 'longue durée formation of the precapitalist colonial elite milieus which [...] is a specific and relatively common feature between the two areas'.[19]

In his essay, Cahen argues specifically that all of the ex-Portuguese colonies share the '"Creole issue," i.e. today's presence of colonial social milieus produced by, or stemming from, the first age of colonization' – something that affords comparison with class formation in Latin America.[20] Nevertheless, when one looks beyond the role played by the formation of extractive elite ('Creole') classes, the place of language offers a different way of comparing structural history over the *longue durée*. This is specifically the case when it comes to the earlier period of colonization, in the era of the trans-Atlantic trade in enslaved persons.

This extractive proto-capitalist class in Africa did not participate in the process of linguistic violence that was a central part of the colonization process in the Americas. Especially in the early period of the Portuguese and Spanish conquest of the Americas, linguistic violence was key to the colonial project. As Walter Mignolo has noted, 'an archaeology of discursive formation would have led to the very root of the massive colonization of language which began in the sixteenth century with the expansion of the Spanish and Portuguese empires.'[21]

As the discussion of Padre António Vieira shows, this change in discourse was central to the violence of colonial conquest in the Americas, where missionaries translated the Bible into indigenous languages and developed

---

[19] Michel Cahen, 'Is "Portuguese-speaking" Africa Comparable to "Latin" America? Voyaging in the Midst of Colonialities of Power', *History in Africa*, 40 (2013), 5–44 (p. 8).

[20] Cahen, '"Portuguese-speaking" Africa', p. 21.

[21] Walter D. Mignolo, 'On the Colonization of Amerindian Languages and Memories: Renaissance Theories of Writing and the Discontinuity of the Classical Tradition', *Comparative Studies in Society and History*, 34.2 (1992), 301–30 (p. 301).

catechisms in those languages. Indeed, as Mignolo notes, 'by colonization of language I mean the actions taken and strategies employed by missionaries and men of letters to (re)organize Amerindian speech by writing grammars, Amerindian writing systems by introducing the Latin alphabet, and Amerindian memories by implanting Renaissance discursive genres conceived in the experience of alphabetic writing.'[22] This combined with formal educational policies and the decimation of the Native American population devastated indigenous linguistic paradigms and their associated metaphysical and cultural worlds.

Nevertheless, this was not the case in Africa in this period, which points to a different dynamic and power relation between African and European languages and cultures. Thus although, as we have stated, the vision of *lusofonia* required the silencing of other languages, this vision was not entirely realized in Africa until the twentieth century, as a variety of factors indicates.

Put simply, the fact that there were no sustained efforts to translate the Bible into African languages until the nineteenth century is a reminder of the recent focus of historians of Africa in this period, which has shown how far Europeans were not in political control and were, in fact, present as tributary guests of African hosts. African political power is an important correlate of the weak linguistic grip that Portuguese as a language held in the era of the trans-Atlantic slave trade. It is a reminder of the comprehensive relationship between language and coloniality, so well discussed by Frantz Fanon in his 1952 *Black Skin, White Masks*, that 'every colonized people – in other words, every people in whose soul an inferiority has been created by the death and burial of its local cultural originality – finds itself face to face with the language of the civilizing nation.'[23] A colonized person 'who has mastered the language, is inordinately feared; keep an eye on that one, he is almost white'.[24] But in a space where people are not colonized, the imperial language will not hold a position of power. And such, in the main, was the case in relation to Portuguese and Spanish in many parts of Africa until the nineteenth century.

This also explains the focus of this section of our article, in which we examine two cases where catechisms were written in African languages, then translated: one in the Fon-speaking region of Allada, put into Spanish in 1660, and the other in Kimbundu from Angola and put into Portuguese in 1697.

[22] Mignolo, 'On the Colonization', p. 304.
[23] Frantz Fanon, *Black Skin, White Masks*, trans. Charles Lam Markmann (London: Pluto Press, 2008), p. 9.
[24] Fanon, *Black Skin, White Masks*, p. 11.

In each case, it is instructive to note that the catechism was produced at a time when the strength of African political control was threatened by various factors relating to climate change, political instability and the trans-Atlantic slave trade. These are rare cases in themselves, and their interjection in each case into the Iberian space makes them useful examples for this article.

The fact that attempts to produce these catechisms occurred at moments of political stress on the African side confirms how important language is in understanding the deep structures of colonialism, and its effects and history in Africa. It also shows how important it is for understanding the place of Portuguese as a language of colonization, to take the connection with Spain and Spanish more seriously. The separation between the two languages and histories is one that has been driven by metropolitan concerns, with the ideals of *lusofonia* and *hispanidad*; from the perspective of Africa, from the 'periphery', the connections are rather more obvious than the differences at play. Indeed, as Cahen writes, 'there is no reason to compare Portuguese-speaking Africa only with Brazil, and why in certain paragraphs we deal with Africa in general, in order to compare it with Latin America and former Portuguese Africa.'[25]

The catechism produced by Capuchin missionaries in Allada was developed following a missionary expedition in 1660. Allada was by then the most important slave trading port on what became known to Europeans as the 'slave coast', at the heart of the area that became the powerful kingdom of Dahomey in the eighteenth and nineteenth centuries (and in the modern republic of Benin). The missionaries appeared following the despatch of an embassy to Madrid by the King of Allada, Tojonu, in 1658.[26] Their work in Allada was not a success but, as part of this work, they did create a catechism; and there seems to have been an element of successful conversion in Allada and its neighbouring kingdom at Hueda, since some seventeenth-century baptismal records were created.[27]

The catechism shows some basic understanding of certain concepts in Fon. It is also an interesting representation of transnational influences at work in Allada by the middle of the seventeenth century. The catechism declares:

---

[25] Cahen, '"Portuguese-speaking" Africa', p. 8.

[26] Mateo Anguiano, *Misiones Capuchinas en África, Vol. II: Misiones al Reino de la Zinga, Benín, Arda, Guinea y Sierra Leona* (Madrid: Consejo Superior de Investigaciones Científicas, 1957), II, 52–53.

[27] We are grateful to Vincent Hiribarren, Department of History, King's College London, for this information about the recording of baptisms.

Creo en Dios Padre	*Midiq; Vodu, mitome*
Todo poderoso	*nu pop*
Los Mandamientos	*Noquè*
De la Sta Madre Iglesia	*Voduque*
Son cinco	*aton.*[28]

The naming of God as *Vodu* represents the religious shrines of *vodun* as one deity. It misrepresents however the religious pluralism that was a fundamental aspect of worship at the different *vodun* shrines of Allada and the neighbouring kingdom of Hueda, where there were plural shrines (*vodunun*). The incorporation of a plural religious outlook within a singular definition in Spanish stands as a powerful symbol of the process of linguistic and cultural simplification enacted by colonial languages. It embodied already at this early time the cultural violence of colonial power, which would stretch into the twentieth century.

From the perspective of Allada's history, it is also noteworthy how in a distinct part of the catechism, Jesus is rendered in Fon as *Lisá*.[29] This illuminates the transnational influences in Allada by the 1660s, with Lisá apparently derived from the Arabic name for Jesus, Issa. The trans-Saharan trade was clearly making substantial inroads into ideas of culture in Allada by this time; indeed the concept of Jesus may not have been new if the name was already being disseminated in Fon circles.

Nevertheless, beyond what the catechism can tell us about both the simplification enforced by proto-colonial languages on African languages, and the transnational influences in Allada by the seventeenth century, it matters that this Fon catechism was developed at a time of considerable local stress. When the missionaries reached the court of the King of Allada in January 1660, and put to him their proposal of evangelization, the report by the Capuchin friars elicited an interesting response:

> He took some time to answer and at length told the missionaries that he was very grateful for the favourable offer which his brother the King of Spain had made him, but that the embassy which he had sent with Bans, a gateman of his palace, was not so that he should change beliefs and adopt a different faith to that which he professed and which had been that of his ancestors; but rather so that they should send him some Christian priests who would be able to conjure away

[28] Anguiano, *Misiones Capuchinas*, App. 3.
[29] Anguiano, *Misiones Capuchinas*, App. 3.

the thick clouds, which were causing great damage in that land, with innumerable bolts of lightning and thunderstorms falling with which many people and animals were dying, and crops and houses were being destroyed.[30]

In other words, the decision to begin the process of catechism and translation occurred at a moment of climatic stress. This was at the height of the Little Ice Age, when there appear to have been numerous climatic shifts across large parts of the world, which may have influenced events such as the overthrow of the Ming dynasty in China, the English Civil War, and the revolution of Portugal's House of Bragança against Spanish rule.[31] In Allada, the ensuing weakness prompted their King's attempt to reach out to Spain. And at this moment of political weakness, the attempt to impose colonial languages and power was initiated: thus language, coloniality, and political power were clearly in dialogue in the Luso-Hispanic worlds of the seventeenth century.

Traditional colonial approaches: Angola and Kimbundu

As regards the second case, in his book *História Geral das Guerras Angolanas*, António de Oliveira de Cadornega (1623–90), a former Portuguese soldier in Angola, stated that there had been a hundred years between the first Portuguese conquest in central West Africa and the time of his writing in 1680, and estimated that one million people from Angola had been shipped to Brazil as enslaved persons.[32]

For the Jesuits in Luanda and Salvador, the human resources required to catechize this vast number of people, and the recruitment of the local clergy sufficient to the task, proved very difficult. The need for this linguistic knowhow, to cater to Angolans newly arrived in Salvador – *boçais* as they were called – then was more obvious in Salvador, Brazil than in Angola. The Jesuit College of Salvador was already training a good number of Angolan priests in the seventeenth century alone and some had already been serving

---

[30] Anguiano, *Misiones Capuchinas*, II, 54; discussed recently in the context of religious practice by Luis Nicolau Parés, *O Rei, O Pai e a Morte: A Religião Vodum na Antiga Costa dos Escravos na África Ocidental* (São Paulo: Editora Schwartz/Companhia das Letras, 2016), p. 123.

[31] See especially Geoffrey Parker, *Global Crisis: War, Climate Change and Catastrophe in the Seventeenth Century* (New Haven, CT and London: Yale University Press, 2013).

[32] Cadornega, *História Geral*, III, 221.

there.[33] Notwithstanding, there was the need for a manual of instruction, for catechism, in particular in the language of Angola.

The hierarchical position – of teacher to student – was possibly reflected in the first bilingual catechism produced in both Kimbundu and Portuguese in 1642, entitled *Gentio de Angola Sificientemente Instruído* [*Heathen of Angola Sufficiently Educated*], by Father Francesco Pacconio et al.[34] Pacconio was an Italian priest, who lived at the Court of Filipe Hari I, King of Pungo and Ndongo, and was his confessor from 1627 to 1640.[35]

This was followed by the work of Pedro Dias, a Jesuit priest who lived in Salvador and Rio de Janeiro, then produced the first grammar of the Kimbundu language spoken in Angola, published in 1697, Lisbon, and entitled *A Arte da Língua de Angola, Oferecida à Virgem Senhora N. do Rosário, Mãe e Senhora dos Mesmos Pretos*.[36] The book was for priests to be instructed in the Kimbundu language to enable them to teach enslaved Angolans in Brazil the basics of Christian faith. It therefore had a political and religious function, and – as with the Allada case – was produced to address people experiencing political difficulties.

Dias's book contains 48 pages. It was not based on Africa as a site of economic and linguistic power, but it was clearly a form of knowledge produced for religious and economic interest. Dias had never been to Angola but produced the grammar through his encounter with Angolans in both Salvador and Rio de Janeiro, in the hospital where he worked.[37] In Dias's book, we have some African words that have entered the Portuguese language such as: *sanzala* 'zenzala' (a big house),[38] *fuba* 'fubá' (cornmeal),[39] *uanda* 'andas' (walk), *mbunda* 'bunda' (seat, behind), *kixima*,[40] *kisibu*, *kixibu* 'cachimbo' (pipe),[41]

---

[33] See Vanicléia Silva Santos, 'As Bolsas de Mandingas no Espaço Atlântico: Século XVIII' (unpublished PhD thesis, Universidade de São Paulo, 2008).

[34] For detailed studies of native languages in the Portuguese contact zones, see Otto Zwartjes, *The Portuguese Missionary Grammars in Asia, Africa and Brazil, 1550–1800* (Amsterdam: John Benjamins, 2011).

[35] Cadornega, *História Geral*, III, 309, 463.

[36] Pedro Dias, *A Arte da Língua de Angola, Oferecida à Virgem Senhora N. do Rosário, Mãe e Senhora dos Mesmos Pretos* (Lisbon: Na officina de Miguel Deslandes, impressor de Sua Magestade, 1697).

[37] See *História Social da Língua Nacional 2: Diáspora Africana*, eds Ivana Stolze Lima and Laura do Carmo (Rio de Janeiro: NAU Editora, 2014).

[38] Cadornega, *História Geral*, I, 621.

[39] Dias, *A Arte da Língua*, p. 5.

[40] See Filipe Zau, 'A Educaçao em África', in *África: Investigadores Multidisciplinares*, ed. Ana Maria Mão-de-Ferro Martinho (Évora: Editorial NUM, 1999), pp. 35–45.

[41] See Cadornega, *História Geral*, I, 612.

'banguê' (stretcher, wheelbarrow, old style sugar mill), 'inhame' (yam), 'dengue' (primness), 'dengoso' (prudish),[42] and *nganga*, which is the Kimbundu term for a 'diviner, medicineman, and a healer, priest' (Catholic priests in both Kongo and Angola were called *nganga*).[43]

The content of the book produced by Dias reflected an interest from the religious point of view and for the benefit of the economic life of the Africans in Brazil. It was a guide for the benefit of the mission. The real contribution of the book in terms of *lusofonia* is to demonstrate the impact of one of the African languages in seventeenth-century Brazil. Margarida Petter remarks that Dias's book reflects first a proof that African languages were in existence in Brazil and, second, that this was a grammar book about the Kimbundu language, produced in Brazil with linguistic data obtained from Brazil.[44] The spread of Kimbundu thus reflects the political influence of Kimbundu speakers in Brazil, and offers an interesting reflection on the Palmares *kilombo* as a maroon community in the seventeenth century, when the book was produced, and in view of Vieira's own contributions to *lusofonia* as outlined in our introduction.

Kimbundu was one of two Bantu languages, widely spoken in Angola at the time, at least in those areas where the Portuguese settlements were, such as Luanda, Bengo, the Cuanza River province, and Pungo AnDongo.[45] The language was widely spoken in the Atlantic in the seventeenth century, particularly in Salvador, Bahia.[46] The Mbundu people of northern Ndongo (Angola) were termed 'Ambundu' and appeared often in the writings of Cadornega during the period. Meanwhile, southerners were called 'Ovimbundu'. Both

---

[42] See José Honório Rodrigues, 'The Influence of Africa on Brazil and of Brazil on Africa', *The Journal of African History*, 3.1 (1962), 49–67.

[43] Cadornega, *História Geral*, I, 615.

[44] See Margarida Petter, 'Línguas africanas no Brasil: vitalidade e invisibilidade', in *História Social da Língua Nacional* 2, eds Lima and do Carmo, pp. 19–40 (p. 20).

[45] Lawrence W. Henderson, *Angola: Five Centuries of Conflict* (Ithaca, NY: Cornell University Press, 1979).

[46] Carta do Padre António Vieira a Roque Monteiro Paim, [Letter from Father António Vieira to Roque Monteiro Paim], *MMA*, XIII, Bahia, 2 July 1691, pp. 221–22. See also Petter, 'Línguas Africanas No Brasil', pp. 19–39; José Honório Rodrigues, 'The Influence of Africa on Brazil and of Brazil on Africa', *The Journal of African History*, 3.1 (1962), 49–67. See also *African Heritage and Memories of Slavery in Brazil and the South Atlantic World*, ed. Ana Lucia Araújo (Amherst, NY: Cambria Press, 2015); Walter Hawthorne, *From Africa to Brazil: Culture, Identity, and an Atlantic Slave Trade, 1600–1830* (Cambridge: Cambridge University Press, 2010); and *Africa and the Americas: Interconnections During the Slave Trade*, eds José C. Curto and Renée Soulodre-LaFrance (Trenton, NJ: Africa World Press, 2005).

groups spoke the same Kimbundu language.[47] It was probably the easiest to learn among the Angolan languages. As the governor of Angola put it at the time, Kimbundu was a language widely spoken among the Portuguese residents in Luanda and they used it for their diplomatic contact with Angolan kings.[48]

The influence of Kimbundu in Brazil offers a different perspective on *lusofonia* from the Allada case, one more in line with the analysis of reciprocal transnationalism offered in the introduction to this chapter. Castro in his analysis on African language influence in Brazil states that there are (i.e. currently) 3,517 recognizable words from African languages in Brazilian Portuguese.[49] From the sixteenth to seventeenth centuries there was a huge need for the use of African languages for instructing Africans about the Catholic faith. The six-month grace given by the crown for the normal period of baptism was becoming increasingly challenging or not feasible for the sheer number of slaves being taken from Africa to the Americas. In São Tomé, there was a school for instructing enslaved Africans before they were taken to Brazil, hence the introduction of African languages for basic instruction prior to baptism. There were many Africans in need of native interpreters or instructors, because there were many different African languages. Jesuits were in charge of ensuring that African languages were used for their missionary purposes as they would enhance learning of the Christian teachings. Those slaves who were proficient in the Portuguese language, in particular from Angola, became costly in terms of the sale price.[50]

All of this helps us to understand the roots of the importance of Kimbundu in the seventeeenth century, both through the grammar and the catechism studied. Kimbundu was probably easier to learn than other languages of the region, but that was not the only reason. Linguistically Kimbundu was widely spoken in Angola and most slaves were also from Angola so, for that reason, it made more headway than other languages. It was influential in Brazil, and knowledge of it was vital for training the native priests who were necessary for expanding the wider mission of *lusofonia*, and its connection to *civilitas*.

[47] Cadornega, *História Geral*, II, 324.
[48] See Cadornega, *História Geral*, III, 147 and 188.
[49] See Petter, 'Línguas africanas', p. 28. Yeda Pessoa de Castro, *Falares Africanos na Bahia* (Rio de Janeiro: Academia Brasileira de Letras, 2001).
[50] André João Antonil (João António Andreoni), *Cultura, e Opulência do Brazil por suas Drogas, e Minas, com Varias Noticias Curiosas do modo de fazer o Assucar; Plantar, & Beneficiar o Tabaco; Tirar Ouro das Minas. & Descubrir as da Prata; e dos grandes Emolumentos, que esta Conquista da America Meridional dá ao Reyno de Portugal com estes, et Outros Generos, et Contratos Reaes* (Rio de Janeiro: Conselho Nacional de Geografia, 1963).

Linguistic power and spread were well recognized as being essential to the power of the Portuguese empire, and it is this relationship between power and language that will be explored more fully in the concluding sections, as the questions that began to be mooted in the early pre-colonial period reached their full flowering in the era of formal colonialism, in the twentieth century.

Language and exchange

During the era of the twentieth-century Estado Novo and formal Portuguese colonialism in Africa, it was a well-known trope of the Salazar regime that what justified Portugal's enduring colonial project was the longevity of Portugal's relations with Africa. The formation of the Sociedade de Geografia in 1875, and the publication of many Portuguese documents on early African relations by Luciano Cordeiro, and then in the twentieth century at the height of the colonial era by António Brásio, were very much a part of this project.[51]

However, when it comes to examining the importance of the place of Portugal and of Portuguese in the shaping of a transnational, globalized world, it is a curious testament to the long reach of Portugal's colonial power that scholars have done little systematic work on the linguistic relationships between Portugal and African languages. Such work, as we will explore in this final section of the essay, may provide new and interesting insights into the balances of power in this early period of Portuguese–African relations, that also remained vital to the ideological project of the Estado Novo, and to Portugal's colonial project in Africa during the twentieth century. There will be two approaches to this in this section: (1) the role of Portuguese in the Kriolu spoken in Cape Verde and Guinea-Bissau; and (2) the relationship between Portuguese and a variety of African languages in what the historian Boubacar Barry called the 'Greater Senegambian region'.[52]

When it comes to the relationship between Portuguese and Kriolu, it is worth noting in the first place the role that colonial hierarchies and categories have played in establishing the parameters for the study of Creole languages. The coloniality of power is deeply present in the categories used to discuss the semantic and syntactic elements of Creoles, viz. the 'superstrate' and the 'substrate'. Superstrate languages are those that have higher status or

---

[51] See, for example, António Brásio, *Monumenta Misionaria Africana: África Ocidental*, 15 vols (Lisbon: Agência Geral do Ultramar, 1953–88); *Viagens, Explorações e Conquistas dos Portuguezes: Collecção de Documentos*, ed. Luciano Cordeiro (Lisbon: Imprensa Nacional, 1881).

[52] Boubacar Barry, *Senegambia and the Atlantic Slave Trade*, trans. Ayi Kwei Armah (Cambridge: Cambridge University Press, 1998).

power in the shaping of Creole languages, associated in the Atlantic world with European languages and especially Portuguese; meanwhile 'substrate' languages refer to those which have lower status, associated in the Atlantic with African languages, which form the syntactical glue which binds the language – and indeed any language – together.

This categorization derives from a colonial model of power, reproduced here in language theory. It is important to note how Creole languages embody power and agency somewhat differently from this conventional model, however: just as Africans did the work and provided many of the skills that built the Atlantic world, the place of African languages in the grammatical structure of Creoles shows how this relationship became internalized socially through language, where African grammatical structures do the linguistic 'work'. In fact, this approach reveals the contrary of the 'top-down' model of development implied in the substrate/superstrate model of linguistics.

Indeed, more cogent analyses of Creole linguistic genesis in the Atlantic world have revealed the weakness of this approach. Anthony P. Grant's analysis of Creoles shows how the substrate/superstrate definition is simplistic, and that recent analysis shows that 'the bulk of the vocabulary may be derivable from one language but [...] the structure of the lexifier language has not been similarly transmitted', and indeed that many Creoles do not fit a model of intertwined languages.[53]

Thus, rethinking the value judgements attributed to linguistic categories helps us to understand African–Portuguese relations in a different way. Indeed, Kriolu helps us to think about African–Portuguese relations in two specific and valuable ways that other historical sources cannot access: the first relates to African history in Cape Verde, and the second to the transnational connections between Cape Verde and the New World.

With regards to the African linguistic presence in Capeverdean Kriolu, it is significant that loanwords in Kriolu come from three main languages: Wolof (the main language spoken in northern Senegal), Mandinga (a very widely spoken language across southern Senegambia and into what is today Mali) and Temne (from Sierra Leone).[54] This offers historical insight into the

---

[53] Anthony P. Grant, 'Language Intertwining: Its Depiction in Recent Literature and its Implications for Theories of Creolization', in *Creolization and Contact*, eds Norval Smith and Tonjes Veenstra (Amsterdam and Philadelphia, PA: John Benjamins, 2001), pp. 81–112 (pp. 82, 97).

[54] Jean-Louis Rougé, 'Apontamentos sôbre o Léxico de Origem Africana dos Crioulos da Guiné e de Cabo Verde', in *Lenguas Criollas de Base Lexical Española y Portuguesa*, ed. Klaus Zimmerman (Frankfurt am Main: Vervuert: 1999), pp. 49–67, (p. 61).

formation of Kriolu, since the Wolof presence in Cape Verde was very small, and dates to the earliest phase of colonization of the islands (1460 to around 1510). There was the settlement on the islands of the family of a Wolof prince, Buumi Jeléen, who visited Portugal in 1488, while some of the earliest trade connections came from this northern part of Senegambia.[55] However, after the turn of the sixteenth century Capeverdean trading connections were oriented exclusively south of the Gambia river, where there are no Wolof speakers.

The presence of Wolof is therefore significant in arguing for the structural importance of early interactions in shaping Kriolu in Cape Verde, and Creole languages in general. Where Mandinga's presence can be understood through its general importance in the adjacent region of Africa – where it was and is widely understood as a second language or lingua franca – the presence of Wolof speaks to the importance of early African–Portuguese relations in establishing the parameters of the language. It is also reflective of why it is crucial to study this early phase of history when considering historical connections between Africa and Portugal: since it was in so many ways a foundational period.

Beyond this, Kriolu's transnational connections are important in understanding the place of language in early colonial power. Here, the relationship between Kriolu and the Papiamentu Kriol language spoken in Curaçao and Aruba is significant. Several recent studies have shown the clear semantic, syntactical and morphological connections between the two Creoles; and indeed it is something one can easily find out by discussing the links with Kriolu and Papiamentu speakers, who are well aware of the similarities. This is explained in Jacobs's analysis by historical connections in the slave trade era between the Cape Verde region, Curaçao and Cartagena in what is now Colombia.[56]

Beyond these transnational connections, one must also consider the connections between Capeverdean Kriolu and the languages spoken in Greater Senegambia. Many of these languages show influence from Portuguese in a range of contexts. In Wolof, the words for key (*caabi* – chave), knife (*paaka*

---

[55] See especially on Bumi Jeleen José da Silva Horta, 'As tradições orais wolof de transmissão cabo-verdiana: a memória de Buumi Jeleen e dos Njaay na ilha de Santiago (séculos XV–XVIII)', in *Les Ruses de l'Historien. Essais d'Afrique et d'Ailleurs en Hommage à Jean Boulègue*, eds François-Xavier Fauvelle-Aymar and Bertrand Hirsch (Paris: Karthala, 2013), pp. 31–46.

[56] Frank Martinus, 'The Origins of the Adjectival Participle in Papiamentu', in *Lenguas Criollas*, ed. Zimmerman, pp. 231–50. Bart Jacobs, 'Linguistic evidence and historiography: the selection of slaves on Curaçao, 1650–1700', *Revista de Crioulos de Base Lexical Portuguesa e Espanhola*, 3 (2012), 1–19.

– faca) and onion (*soble* – cebola) all show Portuguese influence; some of these words are also used in adjacent languages such as Serèèr (in the case of *chabi*).[57] The Pulaar spoken widely across Senegal, the Gambia, Guinea-Conakry and Guinea-Bissau also borrows some words, such as ambergris (*lambere* – ambar).[58]

The language that reveals the strongest influences is Mandinga. In the 1960s, the linguist Von Bradshaw notes a range of Mandinga words that derive from Portuguese, such as *bāndāre* – bandeira,[59] *fani* – pano,[60] *koporo* – cobre,[61] *mesu* – mesa.[62] To Von Bradshaw's analysis can be added certain core words in Mandinga that relate to finance, credit and trade: *fèère* – feira (market), and *júru* – juro (credit/debt).

Reflection on this linguistic discussion allows us to say some crucial things about Portuguese as a language of colonialism in a transnational global context in the era of the slave trade. In the first place, its power related to trade and objects of trade. This explains why words derived from Portuguese relate to the process of trade or are trade/imported goods.[63] Coloniality such as it existed in this era was not related to formal political power, therefore, but to economic colonialism and the construction of economic inequalities (hence the power of the Portuguese namings here).

Connected to this is a second crucial point, which was that part of the power of Portuguese as a language derived from its global reach. The spread of Kriolu to the West Indies and the emergence of Papiamentu testifies to the broader historical and economic process of influence and power which was related to the slave trade. Similarly, the spread of catechisms studied in the previous section speaks to the importance of linguistic power and spread in the ideological buttressing of empire. Underpinning this, however, was a vital element of African work, agency, and skill, which went into shaping the early 'Portuguese' world in the first place – and as emerges in the syntactical

[57] See Benjamin Pinto Bull, *O Crioulo da Guiné-Bissau: Filosofia e Sabedoria* (Bissau: INEP, 1989).

[58] A. T. Von Bradshaw, 'Vestiges of Portuguese in the Languages of Sierra Leone', *Sierra Leone Language Review*, 4 (1965), 5–37 (pp. 13–14).

[59] Von Bradshaw, p. 15.

[60] Von Bradshaw, p. 16.

[61] Von Bradshaw, p. 18.

[62] Von Bradshaw, p. 22.

[63] Indeed, according to Von Bradshaw, the Portuguese influence here was originally greater than can now be determined, for 'there is a tendency for certain loan-words from Portuguese to be superseded by a loan from English (e.g. *mesa*/table). It is plain that the Portuguese content of many vernacular vocabularies was formerly far larger than is now the case' ('Vestiges of Portuguese', pp. 34–35).

place of African grammar in Atlantic Creoles, and the emphasis which seventeenth-century Jesuits placed on learning Kimbundu.

Conclusion: language, hybridity and power

Language is ultimately a route into thinking about power and agency during the era of the trans-Atlantic trade in enslaved persons. As Mignolo reminds us, the question of colonization and language is always connected.[64] This analysis of the role of the Portuguese language in the emergence of linguistic patterns can thus help us to reflect on the question of whether a 'Lusophone' space or a 'Lusotopian' space is a better model for considering these questions. We can begin to reflect on how apposite the concept of 'Portuguese-speaking', and thereby of the CPLP (Comunidade dos Países de Língua Portuguesa), the umbrella transnational political organization uniting all countries with Portuguese as their official language of governance, actually is, in the light of this historical focus on language.

The question of influence and the way in which it relates to the spread of Portuguese is fundamental here. In the first place, Western languages (in this case of Portuguese) did not manifest themselves in their pseudo-universality in Africa during this era. While as Walter Mignolo puts it, through the colonial project 'Western epistemology and hermeneutics (meaning Greek and Latin languages translated into the six modern European and imperial languages) managed to universalize its own concept of universality, dismissing the fact that all known civilizations are founded on the universality of his own cosmology'[65] this did not occur in Africa with Portuguese. This may be, as he notes because 'universality is always imperial and war-driven'.[66]

Portugal did not really have an empire in Africa until the twentieth century, and the spread of its languages was resolutely particular and related to the place of trade in material objects and the trade in enslaved persons. Moreover, if we are to speak of *lusofonia*, and if we are to speak of a 'Community of Portuguese-speaking countries', or CPLP, we have to do so not as some kind of utopian spread of Portuguese culture and ideas, but precisely through this lens of coloniality, power, violence and the universality of the materialistic drive for conquest.

In the end, therefore, a Lusotopian conception gives us a better grasp of both the realities of the idea of Portugal and its realities in African space,

---

[64] Mignolo, 'On the Colonization of Amerindian Languages', p. 307.
[65] Mignolo, 'On Pluriversality' (2013) <http://waltermignolo.com/on-pluriversality/> [accessed 15 October 2018].
[66] Mignolo, 'On Pluriversality'.

especially in the period before formal colonialism in the twentieth century. In writing about a space that is touched by Portuguese power and language but not controlled by it, we reflect better the realities of power before the twentieth century. We can also reflect more deeply on the continuities between the colonial and postcolonial eras, and the political implications in the attempt to enshrine Portugal's former colonies as a 'Lusophone space'. Here one is reminded of the seminal essay on culture by Amílcar Cabral, the leader of Guinea-Bissau's twentieth-century independence movement: 'History teaches us that, in certain circumstances, it is very easy for the foreigner to impose his domination on a people. But it also teaches us that, whatever may be the material aspects of this domination, it can be maintained only by the permanent, organized repression of the cultural life of the people concerned.'[67] A continued emphasis on Portugal's history and language in its former colonies may thus be contributing not to the reality of Portuguese history and the influence of the past, but to its reproduction in the present. And in this perpetuation of Salazarist myth, the realities of language, history and power, are obscured.

[67] Amílcar Cabral, 'National Liberation and Culture', *Transition*, 45 (1974), 12–17 (p. 12).

8

Portuguese as a Transnational Language

Susana Afonso
University of Exeter

Introduction

Transnationalism refers broadly to the movement of people from one nation to another nation or nations, which is characterized not only by sustained links with the home country but also by transformative links with the host country. The term may also refer to the interaction between transnational communities: diasporas interacting with one another and forming social networks.[1] Rather than offering a simple inter-national perspective on the movement of people from one nation-state context to another, transnationalism brings to the study of migration a more dynamic perspective with regard to the role of transnational groups in the 'processes and formations and maintenance [of connections]' involved in the complex process of identity construction.[2] From this perspective, groups are seen as agents of change in both host and home country.

Transnationalism has always been an intrinsic feature of the Lusophone world. Portuguese was a dominant language of trade and diplomacy on a global scale from the Atlantic to the Far East, from the fifteenth to the eighteenth centuries.[3] The colonial enterprise gave rise to an unprecedented movement of populations that formed diasporas across the world. These

---

[1] Nina Glick Schiller, Linda Basch and Cristina Szanton Blanc, 'From Immigrant to Transmigrant: Theorizing Transnational Migration', *Anthropological Quarterly*, 68.1 (1995), 48–63.

[2] Steven Vertovec, *Transnationalism* (London: Routledge 2009), p. 3.

[3] Nicholas Ostler, *Empires of the Word: A Language History of the World* (New York: Harper Collins, 2005).

diasporas varied in nature; traders and (most) explorers formed voluntary transnational communities, whereas slave diasporas held a forced transnational status. It is important to remember that the formation of transnational diasporas did not come to a halt after the end of the Portuguese empire and that Portuguese(-speaking) transnationalism is still a fundamental aspect within the Lusophone space and beyond.

One of the factors that is inevitably affected by movement across national borders is language. During the expansion of the Portuguese empire, new speech communities were established, and new language practices developed, as speakers of Portuguese acculturated to the local context, coming into contact with other languages and cultures as well as sociohistorical realities. As a consequence, local varieties of Portuguese emerged, albeit to different degrees: it became the native language of the majority of the population in Brazil, but it remains largely a second language in Portuguese-speaking Africa,[4] Macau and East Timor. Portuguese-based Creoles (new languages that develop out of very intense contact between demographically disproportionate groups who speak different languages), integrating words from Portuguese and maintaining structural features of the African languages also emerged in Cape Verde, Guinea-Bissau, São Tomé, Macau and East Timor. Given the impossibility of accessing the early stages of contact, this chapter will account for the emergence of new varieties of Portuguese by taking into consideration the social history of the various contact zones and the characteristics of the new speech communities in terms of identity.

The chapter is organized as follows. The next section discusses the relationship between transnationalism and language in general, followed by a section that considers the specific case of Lusophone transnationalism from a historical perspective in Brazil (Afro-Brazilian networks) and in the East (Luso-Asian networks, including Mozambique) and their role in the emergence of the varieties of Portuguese. Some examples of non-standard features of Portuguese will be presented. By way of conclusion, the chapter stresses the importance of studying the language patterns of modern transnational social networks within Portuguese-speaking space.

---

[4] Except in São Tomé and Príncipe where Portuguese became the dominant native language of the population, replacing the local languages. See Tjerk Hagemeijer, 'From Creoles to Portuguese. Language Shift in São Tomé and Príncipe', in *The Portuguese Language Continuum in Africa and Brazil*, eds Laura Álvarez López, Perpétua Gonçalves and Juanito Ornelas de Avelar (Amsterdam: John Benjamins, 2018), pp. 169–84.

Transnationalism and language

Transnational individuals develop alternative language practices to the standard ones in the country of origin. This is in line with one of the conceptual premises of transnationalism, namely that of the mode of cultural reproduction, or the association between transnationalism, hybridity and creolization (for instance), as exemplifying the 'fluidity of constructed styles, social institutions and everyday practices'.[5]

The language repertoires of transnational individuals are reshaped in different ways. To put it in a rather simplistic way, new languages (the official language(s) of the host country) will be added to their repertoire, whereas other languages already in their repertoires may gradually be abandoned or their use limited to specific functions. However, the very concept of 'language' in a language repertoire may take different forms; vernacular uses of a language, most frequently used vocabulary or limited structures might simply become part of the reshaped language repertoire of transnational individuals, particularly when they operate in extremely diverse contexts. Furthermore, the various languages (in whichever form) of the repertoire are far from being clearly delimited. Speakers mix the linguistic forms of their repertoires through what is called code-switching or translanguaging.[6] Language repertoires must therefore be conceptualized as 'emergent and dynamic pattern[s] of practice in which semiotic resources are being used in a particular way'.[7]

New language practices are associated with the construction of new identities through the interaction between internal and external processes that are specific to particular social realities[8] and are 'conveyed, negotiated and regimented',[9] not exclusively but importantly through language. People cluster in different social networks made up of 'idiolects' (use of a language whose

---

[5] Vertovec, *Transnationalism*, p. 9.

[6] Code-switching/translanguaging is the dynamic process in which speakers alternate between languages or language varieties or use resources from different languages in a single conversation. See Angela Creese and Adrian Blackledge, 'Translanguaging in the Bilingual Classroom: A Pedagogy for Learning and Teaching?', *Modern Language Journal*, 94 (2010), 103–15.

[7] Jan Blomaert and Ad Backus, 'Repertoires Revisited: "Knowing Language" in Superdiversity', *Tilburg Papers in Cultural Studies*, 24 (2012), p. 6.

[8] Ulf Hannerz, *Transnational Connections: Culture, People, Places* (London: Routledge, 1996).

[9] Anna de Fina, 'Linguistic Practices and Transnational Identities', in *Routledge Handbook of Language and Identity*, ed. Sian Preece (London: Routledge, 2016), pp. 163–78 (p. 163).

features are unique to an individual), which converge into a recognizable form made up of a set of features selected during the process of contact between members of social networks. These selected features become communal and function as a linguistic mark of a particular social network. The formation of new language varieties is, therefore, a process led by members of a social network operating as agents of change, as they undergo a process by which new identities are formed.[10]

Although transnationalism has been used to refer mainly to mobility in late modernity, it should also be possible to reanalyse historical mobility through a transnational lens. The Portuguese colonial enterprise lasted from the 1500s until the handover of Macau to China in 1999, instigating unprecedented changes in terms of the connectivity between peoples. There were Africans in Portugal and Brazil, Goans in Mozambique, Macanese in Timor, and, of course, Portuguese in all the territories which Portugal controlled, or in which it had commercial interests.

Transnationalism and the emergence of varieties of Portuguese

The ways in which new varieties of Portuguese emerge self-evidently requires investigation from a transnational perspective. The impact of transnational diasporas on the local ecology of languages has varied according to the type of colonization pattern in place. In exploitation colonies, such as the territories in the Far East (Goa, Timor, Macau) and initially in African territories controlled by the Portuguese, Portuguese (or, more precisely, forms of Portuguese) was added to the linguistic repertoire of the local population by the local social elite, serving as a lingua franca but rarely as the vernacular.[11] Multilingualism was thus preserved with a fairly clear distribution of languages according to usage as well as to geographic and ethnographic spread.

The outcomes of language contact are very much dependent on social and historical circumstances[12] and are associated with processes of identity

[10] William Labov, *Principles of Linguistic Change. Vol. 2. Social Factors* (Malden: Blackwell, 2001).

[11] A lingua franca is a language of wider communication used between groups who do not share the same language(s). The vernacular is the everyday, colloquial language spoken by a group as their mother tongue.

[12] Among others, see John Holm, 'The Genesis of the Brazilian Vernacular: Insights from the Indigenization of Portuguese in Angola', *PAPIA*, 19 (2009), 93–122. In relation to world Englishes, see Edgar Schneider, *Postcolonial English. Varieties around the World* (Cambridge: Cambridge University Press, 2007).

formation. A reconstruction of the identity-formation processes of historic transnational social networks that shaped the type of contact between speakers with different language repertoires may be possible through analysing the formation of modern identities. These are described as 'fragmented, multi-vocal, discontinuous and contradictory', as well as hybrid,[13] as individuals interact with contexts in which multiple linguistic resources and 'inventories of identities'[14] are found.

Historical studies have unearthed characteristics of social networks that are crucial to understanding the outcome of contact. Across the Portuguese empire, white Portuguese who were born overseas were considered to be different from the Portuguese in Portugal because they were morally 'corrupted' by their 'local' environment and were, therefore, unable to maintain the hierarchies and value systems of the homeland.[15] What this shows is that the Portuguese born overseas must have undergone a process of constructing a new identity that was sufficiently distinct for it to be contrasted with Portuguese identity as it was seen and accepted in Portugal itself. The complexity of classifying the Portuguese in overseas territories increased the more hybrid they became. As Havik and Newitt put it: 'Mixed' parentage raised legal, cultural and religious problems and, of course, problems of perception and identity' which were 'complex and diverse', while potentially maintaining links with the home culture in Portugal.[16] Evidently, the language also underwent hybridization, although it maintained strong links with European Portuguese.

Across the Portuguese empire, different population groups formed social networks that shaped the linguistic outcome of contact. In the next two sections I will take a transnational approach to discussing the formation of Afro-Brazilian networks and networks in the East, and their role in shaping new forms of Portuguese.

[13] De Fina, 'Linguistic Practices and Transnational Identities', p. 168.
[14] De Fina, 'Linguistic Practices and Transnational Identities', p. 169.
[15] Glenn Ames, 'The Portuguese Province of the North: 'Creole' Power Groups in Urban Centres and Their Hinterlands, c.1630–1680', in *Creole Societies in the Portuguese Colonial Empire*, eds Philip Havik and Malyn Newitt (Cambridge: Cambridge Scholars, 2015), pp. 212–34.
[16] In *Creole Societies in the Portuguese Colonial Empire*, eds Havik and Newitt, pp. 7–9.

Afro-Brazil and the formation of Vernacular Brazilian Portuguese

If there is one language variety in Brazil that encapsulates the complex history of contact between languages throughout the centuries, it is Vernacular Brazilian Portuguese (VBP), which differs considerably from Standard Brazilian Portuguese (SBP).

The main debate regarding the historical development of VBP relates to whether or not its origins are Creole.[17] Portuguese-based Creoles must have emerged in Brazil, given the displacement of approximately four million African slaves to Brazil between the seventeenth and eighteenth centuries to work initially on the plantations and later in the mining industry. They brought with them their languages, particularly Kimbundu and Kikongo, Yoruba and Ewe,[18] and possibly some Creoles and simplified forms of Portuguese. Something that has also been hotly debated in this regard is whether the vernacular is, in fact, a 'post-Creole' (a decreolized form of a previously generalized Creole).

With no records of the development stages of the vernacular, nor any clear evidence of a generalized Creole, historical records that document the demographic composition of Brazil, the kinds of social interactions between transnational members of social networks, and the construction of new identities can shed light on how this new variety came about. Demographic records (Table 8.1) show that the number of black Africans never really substantially outnumbered the number of Portuguese. Throughout history, Brazil underwent a continuous and sizeable influx of Portuguese from different social classes and from several regions, who used vernacular forms of European Portuguese, with which the African-born and Brazilian-born slave populations had contact. What demographic records bring to light, however, is the emergence of new groups: *pardos* (mixed-race, Brazilian-born)

---

[17] See Gregory R. Guy, 'On the Nature and Origins of Popular Brazilian Portuguese', in *Estudios sobre Español de América y Lingüística Afroamericana*, 83 (Bogotá: Instituto Caro y Cuervo, 1989), pp. 227–45; John Holm, 'Popular Brazilian Portuguese', in *Actas do Colóquio sobre Crioulos de base Lexical Portuguesa*, eds Ernesto d'Andrade and Alain Kihm (Lisbon: Colibri, 1992), pp. 37–66; Esmeralda Negrão and Evani Viotti, 'Brazilian Portuguese as a Transatlantic Language: Agents of Linguistic Contact', *InterDISCIPLINARY Journal of Portuguese Diaspora Studies*, 3.1 (2014), 135–54; Heliana Mello, 'African Descendants' Rural Vernacular Portuguese and Its Contribution to Understanding the Development of Brazilian Portuguese', in *Iberian Imperialism and Language Evolution in Latin America*, ed. Salikoko Mufwene (Chicago, IL: University of Chicago Press, 2014), pp. 168–85.

[18] John Lipksi, *A History of Afro-Hispanic Language: Five Centuries, Five Continents* (Cambridge: Cambridge University Press, 2005), p. 258.

and *Creoles* (black or white, Brazilian-born). *Pardos* and *Creoles* were key to the language shift towards Portuguese, giving rise to new varieties.

Table 8.1. Estimated population of Brazil, 1538–1890[19] (emphasis added)

	1538–1600	1601–1700	1701–1800	1801–50	1851–90
African-born	20%	30%	20%	12%	2%
Creole Africans	–	20	21	19	13
Integrated Amerindians	50	10	8	4	2
Mixed	–	10	19	34	42
European-born	30	25	22	14	17
Creole Whites	–	5	10	17	24

Among the slave population, there was a clear social differentiation between African-born slaves and Brazilian-born slaves. The latter enjoyed a more advantageous position: they were assigned specialist roles and even managerial positions in sugar plantations, which could, as a consequence, lead to manumission, or legal freedom.[20] These social distinctions were first and foremost established by the colonists and accepted by the Brazilian-born groups who, like the white colonists, considered the African-born slave, newly arrived in Brazil, to be 'primitive'. In the eyes of the white colonists, the newly-arrived African-born slaves had very little or no communication skills in Portuguese and no culture.[21] The specificity of the identity of the Brazilian-born slaves was inevitably based on the difference between the self and the other groups with which they interacted. Although Brazilian-born slaves, as forcibly transnational individuals, maintained links with their African origins, particularly with regard to religion, 'inalienable from African cosmology, rituals, cultures [that] permeated into value systems and behaviours',[22] other identity markers

---

[19] Alberto Mussa, 'O papel das línguas africanas na história do português do Brasil' (unpublished master's thesis, Universidade Federal do Rio de Janeiro, 1991), p. 163, cited in John Holm, *Languages in Contact: The Partial Restructuring of Vernaculars* (Cambridge: Cambridge University Press, 2004), p. 50.

[20] A. J. R. Russell-Wood, 'Atlantic Bridge and Atlantic Divide: Africans and Creoles in Late Colonial Brazil', in Havik and Newitt, pp. 142–83 (p. 146).

[21] See Antonil (1837) cited in Russell-Wood, 'Atlantic Bridge and Atlantic Divide', p. 154.

[22] Russell-Wood, 'Atlantic Bridge and Atlantic Divide', p. 139.

clearly set them apart from African-born slaves. For instance, 'Afro-Brazilian slave women consciously dressed themselves, adopted hair styles, and wore jewellery'.[23]

Portuguese language skills were also a crucial part of the identity of these new social networks. The adoption of Portuguese by the *pardos* as their vernacular corroborates Mufwene's hypothesis that language change occurs due to socioeconomic pressures on the less powerful members of a social network.[24] Because certain linguistic features are evaluated differently by members of a social network, depending on their socioeconomic vantage point, those features which appeared to be more advantageous were therefore adopted. For the *pardos*, the adoption of (a form of) Portuguese would, in their view, bring them closer to the more powerful sectors of the population, while differentiating them from the powerless African-born slaves. This also meant that the African languages brought to Brazil by the slaves were gradually displaced.[25]

VBP became a new language that reflected the complex make-up of a particular social network whose members were transnational individuals, effectively conveying their newly constructed identities. This contact variety shows innovations at all levels.[26] Due to space restrictions, however, only a few examples can be presented here. Generally speaking, some grammatical innovations may be attributed to the structural influence of the African substrate languages, while others correspond to innovations that are typical of second-language learners. The absence of number agreement in the noun phrase (NP) as (1) shows, as well as double negation, as in (2), are features that can arguably be traced to the Bantu languages, such as Kikongo and Kimbundu, widely spoken in Brazil.

(1) os   menino
     the.pl child.sg[27]
     'The children'

---

[23] Russell-Wood, 'Atlantic Bridge and Atlantic Divide', p. 155.

[24] See Salikoko Mufwene, *Language Evolution: Contact, Competition and Change* (London: Continuum, 2008) and *The Ecology of Language Evolution* (Cambridge: Cambridge University Press, 2001).

[25] See Salikoko Mufwene, 'Globalization, Global English, and World English(es)', in *The Handbook of Language and Globalization*, ed. Nikolas Coupland (London: Blackwell, 2010), pp. 31–55.

[26] See Holm, 'Popular Brazilian Portuguese' and 'The Genesis of the Brazilian Vernacular' for examples of innovations.

[27] The abbreviations used in all examples are the following: sg (singular), pl (plural), NEG (negation adverb), PRES (Present), PAST (Past tense), IMPF (Imperfect tense), INF (Infinitive), REFL (reflexive pronoun), IMP (Impersonal maker).

(2) eu não acredito em religião não.
    I NEG believe.PRES in religion NEG[28]
    'I don't believe in religion'

In (1), number is only marked in the determiner to the left of the head noun (*os*) but not in the head noun (*menino*). This structure is similar to the structure of nouns in Bantu languages, in which the leftmost element identifies the class of the noun, carrying all the identifying features including number, as (3) from Kikongo below, illustrates (the head noun *ana* remains unaltered in 3a and 3b, with the leftmost element – *mw* in 3a and *b* in 3b – carrying the number features). Contact between Bantu languages and Portuguese may have led to Bantu speakers who acquired Portuguese reanalysing the left determiner in the NP and the Bantu noun classifier that would carry the morphological features of the NP, such as number. A similar structure is also observed in Cape Verdean Creole, as illustrated in (4).

(3) a. Mw-ana
    sg child
    'The child'

    b. B-ana
    pl-child
    'the children'[29]

(4) kes menin
    those.pl child.sg
    'Those children'

In the double negation structure in (2), negation is marked in two elements: one before and the other after the verb. This structure is also present in Bantu languages (5) and São Tomense Creole (6).

(5) Ke besumba ko
    NEG buy NEG
    'They don't buy'[30]

---

[28] *Corpus Discurso & Gramática: A Língua Falada e Escrita na cidade do Natal*, ed. Maria Angélica Furtado da Cunha (Natal: EDUFRN, 1998).

[29] Leon Dereau, *Cours de Kikongo* (Namur: A. Wesmael-Charlier, 1955). Available at: <http://web.archive.org/web/20061107172144/http://www.nekongo.org/akongo/docs/langue_culture/cours_kikongo_dereau.pdf> [accessed 15 July 2018].

[30] John Lipski, 'Strategies of Double Negation in Spanish and Portuguese'

(6) I'ñe   na   ka   'tlabanaí fa
    they   NEG PAST work   NEG
    'They did not work here'

Other common features are the elision (denoted Ø) of the pronoun *se* in most types of *se* constructions or generalization of the pronoun to signify all grammatical persons.[31] (7) is an example of an impersonal construction with a null pronoun and (8) shows a generalization of the pronoun in a reflexive construction.

(7) No   Brasil Ø circula   à   direita
    in.the Brazil drive.PRES.3sg   on.the   right
    'In Brazil, (people) drive on the right'[32]

(8) Vou-   se   embora
    go.PRES.1sg REFL.3sg   away
    'I'm going away'

The same innovations are also identifiable in Vernacular Angolan Portuguese (VAP), most probably because, to a large extent, VBP and VAP share the same substrate languages as well as experiencing a continuing influx of Portuguese native speakers throughout history.[33] This means that, despite their specificity from both historical and socioeconomic perspectives, in both contact situations, from a linguistic viewpoint, the pool of features in the contact situation (linguistic variables) must have exhibited similarities.[34]

(unpublished research paper, 2001). Available at: <http://www.personal.psu.edu/jml34/negation.pdf> [accessed 14 July 2018].

[31] See Michael Kliffer, 'The Case of the Missing Reflexive', *Hispania*, 65.3 (1982), 424–27.

[32] Kliffer, 'The Case of the Missing Reflexive', p. 425

[33] See Liliana Inverno, 'A transição de Angola para o português vernáculo: estudo morfossintáctico do sintagma nominal', in *O Português em Contacto*, ed. Ana Carvalho (Madrid, Frankfurt: Iberoamericana, Vervuert, 2009), pp. 87–106; and Maria Fernanda Bacelar do Nascimento et al, 'Aspectos de unidade e diversidade do português: as variedades africanas face à variedade europeia', *Revista Veredas*, 9 (2008), 35–59.

[34] Donald Winford, 'The Interplay of "Universals" and Contact-induced Change in the Emergence of New Englishes', in *Vernacular Universals and Language Contacts. Evidence from Varieties of English and Beyond*, eds Markku Filppula et al (London: Routledge, 2009), pp. 207–30.

Luso-Asian social networks

The type of colonial enterprise pursued in the East was very different from that undertaken in Brazil, since it focused on the monopoly on trade in the Indian Ocean. Trade between Goa, Gujarat and Mozambique had been an important and lucrative feature of the Portuguese intra-Asian commercial network in the late sixteenth and seventeenth centuries.[35] And in the Far East, trade between Macau, Solor (an island at the eastern tip of Flores) and Timor flourished in the seventeenth century. It was also during the seventeenth century that Portuguese migration was at its highest, but, unlike the Brazilian case, never took place on a large scale, and settlers concentrated mostly in coastal and urban areas, with some exceptions, such as Sri Lanka or the Zambezi valley.[36] In all territories where the Portuguese settled, intermarriage with the local population took place, forming new, hybrid social networks that, from a geopolitical point of view, stood at the crossroads between Portugal and the local political networks. The settlers thus aligned themselves both with Portuguese and with local values and languages.

Rapidly these communities became crucial to maintaining control over certain territories, even though their power was to a certain extent personal, without close supervision by the Portuguese crown. For instance, the creation, in the seventeenth century, of *prazos* (large estates leased to the Portuguese settlers by the local kingdoms) in the Zambezi valley, where the first Portuguese had arrived at the beginning of the sixteenth century, was an attempt by the Portuguese, Goans and the mixed-race population to gain control over certain chieftaincies on the margins of the river.[37] The holders of the *prazos*, the *prazeiros*, also played an important role in trade, as they supplied the markets with goods from Goa and Gujarat. In a similar way the social networks of *casados* (married men, some married to local women), also managed to gain control over trade as well as production in Sri Lanka, Goa, Macau and Timor.

Demographic figures show just how hybrid the communities were in the East in the seventeenth century. In fact, in 1635, the black *casados* (mixed-race, Indian-born) (7,635) outnumbered the white *casados* (Indian-born

---

[35] Sanjay Subrahmanyam, *The Portuguese Empire in Asia 1500–1700*, 2nd edn (Oxford: John Wiley, 2012).

[36] See Subrahmanyam, *The Portuguese Empire in Asia*.

[37] See Subrahmanyam, and Allen F. Isaacman, *Mozambique – The Africanization of a European Institution: The Zambesi Prazos, 1750–1902* (Madison, WI: University of Wisconsin Press, 1972).

Portuguese) (4,947).[38] Given the low numbers of Portuguese in the Far East in comparison to the local populations, and the formation of hybrid social networks, it is not surprising that local languages survived and that this was a scenario favouring the emergence of Indo-Portuguese Creoles. According to Clements, contact between the Portuguese and the Indians (through the Eurasian emergent population) led to the emergence of a simplified form of Portuguese (a pidgin), which over time underwent a process of creolization, becoming the native language of a new generation of Indian Christians.[39] The Creoles, or rather forms located on a continuum between Creole and (perceived standard) Portuguese, became very much associated with the new mixed social network whose identity, particularly its religious identity, was distinct from non-Christian social networks.[40]

Alongside migration from Portugal, Chinese and African slaves, mainly from what is present-day Mozambique, were displaced to areas of Portuguese settlement.[41] In the eighteenth century, in Diu alone, for example, slaves represented 17.4 per cent of the total Catholic population, which was, in the main, non-European (by a ratio of more than 13:1).[42] The fact that most slaves were employed as house servants constituted the right context for a shift towards the language of the masters. Compared to the plantation setting, in the homestead society, servants who were distributed in small numbers across households came into close contact with the masters, who spoke, in this case, Indo-Portuguese Creoles.[43]

Creoles also emerged in Macau (Makista) and East Timor (the now extinct Bidau Creole). When the Portuguese established their first settlement, in 1557, the inhabitants of Macau were mainly foreigners, among whom the Portuguese, both *reinóis* (white Portuguese), and a very significant population of *casados*, were politically dominant, but by no means the majority. It is

---

[38] See António Bocarro, *O Livro das Plantas de todas as fortalezas, cidades e povoações do Estado da Índia Oriental*, ed. Isabel Cid, 3 vols (Lisbon: Imprensa Nacional, 1992 [1635]); and Vitorino Godinho, *Ensaios, vol. II (sobre história de Portugal)* (Lisbon: Livraria Sá da Costa, 1968).

[39] J. Clancy Clements, *The Genesis of a Language: the Formation and Development of Korlai Portuguese* (Amsterdam: John Benjamins, 1996).

[40] Hugo Cardoso, 'Linguistic Traces of Colonial Structure', in *Linguistic Identity in Postcolonial Multilingual Spaces*, ed. Eric Anchimbe (Newcastle-upon-Tyne: Cambridge Scholars Publishing, 2007), pp. 164–81.

[41] Hugo Cardoso, 'The African slave population of Portuguese India: Demographics and Impact on Indo-Portuguese', *Journal of Pidgin and Creole Languages*, 25.1 (2010), 95–119.

[42] Cardoso, 'The African Slave Population', p. 111

[43] Robert Chaudenson, *Des îles, des hommes, des langues* (Paris: L'Harmattan 1992).

estimated that the Portuguese only numbered 400 to 900 in the sixteenth and seventeenth centuries, against a majority of Indians, Malay, African and Indian-born black slaves and a growing number of Chinese.[44] Language contact between these groups led to processes of pidginization and creolization, as well as the formation of varieties of Portuguese as a second language (L2), exhibiting varying degrees of influence from Malay and Cantonese. Makista underwent a process of decreolization in the twentieth century, developing into a decreolized Portuguese L2. This variety of Portuguese exhibits similar features to other overseas vernacular varieties of Portuguese (like VBP and VAP), namely variable gender and number agreement (9) and the absence of a pronoun in *se* constructions (10).

(9) China tinha esses coisa hung táu pīng
China have.IMPF.3sg those.pl thing.sg hung táu pīng
'In China they had that thing, *hung táu pīng*'[45]

(10) aquele que tem dois bicos. *Chama* Ø táu lū.
That who have.PRES.3sg two points. Call.PRES.3sg *táu lū*
'That thing which has two edges. It's called *táu lū*'[46]

Makista was also found in East Timor, where it may have influenced the Bidau Creole, since speakers of the Macau Creole settled there due to the flourishing trade that linked Macau to Solor and Timor in the seventeenth century.[47] It was also during this time that the Portuguese presence in Timor was at its strongest and this is when a Eurasian group (known as *Larantuqueiros* or *topazes* – 'black Portuguese'), a mix of Dutch, Portuguese and Timorese, emerged.[48]

Documentation about Bidau is lacking, but there are epistolary sources from the late nineteenth and early twentieth centuries attesting to the presence of a hybrid variety of Portuguese that some of the letters identify as Bidau, while others identify it as L2 Portuguese influenced by Tetun, although the concept of Creole at that time might have been more closely associated with L2 features.[49] What this means is that the variation of Portuguese

---

[44] Alan Baxter, 'O português em Macau: Contacto e assimilação', in *O Português em Contacto*, ed. Carvalho, pp. 277–312.
[45] Baxter, 'O português em Macau', p. 301.
[46] Baxter, 'O português em Macau', p. 301.
[47] Alan Baxter and Hugo Cardoso, 'Early Notices Regarding Creole Portuguese in Former Portuguese Timor', *Journal of Language Contact*, 10 (2017), 264–317.
[48] Subrahmanyam, *The Portuguese Empire in Asia*, p. 220.
[49] See Baxter and Cardoso, 'Early Notices'.

spoken in East Timor was great and, as with Indo-Portuguese varieties, these varieties would be located on a continuum ranging from more Creole features to more standard Portuguese features. Some of the typical Creole features are the absence of articles and lack of gender and number agreement, which are typical of Portuguese L2. Despite the very limited number of speakers of Portuguese in East Timor (as well as the very low number of Portuguese migrants there in the twentieth century), and the banning of Portuguese under Indonesian rule (1975–2002), some forms of Portuguese survived among the old Timorese social elite. These include features that were observed in the nineteenth century, such as morphological simplifications (lack of gender and number agreement), and innovative uses of the *se* constructions:[50] elision of the pronoun *se* (14) (also observed in VBP, VAP, and Vernacular Mozambican Portuguese, see below) and double marking in some types of *se* constructions, for example the impersonal *se* construction in (15).[51]

(14) Mambae, né?   Também só   Ø fala   em casa.
     Mambae right? Also   only speak.PRES.3sg at home
     (lit.) 'Mambae, right? Only speak at home' ('It is only spoken at home')

(15) *Eles* foram   fazer-   se   um levantamento...
     they go.PAST.3pl   make.INF   IMP a survey...
     'They made a survey'

Portuguese is also mostly a second language in Mozambique, spoken by 39.7 per cent of the population in 2007, according to the census. Most Portuguese speakers (L1 and L2) are to be found in the cities, where a nativized variety of Portuguese is emerging, as a contact variety, despite the high variation in the idiolects of the speakers.[52] Since the very beginning of Portuguese settlement

---

[50] See Susana Afonso and Francesco Goglia, 'Linguistic Innovations in the Immigration Context as Initial Stages of a Partially Restructured Variety: Evidence from SE Constructions in the Portuguese of the East-Timorese Diaspora in Portugal', *Studies in Hispanic and Lusophone Linguistics*, 8.1 (2015), 1–33. See also Susana Afonso, 'Impersonal SE Constructions in the Portuguese of East Timor: Notes on the Relation Between Language Contact and Second Language Acquisition', in *Ibero-Romance Languages in Contact and in Contrast: Linguistic Convergence*, eds Miriam Bouzouita and Renata Enghels (Berlin: De Gruyter, forthcoming).

[51] These examples are taken from a corpus of Portuguese spoken by East Timorese living in Portugal collected in 2010 and 2011. See details of the data collection in Afonso and Goglia, 'Linguistic Innovations'.

[52] Perpétua Gonçalves, 'Towards a Unified Vision of Classes of Language Acquisition

in Mozambique in the sixteenth century and the establishment of *prazos*, Portuguese has come into contact with the local languages. At that point, there was no colonial system to impose the European language as would happen in the nineteenth century, after the Berlin Conference of 1884–85, which led to the effective occupation of Mozambique by the Portuguese. The way that the locals and the mixed population used Portuguese (on a continuum between simplified forms of Portuguese and standard Portuguese) developing out of face-to-face encounters between populations, changed when a centralized colonial system was established. The *prazos* system was abolished at the beginning of the nineteenth century resulting in the *prazeiros*' loss of local influence.

It is very likely that those hybrid forms survived in inland rural areas where the Portuguese did not penetrate. However, the current local variety of Portuguese is associated with another kind of social network that began to emerge in the late nineteenth and early twentieth centuries, made up of a local social elite, the *assimilados*, who were educated in Portuguese and embraced Portuguese values and religion. As Portuguese became associated with social mobility, there was some eagerness to acquire the language. The *assimilados*, however, never fully abandoned local practices, including polygamy, despite being Roman Catholic.[53]

This hybrid identity is also expressed in the use of language. The Mozambican Portuguese variety (or, more accurately, varieties, given the high variability) is influenced by features of the local African languages at all levels as well as by innovations typical of the linguistic strategies of L2 speakers.[54] At the structural level, some forms of Mozambican Portuguese show the elision of the pronoun *se* in some construction types (16) (similarly to VBP, VAP and Portuguese in East Timor), but it also shows innovative uses of the same pronoun (17). Also identifiable is the lack of number agreement in the NP (as happens in VBP and VAP) (18).

---

and Change: Arguments for the Genesis of Mozambican African Portuguese', *Journal of Pidgin and Creole Languages*, 19.2 (2004), 225–59 (p. 233).

[53] André Mindoso, 'Os Assimilados de Moçambique: Da situação colonial à experiência socialista' (unpublished PhD thesis, Universidade Federal de Paraná, 2017). Available online at: <https://acervodigital.ufpr.br/bitstream/handle/1884/46471/R%20-%20T%20-%20ANDRE%20VICTORINO%20MINDOSO.pdf?sequence=1> [accessed 31 July 2018].

[54] See Gonçalves, 'Towards a Unifed Vision', and Perpétua Gonçalves, 'Tipologia de "erros" do Português Oral de Maputo: um primeiro diagnóstico', in *Panorama do Português Oral de Maputo. Vol. II. A Construção de um Banco de 'Erros'*, eds Christopher Stroud and Perpétua Gonçalves (Maputo: INDE, 1997), pp. 35–67.

(16) O navio afundou   Ø
 The ship sink.PAST.3sg
 'The ship sank'[55]

(17) Quando me   acabei   com o curso.
 When REFL finish.PAST.1sg with the degree
 'When I finished the degree'

(18) Há   muitas dificuldade.
 There.is many.pl difficulty.sg
 (Lit.) There are many difficulty ('there are many difficulties')

Conclusion

This chapter has presented a historical perspective on transnational Lusophone social networks and their active role in the emergence of varieties of Portuguese. Speakers are the agents of change and changes occur at the level of the 'individual communicative acts of [its] speakers' via contact that occurs not between languages but really between the idiolects of speakers.[56] Furthermore, the direction of the evolution of language is determined by the socioeconomic context in which speaker's communicative acts evolve and the pressures a particular context places on the members of social networks, also known as the language ecology. Due to the history of sustained contact between the idiolects of the speakers of Portuguese and the idiolects of speakers of other languages that took place in the particular language ecologies of the territories the Portuguese settled, the outcomes of contact, in particular the emergence of new varieties of Portuguese, must be discussed with reference to the social, demographic and linguistic configuration of the newly-established networks. With no direct access to the language repertoires or language practices of the transnational individuals who were part of the transnational social networks, nor to what kind of interactions they engaged in, historical documentation of the Portuguese empire, including the displacement of people across the Portuguese empire, is instrumental in hypothesizing about how the configuration of the groups and their interaction impacted directly on the outcomes of contact.

---

[55] Example (17) is adapted from Gonçalves, 'Towards a Unified Vision', p. 249. Examples (18) and (19) are adapted from Gonçalves, 'Tipologia de "erros"', p. 51 and p. 60, respectively.

[56] See Mufwene, *Language Evolution*; and *The Ecology of Language Evolution*; and William Croft, *Explaining Language Change. An Evolutionary Approach* (London: Longman, 2000).

What can be identified across the Portuguese empire is the creation of hybrid social networks arising through the intermarriage between Portuguese migrants and local people, the formation of hybrid identities, and, consequently the emergence of hybrid languages: new varieties of Portuguese and Creoles, depending on the speaker's particular demographic and socioeconomic circumstances.

Transnationalism continues to be a pervasive feature of and within the Lusophone territory and beyond, with new social networks and specific identities continuing to emerge.[57] Today, transnational communities are perhaps far more complex than ever before. These social networks are connected both to their local environment and to their original social networks in the home country and, at the same time, with the advent of social media, with other social networks elsewhere. Social media, therefore, enables a more diverse configuration of social networks, which are no longer limited to face-to-face contact, and facilitates the maintenance of stronger ties with the original social networks at home. The impact of these two aspects on the language, not only on the idiolects of the transnational individuals but also on the original social networks at home, is a topic that merits future research.

---

[57] See, for example, Lilia Abadia, Rosa Cabecinhas, Isabel Macedo and Luís Cunha, 'Interwoven Migration Narratives: Identity and Social Representations in the Lusophone World', *Identities. Global Studies in Culture and Power*, 25.3 (2018), 339–57; Lurdes Macedo, Moisés de Lemos Martins, Rosa Cabecinhas and Isabel Macedo, 'Researching Identity Narratives in Cyberspace: Some Methodological Challenges', in *Narratives and Social Memory: Theoretical and Methodological Approaches*, eds Rosa Cabecinhas and Lilia Abadia (Braga: Universidade do Minho, 2013), pp. 119–33.

9

Beyond Comprehension

Language, Identity and the Transnational in Gil Vicente's Theatre

Simon Park
St Anne's College, University of Oxford

A witch, a Picardese-speaking demon, a handful of fairies, and a black man from Guinea: these are my *dramatis personae*. They all come from plays by the sixteenth-century writer, Gil Vicente (c. 1465–c. 1536), and, as you can tell, hail from quite different places and possess quite different powers. This little list – only a fraction of Gil Vicente's total cast of characters – foregrounds an aspect of his work that has long fascinated critics: the varied languages and origins of the characters in his plays.[1] They travel as far as India, and they come to Portugal from across Europe; they speak (or give the appearance of speaking) Portuguese, Castilian, French, Italian, Latin and German. In these respects, Gil Vicente's plays reflect his age. Lisbon was, in his lifetime, one of the most populous cities in Europe and a hub of global exchange. Following the so-called 'Discoveries' made in Africa, Asia and South America, the Portuguese capital bustled with people and goods from the world over. As ships set sail for Antwerp or Goa, communities speaking many different languages settled in or passed through Portugal. Foreign visitors to the capital

---

[1] Gil Vicente's language has been a consistent preoccupation for critics. The classic study is Paul Teyssier, *La langue de Gil Vicente* (Paris: Klincksieck, 1959). See also: Giulia Lanciani, 'O plurilinguismo no teatro de Gil Vicente', in *Gil Vicente 500 anos depois*, eds Maria João Brilhante et al, 2 vols (Lisbon: INCM, 2003), I, 45–52; Marian Leanna Smolen, 'Bilingualism as Semiotic Code in the Theatrical Code Systems of the Theater of Gil Vicente' (unpublished doctoral dissertation, Arizona State University, 1990); and Marie-France Antunes-Fernandes, 'Gil Vicente: un espagnol portugais du début du XVIe siècle', in *Langues et identités dans la Peninsule Ibérique*, ed. Alain Milhou, Cahiers du C.R.I.A.R., 9 (Rouen: Université de Rouen, 1989), pp. 23–50.

in the sixteenth century commented on the population's diversity – particularly the high number of black inhabitants.[2]

In trading throughout their expanding empire, negotiating new diplomatic relations and conquering new territory, the Portuguese had to operate across multiple languages, often by means of interpreters or *linguas*.[3] As the Jesuit, Luís Fróis, underlines in his history of the Society of Jesus's mission in Japan, language skills were essential for bridging cultural divides (and for effective proselytizing): 'discovering an understanding of the language and the communication between men', he writes, granted the missionaries access to 'the secrets that vision alone cannot grasp'.[4] Fróis highlights in his history the difficulties early missionaries faced because they could not communicate effectively with the Japanese. Indeed, lives and limbs could be lost through mistranslations or failure to understand etiquette. Fernão Mendes Pinto describes in his 1614 *Peregrinação* [*Peregrination*] how a messenger sent by the Portuguese to a Chinese mandarin had his ears cut off for delivering a message expressed in the diplomatic language of friendship common to European relations, which was read as an unforgivable insult to the emperor who thought all other kingdoms subordinate and whose representatives should therefore address him as supplicants.[5] Despite such challenges, the spread of the Portuguese language was thought to be an essential component of empire-building. The humanist scholar and official historiographer of the Portuguese empire in Asia, João de Barros, argued with prescience that language lasts longer than any material marker of empire: 'the arms and columns set up in Africa and Asia [...] are material, and time can thus erode them, but it will not erode the learning, customs, language that the Portuguese have left in these lands'.[6] Linguistic exchange, however, was reciprocal. Attempts to grapple

---

[2] See Kate Lowe, 'The Global Population of Renaissance Lisbon: Diversity and its Entanglements', in *The Global City: On the Streets of Renaissance Lisbon*, eds Annemarie Jordan Gschwend and K. J. P. Lowe (London: Holberton, 2015), pp. 57–75 (p. 61).

[3] See Dejanirah Couto, 'The Role of Interpreters, or *Linguas*, in the Portuguese Empire During the 16th Century', *e-Journal of Portuguese History*, 1.2 (2003), 1–10 <http://www.brown.edu/Departments/Portuguese_Brazilian_Studies/ejph/html/winter03/html/couto_main.html> [accessed 10 September 2018].

[4] Luís Fróis, *História de Japam*, ed. Josef Wicki, 5 vols (Lisbon: Biblioteca Nacional, 1976–1984), I (1976), pp. 2–3. All translations in this chapter are my own.

[5] See Fernão Mendes Pinto, *Peregrinação*, 2 vols (Lisbon: Relógio d'Água, 2004), I, 202.

[6] João de Barros, *Gramática da língua portuguesa: cartinha, gramática, diálogo em louvor da nossa linguagem e diálogo da viciosa vergonha*, ed. Maria Leonor Carvalhão Buescu (Lisbon: Faculdade de Letras da Universidade de Lisboa, 1971), p. 405.

with the new climes and cultures encountered brought foreign words into Portuguese as much as Portuguese gained new speakers and its own words migrated into other languages.

Closer to home, a series of marriages between Spanish princesses and Portuguese kings embedded Castilian into the Portuguese court: it held prestige as a literary language and most of the writers from the period wrote both in Castilian and Portuguese. Latin was the international language of erudition and of the Catholic Church; classical texts formed the basis of schooling and infused almost every part of elite written culture. Italian also provided Portuguese writers with models to follow (and challenge) and some of the major cultural figures of the day, such as Francisco de Sá de Miranda (1481–1558), spent time in Italy. An indicative expression of this elite multi-lingualism is the record of a 1588 poetry competition that awarded prizes for compositions in each of the four languages I have mentioned: Portuguese, Castilian, Latin and Italian.[7] Citation, imitation, translation, parody and commentary were all key textual practices that brought together writing in different languages and people in different places.

To understand this period and its texts at all, then, one has to acknowledge the movement of writers, their texts, and ideas between languages and across borders. Early modern literary studies have thus long had a transnational dimension. Readers of Gil Vicente have certainly always been confronted by what we can call transnational phenomena, because of plays such as *Auto da Fama*, which features a Castilian, an Italian and a Frenchman all trying to woo Fame out of Portugal – and, of course, failing. One has to allow for some looseness in the 'national' element of 'transnational', though, since 'nations' as we now know them did not fully emerge before the eighteenth century and focusing too hard on the national can lead us to overlook other kinds of border that were equally, and in some cases, more important. That said, nations and national identity were not born overnight: Portugal's geographic borders have remained to this day very similar to those set out in the 1297 Treaty of Alcañices, the country had a single currency since the time of D. Afonso III (r. 1248–79) and, in the sixteenth century, narratives were increasingly being written about its people's origins, language and character, so thinking 'nationally' has some purchase.[8]

---

[7] See *Relaçam do solenne recebimento que se fez em Lisboa às santas reliquias q[ue] se leuáram à igreja de S. Roque da companhia de Iesu aos 25 de Ianeiro de 1588* (Lisbon, 1588).

[8] For a deeper exploration of the extent to which we can speak of 'nations' in relation to early modern Portugal, see José Manuel Sobral, 'A formação das nações e o nacionalismo: os paradigmas explicativos e o caso português', *Análise social*, 37 (2003), 1093–126.

Auto da Fama itself suggests something of a nascent national identity in its personifications of Castile, Italy and France.

While the 'national' aspect of the transnational must therefore come with some caveats, the term is productive as a 'way of seeing' that trains our eyes on 'movements, circulations, flow', be that of people, objects, texts or ideas.[9] This means, as Patricia Seed argues, prioritizing not just what or who moves, where they go and why, but what happens when they get where they are going or decide to head home, what happens to those left behind and what goes on when in transit.[10] These issues subtend much of Gil Vicente's theatre, because most of his single act plays, known as *autos*, have a processional structure, wherein a series of arrivals, sometimes from far afield, propels the performance forward. In this article, I will explore two such arrivals by characters coming from outside Portugal. I draw out how the figures concerned – and the other characters they are confronted with – respond, in these initial interactions, to different ways of speaking. The geographical movements here are transnational in that the characters come from outside Portugal, but the linguistic differences that emerge have, in the end, more to do with social, racial and supernatural concerns than with the national origins of the speakers or the fact that they cross national boundaries. What I highlight, then, is how moments of arrival constitute critical junctures when linguistic differences are negotiated. My examples also reveal how, historically, language has been constituted as a marker of identity and, particularly, how it related to other identity markers, such as skin colour. Both scenes involve failed assimilation: a devil refuses to speak the language of his summoner, and the whitening of a black man's skin fails to make him the marital catch he wishes he were, because of the way he speaks. These episodes thus foreground the struggles to resist or fit in that can accompany transnational (or indeed any) movement from one place to another.

Speak Portuguese, dammit!

Auto das fadas [*The Farce of the Fairies*] features one of Gil Vicente's most famous multilingual moments: a dialogue between the witch, Genebra Pereira, and a devil who speaks Picardese. The exact year of the first performance of the play remains unknown, but we know it took place during the reign of D. Manuel I (r. 1495–1521) and in the presence of Prince João (b. 1502).

The play opens with the arrival of the witch, who has come to the court to plead the benefits that sorcerers like her bring to society. After a long

---

[9] C. A. Bayly et al, 'AHR Conversation: On Transnational History', *American Historical Review*, 111 (2006), 1440–64 (pp. 1454, 1444).

[10] Bayly et al, 'On Transnational History', p. 1443.

monologue, she summons a devil to give a practical demonstration of her (supposedly harmless) witchery. A devil appears, speaking, we are told, 'in the Picardese tongue' and the farcical miscommunications commence.[11] The witch wants the devil to fetch some fairies [*fadas*] to read the audience's fortunes, but instead he brings friars [*frades*] who deliver a burlesque sermon on the Virgilian theme of 'love conquers all' in Castilian. Here, Castilian's poetic associations lend themselves to comedy in the mouths of the inappropriately lovelorn friars. Once the friars have concluded, Genebra Pereira finally manages to make the devil comply with her wishes, transporting the fortune-telling fairies to the stage.

On the one hand (the devil's), the play dramatizes the pressure to speak the language of a new environment and the (limited) resistance possible through refusing to do so. On the other (the witch's), it stages a character's response to a language she cannot understand: her attempts to identify it and to make sense of its strangeness. Like many of Gil Vicente's plays, *Auto das fadas* has no fourth wall: Genebra Pereira addresses the audience, the friars' sermon nods at the dalliances of members of the court, and the fairies read the audience's fortunes. These onlookers add to the stresses of deciphering the devil's words and getting him to obey her, because she wants to impress them.

Devils were, perhaps, the early modern transnational agents *par excellence*, because they could travel anywhere in an instant. Indeed, as Thibaut Maus de Rolley has shown, a great deal of anxiety on the part of early modern demonologists stemmed from this perceived ability of devils to travel freely across the world and do evil things wherever they might choose.[12] Even in this play, for instance, the devil dashes off to the 'lost islands' to fetch the fairies and transvects the two priests onto the stage from Hell. What is more, devils were also associated with an ability to speak foreign tongues: a telltale sign of possession was someone breaking out into a language they had not learned.[13] Devils were, then, the disturbing embodiment of the mobile and multilingual.

At first, the dialogue between the witch and the devil seems to parallel an archetypal episode of transnational migration: the arrival of someone new, who does not speak the language of the environment they find themselves in,

---

[11] Gil Vicente, *Obras completas*, ed. Manuel Marques Braga, 6 vols (Lisbon: Sá de Costa, 1943–44), V (1944), 187. Further references to this edition follow in the text.

[12] Thibaut Maus de Rolley, 'Putting the Devil on the Map: Demonology and Cosmography in the Renaissance', in *Boundaries, Extents and Circulations: Space and Spatiality in Early Modern Natural Philosophy*, eds Koen Vermeir and Jonathan Regier, *Studies in History and Philosophy of Science*, 41 (Switzerland: Springer, 2016), pp. 179–207 (p. 186).

[13] Stuart Clark, *Thinking with Demons: The Idea of Witchcraft in Early Modern Europe* (Oxford: Oxford University Press, 1999), p. 401.

and whom the 'hosts' attempt to figure out. Here, the twist is that the devil can understand Portuguese, but chooses not to. The devil's refusal to comply linguistically puts Genebra Pereira on the back foot in her attempts to impress her courtly onlookers. She wonders at one point whether her magical ingredients were polluted with swallow poo because the devil is so disobedient. I think, however, and this has gone unremarked by critics, that it has more to do with erotics than failed witchcraft, given that she plucked him, pants down (V, 187, l. 12), from an orgiastic witches' Sabbat to do the bidding of a proudly chaste sorceress.[14] The humour of the play depends on the misogynist polarity whereby women are cast as either virgins or whores and on the fact that Genebra Pereira does not sit in this dichotomy where the devil and the audience expect her to. In a reversal of the traditional association of witches with a dangerous kind of sexuality, Genebra Pereira rejects sex and gets visibly annoyed with the friars who, in another comic overturning of expectations, have clearly broken their vows of celibacy. Gil Vicente paints the witch as a comical aberration whose lack of interest in sex goads the devil into insubordination.

Her initial response, though, to the devil is to try to identify which language he speaks:

> Que linguagem he essa tal?
> Hui, e elle fala aravia!
> Olhade o nabo de Turquia!
> Falade aramá Portugal. (V, 188, ll. 1–4)

> [What language is this, then?
> Ugh, he's speaking gobbledygook!
> Look at that Turkish snout!
> Speak Portuguese, dammit!]

Scholars have deciphered much of the devil's Picardese, but with historical distance, Gil Vicente's questionable grasp of the language to start with, and only a printed edition produced after Vicente's death to go on, certain words

---

[14] The fact that the devil is summoned with his pants down suggests he has been dragged from a Sabbat, where witches and demons were said to fornicate. Genebra Pereira, however, wants to 'be single because it is a state of more grace' (V, 184, ll. 1–2) and the devil appears to mock her for this with his opening words, calling her 'human falsity' (187, l. 15), before alluding to her unmarried state (187, l. 16). For more on the Sabbat, see Walter Stephens, *Demon Lovers: Witchcraft, Sex, and the Crisis of Belief* (Chicago, IL: University of Chicago Press, 2002).

and phrases still remain frustratingly opaque.[15] João Nuno Alçada's reading of the scene as a critique of the witch's heterodoxy, hypocrisy and false virtue is compelling: the devil certainly questions her authority and the virtuous story she has told about herself in her opening monologue.[16] Where his analysis does not persuade, however, is in the emphasis he lays on the 'impossibility of an understanding' between the two characters.[17] To do so risks overlooking the attempts that the witch makes to understand the devil. For instance, in light of all the confusion, editors tend to gloss the word *aravia* in my quotation as 'nonsense'. But if we take *aravia* in the context of what the witch goes on to say, another potential meaning emerges. *Aravia* (gobbledygook) derives from the word *arabia* (Arabic). This etymological connotation might still be active here, as in the very next line the witch identifies the devil as having a Turkish nose, in alignment with early modern stereotypes that modelled demonic physiognomy on that of the 'Moor' or Black Muslim.[18] She attempts to identify him through a combination of how he speaks and how he looks, matching up the two. Some linguistic evidence suggests *aravia* is an alternate spelling for *arabia* and, if this is the case, this moment becomes less about declaring that the devil's speech means nothing and more about trying to pinpoint which language it is.[19] Indeed, to simply say that she equates the devil's words with babble would ignore the fact that she asks explicitly and more than once: 'what language is this?'

Coupled with her later guesses of Latin and German (V, 188, l. 16; 189, l. 12), the witch's speculations about the devil's language have much to tell us. These guesses sketch out the frontiers of the linguistically unfamiliar, giving us an insight into which languages were perceived to be 'accessible' to her.[20] Speakers have notions of which languages are more or less distant from those

---

[15] See the discussion about the philological challenges in Teyssier, pp. 281–90.

[16] João Nuno Alçada, *Por ser cousa nova em Portugal: oito ensaios vicentinos* (Coimbra: Angelus Novus, 2003), pp. 311–92.

[17] Alçada, p. 339, see also p. 343. For a similar viewpoint, see Salvato Trigo, 'Gil Vicente e a teatralização das linguagens', *Revista da Faculdade de Letras*, 1 (1984), 209–25 (p. 218).

[18] Sophia Rose Arjana, *Muslims in the Western Imagination* (New York: Oxford University Press, 2015), p. 67. Note that in *Macbeth*, the witches drop 'nose of Turk' into their magical broth, see William Shakespeare, *Macbeth*, ed. Nicholas Brooke (Oxford: Oxford University Press, 1990; repr. 2008), p. 169.

[19] See *Corpus de testimonios de convivencia lingüística (ss. XII–XVIII)*, eds Emma Martinell Gifre, Mar Cruz Piñol and Rosa Ribas Moliné (Kassel: Reichenberger, 2000), pp. 129, 214, 217; and Bento Pereira, *Thesouro da lingoa portuguesa* (Lisbon, 1647), fol. 13v, which gives *aravia* as *sermo Arabicus*.

[20] My thinking here is indebted to Terence Cave, *Pré-histoires II: langues étrangères et troubles économiques au XVIe siècle* (Geneva: Droz, 2001), pp. 74–75.

they speak. In a different context, Gonzalo Fernández de Oviedo, one of the chroniclers of the Spanish conquests in the New World, points to this idea when comparing the difficulties faced by Indian interpreters in the New World with communication problems faced in Europe: one interpreter, he observes, in attempting to understand another tribe, 'did not understand them better than a Biscayan talking Basque could make himself intelligible to a person speaking German or Arabic, or any other strange [*extremado*] language'.[21] Whatever the continent, then, the pattern is the same. Note that here too German and Arabic stand as placeholders for the incomprehensible, as they do for Genebra Pereira.

The witch's guesses are also perhaps a gag, given that audience members might well have had an idea of how far they were off the mark. Genebra Pereira's guess of Latin, a language the audience would to some extent be familiar with, positions her at the margins of society and certainly low down the ranks: she is evidently unfamiliar with the liturgy and not in contact with Latin in other contexts, otherwise she would know the devil's language was definitely not Latin. Her gender, allegiance with the occult and the languages she does not know all mark her as an outsider.

As the scene continues, tensions rise. The potential threat of not knowing what the devil is saying becomes very clear in the witch's next remarks:

> Dize, má trama te naça,
> que dizes que não t'entendo?
> Fazes escarneo de mim? (V, 188, ll. 7–10)

> [Tell me, a plague on you,
> What are you saying that I can't understand?
> Are you mocking me?]

The witch's concern that the devil is mocking her presupposes that she thinks he is not just spouting nonsense, but really communicating something. At the end of the scene, she gives up trying to identify the devil's language and refers to his words as 'estes tons' ['these noises'] (V, 202, l. 10). This perhaps indicates less that Gil Vicente intended it to be babble all along and more that the witch's powers of deduction have reached their limit. It points also to the fact that named languages hold a certain status and that Europeans have tended to struggle to deal with tongues whose names they do not know.[22] And yet,

---

[21] Quoted in Stephen Greenblatt, 'Learning to Curse: Aspects of Linguistic Colonialism in the Sixteenth Century', in *Learning to Curse: Essays in Early Modern Culture* (London: Routledge, 2007), pp. 22–51 (p. 27).

[22] For the troubles faced by linguists where a single name for a language does not

along the way, Genebra Pereira does manage to make some sense of what the devil says. His language teeters on the edge of comprehensibility:

> DIABO   Tu nas oy tene vergonhe?
> FEITICEIRA   Que fiz eu? (V, 188, ll. 18–19)
>
> [DEVIL   Didn't you hear? Shame on you.
> WITCH   What've I done?]

The witch's question suggests that she has recognized the word 'tu' (shared between Portuguese and Picardese) and understands (correctly) that the devil is talking about her, but she needs clarification about what he is implying. Later in their conversation, she picks out a word that puzzles her:

> DIABO   Tu aspete de bem la mer.
> FEITICEIRA   Hui! *pete* que póde ser? (V, 189, ll. 1–2)
>
> [DEVIL   Your magic is as effective as farting in the sea.
> WITCH   Ah! What could *arting* mean?]

That she can pick out sounds and some words correctly suggests that the language hovers, frustratingly, on the edge of the known. Indeed, the most persuasive parsing of the devil's line to date reads 'tu aspete de bem la mer' as 'tu as pété dedans la mer' ['you farted in the sea'], which would mean she correctly picked out an individual word ('pété') in its entirety.[23] In other words, in performance she might seem sharper than in print.

Although she makes her linguistic troubles quite clear in these lines, Genebra Pereira does not want to lose face by making too much of a fuss about her failure to understand, so, at one point, she tries to brush it off, asking him to tell her later what he meant (V, 188, ll. 21–22). Her 'tell me later' strategy is a way of wriggling out of the subordinate position she finds herself in through not understanding. Frustrated as she may be, she cannot get angry as it might make it look to the audience like she has lost control.

Eventually, however, she snaps. With a curse, she manages to make him speak, momentarily, in Portuguese (V, 189, ll. 20–26). This is a moment that makes the alignment of power and language use very clear. To speak Portuguese is to submit; to speak Picardese is to rebel. Trying to avoid

---

exist in a community, see the discussion of Khoisan languages in Tore Janson, *Speak: A Short History of Languages* (Oxford: Oxford University Press, 2002), pp. 18–24.

[23] Teyssier, pp. 284–85.

awkwardness, though, the witch quickly changes her tune and turns on the charm to paper over her failures. She keeps trying different tactics to get him to change language:

FEITICEIRA	Quero-vos, mano, entender.
	Minha rosa, vinde ca,
	meu quebranto, dae-ma a fé
	que me não faleis por lá,
	e adoro o rabo de boi.
DIABO	Té toi, té toi.
	Tumerum la caboxes.
FEITICEIRA	Falai aramá Portugues:
	atéqui estou zombando;
	tu has d'ir onde t'eu mando.
DIABO	Irei indaque me pes. (V, 190, ll. 1–11)
[WITCH	I want to understand you, honey.
	Sweetie-pie, come here,
	My evil spirit, promise me you won't talk like that,
	I love your cow's tail.
DEVIL	Shut up, shut up,
	You're doing my head in.
WITCH	Speak Portuguese, dammit!
	I'm getting cross now;
	You have to go where I tell you.
DEVIL	I'll go wherever you say.]

Usually, it is the recent arrival who has everything to lose by failing to speak the language of their new environment. Here, it is the other way around. She calls the devil 'sweetie-pie' and compliments him on his tail, but her attentions repulse rather than attract him, as he tells her to shut up. The final line in this quotation (once more in Portuguese) reminds us that his linguistic defiance has its limits: she does, ultimately, have the power to compel him to do her bidding.

He pushes his luck quite far, though, by bringing friars (a social group usually hostile to witches) and not fairies to her (V, 194, ll. 14–18). By this stage, we know the devil can understand what she is saying but pretends he does not. The tension dissipates once the fairies have arrived and the members of the court hear their fortunes. Indeed, we must not forget the theatrical function of their miscommunication: it has been a way to draw out the drama, allow for the burlesque interlude with the friars (because of the *frades/fadas* mixup), and to make the whole *auto* quite comic, as much as it also imaginatively stages the power plays involved in communication and how talking about language indexes one's place in society.

What's the point of being white?

Frágoa de amor [*The Forge of Love*], from which I take my second example, is a festive play that celebrated the betrothal of D. Catarina to D. João III in 1524. Its *raison d'être* is thus fundamentally transnational: a marriage between kingdoms. In anticipation of the new queen's arrival, Portugal, it is imagined, must be made worthier. Characters in the play are hammered into better shape in the eponymous forge of love, set up by Cupid and his mythological band. Justice, for instance, in the guise of an old lady, enters the forge to have her crooked ways straightened out. Viewed in a transnational frame, though, the play's imaginative conceit of the 'forge' raises a key question about transnational mobility: who adapts to whom and how? Here, it is the destination nation that must step up to the moral superiority of its future royal arrival. Indeed, distinctions between unworthy Portugal and praiseworthy Castile are emphasized by the languages that the characters speak: the mythological figures all speak Castilian, while those in need of improvement all speak varieties of Portuguese, including Fernando, the black man, who has travelled from Spain. It is his role in the play that I want to examine in greater detail, because his speech is clearly distinguished from the Portuguese norm by a set of linguistic features, such as loss of final *r*, *s*, and *l* or additional vowels after final *r* and *s*, pointing to the close connection between racial differences and language, on which the characters comment in revealing ways.[24]

As Fernando walks on stage, Venus immediately questions him:

> VENUS Prieto, vienes de Castilla?
> NEGRO Poro que puruguntá bos esso?
>   Mi bem lá de Tordesilha;
>   que tem bos de ver co'esso,
>   qu'eu bai Castilla qu'eu bem Castilla? (IV, 106, ll. 9–13)
>
> [VENUS Have you come from Castile, black man?

---

[24] For a list of all the variations that characterize the black characters' speech, see Teyssier, pp. 243–49.

178   Simon Park

>   BLACK MAN   What are you asking me that for?
>   I've come from Tordesillas,
>   But what it's got to do with you
>   Whether I'm coming or going?]

Fernando's defensive reaction to the goddess highlights how charged the question 'Where do you come from?' can be. Venus wants to know if he has come from Castile in case he has any news about the future queen, but Fernando thinks the question impertinent. Learning that he has come from Tordesillas of all places (exactly where the new queen, D. Catarina, was), Venus excitedly asks whether he has any updates for her. But Fernando is, unfortunately, not on the same wavelength:

>   VENUS   Y qué nueva hay allá?
>   NEGRO   Nova que uba ja maduro
>   ja vindimai turo, turo.
>   Tordesilla tanto vinha
>   a mi faratai puro vida minha:
>   lá he tera mui segura.
>
>   VENUS   En viñas te hablo yo? (IV, 106, ll. 15–20)
>
>   [VENUS   What's the news from there?
>   BLACK MAN   The grapes are ripe,
>   They've all been harvested, every last one.
>   Tordesilla has so many vines
>   That, for the life of me, I'm fed up:
>   It's fertile land there.
>
>   VENUS   What've vines got to do with anything?]

Venus's question was open, so her vexed reply is a little unreasonable. But Fernando's failure to catch the implications underlying Venus's questions, which the audience grasps from being party to the play's opening, has comic and community-forming effects: he is cast as stupid and far from the royal preoccupations of the other characters. Further confusion ensues as Fernando appears to go on to declare his love for Venus, playing with the motifs of servitude that featured heavily in sixteenth-century love lyrics. For instance, he responds to Venus's question about who his master is, by saying he now only serves her, punning on the potential dual meaning of this verb for a lover who is also a slave [*cativo/cravo*]. It is then Venus's turn to misunderstand:

'Niegro' ['Black man'], she says, 'no t'entiendo cosa' (IV, 108, ll. 24–25) ['I don't understand a word you're saying']. Given she is the goddess of love, it seems surprising she would not understand the wordplay. It cannot be his stereotypical pronunciation that causes the problem either, considering she has more or less followed what he has said up to this point (IV, 109, ll. 4–5).[25] In contrast with the scene from *Auto das fadas*, then, miscomprehension has less to do with vocabulary and more to do with contextual inference, that is, she does not follow because the idea that a black man could love her is unfathomable.

Perhaps because of his failed attempts to woo Venus, Fernando jumps at the chance to be remade in Cupid's forge, which has disturbing powers, we are told, to ethnically and socially 'renew' and 'refine' (IV, 113, ll. 1–10; 114, ll. 8–17). Not only does Fernando want his skin whitened, but his nose to be made slimmer and his hands prettier (IV, 114, ll. 23–28). This curiously echoes Genebra Pereira's comment in *Auto das fadas* on the devil's nose as a potential ethnic marker, pointing to the age's interest in facial features as signs of the people's origins and character. The forge does indeed make his skin white, but we are told by the stage directions that it cannot remove a black man's way of speaking. Fernando immediately regrets his decision:

> Se fala meu he negregado,
> e não fala Portugás,
> para que mi martelado?
> [...]
> Da caminha negro tornae:
> se mi fala namorado
> a muier que branco sae,
> ella dirá a mi – bae bae,
> tu sá home ó sá riabo?
> A negra se a mi falae
> dirá a mi sá chacorreiro. (IV, 116, ll. 6–8, 11–15)

> [If I still speak like a black man,
> And don't speak like a Portuguese,
> What was the point of going in the forge?
> [...]

---

[25] For examples of when interpreters had to be called in because the speech of those who had spent some time in Portugal was still incomprehensible to white Portuguese, see A. C. de C. M. Saunders, *A Social History of Black Slaves and Freedmen in Portugal, 1441–1555* (Cambridge: Cambridge University Press, 1982), pp. 98–102.

Make me black again:
If I try to chat up
A white woman
She'll say to me – 'go away,
Are you a man or a devil?'
And if I talk to a black woman,
She'll ask if I'm a joker.]

His anger stems from the mismatch between how he looks and how he speaks. The situations that he presents Cupid with to persuade the god of love to let him turn his skin black again indicate how this apparent misalliance of skin and voice would be interpreted differently by different people: it might be viewed as a joke or an abomination. The associations between black people and devils, and between devils and speaking in tongues, that were at play in *Auto das fadas* return here, as Fernando imagines a white lady wondering whether he was a man or some evil, supernatural creature, given the way he would talk to her and its supposed incongruence with how he now looks.

In the sixteenth-century court, black people were often the butt of jokes and subject to a host of negative stereotypes.[26] One story from an illuminating set of anecdotes from the court, though, suggests a different way that a mismatch between how a black man looks and how he is expected to speak could play out. In it, a white man from the countryside who mocks a black man's speech – indicating that the language stereotypes evinced in Vicente's play were widespread – ends up being humiliated when the black man in question asks his companions (in 'perfect' Portuguese) why this 'bumpkin can't speak Portuguese and wants to speak like a black man'.[27] The black man who got the better of the bumpkin moved in court circles: he was a musician to D. Teodósio, Duke of Bragança, which points to how social status and race might intersect in interesting ways for the period, although his name, Jácome Feio (Ugly Jake), insinuates that people did not take him entirely seriously.

For some medieval and early modern thinkers, language was considered the most primordial part of a person and the surest indicator of identity, be

---

[26] See A. C. de C. M. Saunders, 'The Life and Humour of João de Sá Panasco, *O Negro*, Former Slave, Court Jester and Gentleman of the Portuguese Royal Household (fl. 1524–1567)', in *Medieval and Renaissance Studies on Spain and Portugal in Honour of P. E. Russell*, eds F. W. Hodcroft et al (Oxford: Society for the Study of Medieval Languages and Literatures, 1981), pp. 180–89.

[27] *Ditos portugueses dignos de memória*, ed. José H. Saraiva (Mem Martins: Europa-América, 1979), p. 197.

it ethnic (as in *Frágoa de Amor*) or national.[28] Elisheva Carlebach points out how, for early modern Jews, it was not just their language, but, allegedly, the sounds they made and their intonation that marked them apart, in much the same way as Fernando separates 'fala negregado' from 'fala Portugás' in large part because of pronunciation: 'Long before the aesthetics of "looking Jewish" became a marker for identifying Jewishness, those of "sounding Jewish" became the most significant sign of Jewish birth.'[29] Further, as Carina Johnson explores, language was used to triage defendants in Spanish Inquisitorial cases and to determine whether the accused fell under their jurisdiction. Faced increasingly with individuals who claimed not to be Spanish, but who spoke the language fluently, physiognomy came, over the course of the century, to replace language as the determining piece of evidence in ascertaining an individual's origin.[30] Bodies and voices were consistently scrutinized for what they could reveal about a person. At a broad level, Gil Vicente's plays reflect this close connection between language and collective character: his witches, gypsies, black people, Jews, peasants and courtiers all have distinctive ways of speaking. As we have seen, *Frágoa de amor* suggests that language inheres so deeply in a person that even a magical forge cannot melt that bit of a person down. The example of Fernando and the forge of love suggests, therefore, how historically contingent and socially determined ideas about language and identity are. Along the same lines, linguists, such as Deborah Cameron, have challenged gendered language myths that claim to have 'natural' or 'biological' bases, but are, in fact, a product of society.[31] Fernando's interactions with Venus – and imagined ones with black and white lovers – also underscore the remarkable extent to which what one looks like and how one pronounces one's words impact what interlocutors hear and understand.

[28] See Robert Bartlett, 'Medieval and Modern Concepts of Race and Ethnicity', *Journal of Medieval and Early Modern Studies*, 31 (2001), 39–56; and Peter Burke, *Languages and Communities in Early Modern Europe* (Cambridge: Cambridge University Press, 2004), pp. 160–61.

[29] Elisheva Carlebach, *Divided Souls: Converts from Judiasm in Germany, 1500–1750* (New Haven, CT: Yale University Press, 2001), p. 257

[30] Carina L. Johnson, 'Heritable Identity Markers, Nations, and Physiognomy', in *The Routledge History of the Renaissance*, ed. William Caferro (Abingdon: Routledge, 2017), pp. 152–66 (especially pp. 153–54).

[31] See Deborah Cameron, *The Myth of Mars and Venus* (Oxford: Oxford University Press, 2007).

* * *

What, then, can we conclude from *Frágoa de amor* and *Auto das fadas*? On a simple level, we can take away that how a character speaks has consequences. The use of a particular language by one character or another indicates which group they belong to, as with the stark contrast in *Frágoa de amor* between those supposedly in need of renewal and those doing the renewing. But we have to avoid attributing a preordained set of connotations to a particular language, because interaction between characters can do surprising things to those assumptions. Depending on the circumstances, the language someone speaks can flummox or show finesse, cause laughter or revulsion; connotations are variously activated, redeployed and dismissed during conversations. Even awareness of languages a character does not speak, as in *Auto das fadas*, can say something about their place in the world.

I focused in this essay on two plays that feature miscommunication, because these scenes of confusion set the stakes particularly high, thereby bringing to the fore the frictions between speakers of different languages, the comedy of such interactions and the effects of that comedy. Miscommunications in these examples made it startlingly clear how attempts to understand another person depend on more than just words. Cross-lingual confusion provides clues to the preconceptions and prejudices that underpin social interactions.

Given that the names attached to languages often relate to the name of a country or region, it can be easy to map geographical origin to language spoken and see language use as primarily an indicator of the place the character came from. However, in both the plays above, transnational travel sets in motion not the encounter between 'national languages' and the difficulty in understanding foreign tongues, but a dynamic negotiation of ethnic, racial, religious, gender and social differences through language. There is, in other words, a great deal to explore in Gil Vicente's plays beyond comprehension.

10

Dialects in Translation

Travelling in Space and Time in the Portuguese-Speaking World with *Pygmalion* and *My Fair Lady*

Sara Ramos Pinto
University of Leeds

In language teaching contexts, translation is often thought of as a language exercise. However, if that were true, the information found in any good dictionary would be sufficient to ensure complete communication and to translate any text in the world. Translating is about much more than language. It is also about discourse and context: knowing the what, the who, the where and the why, in order to ensure successful communication. This volume focuses on transnational communication and, given that transnational communication often happens through translation, it is important to acknowledge the role translation plays in establishing contact with new ideas and to understand how it participates in shaping contexts and literatures.

In this article, I will examine how translation can participate in movements that either confirm or challenge existing norms and practices – with the aim of highlighting translation as a privileged pathway to transnational communication and the consequent transfer of ideas, authors, texts and practices. I will use the Portuguese and Brazilian translations of George Bernard Shaw's play *Pygmalion* (1913) and Alan Jay Lerner's lyrics for the musical *My Fair Lady* (1956) to illustrate these trends and discuss how alternative practices brought into the Portuguese and Brazilian systems through translation contributed towards rethinking existing literary norms and became, at times, promoters of innovation.[1] Focusing on the issue of

---

[1] George Bernard Shaw and Alan Jay Lerner will be referred to as Shaw and Lerner for the remainder of the article. References to the source texts will be made using the

the translation of dialects, I will show how the decision to import these texts and the strategies used to translate dialects affected attempts to bring Portuguese and Brazilian literatures more in line with a wider transnational trend by promoting a literary discourse that is less dominated by the standard variety. This will enable me to show how the translation of dialects opened the door to new literary practices that, going against conventional practices, facilitated the renovation of literary discourse. Given that we will be examining translations from Portugal and Brazil across the twentieth century, we will be able to see how this change evolved over time and, consequently, to discuss the (non)existence of flows of communication and influence within the Portuguese-speaking world.

The transnational through translation

Translation is a culturally embedded and mediated activity that reflects the social and cultural frameworks of the target system in which it occurs. As translations happen in contexts where choices must be made in regard to what is important and relevant to be translated, it is crucial to examine what is selected to travel across geographical and linguistic borders and who makes those decisions, in order to better understand the reception and appropriation of texts, as well as transnational flows of influence. In this sense, the assumption that translation is a cultural product embedded in a specific context paves the way towards accepting that the study of translation can, in turn, be viewed as a gateway to understanding how cultures communicate and identifying the factors mediating that communication.

It could, therefore, be stated that the idea of transnationalism arises regularly (or naturally) in discussions within Translation Studies. This is certainly the case since Even-Zohar,[2] Bassnett and Lefevere,[3] and, more recently, Damrosch[4] and Apter,[5] who have characterized translations as cultural products and cultural imports, highlighting the need to consider the flows and patterns in the exchange of ideas constantly occurring across

following editions: Shaw, *Pygmalion* (London: Penguin Books, 2003); and Lerner, *My Fair Lady* (London: Penguin Books, 1959).

[2] Itamar Even-Zohar, 'The Position of Translated Literature within the Literary Polysystem', *Poetics Today*, 11.1 (1990), 45–52.

[3] Susan Bassnett and Andre Lefevere, *Translation, History and Culture* (London and New York: Pinter Publishers, 1990).

[4] David Damrosch, *What is World Literature?* (Princeton, NJ: Princeton University Press, 2003).

[5] Emily Apter, *Against World Literature: On the Politics of Untranslatability* (London and New York: Verso, 2013).

borders. The ways in which those ideas are translated is undoubtedly of interest to translation scholars, but it is equally important to look at *what* is being translated, *when*, and *who* initiated the transfer process, for example. When examining several translations of the same text existing within the same system, as this chapter does, it is also important to examine *who* and *what* could be motivating the development of new translations. After all, if one translation is available, why do we need a second or third, which are simply retranslations of the same source text? Why are there so many different translations of the same text in Portugal and Brazil when the countries share the same language? The unique subtleties of retranslations are not easy to unravel, and they can certainly be understood as iterations of a simple repetitive action. However, if we assume a translation to be a product of specific sociocultural contexts, then it stands to reason that retranslations of it can be used to map changing social ideologies and literary norms in the target culture.[6]

Nonetheless, it is important to recognize that translation is not a completely norm-governed event, and also to consider more complex contexts in which different norms and ideologies may co-exist in a given time frame, and several agents exert influence. These include the translator and the translation commissioner who have to decide whether to adhere to or contravene the normative or ideological practice. Anthony Pym proposes a distinction between active and passive translations to account for situations in which translations challenge or accept the validity of the previous translation.[7] Some examples of active translations are ones that update the discourse of a translation presumed to be 'dated' or correct a previous version.

In this chapter, we will examine Portuguese and Brazilian translations of *Pygmalion* and *My Fair Lady* and try to map changing social ideologies and literary norms by uncovering the translation strategies adopted for the translation of dialects and the role they were expected to play.

Translating dialects

The use of dialects is a powerful literary resource in the portrayal of characters and situations, one that conveys the sociocultural meanings associated with those dialects. These meanings, commonly understood by the readership, indirectly help to define the sociocultural outline of the character in addition to his/her position in the sociocultural fictional context. If dialects are

---

[6] Siobhan Brownlie, 'Narrative Theory and Retranslation Theory', *Across Languages and Cultures*, 7.2 (2006), 145–70.

[7] Anthony Pym, *A Method of Translation History* (Manchester: St Jerome, 1998).

intrinsically embedded in the source system, their use in a fictional work is also always imbued with a pragmatic and semiotic significance and is dependent upon the author's aesthetic, narrative, thematic or stylistic objectives.

The presence of dialects is a core device in *Pygmalion* and *My Fair Lady* not only because several characters speak Cockney (most prominently the main character, Eliza), but also because the link between dialects and the social fabric under scrutiny in the original play is one of its central topics. In translation, this produces an immediate tension between the foreign and the self for two main reasons: on the one hand, the translator is faced with the challenge of not having adequate resources in the target language to provide for an equivalent target text. In other words, the source language reflects a close relationship between the speaker, the medium and the context, which the target system and language might not be able to capture in a similar fashion.

On the other hand, the very little prestige attributed to dialects in most cultures has often led to dialects being excluded from written and literary discourse. Dialects are often explicitly censored by authors, translators or commissioners, who reject the idea of using less prestigious discourse in literature, or by institutional censors wishing to preserve the norm and its associated ideology. It is thus not surprising that the tendency for discourse standardization has often been identified in translated texts: most translations carry out an attenuation or complete elimination of the source text's linguistic variation. This is certainly true in the case of translated texts in Portugal and Brazil.[8]

Bearing all this in mind, plays such as *Pygmalion* and *My Fair Lady* are particularly relevant examples to help us uncover the ways translation participates in transnational movements of communication, influence and change in literary discourse. How have translators responded to the challenge of translating the Cockney dialect? Have they conformed to or gone against the norms and expectations of the target context? If the latter, why choose a strategy that risks rejection?

---

[8] See Vanessa Hanes, 'A Tradução de Variantes Orais da Língua Inglesa no Português do Brasil: Uma Aproximação Inicial', *Scientia Traductionis*, 13 (2013), 178–96; Kátia Hanna, 'Tradução do Dialeto Literário de Burma Jones, da obra *A Confederacy of Dunces* de John Kennedy Toole' (unpublished PhD thesis, Universidade de São Paulo, 2007); Sara Ramos Pinto, 'Tradução no Vazio: A Variação Linguística nas Traduções Portuguesas de *Pygmalion*, de Bernard Shaw, e *My Fair Lady* de Alan Jay Lerner' (unpublished PhD thesis, Universidade de Lisboa, 2010); Alexandra Assis Rosa, 'Tradução, Poder e Ideologia: Retórica Interpessoal no Diálogo Narrativo Dickensiano em Português (1950–1999)' (unpublished PhD thesis, Universidade de Lisboa, 2004).

I will examine both textual and paratextual elements. Translation strategies and patterns of behaviour in the translators' choices can be identified using textual elements, whereas paratextual and extratextual elements will enable us to investigate who was involved, what the finished product looked like, how it was marketed and received and, finally, to uncover the reasons behind the production of each new translation.

Pygmalion and My Fair Lady in context

For those unfamiliar with Shaw's *Pygmalion*, it is a comedy about a professor of phonetics (Professor Higgins) who makes a bet with his friend (Colonel Pickering) that in six months he can train a dishevelled Cockney flower girl (Eliza Doolittle) to pass for a duchess at an ambassador's garden party, by teaching her to assume a more genteel manner and what we might call 'impeccable' discourse. Eliza, unaware of the bet, embarks on this venture because speaking 'properly' will allow her to work in a flower shop. The play is a harsh satire on the rigid British class system of the day and a visible attempt to highlight the issue of women's independence. Central to the plot is the use of Cockney, a non-standard variety of British English and one of the main elements driving the play's social critique.

Pygmalion is one of Shaw's most important and best-known plays and one that received immediate approval from both audience and critics. Confirmation of this can be found in its many translations into different languages since it was first performed, in Vienna, in 1913, as well as its adaptations for film and musical theatre, most famously as *My Fair Lady*.[9] All these adaptations follow the original script very closely with one notable change: the ending. In accordance with Shaw's intended social critique and discussion of women's emancipation, at the end of the play, unexpectedly, Eliza and Higgins become friends. In the film and musical adaptations, on the other hand, Eliza has to surrender to romantic ideals and falls into his arms.

Even though *Pygmalion* was an instant success, its introduction into the Portuguese literary system only happened almost 20 years after the first publication of the play in London. In 1945 Shaw was still an unknown author to a Portuguese audience, despite the international success of his plays (particularly *Pygmalion*) and the Nobel Prize for Literature awarded

---

[9] The 1938 film version of *Pygmalion*, directed by Anthony Asquith and Leslie Howard, included extra material by Shaw. It won the Academy Award for Writing (now Best Screenplay) that year and formed the basis for the musical stage play *My Fair Lady* (1956) by Alan Jay Lerner (book and lyrics) and Frederick Loewe (music) and the film *My Fair Lady* (1964) directed by George Cukor.

to him in 1925. The social critique embedded in his plays along with his more openly socialist writings made him an author *non grata* for the Estado Novo dictatorial regime of the time, and a prime candidate for censorship. The fact that his works often included dialects made things even worse: his works were difficult to translate, and forced the translator to adopt a deviant discourse not well received by censorship or by readers. It was interpreted as 'bad Portuguese' and, therefore perceived as disconnected from written and literary discourse.

Given that there is not an established tradition of publishing drama in the Portuguese system,[10] it is perhaps not surprising that both *Pygmalion* and Shaw were introduced to the Portuguese repertoire via the stage, and not the medium of literature. Nor is it surprising that the romanticized and more toned-down version of the story found in *My Fair Lady* (which was more appealing to Portugal's gender conservatism at the time) was selected for publication before *Pygmalion*. The first translation of *Pygmalion* appeared in 1945, intended only for use as the script for a stage performance put on by brothers António and Francisco Ribeiro Lopes (also known as 'Ribeirinho').[11] In 1961, the play was translated again by Marina Prieto as part of her undergraduate dissertation during her studies at the University of Lisbon. There were only ever 500 copies of this translation and it was never made available in bookshops. In 1966, *My Fair Lady* was published for the first time by H. Silva Letra and Gervásio Lopes.[12] It was only in 1972 that *Pygmalion* was published in book form.[13] A reputable publisher, Editorial Verbo, invited well-known university lecturer Fernando de Mello Moser, to translate the play and publish it in the series 'Livros RTP, Biblioteca Básica Verbo' (RTP Books, Verbo Basic Library). This series was organized in partnership with the state television channel RTP in an attempt to bring major works of literature to all households in Portugal. Shortly afterwards, in 1974, director and television producer Artur Ramos decided to stage *Pygmalion* in Lisbon using a translation by Luís Francisco Rebelo and José Palma e Carmo, which is no longer

[10] Sara Ramos Pinto, 'Quando a Página e o Palco se Encontram', in *Depois do Labirinto: Teatro e Tradução*, eds Manuela Carvalho and Daniela di Pasquale (Lisbon: Nova Vega, 2012), pp. 213–50.

[11] Shaw, *Pigmalião*, translated by António Lopes Ribeiro (unpublished typescript, 1945). António Lopes Ribeiro was a famous director of theatre and cinema. His brother was a well-known comic actor who was also a respected theatre director and manager.

[12] Lerner and Loewe, *My Fair Lady, Comédia Musical em Dois Actos Baseada no Pygmalion de Bernard Shaw*, trans. H. Silva Letra and Gervásio Lopes (Lisbon: Portugália, 1966).

[13] Shaw, *Pigmalião: Romance em Cinco Actos*, trans. Fernando Mello Moser (Lisbon: Verbo, 1972).

available. Rehearsals started in the Maria Matos theatre, but the play was replaced at the last moment by a work by left-wing Portuguese playwright Bernardo Santareno. In the wake of the April 1974 Carnation Revolution, and the lifting of censorship, there was a move to stage plays that had previously been forbidden. *Pygmalion* was chosen for its veiled satire, and social and linguistic critique, but also because its international renown enabled it to bypass the censors. After the revolution, such tactics were no longer necessary and directors were eager to stage plays that had been forbidden mostly for their more direct social critique. This is, however, far from being the end of the story. In 1987, *Pygmalion* was translated again by Mário Abreu and published by Europa-América.[14] Then, in 2003, a new theatre production of *My Fair Lady* was staged at the Politeama theatre in Lisbon under the direction of Filipe La Féria and published in book form by Europa-América.[15]

In Brazil, the context is simultaneously very similar and very different: similar because the play was also introduced to the Brazilian repertoire through theatre; yet, very different because, even though Brazil experienced periods of dictatorship during the twentieth century, Shaw's socialist writings do not seem to have caused much concern to the censors there. In 1949, the publisher Melhoramentos acquired the rights to translate and publish all of Shaw's works and most of his plays and social writings were then published over the following decades. The first translation, however, had been done in 1942, by the famous actor and director Miroel Silveira.[16] His text was later published in 1955 by Melhoramentos and reprinted in 1964 by Delta as well as in 1971 and 1973 by Opera Mundi. The only other published translation of *Pygmalion* in Brazil was produced in 1995 by well-known comic writer Millôr Fernandes, and published by L&PM.[17] Interestingly, like Silveira, Fernandes had also completed his translation years earlier, for a performance of the play in 1963. Despite the fact that these are the only two published translations of the play, many adaptations have been produced for theatre, television series and *telenovelas*.

My Fair Lady was translated (by an unknown translator) and performed in Brazil in 1962, and again in 2007 using a translation by Claudio Botelho and directed by Jorge Takla. The same translation was used by Takla in 2017

---

[14] Shaw, *Pigmalião*, trans. Mário de Abreu (Mem Martins: Publicações Europa-América, 1987).

[15] Lerner and Loewe, *My Fair Lady, Minha Linda Senhora*, trans. Filipe La Féria and Helena Rocha (Lisbon: Publicações Europa-América, 2001).

[16] Shaw, *Pigmalião: Comédia em Cinco Actos*, trans. and adapt. Miroel Silveira (São Paulo: Melhoramentos, 1955).

[17] Shaw, *Pigmalião*, trans. Millôr Fernandes (São Paulo: L&PM, 2005 [1995]).

190 Sara Ramos Pinto

for a new production. Unfortunately, I have not managed to obtain these translations, so they have not been included in the corpus. Given that the focus of the chapter is on flows of influence, I will analyse only those translations that became known through theatre performance or wide publication, and I will do so in chronological order.

Textual and extratextual analysis

Pigmalião *(1945), by Francisco Ribeiro (Portugal)*

The textual analysis of this first Portuguese translation for the stage shows a clear preference for re-creating dialects in the target text and maintaining the harsh social critique of the source text. Elisa's outburst 'Ora amostre lá o que bocemecê 'screbeu de mim' ['You just shew me what you've wrote about me'][18] is a typical example of how the translator selected lexical, morphosyntatical and orthographic features generally perceived as being indicative of a low educational level and low social status.

The deviant orthography often followed shows the intention that the characters' spoken discourse on stage should also assume a non-standard pronunciation. For non-standard discourse to be spoken on stage is not unheard of in Portuguese theatre (canonical playwrights such as Gil Vicente (c. 1435–c. 1536) and Almeida Garrett (1799–1854) immediately come to mind), but for it to appear in a foreign play and to clearly serve the purpose of critiquing contemporary society was certainly, at the time, considered to be going against the norm.

Paratextual elements seem to support this assumption: the page-length reviews that appeared on three consecutive days in the *Diário Popular* (30–31 October 1945 and 1 November 1945) show that, despite the performance's very positive reception, the translation caused quite an uproar. Articles about translations were not usually to be found in newspapers, so the fact that this one received so much attention proves just how unexpected it was to hear non-standard discourse on stage at the time. One of those articles, which included an interview with the translator/director, conveys how carefully the translator placed this strategy in context, in order to avoid censorship. He explicitly presented Shaw as one of the canonical authors of English literature, along with others such as Shakespeare, and himself as a faithful servant of the author without the authority to do anything other than translate every word of the source text. Ribeiro was far from naive. However, positioning himself as a humble translator allowed him to build on the symbolic capital, i.e. the 'accumulated prestige, celebrity [and]

[18] Shaw, *Pigmalião*, trans. Ribeiro, p. 5; Shaw, *Pygmalion*, Act I, p. 14.

honour',[19] that English literature enjoys in the Portuguese system as well as on Shaw's international reputation, allowing him to secure the necessary permission from the censors to introduce to the country an author who had until then been conspicuously absent from Portuguese stages, bookshelves and university curricula. His tactic also seems to have secured a positive reception towards the presence of non-standard discourse on stage.

In this context, it is possible to conclude that behind this translation there was a clear intention to introduce Shaw to the Portuguese system and thus reinvigorate the country's theatrical repertoire. Furthermore, Ribeiro's translation represents an aim to renovate the performance of discourse on stage and challenge norms by opening it up to the different linguistic varieties one might hear in the streets, thereby making it less dominated by the standard variety.

Pigmalião *(1955 [1942]), by Miroel Silveira (Brazil)*
A similar attitude can be found in the first Brazilian translation, presented as a translation and an adaptation: the setting is transposed from London to Rio de Janeiro. In the words of the translator, who selected the text for translation and directed the performance, the challenge of translating dialects could only be overcome if the play were to be relocated to Brazil. Keeping the original setting would mean failing to transfer the social critique, since the action on stage would be too distant from the audience's lives. As a result, the linguistic variation was re-created in a similar manner to that found in the source text, using dialects from Rio de Janeiro. The translator employed lexical and morphosyntactical features as well as non-standard orthography markers generally perceived as indicative of a low educational level and low social status: 'Então esse cara é seu filho. Por que é que a madama não deu mais milhor educação pra êle?' ['Ow, eez ye-ooa san, is e? Wal, fewd dan y' de-ooty bawmz a mather should'].[20]

Silveira's introduction to the 1955 edition informs us that relocating the action to Brazil challenged the norm and the audience's expectations, leading some critics to express their dislike and leading the translator to justify his decision. In addition to affirming his status as an expert in English theatre and an established translator and director, Silveira builds on the symbolic capital of other translations (namely the French translation by Henriette and Augustin Hamon, which moves the play to Paris), and revered figures such as the author Mário de Andrade to support his decision: 'I followed the example

---

[19] Pierre Bourdieu, *The Rules of Art: Genesis and Structure of the Literary Field* (Stanford, CA: Stanford University Press, 1996), p. 7.
[20] Shaw, *Pigmalião*, trans. Silveira, p. 231; Shaw, *Pygmalion*, Act I, p. 11.

of the majority of the translators of *Pygmalion* into other languages, who were authorized to by Shaw. If something was lost as a result, it is not my fault – my conscience is clear, but also put to rest by Mário de Andrade. It is possibly our language's fault.'[21]

Despite the strange reaction it provoked, it is important to note that this was a well-received translation, which came to be published as a book and reprinted several times. The fact that Miroel Silveira was well-known to the Brazilian public as a reputable critic and director certainly contributed to the play's favourable reception. The fact that he is still seen today as one of the main promoters of change and renovation in Brazilian drama in the 1950s has reinforced the relevance and credibility of this translation and ensured its continued presence in bookshops.

Silveira's translation seems to play a similar role to Ribeiro's: it introduced *Pygmalion* and Shaw to the Brazilian system, renovating the theatre repertoire and marking a moment of social critique. I could not find any references to this translation strategy representing an act of defiance. However, given the conclusions drawn by previous studies (see note 10) regarding the tendency towards discourse standardization in Brazil, we can conclude that by including dialect Miroel Silveira was challenging the conventions of translated discourse, if not original literary discourse.

Minha Querida Senhora *(1966), translated by H. Silva Letra and* Gervásio Lopes *(Portugal)*

A very different attitude can be found in the first translation of *My Fair Lady* in Portugal. H. Silva Letra and Gervásio Lopes's translation shows a clear preference for discourse standardization and a softening of the social critique. The strong presence of dialectical discourse is reduced to a few oral discourse features, as we can see when Elisa says 'Então porque é que assentou as minhas palavras?' ['Then what did you take down my words for?'].[22]

This translation seems to confirm the target system norms. Despite bringing a new author and text to the Portuguese repertoire, it functions as a conservative force because it conforms to the existing practice and domesticates the foreign. The priority given to ensuring a successful and well-received translation is further confirmed by the fact that this is an edition that, for commercial purposes, builds on the symbolic capital associated with the 1964

---

[21] Shaw, *Pigmalião*, trans. Silveira, pp. 221–22. All translations into English are mine, unless otherwise indicated.

[22] Lerner, *Minha Querida Senhora*, trans. Letra and Lopes, p. 5; Lerner, *My Fair Lady*, Act I, p. 14.

film, as it includes a prominent picture of Audrey Hepburn, who played Eliza, on the cover.

Pigmalião *(1972), translated by Fernando Mello Moser (Portugal)*

Since the first translation of the play in book format was completed as part of an undergraduate dissertation, we can consider this second translation of *Pygmalion* to be the one that actually introduced *Pygmalion* and Shaw to the Portuguese literary system. We should also bear in mind that it had been performed on stage almost 30 years before, but only in three cities, and had therefore been limited to the audience members who could afford to purchase the theatre tickets. Shaw and his play were virtually unknown elements to wider Portuguese society and were not even recognized there as canonical elements in either English or world literature. It is, thus, quite surprising that this text was selected to be part of the 'Biblioteca Básica Verbo' series, which sought to make canonical world literature easily available to Portuguese readers. It is even more surprising that analysis of the text shows a clear intention to maintain dialects and to include Shaw's preferred ending. The translator employed lexical and morphosyntatical features generally perceived as indicative of a low educational level and low social status. There were few orthographic markers, but italics were used to mark the non-standard elements: 'Atão, pra que é que vossemecê se pôs a 'screver o que eu *dezia*?' ['Then what did you take down my words for?'].[23]

This is clearly a translation in defiance of the target system norms, and one that contributed towards the renovation of the literary canon as well as of the linguistic practices in written discourse. There is no translator's note included in the edition to confirm this conclusion, but in 1984 (ten years after the revolution), Moser published an essay commenting on his translation. In the essay he explains that he thought it essential to raise the profile of the playwright, and promote his innovative discourse and his social critique, as presented in the play. An informal email interview I conducted with the director of publishing house Verbo in 2006 confirmed the generally accepted view that this collection was ground-breaking, not just because it made essential authors and texts available at extremely affordable prices, but also because these were translations of canonical authors done by distinguished translators (Moser was a well-respected university lecturer, for example), which enabled the publisher to overcome censorship and publish something innovative at every level.

---

[23] Shaw, *Pigmalião*, trans. Moser, p. 6; Shaw, *Pygmalion*, Act I, p. 13. In 'correct' Portuguese this would be 'Então, para qué é que vossa mercê se pôs a escrever o que eu dizia?'.

Pigmalião *(1987), translated by Mário Abreu*

Building on the innovative path opened up by previous translations, Abreu's retranslation of *Pygmalion* uses a similar strategy of re-creation of dialect in a very different political and social context. As in the previous case, his Eliza boasts very distinctive speech in which it is possible to find frequent lexical, morphosyntatic and orthographic markers that distinguish her as non-educated: 'Atão pra que é que bossemecê estebe a escrever o que eu disse?' ['Then what did you take down my words for?'].[24]

After the 1974 revolution, censorship had been lifted, women had taken visible steps towards emancipation and social hierarchies had been shaken to the core. Attitudes towards dialects, as well as written and literary discourse, had also progressively changed making it more acceptable to find dialectical features in literature and written discourse in general. The effort to maintain Eliza's non-standard discourse in this translation does not constitute, therefore, an innovative move but one that confirms newly implemented discourse and translation practices that were increasingly becoming the norm. This, however, begs the question that if the purpose was simply to confirm practices, why commission a new translation?

According to the translator's note included in this edition, one reason was to update the discourse of the last translation, which by 1984 was considered outdated. According to an informal email interview with the director of the publishing house Europa-América in 2006, another motivation was that this was now considered to be a classic play by a canonical author. Knowledge of the play and its author was considered to be essential for a Portuguese audience that no longer had easy access to the out-of-print 1972 edition. In this sense, Abreu's translation confirms the central status of the author and play, which are still well-known in the Portuguese system but which could have been forgotten had the text disappeared from bookshops. The fact that it acknowledges the previous translation and updates it by employing similar strategies, whereby linguistic variation is preserved (without using italics as a safeguard), suggests that the practices of renewal introduced in the 1970s translation are accepted as the norm or, at least, as a more common practice.

Pigmaleão *(1963; 1995), translated by Millôr Fernandes (Brazil)*

While several translations of *Pygmalion* and *My Fair Lady* had been published or staged in Portugal by 1963, in Brazil there is a glaring gap between the first and the second translation of *Pygmalion*. Rather than relocating the action to Rio de Janeiro, Millôr Fernandes maintains the London setting in his Brazilian retranslation of *Pygmalion*, clearly showing an alternative attitude towards the

---

[24] Shaw, *Pigmalião*, trans. Abreu, p. 5; Shaw, *Pygmalion*, Act I, p. 13.

source text. The translator replaces Shaw's note about Eliza's appearance and demeanour, which appears after her third speech,[25] and includes an extensive note of his own explaining his choices: 'The translator warns that, clearly, it is impossible to translate cockney into Portuguese. [...] So he will try to create a language which, coming from nowhere, might suggest the idea of cockney, a kind of linguistic baseness that leads representatives of the elite to reject more intimate liaisons [...] with people of such ignorance.'[26]

Fernandes utilized lexical, morphosyntactic and orthographic features that anyone in Brazil would interpret as expressing a low level of education and low social status, as one can find in speeches such as: 'Mãe boa, hein, qui insina êssis modus pru filho; bota as fror tudo no artolero i corri sim nim pargá' ['Wal, fewd dan y' de-ooty bawmz a mather should, eed now bettern to spawl a pore gel's flahrzn than ran awy atbaht pyin'].[27] The main challenge was to find a way to re-create the dialect without using any specific Brazilian dialect, which might then promote an immediate incongruence between discourse and setting. The portrayal of the characters as uneducated and working-class is, however, also achieved through the insertion of additional lines and the exaggeration of certain comedic moments.[28] This strategy shows a clear intention to maintain Shaw's social critique, but also the need to update the discourse for a contemporary Brazilian audience. This illustrates a different type of textual intervention, but one that has also been overwhelmingly well received. Fernandes, known for his translations of Shakespeare, Chekhov and Molière, was a key figure in orchestrating that positive reception, a fact confirmed by the appearance of his name on the book's front cover.

Minha Linda Senhora *(2003), translated Filipe La Féria and Helena Rocha*
The most recent translation into Portuguese of Eliza's story to date was done in Portugal, by Filipe La Féria and Helena Rocha, who wanted to bring the now canonical musical *My Fair Lady* into the Portuguese repertoire. The translation was developed for both book publication and theatre performance,

---

[25] 'Here, with apologies, this desperate attempt to represent her dialect without a phonetic alphabet must be abandoned as unintelligible outside London', Shaw, *Pygmalion*, Act I, p. 11.

[26] Shaw, *Pigmaleão*, trans. Fernandes, p. 17.

[27] Shaw, *Pigmaleão*, trans. Fernandes, p. 16; Shaw, *Pygmalion*, Act I, p. 11.

[28] Luciane Dos Santos Fortes, 'Duas Traduções Brasileiras da peça *Pygmalion* de Bernard Shaw: Uma análise inicial a partir dos Estudos Descritivos da Tradução', *In-Traduções*, 3.4 (2011), 85–95 <http://incubadora.periodicos.ufsc.br/index.php/intraducoes/article/view/179> [accessed 23 January 2017].

something quite uncommon until the early 2000s.[29] It gave prominence to the name of the director of the performance, building on the success of the show and the director's symbolic capital. If we consider information from television interviews given by La Féria at the time of the première and the theatre programme, but also bear in mind that the last performance was 40 years earlier, in 1961, and that the 1966 book version was out of print, we can conclude that this translation was done to revive and revitalize *My Fair Lady* in both Portuguese theatre and its literary repertoire. The play was frequently referred to as a classic, as confirmed by the inclusion of the translation in a series entitled 'Great Classics of the Theatre'.

Distancing itself from the previous translation of *My Fair Lady*, the La Féria and Rocha version shows a clear preference for re-creating dialects in the target text and in the performance. In fact, there are many more non-standard features than in the source text, demonstrating clear support for a social critique that was also more visible than in the source text. Lines such as 'Deixe cá vegue essa poga. [...] Mas que gaio de gatafunhos mais asquesitos são estes?' ['You just shew me what you've wrote about me. [...] Whats that? That ain't proper writing'],[30] confirm that although *My Fair Lady* was usually presumed to be a 'lighter' version of *Pygmalion*, this translation seems to infuse the text with all of Shaw's original intentions. The discourse is more deviant and new lines have been introduced as a necessary step to update the play so that a twenty-first-century Portuguese audience could appreciate the social critique. This is particularly visible in the following passage:

> Senhora Eynsford-Hill: Pronto. Parou de chover. Já não precisamos de nenhum táxi. Vamos de autocarro, ouvistes, Clara?
> Higgins: Ouvistes?!!!
> Transeunte: Pela boca morre o peixe![31]
>
> [Mrs Eynsford-Hill: Very well. It has stopped raining. We no longer need a taxi now. We'll take the bus, Clara, do you hear me?
> Higgins: Do you hear me?!!!
> Bystander: Careful what you say! (Literally: fish are caught by the mouth.)][32]

---

[29] See Ramos Pinto, 'Quando o Palco e a Página se Encontram'.
[30] Lerner, *My Fair Lady*, trans. La Féria and Rocha, p. 5; Lerner, *My Fair Lady*, Act I, p. 15.
[31] Lerner, *My Fair Lady*, trans. La Féria and Rocha, p. 3.
[32] These lines have been added to the source text, so this is my translation.

This translation shows a clear intention to challenge the norms of discourse on stage in order, in turn, to challenge the audience and to recreate the intended impact of social critique. As the director explained in the programme notes:

> This *My Fair Lady* is less academic than the original, it's harsher and funnier, with Shaw's irony and worries underlined in red. By mounting it on the Portuguese stage, we are talking about Portugal too, our rich, our poor and our fake rich, who pretend to be rich but forget that 'pela boca morre o peixe', in other words, the way they speak betrays their true origins.[33]

Conclusion

Looking at all seven translations we can clearly identify two distinct groups: one in which translation strategies conform to the target context ideology and norms; and the other that adopts the opposite strategy in clear defiance of target context practices. It is also evident that the decision whether or not to re-create dialects is strongly mediated by particular contexts and the specific conditions necessary for translations to be more experimental. The paratextual analysis has shown that, despite the reputation and fame of both texts and authors, only established translators had enough symbolic capital to be able to publish translations that adopted challenging strategies such as re-creating Shaw's use of dialect. Such choices, however, need to be seen within a larger context. On the one hand, other agents from the series editor to the publisher will necessarily have been involved in the process of deciding to challenge existing practices. On the other hand, it is important to consider where these practices stand within a wider transnational context. The fact is that even though apparently unique and exceptional when examined within the national boundaries of Portuguese and Brazilian literatures and cultures, these alternative literary practices follow a more widespread Western trend in the 1960s and 1970s towards serious discussions about linguistic hierarchies, the standardization of literary discourse, distinctions between highbrow and lowbrow literature, and discourse's relationship with social inequality.[34] Translation was, thus, the gateway found by specific agents (translators, commissioners, etc.) to incentivize new dialogues with the 'foreign' and introduce new practices (and the ideologies behind them) by building on the symbolic capital of the source culture, text and author.

---

[33] Programme notes, Filipe La Féria, *My Fair Lady, Minha Linda Senhora* (Lisbon: Teatro Politema, 2003), p. 4.

[34] See Rosa; and Hanes.

I have used the translations of *Pygmalion* and *My Fair Lady* here as an illustrative example, but similar attitudes of challenge and flows of influence have been recognized in both the Portuguese and Brazilian systems in translations of Anglophone authors such as Charles Dickens, Mark Twain or Anthony Burgess.[35] One of the Brazilian translators of Mark Twain's *Huckleberry Finn* highlights her strategy to maintain the dialects in her translations as a deliberate choice in order to avoid subverting the literary work or 'civilizing' characters who were literally trying to set themselves free.

The influence from Northern European literary systems (such as the English or the French) seems obvious, but can flows of influence be identified within the Portuguese-speaking world? Considering that the Portuguese and Brazilian systems share part of their history and the same language, it is striking that Brazilian and Portuguese translators are unaware of each other's work. They all mention foreign translations or previous translations produced in the respective context, but pertinent solutions found in countries sharing the same language do not seem to be of relevance. This could simply be a case of translators only referring to those sources they found useful or supportive of their own choices; however, the fact that different translations are produced in each country and yet there is no cross-distribution seems to point to the fact that these are quite independent circuits of production and distribution and that the flows of influence from central European systems are much stronger than those within the Portuguese-speaking world. This is probably the result of a very nation-based idea of community and of the Portuguese language, which has only recently become more open.

Transnational approaches to literature and language highlight the need to consider the national while at the same time looking beyond national borders. The fact that much of that movement beyond borders happens through translation has highlighted the importance of examining global flows, circuits and exchanges through which cultures and texts travel, are translated and give way to new hybrid forms that, as a result, establish further avenues of communication and transnational flows of ideas, practices and people.

In this chapter, I have assumed translation to be a product of its context and highlighted the importance of scrutinizing the different dialogues that translation promotes between the cultures involved, the agents and ideologies participating in and mediating that dialogue and, finally, how such events and movements fit into larger flows of communication. Textual analysis has enabled us to identify the variety of translation strategies followed and conclude that these reflected either a tendency towards conformity with the dominant ideology or a tendency to challenge it. The latter clearly showed

[35] See Rosa; Hanes; and Hanna.

an active effort to innovate and challenge current practices and ideology regarding the use of dialects in literary discourse, social linguistic hierarchies and, to a certain extent, women's position in society. Both *Pygmalion* and *My Fair Lady* foreground the ways in which class politics mediates linguistic choices and challenges (through irony and humour) the social context behind the linguistic hierarchies it unveils throughout the play. Some of the abovementioned publications and performances aimed to import those elements to the Portuguese and Brazilian contexts with the clear intention of being disruptive and provocative and, through translation, offered examples of alternative literary practices as well as alternative discourses and social models.

The paratextual and extratextual analysis enabled us to contextualize the choices behind the strategies and examine the translators' motivations. It also helped us to understand that translation can, in specific contexts (institutional censorship, for example), be an authoritative voice which, by building on the symbolic capital of the text, author or source culture, can introduce alternative practices, voices and ideas.

This chapter has shown that while translation is a space of contact with the foreign and has the potential to disrupt canons and provoke a questioning of norms and traditions, it is also a space where distinctions between the domestic and the foreign become diluted and transnational flows of influence can be introduced.

11

The Duality and Ambiguity of Mega-Events in Rio de Janeiro

Local and Transnational Dimensions of Urban Transformations in the Webdocumentary *Domínio Público*

Tori Holmes

Queen's University Belfast

Just as the concept of the transnational has been attracting increasing attention in Modern Languages, it has also been a theme of research on so-called 'mega-events', defined by Maurice Roche as 'large-scale cultural (including commercial and sporting) events which have a dramatic character, mass popular appeal and international significance', usually organized by national governments in conjunction with international non-governmental bodies.[1] For Roche, mega-events such as the World Cup and the Olympic Games are 'systematically dualistic and thus ambiguous phenomena', which function along three main interlinked axes: the modern/non-modern, the national/non-national, and the local/non-local (or urban/mediated).[2] Mega-events are thus both nationally and internationally significant, and can be viewed from both historical and contemporary perspectives, since they have 'represented and continue to represent key occasions in which [...] a national past, present and future [...] could be invented and imagined not just by and for leaders and citizens of the host nation, but also by and for the publics of other nations'.[3] While the local dimension of mega-events offers opportunities for

---

[1] Maurice Roche, *Mega-Events and Modernity: Olympics and Expos in the Growth of Global Culture* (London and New York: Routledge, 2000), p. 1.
[2] Roche, *Mega-Events and Modernity*, p. 8.
[3] Roche, *Mega-Events and Modernity*, p. 6.

'concrete embodied spectatorship and participation', as well as the transformation and (re)branding of the urban setting(s) hosting the event,[4] it is also important to understand their status as media events and how both official and contestatory discourses about mega-events can be projected and amplified beyond the local via media technologies. Opposition to mega-events similarly combines 'a set of domestic determinants and dynamics, as well as an international enabling context'.[5] Overall, mega-events 'provide a political space in which the transnationalization of local issues and the localization of transnational dynamics occur simultaneously'.[6]

Modern linguists are well placed to contribute to the study of mega-events in non-Anglophone settings, given our ability to interpret such events, particularly their cultural manifestations, in the social, historical, political, and cultural context of a given host nation. Taking a transnational modern languages approach in turn allows for consideration of interactions and repercussions beyond the nation state.[7] In this chapter, I apply such a dual focus to the analysis of a Brazilian webdocumentary produced in response to Rio de Janeiro's recent hosting of the 2014 FIFA World Cup and the 2016 Olympic Games. The *Domínio Público* [*Public Domain*] project was set up in 2011 by Brazilian audiovisual collective Paêbirú Realizações Coletivas to investigate urban change linked to these mega-events, focusing particularly on the UPP (Police Pacifying Unit) public security initiative[8] and housing removals in Rio's *favelas*, the privatization of public space across the city, and associated popular resistance. After a successful crowdfunding campaign on Brazilian website Catarse in 2012, as part of which it circulated several short videos, the project released its feature-length documentary in June 2014 on the eve of the World Cup. The release had been delayed to allow the film-makers to include

[4] Roche, *Mega-Events and Modernity*, p. 10.

[5] Scarlett Cornelissen, '"Our Struggles Are Bigger than the World Cup": Civic Activism, State-Society Relations and the Socio-Political Legacies of the 2010 FIFA World Cup', *The British Journal of Sociology*, 63.2 (2012), 328–48 (p. 331).

[6] Richard Giulianotti and Susan Brownell, 'Olympic and World Sport: Making Transnational Society?', *The British Journal of Sociology*, 63.2 (2012), 199–215 (p. 206).

[7] Derek Duncan, 'Transnational', *Sound Cloud* (n.d.) <https://soundcloud.com/user-674977235/derek-duncan-transnational> [accessed 11 July 2017].

[8] The UPP scheme was initiated in December 2008, with the occupation of the Santa Marta *favela* in Rio's Botafogo neighbourhood. The aim of the initiative is to create 'a force-within-a-force', made up of new recruits without prior experience in the police, who receive training on human rights and community policing. See Adam Isacson and Observatório de Favelas, 'Pacification', in *The Rio de Janeiro Reader: History, Culture, Politics*, eds Daryle Williams, Amy Chazkel and Paulo Knauss (Durham, NC: Duke University Press, 2016), pp. 344–53 (p. 347).

footage of the Brazilian street protests of June 2013, known as the 'June Journeys', in the film. *Domínio Público* also included a range of 'paratextual' content,[9] notably a page on Facebook, which continued to post content about the documentary and its themes well into 2016. As its name suggests, a key feature of *Domínio Público* was an effort to circulate its outputs as widely and openly as possible; as well as being freely available online, its audiovisual outputs were disseminated via screenings, including outside Brazil.[10]

My analysis of *Domínio Público* pays attention to both its content ('meaning') and circulation ('motion').[11] I draw on work by Brian T. Edwards on the circulation of American cultural products in the Middle East and North Africa which combines close reading with data on circulation and 'uptake' gathered via fieldwork.[12] Edwards is sensitive to how digital culture constitutes 'a more complex circumstance' for cultural works than the analogue age,[13] which can involve unpredictability and fragmentation but also offer rich data on the relationship between texts and contexts, 'unsettl[ing] a more bounded or provincial sense of "the text"'.[14] Nonetheless, he strongly emphasizes the need for 'a balance of attention between moments of transnationally inspired cultural encounter and that which remains local and difficult to translate',[15] recalling Roche's characterization of mega-events as dualistic and ambiguous. In this chapter, I use the theme of language to structure my discussion of *Domínio Público*, focusing on how the project employs

[9] On the relevance of the term 'paratext' in media and cultural studies, see Jonathan Gray, 'Television Pre-Views and the Meaning of Hype', *International Journal of Cultural Studies*, 11.1 (2008), 33–49. On paratexts in webdocumentaries, see Siobhan O'Flynn, 'Documentary's Metamorphic Form: Webdoc, Interactive, Transmedia, Participatory and Beyond', *Studies in Documentary Film*, 6.2 (2012), 141–57.

[10] *Domínio Público* was screened in the UK, Austria, Switzerland, France and Argentina. For more on this, see Tori Holmes, 'Giving Visibility to Urban Change in Rio de Janeiro through Digital Audio-Visual Culture: A Brazilian Webdocumentary Project and Its Circulation', *Journal of Urban Cultural Studies*, 4.1–2 (2017), 63–85.

[11] See Brian T. Edwards, 'Tahrir: Ends of Circulation', *Public Culture*, 23.3 (2011), 493–504.

[12] See Brian T. Edwards, *After the American Century: The Ends of US Culture in the Middle East* (New York: Columbia University Press, 2016). My digital ethnography of *Domínio Público* involved 'following' content posted on the project's Facebook page; internet research into screenings and media coverage of the project; interaction and interviews via Facebook messaging, email, Skype and in person; participant observation at a screening; and close textual and visual analysis of relevant digital and audiovisual content.

[13] Edwards, *After the American Century*, p. 24.
[14] Edwards, *After the American Century*, p. 27.
[15] Edwards, *After the American Century*, p. 37.

interviews and archival content to communicate both local and transnational aspects of the mega-event conjuncture in Rio, how the project's approach to subtitling both facilitated and frustrated a transnational gaze and, finally, how the project's transnational reach has been amplified via coverage on English-language websites.

Given the focus of this volume, the chapter will also consider whether *Domínio Público* can be considered a 'transnational documentary' *per se*. This term, put forward in a 'Manifesto' on the same subject,[16] might initially seem to apply only to documentaries with an explicit and self-conscious transnational orientation or configuration (for example in subject matter, funding and/or production context); indeed, the authors refer to the emergence of 'new global documentaries'[17] as a counterweight to the growth of transnational media corporations. They also contrast the transnational mode of documentaries with another strategy for independent media production in a globalized context, namely a 'local' approach involving 'the use of small-format video by activist communities'.[18] Associating this movement with a 'search for a foundational identity', which can be progressive or regressive, they argue instead for a 'radical, communal transnational' approach that 'reject[s] a notion of the nation as an essentialist given' and encompasses films that 'supersede the opposition between the first and third world, between the center and the periphery'.[19] However, elsewhere in the 'Manifesto' Hess and Zimmerman observe:

> Films, videos, Web sites and CD-ROMs are emerging that operate within this new epistemological nexus – work that refigures the relationship between the local, regional, national and global as one of endless mediation, integration and negotiation rather than separation. It deploys multiple languages, hybridities and strategies to deconstruct the smoothness of the transnational and to unpack its sedimented layers with frissure [*sic*] and conflict.[20]

This more fluid and inclusive formulation allows for a potentially wider application of the term 'transnational documentary', as I will show here in relation

---

[16] John Hess and Patricia R. Zimmermann, 'Transnational Documentaries: A Manifesto', in *Transnational Cinema: The Film Reader*, eds Elizabeth Ezra and Terry Rowden (London and New York: Routledge, 2005), pp. 97–108.
[17] Hess and Zimmermann, 'Transnational Documentaries', p. 101.
[18] Hess and Zimmermann, 'Transnational Documentaries', pp. 102–03.
[19] Hess and Zimmermann, 'Transnational Documentaries', p. 103.
[20] Hess and Zimmermann, 'Transnational Documentaries', p. 100.

to *Domínio Público*. Although made by film-makers from and based in Brazil, and clearly focused on Brazil, this chapter will contend that there is some scope for approaching *Domínio Público* also as a transnational documentary, given the transnational dimensions of its subject, and that applying a transnational lens to the project can be productive, even if some aspects of the project remain resolutely embedded in its local setting.

Blending the local and the transnational: interviews and remediation

One way that *Domínio Público* communicates the binary nature of its subject matter is through interviews. Although the majority of those interviewed by the project are Brazilian, the feature-length version of the documentary includes an interview in English with US-based geographer David Harvey, as well as commentary in Portuguese by non-native speakers (the Austrian owner of a hostel in the Vidigal *favela* and the American geographer Christopher Gaffney). The interviews with the hostel owner and Gaffney are used to highlight local impacts of Rio's hosting of international mega-events – increases in property prices in *favelas* and temporary changes to local legislation required by FIFA respectively – although growth in *favela* tourism predates the mega-event conjuncture.[21] While Gaffney has long worked on Brazil, David Harvey offers a broader perspective, speaking about global trends in mega-event infrastructure development, and the financial consequences for host nations. Footage of these same two interviewees reappears towards the end of the film in the segment on the 2013 protests, when both comment on perceived parallels with protests in Turkey; we then hear Harvey speaking about global movements against inequality and capitalism as we view footage of the Brazilian protests. In this way, non-Brazilian interviewees are used to suggest a transnational context for the Brazilian protests.

This transnational context and the connection between the protests and the mega-event conjuncture have been debated in the academic literature. For Alonso and Mische, Brazil's hosting of mega-events was one of five factors that contributed to the protests; they consider this to be an 'internal' factor 'connected to the international scene', which 'brought a discussion of state priorities to the public sphere'. This discussion, across different media, 'generat[ed] a "discursive opportunity" to frame grievances in terms of a "FIFA standard" in public services'.[22] A second factor listed by the authors

---

[21] See Bianca Freire-Medeiros, '"I Went to the City of God": Gringos, Guns and the Touristic Favela', *Journal of Latin American Cultural Studies: Travesia*, 20.1 (2011), 21–34.

[22] Angela Alonso and Ann Mische, 'Changing Repertoires and Partisan Ambivalence

is explicitly transnational: perceived similarities with other 'anti-austerity, anti-autocracy and anti-inequality protests'[23] that had taken place in different countries over the preceding five years, including youth participation and use of social media, as well as a strong 'rejection of partisanship'[24] and an 'anti-institutionalist stance'.[25] Despite these similarities, however, there were also differences between the Brazilian protests and those in other locations. For example, Sotero emphasizes that unlike protests in Tunisia, Egypt, Turkey, and Libya, Brazilians were not (only) protesting against the national government but rather 'marching strongly against the policies of local and state administrations run by rival political parties'.[26] This included local impacts of transnational mega-events.

The other three factors identified by Alonso and Mische refer more directly to national socio-political circumstances: the weakening appeal of the left-wing Partido dos Trabalhadores (PT) government; the lack of effective channels and outlets for dialogue and mobilization by civil society and social movements under successive democratic governments that had incorporated social agendas into their programmes; and the widespread repudiation of heavy-handed violence used in protests in São Paulo against public transport price rises in early June 2013, which set in motion the larger, more broad-based protests seen later that month.[27] Overall, Alonso and Mische highlight both 'historical patterns' of national protest and 'broader trends in global protest' as influences on Brazilian protesters.[28] Here we see a blending of influences from different scales that again recalls Roche's designation of mega-events.

Brazilian interviewees in *Domínio Público* signal transnational dimensions of the mega-events at the same time as they stress the historical continuities of local urban transformations. Two topics manifesting this duality are public security policy and removals. In the feature-length film, civil policeman[29]

---

in the New Brazilian Protests', *Bulletin of Latin American Research*, 36.2 (2017), 144–59 (p. 147).

[23] Alonso and Mische, 'Changing Repertoires', p. 147.
[24] Alonso and Mische, 'Changing Repertoires', p. 145.
[25] Alonso and Mische, 'Changing Repertoires', p. 158.
[26] Paulo Sotero, 'Brazil's Stunted Revolt', *Georgetown Journal of International Affairs*, 15.1 (2014), 5–13 (p. 7).
[27] Alonso and Mische, 'Changing Repertoires', pp. 147–48.
[28] Alonso and Mische, 'Changing Repertoires', p. 145.
[29] There are different police forces in Brazil, with different remits. As Erika Robb Larkins explains, 'The civil branch is responsible for *investigating* crimes, while the military branch is responsible for maintaining public order and stopping *crimes in progress*' (original emphasis). See Erika Robb Larkins, 'Performances of Police Legitimacy in Rio's Hyper Favela', *Law & Social Inquiry*, 38.3 (2013), 553–75, (p. 562).

Orlando Zaccone quotes the book *Planet of Slums*[30] when arguing that the military occupation of poor urban areas in Rio is 'a transnational process'[31] with parallels to initiatives in Haiti, Colombia and the West Bank. Speaking about state-led initiatives in *favelas*, Alan Brum Pinheiro, a resident of the Complexo do Alemão *favela* and executive secretary of a local NGO, recalls a previous phase of urban change in the city, itself an event with transnational dimensions: the transfer of the Portuguese court to Rio in 1808, fleeing the arrival of Napoleon's troops in Lisbon. Scholarship has shown that the period of 13 years during which Rio served as the capital of the Portuguese empire, until 1821, was characterized by encounters and juxtapositions of different systems and practices, which 'were brought together in one city'.[32] Transitioning from slave port to the seat of imperial power, Rio underwent accelerated transformations, and moved towards economic independence and a heightened international profile.[33] In the documentary, Brum Pinheiro observes that there are parallels between how the Portuguese court went about 'modernizing' Rio in the nineteenth century and contemporary policies targeted at *favelas*: 'it is exactly the same institutions that arrive first. The police arrive, and the banks arrive. After that they think of other things.'[34] In relation to housing, interviewee Juca Kfouri, a sports journalist, compares removals in Brazilian World Cup host cities with those that took place in Cape Town around the 2010 World Cup, and other interviewees refer to previous phases of removals of the urban poor in Rio. These commentaries suggest that interventions associated with international mega-events need to be understood through Rio's history of urban change, itself shaped by both local and transnational forces.[35]

Domínio Público also communicates the binary nature of the mega-event conjuncture (in particular its national/non-national and urban/mediated characteristics) through its incorporation of archival material, both digital and analogue. This includes media content in languages other than Portuguese.

[30] Mike Davis, *Planet of Slums* (London: Verso, 2006).
[31] All translations are my own.
[32] Patrick Wilcken, *Empire Adrift: The Portuguese Court in Rio de Janeiro, 1808–1821* (London: Bloomsbury, 2005), p. 257.
[33] For more on this period and the changes it entailed, see Wilcken, *Empire Adrift*, and Kirsten Schultz, *Tropical Versailles: Empire, Monarchy, and the Portuguese Royal Court in Rio de Janeiro, 1808–1821* (London and New York: Routledge, 2001).
[34] Larkins has argued that this period continues to shape policing in Rio today. See Larkins, 'Performances of Police Legitimacy', p. 561.
[35] See Bruno Carvalho, 'Introduction – Rio, City of Epithets: Olympic Urbanism in Context', in *Occupy All Streets: Olympic Urbanism and Contested Futures in Rio de Janeiro*, eds Bruno Carvalho, Mariana Cavalcanti and Vyjayanthi Rao Venuturupalli (New York: Terreform, 2016), pp. 20–29.

The feature-length documentary displays a screenshot of an article from the online version of *The Sun* newspaper with the headline 'Riover and out' and the sub-headline 'Families' agony as 30,000 are evicted from their homes in £11bn slum facelift' as part of a segment on removals, and an article in Spanish from *El País Internacional* with the headline 'Brazil rises up in protest against the increase in transport prices' and sub-headline 'The protests come at a time of economic crisis, with high inflation and falling markets' appears towards the end of the film. Although relatively limited compared to the presence of Brazilian media content, the inclusion of international news highlights mediated dimensions of mega-events, especially the heightened interest in local issues from the international media during the mega-event period. As César Jiménez-Martínez has noted in his work on media coverage of the 2013 Brazilian protests, the contemporary media landscape is shaped by 'blurred boundaries between the local, the national and the transnational',[36] and 'access and interplay between images [of the nation] produced within and outside Brazil constituted an important characteristic of the media coverage during the June Journeys'.[37] Overall, *Domínio Público*'s borrowing from other media can be understood as a form of 'remediation',[38] which comments on and foregrounds the role of different types of media in Rio's mega-events and associated transformations. The example that follows combines digital and analogue content in a thematic sequence on public security. It thereby highlights the global context and forces shaping Rio's urban transformations, at the same time as it historicizes them in a local context.

In a sequence coming within the first ten minutes of the feature-length documentary, *Domínio Público* first presents old footage of Brazilian 'former billionaire' Eike Batista[39] being interviewed on the *Roda Viva* television programme in 2010.[40] The archival status of the footage is explicitly flagged

---

[36] César Jiménez-Martínez, 'Nationhood, Visibility and the Media: The Struggles for and over the Image of Brazil during the June 2013 Demonstrations' (unpublished PhD thesis, London School of Economics, 2017), p. 201.

[37] Jiménez-Martínez, 'Nationhood, Visibility and the Media', p. 204.

[38] Jay David Bolter and Richard Grusin, *Remediation: Understanding New Media* (Cambridge, MA: MIT Press, 2000).

[39] Eike Batista, 'once Brazil's richest man', was sentenced to 30 years in prison in July 2018 for bribery, when already under house arrest for other charges. In 2019 he was temporarily detained, then released, as part of ongoing corruption investigations in Brazil known as Operation Car Wash. See Mario Sergio Lima, 'Former Billionaire Eike Batista Released From Prison in Brazil', *Bloomberg* (11 August 2019) <https://www.bloomberg.com/news/articles/2019-08-11/former-billionaire-eike-batista-released-from-prison-in-brazil> [accessed 21 September 2019].

[40] This traditional interview programme, which involves interviewees responding

by the decision to show it playing on the *Roda Viva* channel on YouTube, on a computer screen. In the segment, Batista discusses his role in financing the UPP *favela* pacification scheme, alongside other partners like Coca-Cola and the Brazilian Football Federation (CBF), as well as transnational precedents for the UPP scheme (Rudy Giuliani's 'Zero Tolerance' policy in New York and public security policy in Medellín). After brief aerial footage of a *favela*, a second piece of archival material is introduced, this time a television advertisement for the UPP scheme, produced by the Rio state government, which is shown playing on a small, old-fashioned square television set in what appears to be a humble *favela* home. The advertisement combines a talking head interview with a UPP policeman and idyllic footage of everyday life in a *favela*, the latter accompanied by a samba soundtrack about the fight between good and evil (a version of 'Juízo Final' by Nelson Cavaquinho and Élcio Soares from 1973). There is then a cut to what appears to be original footage of a protest about police violence in a *favela*, now occupying the full screen with no intermediary framing, which shows protesters playing a funereal beat on percussion instruments as members of the crowd clap along, an installation/performance involving candles, placards bearing the names of victims, a person dressed in black lying down as if dead, and an activist speaking from a stage, above a banner saying 'NO MORE STATE VIOLENCE'.

The three components of the sequence establish a contrast between the official discourse and ideals of the UPP scheme and how it is promoted, and the reality in which historical patterns of policing and state violence in Rio persist, and generate protest. The sequence thus illustrates the intertwining of global and local elements in public security initiatives associated with the Rio mega-events, as asserted by anthropologist Erika Robb Larkins: 'Pacification depends on a new rationale – what I call the Olympic exception – for the same old variety of oppressive state action in the favela.'[41] While the use of 'frames within frames'[42] seen in this sequence was initially an improvised solution to deal with practical difficulties during production, it was eventually adopted as a feature of *Domínio Público*'s 'language',[43] because of the way it

---

to questions from journalists seated in a circle around them (hence the name, which can be translated literally as *Live Circle*), is broadcast weekly on the São Paulo-based public television channel TV Cultura.

[41] Erika Robb Larkins, *The Spectacular Favela: Violence in Modern Brazil* (Oakland: University of California Press, 2015), p. 139.

[42] Caitlin Manning and Julie Shackford-Bradley, 'Global Subjects in Motion: Strategies for Representing Globalization in Film', *Journal of Film and Video*, 62.3 (2010), 36–52 (p. 48).

[43] Fausto Mota (Paêbirú audiovisual collective), interview with Tori Holmes, 8 September 2014.

foregrounded the media as part of the film's subject matter, via a faceless character shown carrying out internet research and reading/viewing relevant material. It also allowed the film-makers to incorporate the voices of people that they were not able to interview directly, in such a way that the external origin of this material was clear.

Partial translation and a local visual literacy environment

Subtitling of digital audiovisual material, often by amateurs, has not yet been a very prominent subject for digital culture research,[44] but it is centrally important for ensuring that activist content is visible and accessible to viewers and activists in other places.[45] While there is not scope for an in-depth examination of subtitling in *Domínio Público*, some consideration of this aspect of the project can help in ascertaining whether or not the 'transnational documentary' nomenclature is appropriate.

Thanks to the efforts of volunteers, core elements of *Domínio Público*'s 2012 crowdfunding campaign were translated into languages other than Portuguese. The campaign video had subtitles in English, French and Spanish, and the core information about the project on crowdfunding site Catarse was also translated into the same three languages. The feature-length version of the documentary, from 2014, was initially released with subtitles in English and Spanish, with French, Italian and Portuguese added later, the latter to increase accessibility within Brazil. As Fausto Mota from Paêbirú told me, transnational visibility was considered an advantage by the film-makers because it could potentially boost interest at home: 'often achieving visibility abroad, attracting the attention of the foreign media causes more repercussion in Brazil, especially because the mainstream press here will not say anything about a film like ours.'[46]

Statistics from the Vimeo video platform, captured in May 2015 and sent to me by Paêbirú, confirm the transnational reach of the crowdfunding video with English subtitles, which was 'loaded'[47] over one million times by users in

---

[44] Luis Pérez-González, 'Amateur Subtitling as Immaterial Labour in Digital Media Culture: An Emerging Paradigm of Civic Engagement', *Convergence: The International Journal of Research into New Media Technologies*, 19.2 (2013), 157–75.

[45] Alexandra Crosby and Tanya Notley, 'Using Video and Online Subtitling to Communicate across Languages from West Papua', *The Australian Journal of Anthropology*, 25.2 (2014), 138–54; Mona Baker, 'The Prefigurative Politics of Translation in Place-Based Movements of Protest: Subtitling in the Egyptian Revolution', *The Translator*, 22.1 (2016), 1–21.

[46] Mota, interview, 8 September 2014.

[47] At the time, a 'load' on Vimeo was when 'the video player fully loads on any web

more than 150 countries, led by Brazil, the USA, Portugal, Germany and the UK. Data about the project's crowdfunding campaign available on Catarse shows that around 40 per cent of its funders listed their location as 'other' as opposed to a named Brazilian state (23 per cent listed Rio, and a combined 46 per cent listed states in the southeast region of Brazil – Rio, Espírito Santo, Minas Gerais and São Paulo; 22 other federal units were listed, meaning that only two Brazilian states were not represented). While the 'other' list is likely to include some funders who preferred not to disclose a location, review of the itemized list of crowdfunders shows that a small handful did list a location recognizable as being outside Brazil. Clearly the conclusions that can be drawn from this kind of data are limited, but the statistics showing the crowdfunding video was loaded outside Brazil combined with the evidence that there were some foreign-based crowdfunders indicate that the project reached a transnational audience, at the same time as it had strong appeal and resonance for domestic viewers, particularly those geographically close to Rio.

Nonetheless, there are other elements of the audiovisual outputs of *Domínio Público*, and particularly its paratextual content, that are not translated and that therefore potentially limit its designation as a transnational documentary. For example, updates about the project posted on Catarse during and after the campaign were only available in Portuguese,[48] as was the information on Paêbirú's own website,[49] although the title of the page (the same as the title of the video on Vimeo), hints at the possibility of other languages: '*Domínio Público* / Public Domain – Full – With Subtitles'. The extensive content posted on the project's Facebook page is also almost entirely in Portuguese, except on the rare occasions when third party content in another language has been shared (for example about screenings outside Brazil). The transnational label is therefore harder to justify when *Domínio Público* is understood as a multifaceted webdocumentary project, rather than just a film.[50] Despite the film-makers' efforts to make available subtitled

---

page, either on vimeo.com or wherever the video is embedded'. This was different to a 'play', which was when 'someone starts to play a video'. Information from: <https://help.vimeo.com/hc/en-us/articles/224822287-What-is-the-difference-between-an-impression-and-a-play-> [accessed 20 September 2018]. 'Loads' are now known as 'impressions' and 'plays' as 'views', see <https://vimeo.zendesk.com/hc/en-us/articles/115004386887-Video-Manager-analytics-panel> [accessed 21 September 2019].

[48] <https://www.catarse.me/dominiopublico#posts> [accessed 20 September 2018].

[49] Previously available at: <http://www.paebiru.com/dominiopublico> (domain no longer active).

[50] See Elizabeth Coffmann, 'Spinning a Collaborative Web', in *New Documentary Ecologies: Emerging Platforms, Practices and Discourses*, eds Kate Nash, Craig Hight and Catherine Summerhayes (Basingstoke: Palgrave Macmillan, 2014), pp. 105–23.

versions of the project's main audiovisual outputs, and their stated interest in attracting international attention to the issues portrayed in *Domínio Público*,[51] the project's non-audiovisual digital paratexts largely escaped translation and thus remained accessible only to Portuguese-speaking audiences. The transnational aspects of the project were thus more static than its local paratextual flows, which continued to be generated and circulated after the release of the feature-length film, suggesting an 'afterlife'.[52] At the same time, it is important to recognize the burden of translation and how this could slow down and complicate a project such as *Domínio Público* if absolutely all its content were to be translated, unless planned and resourced from the outset.

Other features of *Domínio Público*'s audiovisual outputs themselves also potentially complicate full access by a non-local audience. Both the short and feature-length versions of *Domínio Público* are notable for containing a large amount of written Portuguese throughout, in footage of official signs (often for infrastructure and construction works), graffiti and street art, cartoons, t-shirts, online news articles, websites, social media content, protest placards and banners, and even a business card (Figure 11.1). The marked presence of a 'visual literacy environment'[53] offers traces of literacy practices in varied arenas relating to the mega-event conjuncture (regulatory, commercial, vernacular, contestatory). This reveals how written language is central to divergent discourses and activities relating to urban transformations and mega-events, whether those of the authorities and contractors promoting them, or those of actors engaged in oppositional practices. Indeed, *Domínio Público* suggests that language is a realm in which disputes between these groups are played out.

These written texts are sometimes translated in subtitles, and sometimes not; even when they are translated this is often only partial. In *Domínio Público*, there is an attempt to subtitle the most important elements of written language (for example, the headlines of news articles tend to be translated, but not the sub-headlines or extracts shown on screen), but when written texts appear on screen at the same time as an interviewee is speaking, priority is given to the speaker. In the project's crowdfunding

---

[51] For example, in the crowdfunding video, Raoni Vidal, one of the film's directors, makes an appeal to potential crowdfunders, saying 'The whole world needs to know about the injustices committed against the Brazilian people'.

[52] Janet Harbord, *Film Cultures* (London: SAGE, 2002), p. 5. For more on *Domínio Público*'s 'afterlife', see Holmes, 'Giving Visibility'.

[53] David Barton and Mary Hamilton, *Local Literacies: Reading and Writing in One Community* (London: Routledge, 1998), p. 42.

Local and Transnational Dimensions of Urban Transformations 213

Figure 11.1. Activist graffiti on a promotional hoarding for construction work relating to the Rio Olympics. Still taken from *Domínio Público* crowdfunding video, 2012. Producer: Paêbirú Realizações Coletivas. Directed by Fausto Mota, Raoni Vidal and Henrique Ligeiro.

video, this means, for example, that during an interview with former footballer and then federal deputy (now senator) Romário, a newspaper front page in Portuguese on overspending on World Cup stadia is shown without any translation at all. Later, during an interview with Rio politician Marcelo Freixo, footage of a newspaper headline on political intimidation by militias (paramilitary groups), and an official sign for the TransCarioca highway stating 'The city government is building a more developed, fairer and more integrated Rio', are not translated. The end of the Freixo audio is followed on screen by footage of several more news items about Eike Batista's funding of the Rio 2016 bid and a contract being awarded without tender to a supporter of Rio mayor Eduardo Paes's campaign; this time, as no-one is speaking, the headlines are translated.

As Stefan Solomon has pointed out in relation to Brazilian documentary *Proxy Reverso* (Guilherme Peters and Roberto Winter, 2015), which is filmed on a computer desktop and made up entirely of digital content, a complete approach to subtitling can 'add another layer of text to an already crowded screen' and leave the viewer in 'doubt over which are the most important words and images on the screen'.[54] In *Domínio Público*, there are occasions when understanding – or even just recognizing the relevance of – the textual content of a particular shot is arguably not essential for following the narrative thread (such as when interviewees appear wearing t-shirts with written language on them), but in other cases, the textual content can add extra layers of meaning. For example, in a sequence showing footage of a July 2013 protest against police violence in the Maré *favela* in the feature-length documentary, subtitles are given for the funk song being performed live and for the chants by protesters, but not for the intertitle saying what the event is, nor for the placards shown. Here again the human voice is given priority over written language in the approach to subtitling. Although the project demonstrably achieved transnational reach without being fully subtitled, the dominance and recurrence of written language in the films suggests this is an integral part of its narrative on urban transformations, and particularly important for understanding their local dimensions. The linguistic and socio-cultural expertise of Modern Languages scholars can be crucial in accessing and interpreting this type of textual data, contributing an additional layer of analysis.

---

[54] Stefan Solomon, 'Two Ways of Filming a Crisis: Brazilian Political Cinema Today', *Lola*, 7 (2016) <http://www.lolajournal.com/7/brazil.html> [accessed 2 January 2017].

Transnational amplification through a 'bridgeblog'

Translation was also central to another mechanism for amplifying the transnational visibility of *Domínio Público*. Content about the project appeared on RioOnWatch, a project set up in 2010 'to bring visibility to *favela* community voices in the lead-up to the 2016 Olympics'.[55] From 2010 to 2016, it published 'the perspectives of community organizers, residents, international observers, and researchers on the fast-paced urban transformations that characterized pre-Olympic Rio'; a broader editorial line was adopted in 2017.[56] The project also uses social media platforms, such as Twitter, to disseminate its content. Although not a blog in the strict sense, RioOnWatch can be understood as an example of 'bridgeblogging', a practice that aims to 'reach across gaps of language, culture and nationality to enable interpersonal communication', producing content that is 'intended to be read by an audience from a different nation, religion, or culture'.[57] I suggest here that, following Dayan, it can also be termed a 'visibility entrepreneur', a citizen initiative that contests and questions the hegemony of the mainstream media in 'conferring visibility' in the public sphere.[58] In this case the visibility is that of *favelas*, stigmatized urban spaces often represented with reference to negative stereotypes of crime, violence and poverty.[59] According to Bailey et al, 'new media outlets and organizations' such as RioOnWatch 'helped to bring a number of previously unexamined questions to the attention of the international media' before and during the Rio mega-events.[60]

RioOnWatch published an article mentioning *Domínio Público* in June 2013, and a series of tweets about a screening of the documentary in August

---

[55] RioOnWatch, 'About', *RioOnWatch* (2014) <http://www.rioonwatch.org/?page_id=14992> [accessed 5 July 2017].

[56] RioOnWatch, 'About', n.p.

[57] Ethan Zuckerman, 'Meet the Bridgebloggers', *Public Choice*, 134.1–2 (2008), 47–65 (p. 48).

[58] Daniel Dayan, 'Conquering Visibility, Conferring Visibility: Visibility Seekers and Media Performance', *International Journal of Communication*, 7 (2013), 137–53 (p. 144).

[59] For more on this, see Silvia Ramos and Anabela Paiva, *Mídia e violência – Novas tendências na cobertura de criminalidade e segurança no Brasil* (Rio de Janeiro: IUPERJ, 2007); Janice Perlman, *Favela: Four Decades of Living on the Edge in Rio de Janeiro* (Oxford: Oxford University Press, 2010).

[60] Kyle Bailey, Robert Oliver, Christopher Gaffney and Korine Kolivras, 'Negotiating "New" Narratives: Rio de Janeiro and the "Media Geography" of the 2014 FIFA World Cup', *Journal of Sport and Social Issues*, 41 (2017), 70–93 (p. 84). See also Jiménez-Martínez, 'Nationhood, Visibility and the Media'.

2015. The project was not the main focus of the article, but it was mentioned as part of a text about the activities of the *Favela Não Se Cala* [*Favelas* Won't Keep Quiet] social movement, which later featured in *Domínio Público*. The article highlights the importance of audiovisual and media production in activism against negative social impacts of mega-events in Rio: 'Photographers and videographers flitted about the discussion circle, including the crew of *Dominio Público* [sic], the investigative project currently being filmed about the privatization of Rio. *Favela* residents shared their experiences of state policy toward their communities and efforts to counter some of those policies.'[61] The words *'Domínio Público'* contain a hyperlink to the project's crowdfunding video on Vimeo, albeit the version without subtitles.

In August 2015, one of the Twitter accounts managed by RioOnWatch, known as RioOnWatch Wire (an 'English-language hourly newswire service on and from Rio's favelas'),[62] posted a series of tweets directly or indirectly about a screening of *Domínio Público* in the Rio neighbourhood of Lapa, over several days, before, on, and after the day of the screening.[63] The first tweet, on 8 August, prefaced by the word 'EVENT' in capitals, announced the screening of *Public Domain* (using its English title), a film about 'transformations brought about by mega-events', with an abbreviated link to the event page on Facebook. Later the same day, a second tweet beginning with the word 'BACKGROUND' stated 'Discussion following the #film screening will feature #VilaAutódromo resident MariaDaPenha among others.' The tweet also included a photo of Penha, an activist against removals from Rio's west zone, close to the Olympic Park, with blood on her face after a confrontation with police. Two days later, on 10 August, the first tweet, beginning 'EVENT' was repeated. It was immediately followed by two further 'BACKGROUND' tweets, this time with different content. The first mentioned another documentary about the impact of the World Cup on women in Rio, linking to an interview with its director on the RioOnWatch website (in English). The second stated 'Favela residents have a rich tradition as producers and subjects of #film', and linked to the '#film' tag on the RioOnWatch website. On 11 August, there was another tweet announcing the screening, again accompanied by the flyer, stating 'EVENT tomorrow...'. The background tweet about films by/about *favela* residents was repeated, and two further tweets about the importance

---

[61] Catherine Osborn, 'Favela Não Se Cala Continues Mobilizing Awareness in Providência & Horto', *RioOnWatch* (2013) <http://www.rioonwatch.org/?p=9116> [accessed 5 July 2017].

[62] See <https://twitter.com/rioonwire> [accessed 20 September 2018].

[63] See Holmes, 'Giving Visibility', for a discussion of other aspects of that screening, which I attended in person.

of public space in Rio may have been intended as background to the screening tweets, but this is not clear due to other stories covered the same day. The tweet posted on 12 August, the day of the screening, was almost identical to previous posts advertising the event, but included the word 'NOW' rather than 'EVENT'. This was again followed by the background tweet on *favela* residents as producers/subjects of films. Further tweets on this day about the port area and the high price of World Cup tickets may also have been intended as background to the screening, but again this is not clear. Finally, on 13 August, the day after the screening, a recap tweet was posted stating 'Yesterday saw #PraiaDoSossego families forcibly #evicted and "Public Domain" #film screening.'

An article on Catalytic Communities' website about RioOnWire provides some context and rationale for these tweets in English, stating that the initiative, which ceased activities at the end of August 2016, sought to post 'hourly content on favelas, mega-events, public policy and urban developments in Rio de Janeiro'.[64] Described as a 'carefully manicured Twitter feed' targeted at international journalists, the aim was to provide a 'traditional English-only Wire service' combining 'the latest and breaking *favela* stories in Rio' and 'follow-up posts after each providing contextual depth'. In line with the overall objectives for RioOnWatch, the aim of the service was to 'reduce stigmatizing and superficial reads on Rio and increase the amount of helpful coverage'. In addition to covering news *per se*, the account 'served as a platform for announcing positive community news and local events', like the screening of *Domínio Público*. In the almost complete absence of 'likes' and 'retweets' of the tweets about the event, however, it is difficult to ascertain whether this sequence of tweets did generate any journalistic coverage of *Domínio Público* or the issues it raises, or whether it informed the media in other ways. Nonetheless, the tweets constituted an attempt, by a group other than the documentary's original makers, to amplify its visibility beyond the local setting, and to an English-speaking audience.

Conclusion

As my analysis has shown, *Domínio Público* includes both national and non-national, local and non-local (urban and mediated), and modern and non-modern elements in its portrayal of Rio's preparations for hosting the 2014 World Cup and 2016 Olympics. The composition of the webdocumentary,

---

[64] Catalytic Communities, 'RioONWire Favela News Wire Wraps Up 17 Months of Hourly Coverage', *CatComm* (2016) <http://catcomm.org/rioonwire-wraps-up/> [accessed 6 July 2017].

therefore, mirrors the dualistic and ambiguous nature of mega-events set out by Roche. The 'transnational documentary' label proposed by Hess and Zimmerman fits some aspects of the project and allows for 'mediation, integration and negotiation rather than separation' between different geographical scales,[65] in keeping with its subject matter. Nonetheless, *Domínio Público* is not just a transnational documentary and cannot be reduced to this term, which effaces the local embeddedness of the project and its response to the mega-events, and does not account for elements – such as its many digital paratexts, and prominent use of written texts within audiovisual outputs – which cannot travel so easily or be translated. The project's approach to its international visibility can itself be understood as dual and ambiguous, simultaneously facilitating the access of transnational audiences to its audiovisual outputs through subtitling, while potentially limiting full non-local access to the additional detail and nuance contained in elements of the project available only in Portuguese, including the updates published after 2014. In this way *Domínio Público* serves to highlight that the tensions and conflicts surfaced by the transnational mega-events in Rio have a long local and national history and will continue to make themselves felt long after the international spotlight has shifted to other locations.[66]

---

[65] Hess and Zimmermann, 'Transnational Documentaries', p. 100.

[66] See Julia Michaels, 'Não interessa mais', *Revista Piauí* (2017) <http://piaui.folha.uol.com.br/nao-interessa-mais/> [accessed 12 July 2017]; Cornelissen, '"Our Struggles Are Bigger than the World Cup"'.

Part III

Temporality

12

Mining Memory's Archive

Two Portuguese Documentaries about the Second World War

Ellen W. Sapega
University of Wisconsin, Madison

In 1949, José Cardoso Pires published a story titled 'Amanhã, se Deus quiser' ['Tomorrow, God Willing']. This short text that recounts the grim experiences of a working-class family in Lisbon during the years of the Second World War was among the first publications by a writer who would become one of the strongest voices in the development of the novel in Portugal during the second half of the twentieth century. Diverging from neo-realist models that had shaped Portuguese literature in the previous decade, Cardoso Pires began his literary career with a series of tersely dispassionate narratives that blurred the lines between cause and effect, inviting the reader to enter the play of fiction.[1] While the characters in the story 'Tomorrow, God Willing' never explicitly mention the war, their comments, together with several descriptive elements included by the first-person narrator, alert the reader to a wider international context in which the protagonist experiences his present as a frustrated time of waiting for political change, the possibility of which is clearly outside the realm of his own power or volition.

The 1949 version of this story obliquely references government-imposed rationing policies, the high cost of food and medical items, and a pervasively

---

[1] The story first appeared in *Os caminheiros e outros contos* (Lisbon: Centro Bibliográfico, 1949). An English translation by Giovanni Pontiero, entitled 'Tomorrow, God Willing', is published in *Passport to Portugal*, eds Mike Gerrard and Thomas McCarthy (London: Serpent's Tail, 1994), pp. 90–99. All other translations into English are my own unless otherwise stated. See also Sílvia Oliveira, 'The Non-Sense of an Ending: José Cardoso Pires and the Neorealist Short Story in Portugal', *Romance Quarterly*, 57.3 (2010), 231–42 (p. 237).

corrupt network of patronage. A reworked version that Cardoso Pires published more than a decade later describes the difficulties of this time in even greater detail: through the addition of a number of interpolated passages, the narrator also alludes to the prevalence of Nazi-type emblems and ceremonials, a blackout enforced by 'os legionários da Defesa Civil' ['the Civil Defense legionnaires'], and the sound of Big Ben as a neighbour, illegally, tunes into the wartime BBC broadcast.[2] These additions, which situate the story in a more explicit historical context, might lead us to conclude that by 1963 Cardoso Pires, and other Portuguese like him, had achieved a sufficient distance from the lived events of the war years to begin an assessment of that time and to evaluate its impact on the collective imagination. This was not the case, however; in fact, Cardoso Pires's short story is something of an anomaly, one of only a handful of literary texts that explicitly reference Portuguese experience during the Second World War.

Mentions of daily life in wartime Lisbon are notable for their absence from Portuguese literature and art both in the 1940s and during the subsequent decades. At a time of great mobility, when refugees, exiles, and spies crossed multiple national borders, the Portuguese capital constituted a neutral space where diverse populations would mix, often on a daily basis. Although the city and its environs experienced a cosmopolitan moment that was unprecedented, perhaps, since the sixteenth century, cultural production in Portugal tended not to reflect a view of Lisbon as a place of transit or a temporary home for diverse populations seeking to flee or to profit from the war. Reticence about Lisbon's importance as an international crossroads might be explained, in part, as the result of the Portuguese government's prevailing culture of censorship and nationalist propaganda. Signs of the war that raged in Europe were common throughout the capital city, and fears of its impending violence were widespread, yet a significant number of events associated with the conflict were difficult for Lisbon's residents to interpret, due to the limited access to information allowed by their government. Since the early 1930s, restrictions had been placed on free expression, and the state's well-oiled propaganda machine promoted a decidedly nationalist image of Portugal as a racially and culturally homogenous place where the shared values of 'Deus, Pátria e Família' ['God, Fatherland, and Family'] united its citizens and protected them from external demands.

If writers and artists working in the 1940s found it difficult to openly address the topic of the war, the continued silence about that epoch in the

---

[2] The revised version of the Cardoso Pires story was reprinted in *Jogos de azar* (Lisbon: Arcádia, 1963). See also Robin Warner, 'Narration as Critique in Some Short Stories of José Cardoso Pires', *Romance Quarterly*, 39 (1992), 361–71 (p. 363).

decades that followed might be ascribed to renewed government repression in its wake. The Second World War constituted a historical watershed for much of the world, with its end ushering in significant cultural and political changes across Europe, Asia and Africa. The Portuguese situation was barely altered, however, much to the chagrin of the opponents of Salazar's Estado Novo [New State]. At a moment when the European allied powers were taking steps towards decolonization, Portugal's imperial ethos was strengthened and discursively repackaged, cloaked in a new semantic terminology that rebranded its colonies as 'overseas provinces'. At the same time, laws aimed at circumventing the free circulation of information were tightened in the 1950s and 1960s, and strict censorship of the press and other media remained in effect until the fall of the regime in April 1974.[3] In the aftermath of the war, there was no public space in Portugal in which the experience of the previous decades could be openly discussed or analysed. For many throughout Europe and beyond, the events surrounding the Second World War gave rise to a sort of transcultural memory that would unfold across and beyond cultures.[4] In Portugal, the confines of national boundaries remained officially closed and much information about the war years became virtually inaccessible. To speak of the transnational would constitute a challenge to the state's authoritarian doctrine; to extol it could be deemed a traitorous act.

More recently, however, Portuguese writers, historians and film-makers have begun to revisit the war years in order to expose the dynamics of ignorance that the regime had promoted. Works such as those by Marina Tavares Dias (*Lisboa nos anos quarenta: longe da Guerra* (1996)) and Irene Flunser Pimentel (*Judeus em Portugal durante a Segunda Guerra Mundial* (2006)) and João Madeira, Irene Flunser Pimentel and Luís Farinha (*Vítimas de Salazar: O Estado Novo e a violência política* (2007)) began to remedy this situation through the creation of an archive of memories and documentary evidence about the Second World War that, until, quite recently, was not available in Portugal.[5] In the present essay, I look at two documentary films

---

[3] See A. H. de Oliveira Marques, 'Until 1949, the regime undoubtedly faced a serious crisis. Many people expected the Allies to adopt, in regard to Portugal, the boycott policy they were using in regard to Spain... At home there was uneasiness, many rumors, aborted conspiracies, and increasing repression. Schoolteachers and university professors were being fired. The concentration camp at Tarrafal (Cape Verde Islands) reopened its gates for the first political prisoners, most of them Communists or Communist sympathizers.' *History of Portugal*, 2 vols (New York: Columbia University Press, 1972–76), II, p. 218.

[4] Astrid Erll, 'Travelling Memory', *Parallax*, 17.4 (2011), 4–18 (p. 9).

[5] Marina Tavares Dias, *Lisboa nos anos 40: longe da guerra* (Lisbon: Quimera, 2005); João Madeira, Irene Flunser Pimentel and Luís Farinha, *Vítimas de Salazar:*

that put this archive to public use as they reassess 1930–40s Portuguese culture from standpoints that mesh the personal and the collective.[6] Daniel Blaufuks's DVD of 2002 titled *Sob céus estranhos* [*Under Strange Skies*][7] and a more recent film, *Fantasia Lusitana* [*Lusitanian Fantasy*] (2010), by João Canijo, ask viewers to revisit the epoch and to question the Portuguese leader's motives for maintaining neutrality during the Second World War. As they implicate Salazarism in ethical debates about knowledge and ignorance, or action and inaction, these films serve as correctives for the collective act of 'forgetting', which the state actively encouraged after the war.

Blaufuks and Canijo explicitly place questions of mediation at the centre of their revisitation of a collective past by making use of public images and shared narratives of national identity. They do so, however, in very different ways. Both film-makers acknowledge the temporal distance that separates them from the era they depict. Canijo and Blaufuks are, in this sense, products of the 'generation after'.[8] In their attempts to connect the viewer to the past by means of images and stories – photographs, films, documents and narratives – their work demonstrates the awareness that modern memory is both highly mediated and dependent on a variety of national and transnational sources. They juxtapose multiple examples of the Estado Novo's nationalist propaganda with other archival elements to draw attention to the transnational flows that impacted Portuguese experience at that time. As they draw upon these sources, their films display several of the dimensions of movement that Astrid Erll identifies as central to the dynamics of travelling memory.[9]

Born in Lisbon in 1963, Daniel Blaufuks is the grandson of a German Jewish couple who moved to Portugal in April 1936. In his film (Figure 12.1), he strives to recall his grandparents' experience and to preserve their memories. As this

---

Estado Novo e Violência Política; (Lisbon: Esfera dos Livros 2007); Irene Flunser Pimentel, *Judeus em Portugal durante a Segunda Guerra Mundial* (Lisbon: Esfera dos Livros, 2006). Other books that have added to this archive include: Irene Flunser Pimentel and Cláudia Ninhos, *Salazar, Portugal e o Holocausto* (Lisbon: Temas e Debates, 2013); Filipe Ribeiro de Meneses, *Salazar: A Political Biography* (New York: Enigma Books, 2009–10); and Neill Lochery, *War in the Shadows of the City of Light, 1939–1945* (New York: PublicAffairs, 2011).

[6] Susan Rubin Suleiman, *Crises of Memory and the Second World War* (Cambridge, MA: Harvard University Press, 2006), p. 8.

[7] This DVD is included in the volume of memories and photographs of the same name (2007). Images and texts from the book can be accessed at: <http://www.danielblaufuks.com/> [accessed 9 September 2018].

[8] Marianne Hirsch, 'The Generation of Post-Memory', *Poetics Today*, 29.1 (2008), 103–28 (p. 105).

[9] Erll, 'Travelling Memory', p. 12.

personal story begins, the video presents a silent opening sequence in which the camera pans a view of a cemetery in which we see graves inscribed with names written in Hebrew. Appearing on screen even before the title credits, these silent images constitute a mnemonic form that evokes the trauma of the Holocaust.[10] The film-maker draws here upon what Erll has referred to as the 'cultural content' of transcultural memory in which shared images and narratives are subject to ongoing interpretations and renewal.[11] It is disconcerting, therefore, when the narrator's voice-over identifies and locates the graveyard in Lisbon. Explaining that he recognizes almost all of the names inscribed on the tombs, Blaufuks describes the space as a sort of 'village cemetery' and adds that of the '50 to 200 thousand people who passed through Lisbon, only 50 remained here'. This opening sequence not only provides information that partially explains why memories of the Jewish presence in wartime Lisbon could be all but erased from the national imagination after 1945. It also inserts Portugal and its history into a story or stories of transnational dimensions.

Blaufuks then turns his attention to reconstructing his grandparents' story, recounting their 1936 departure from the German city of Magdeburg and their arrival a week later in Lisbon. Throughout the video, the narrator incorporates excerpts from his grandfather's letters and diaries (read in the original German) and supplements them with his own recollections of events that he witnessed as a child or of stories that were passed down to him. The images that accompany this text include family photographs and letters, as well as slow-motion footage, much of it out of focus, evidently taken from home movies made when Blaufuks was a small child. Drawing on structures of mediation and representation that Marianne Hirsch associates with the concept of familial post-memory,[12] Blaufuks subsequently embeds these structures in a larger story, as observations from the recollections of other refugees, such as Arthur Koestler, Hermann Grab and Hans Sahl, are woven into the narrative fabric. Visually, these portions of the video are accompanied by silent movie footage that captures street scenes of central Lisbon, and each author is only identified at the end of the passage. Additionally, the video includes fragmented images of documents and newspaper headlines; some of the documents are identified – police reports and files from the PVDE,[13] diplomatic dispatches, etc. – while others are not.

---

[10] Erll, 'Travelling Memory', p. 13.
[11] Erll, 'Travelling Memory', p. 13.
[12] Hirsch, 'The Generation of Post-Memory', p. 115.
[13] The *Polícia da Vigilância e Defesa do Estado* [Police for the Vigilance and Defence of the State] was a special political force created in 1933 that was charged with ensuring the security of the state.

226 *Ellen W. Sapega*

As private recollections are connected to public memories, Blaufuk's video illustrates Hirsch's observation that 'even the most intimate family knowledge about the past is mediated by broadly available public images and narrative'.[14] In this particular case, as many of the public images included are photographs housed in Portuguese archives, their provenance would be familiar to students of the time period. By placing them in juxtaposition with the narrator's family story, however, the history registered in these documents is personalized in a way such that it becomes 'embodied knowledge', to borrow a term from Diana Taylor.[15] This embodiment is explicit, in fact, in the framing of many of the family photographs, which are shown as held in someone's hand (presumably the narrator's).

Figure 12.1. Still taken from *Sob céus estranhos*.
Directed by Daniel Blaufuks. © Lx Filmes. 2002.

---

[14] Hirsch, 'The Generation of Post-Memory', p. 112.
[15] Diana Taylor, *The Archive and the Repertoire: Performing Cultural Memory in the Americas* (Durham, NC: Duke University Press, 2003). Cited in Hirsch, 'The Generation of Post-Memory', p. 105. For Taylor, embodied knowledge involves performance and the repertoire of embodied knowledge that is absent from the archive.

Indeed, the act of revisiting the archive in order to inject it with the subjective perspective of personal memory is an important dynamic of Blaufuk's video. In his attempt to 'mine' the archive, inscribing his grandparents' experiences of the war years within it, Blaufuks for the most part avoids incorporating references to the official discourses of a glorious past that shaped a good deal of the Estado Novo's nationalist rhetoric at that time.[16] Instead, he chooses to uncover documentary evidence about the treatment of Jewish refugees in Portugal that highlights some of the ambiguities that informed the regime's neutral stance. As the narrator observes, in order to assure that Portugal would be no more than a country of transit, and not a place of exile, Lisbon was transformed into an 'uncomfortable waiting room'. In a few telling instances, nonetheless, documentary footage from the state propaganda archive is incorporated. A Portuguese newsreel that opens the video, appearing just before the segment that shows the images of Lisbon's Jewish cemetery, recalls the experience of watching previews and other shorts within a public cinema. It also serves as a sort of preface to the story that will follow. After the announcement that the footage to follow had been approved by the state's official censors, the first part of the newsreel reports on the arrival in Lisbon harbour of the German warship *Deutschland*; this clip then is followed by another account on the visit of the British home fleet. With this preface, the viewer is thus alerted to details about the wider sociopolitical context in which, ironically, the general populace's access to the information that Blaufuks goes on to provide was significantly limited.

By placing these clips at the video's opening, the time and place of the story that will be told is clearly established. The equivocal and contradictory stance assumed by the Salazar government in regard to the belligerent parties involved provides a frame for the memories that will follow. After this segment, Blaufuks's private memories will take precedence, nonetheless, with very little recourse made to the official archive of national experience that the Estado Novo created, preserved and promoted during the 1940s and 1950s. This element – the repeated assertion of the importance of intimate family knowledge about the past – places Blaufuks's documentary squarely within transnational narratives centring on memories of the Holocaust that have been transmitted from one generation to another. It also distinguishes *Sob céus estranhos* from João Canijo's documentary of 2010, *Fantasia Lusitana*.

Like Daniel Blaufuks, João Canijo, born in 1957, belongs to a generation that experienced the years of the Second World War only indirectly. His film (Figure 12.2) revisits the same historical moment and also incorporates voice-overs drawn from the memoirs of refugees and exiles that passed through

---

[16] Most of these 'official' discourses invoked Portugal's glorious Age of Discovery.

Lisbon. However, in its complex juxtaposition of this material with official Estado Novo propaganda and documentary film clips, *Fantasia Lusitana* engages more directly with the Portuguese state's propaganda apparatus and the Salazar government's subsequent attempts to shape collective memory about its actions during this time. In contrast with Blaufuks's work, Canijo's documentary has no narrator. The images shown in *Fantasia Lusitana* are drawn almost exclusively from documentary footage, most of which is taken from movies and newsreels produced by the Estado Novo. As Manuel Halpern has noted, João Canijo, in making this film, 'never once picked up a camera, nor did he write any text'.[17] In addition to the documentary's soundtracks, the director provides excerpts of speeches written and delivered by Salazar, while words written by Erika Mann and Alfred Döblin, two authors whose works were included in *Sob céus estranhos*, are also read aloud in the original German. Additionally, passages from Antoine de Saint-Exupéry's text 'Lettre à un otage' ['Letter to a hostage'] (1944) make up part of the soundtrack.

The 'story' that Canijo tells emerges from the confrontation of the different foreigners' views of the capital and the images and voice-overs employed by the Estado Novo's propaganda machine, with the 1940 Exposição do Mundo Português [Exposition of the Portuguese World] acting as a sort of centrepiece. Clips are shown from several now familiar promotional films produced about this event, which, often referred to as the 'staging of the regime', served as an occasion for the government to stage or project an authorized version of Portugal's past and its present.[18] However, in their juxtaposition with comments by Saint-Exupéry, Döblin and Mann about the exposition, the absurdity of the official views projected in such state-sponsored events comes to the fore. These multilingual voice-overs oppose Salazar's nationalist discourses every bit as much as the montage of images does, and the transnational experiences narrated in these passages belie the nationalist discourses promoted by the Estado Novo. In the documentary's final segments, the technique of presenting disparate images under a soundtrack that contradicts what the viewer sees is further developed, as a series of still photos depicting state violence and the abject poverty suffered by many Portuguese during this

---

[17] Manuel Halpern, writing in the *Jornal de Letras*, was cited in Ana Salgueiro Rodrigues, 'Fantasia? Lusitana? Cinema, história(s de vida) e ética artística am Daniel Blaufuks e João Canijo', *Doc On-Line*, 9 (2010), 60–79 (p. 71) <www.doc.ubi.pt> [accessed on 9 September 2018].

[18] For more information about the Exposition of the Portuguese World, see Ellen W. Sapega, 'Staging Memory: "The Most Portuguese Village in Portugal" and the Exposition of the Portuguese World', in *Consensus and Debate in Salazar's Portugal* (Philadelphia: Pennsylvania State University Press, 2008), pp. 9–45.

Figure 12.2. Still taken from *Fantasia Lusitana*. Directed by João Canijo.
© Periferia Filmes. 2010.

time is accompanied by recordings of Salazar alternately inveighing against communism or assuring the nation's citizens that they are fortunate to live in a nation that zealously cares for them and protects their interests.

With this technique of montage, Canijo's documentary emphasizes the interplay between 'state-operated institutions of memory and the flow of mediated narratives within and across state borders'.[19] It invites the viewer to assess the divide that separated official discourse from the personal experience of many who lived in, or passed through, Portugal at that time. It was this official discourse that helped to shape (or warp) collective memories of that era or, to put it a bit differently, that played a key role in facilitating the subsequent amnesia that has developed about the years in question. The main achievement of *Fantasia Lusitana* lies in the ways that it furthers the spectator's understanding of how the Portuguese government sought to deceive its citizens by impressing upon them a very skewed picture of the

[19] Chiara De Cesari and Ann Rigney, 'Introduction', in *Transnational Memory: Circulation, Articulation, Scales*, eds Chiara De Cesari and Ann Rigney (Berlin: De Gruyter, 2014), pp. 12–41 (p. 16).

nation and its exploits. João Canijo's documentary is not only about present-day collective memory, about what has been remembered and/or forgotten by those Portuguese who lived through the years of the Second World War and by the generations who came after; as its title reflects, it is also a meditation on how memory was manipulated and turned into a fantasy, when it was used explicitly as a propaganda tool by the Salazar government.

Sob céus estranhos and *Fantasia Lusitana* reassess 1930–40s Portuguese culture from standpoints that mesh the personal and the collective, as both film-makers seek to make sense of and provide a context for the silences, ambiguities, and ambivalences that have characterized many recollections of these years. Likewise, both draw on similar visual materials, using the register of memory to interpellate the viewer. By personalizing the archives that they mine and inviting viewers to revisit the collective past, the two documentaries avoid the impassive perspectives of academic authority. However, even though both 'texts' draw on some of the same national and transnational sources, each uses a significantly different frame of reference.

Blaufuks's video, with its emphasis on the lived experiences of the narrator's grandparents and their relatives, seems to fall quite neatly into the category of 'familial post-memory', which, according to Marianne Hirsch, is based upon 'a *structure* of inter- and trans-generational transmission of traumatic knowledge and experience'.[20] In fact, *Sob céus estranhos* seems a particularly apt illustration of Hirsch's observation that: 'Family life, even in its most intimate moments is entrenched in a collective imaginary shaped by public, generational structures of fantasy and projection and by a shared archive of stories and images that inflect the transmission of individual and familial remembrance.'[21] Many of the events entrenched in the collective imaginary that Daniel Blaufuks invokes include the experiences of others who, like his grandparents, found themselves in Lisbon during the war years. Thus, his documentary inserts the transnational narratives of the Holocaust and of Jewish memory in exile into the context of Second World War Lisbon to tell a wider story about Portugal during this time.[22] For this viewer, the moment perhaps in which personal or familial remembrances most effectively mesh with the history of Portugal, occurs towards the video's end, when a letter written by Blaufuks's grandfather relating the public elation experienced at the end of the war is followed by the image of a newspaper article that communicates Salazar's orders, upon learning of Hitler's death, that all flags in Portugal be flown at half-mast. Blaufuks then provides archival

[20] Hirsch, 'The Generation of Post-Memory', p. 106.
[21] Hirsch, 'The Generation of Post-Memory', p. 114.
[22] Erll, 'Travelling Memory', pp. 12–13.

documentation that substantiates Salazar's knowledge of the concentration camps, commenting that: 'By then he had surely read the extensive report on the camps of Auschwitz and Birkenau, sent to Lisbon in August 1944 by the Portuguese consul in Bucharest. The document described the organization of the extermination camps and included detailed victim numbers and the exact location of the buildings.'

In Blaufuks's video, we find an example of the blending of archival documentation with the 'vertical identification' that occurs within the family, between child and parent. It is tempting, in this light, to then regard *Fantasia Lusitana* as an example of a complementary category of post-memory and to treat that film as an instance of the horizontal identification that Hirsch associates with 'affiliative post-memory'. Canijo's depiction of this time certainly does incorporate structures of mediation that are 'broadly appropriable, available and, indeed, compelling enough to encompass a larger collective in an organic web of transmission'.[23] In Canijo's film, we *see* many examples of the fascistic militarization that the writer José Cardoso Pires recalled of his adolescence.[24] We are therefore reminded that, in the late 1930s and early 1940s, the Salazar government sympathized much more with the Axis powers than it cared to admit in the years that followed the war. Additionally, *Fantasia Lusitana* demonstrates quite explicitly how the Salazar regime set about changing the story of its sympathies and alliances in the immediate aftermath of the Second World War. However, as *Fantasia Lusitana* includes reflections on the act of forgetting and on the ways that memory can be and has been manipulated in both the past and in the present, it also seems to problematize the very concept of 'contemporaneity and generational connection with the literal second generation' that is usually considered a characteristic of affiliative post-memory.[25]

In both instances, the makers of these films entered the archive to work and rework the growing body of materials to be found there and the results of their exercise open a space for the transnational in the burgeoning 'culture of memory'[26] operating in Portugal today. These personalized and idiosyncratic

---

[23] Hirsch, 'The Generation of Post-Memory', pp. 114–15.

[24] In a long interview published in 1991, Cardoso Pires was asked to describe the image that he retained of the Lisbon of his childhood. In his reply, he recalled 'A frightened city, waiting to be thrown into the war. Unemployment. Fascist legionnaires, shop windows with Nazi propaganda on every corner', adding that it was this climate of stasis, inactivity, and mindful waiting that he depicted in his short story 'Amanhã, se Deus quiser'. Artur Portela, *Cardoso Pires por Cardoso Pires* (Lisbon: Publicações D. Quixote, 1991), p. 19.

[25] Hirsch, 'The Generation of Post-Memory', p. 115.

[26] Andreas Huyssen, *Present Pasts: Urban Palimpsests and the Politics of Memory* (Stanford, CA: Stanford University Press, 2003), p. 15.

visits to the archive make important contributions to contemporary debates surrounding the 'ethics of memory', asking not only how memory is enacted but to what good end?[27] As they participate in contemporary conversations about the Second World War that transcend national borders, the directors invoke new frames of collective remembrance that have been emerging as alternatives to the nation.[28] They serve as correctives for any nostalgic or apologetic views regarding the actions of the Estado Novo that may be gaining currency in the popular imagination. Moreover, and perhaps more importantly, both Daniel Blaufuks and João Canijo alert their viewers to the fact that the 'generation of post-memory' must follow a different route in Portugal, given that the very structures of mediation that are at post-memory's core were, for the most part, absent or suppressed from public discourse for many decades.

---

[27] Suleiman, *Crises of Memory*, p. 8.
[28] De Cesari and Rigney, 'Introduction', p. 13.

13

Disjunctive Temporalities of Migration in Photobooks from Brazil

Edward King
University of Bristol

The photobook has always been a medium of movement and mobility. As an object of study, it is restless and hard to pin down. While critics largely agree on its two defining characteristics being the emplacement of photographic images in meaningful sequences and combinations of photographs with text (see Patrizia Di Bello and Shamoon Zamir, discussed further below), the origins and forerunners claimed on behalf of the contemporary photobook are more diverse. The various competing genealogies of the form are closely connected to experiences of travel, migration and displacement from the nineteenth century to the present. In their curated global history, Martin Parr and Gerry Badger point out that the dominant themes of the earliest photobooks produced in France in the middle of the nineteenth century by the Imprimerie Photographique in Lille were 'studies of travel, picturesque landscapes, ancient monuments and [...] ethnographic documents' serving the interests of the colonizing agendas of the day.[1] Publications such as Maxime Du Camp's *Egypte, nubie, palestine et syrie* (1852) acted as orientalist legitimizations of colonization and exotic enticements to travel. The dominant forms of the family album, a vernacular cousin of the photobook, also have close connections with movement and migration. Elizabeth Siegel points out that the first family albums in the USA emerged in the wake of the Civil War in the context of the shattering of family structures by mourning and westward migration. Family albums functioned as an imaginary suture, a fantasmatic unification of the family in the face of its shattering.[2] Photographic practices

---

[1] Martin Parr and Gerry Badger, *The Photobook: A History*, 3 vols (London: Phaidon Press, 2004), I, p. 16.
[2] Elizabeth Siegel, 'Talking through the "Fotygraft Album"', in *Phototextualities:*

of the nineteenth century in Brazil were also either agents of or reactions against mobility of various kinds, whether it be the prominent role of European immigrants in early experiments with the form or the production of exotic images of nature and slavery to feed the growing tourist industry during the latter half of the century.[3] Photobooks confront us as readers and critics working within the field of modern languages with the urgency of placing texts, images and technologies within the contexts of transnational movement and inter-cultural encounter from which they emerge.

Photobooks have often served to reinforce the positivistic desires that accompany colonial travel and naturalize the temporalities or culturally and historically specific conceptions of time that undergird the projects of empire. This is partly due to early associations between the form and ethnographic projects aimed at producing colonized others as knowable and controllable. As Johannes Fabian argues in *Time and the Other*, ethnographic discourses have an important temporal dimension since they position the authors as speaking from the modern present (the 'here and now') and their objects of study as existing in a timeless pre-modern past (the 'there and then').[4] Esther Gabara points out how photography has so often been a technology of what Fabian terms 'allochronism' in Latin America, the denial that takes place in the narrativization of ethnographic encounters of the fact that both author and object exist within the same time frame (an effect that Fabian describes as the 'denial of coevalness').[5] Photographic technologies were quickly seized upon by practitioners of the racial sciences during the second half of the nineteenth century. The triptychs of slaves produced by Augusto Stahl under commission from the Harvard-based zoologist Louis Agassiz, for example, attempted to present their objects as ahistorical racial types, free from social and political contexts.[6]

Intersections of Photography and Narrative, eds Alex Hughes and Andrea Noble (Albuquerque: University of New Mexico Press, 2003), pp. 239–53 (p. 242).

[3] See, for example, Natalia Brizuela, *Fotografia e império: Paisagens para um Brasil moderno* (São Paulo: Companhia das Letras, 2012); and Marcus Wood, *Black Milk: Imagining Slavery in the Visual Cultures of Brazil and America* (Oxford: Oxford University Press, 2013).

[4] Johannes Fabian, *Time and the Other: How Anthropology Makes its Object* (New York: Columbia University Press, 2014).

[5] Esther Gabara, 'Recycled Photographs: Moving Still Images of Mexico City, 1950–2000', in *Photography and Writing in Latin America: Double Exposures*, eds Marcy E. Schwartz and Mary Beth Tierney-Tello (Albuquerque: University of New Mexico Press, 2006), pp. 139–70 (p. 165).

[6] See Brian Wallis, 'Black Bodies, White Science: Louis Agassiz's Slave Daguerreotypes', *American Art*, 9.2 (1995), 38–61.

It could also be argued that the distinguishing formal dimensions of the photobook serve to naturalize this temporality.

Attempts to define the form vary widely both in terminology and emphasis. In their study of the form, Patrizia Di Bello and Shamoon Zamir avoid strict definitions of the medium but point to a constellation of formal tendencies that should guide study of this most unstable of cultural objects. These include 'a [photographic] image's interactions with another, or its place in a group or sequence' and the 'dialectical coexistence' between photographic images and text.[7] The combination of text and images has often been used as a tool in the construction of allochronistic temporality. The captions frequently used in pre-photographic books of paintings and engravings produced by European traveller-artists in Brazil function as a vehicle for a voice of scientific authority. This is clearly the case in Jean Baptiste Debret's *Viagem pitoresca e histórica ao Brasil* (1834–39) in which the captions reinforce the elision between the geographically and temporally exotic carried out in the title. This promise to harness the power of images and direct them towards specific political goals was a reason why, as Parr and Badger point out, the photobook became an 'essential tool' of the documentary movements in the USA, Western Europe and the USSR in the 1920s and 1930s.[8]

The other dominant formal quality identified by Di Bello and Zamir, the placement of photographs in sequence, also lends itself to attempts to construct time as knowable for reasons of political control. The sequencing of images in photobooks contains a strong formal echo of attempts by scientists during the second half of the nineteenth century to render the passing of time visible and knowable. Eadweard Muybridge's spatialization of time in his stop-motion photographs of moving animals and human figures from the 1870s finds its counterpart in a range of narrative forms of the day, including comic strips, photographic books and family photograph albums, that evoke the passing of time through a series of static images. Jonathan Crary points out that over the course of the nineteenth century, at a time when 'the control of time becomes synonymous with new modalities of power', temporality and vision become increasingly connected.[9] On the one hand, the 'new abstraction and mobility of images' brought about by emerging communication technologies entailed a temporal explosion. But this explosion is met by an 'inverse

---

[7] Patrizia Di Bello and Shamoon Zamir, 'Introduction', in *The Photo Book: From Talbot to Ruscha and Beyond*, eds Patrizia Di Bello, Colette Wilson and Shamoon Zamir (London: I. B. Tauris, 2012), pp. 1–16 (p. 1).

[8] Parr and Badger, *The Photobook*, p. 10.

[9] Jonathan Crary, 'Techniques of the Observer', *October*, 45 (1988), 3–35 (p. 14).

disciplining of the observer in terms of rigidly fixed relations to the image' that grounded a stable temporality.[10]

However, it is these same qualities that have led to the form being used to unsettle and propose alternatives to these hegemonic temporal constructions. The photobook, as a site of creative intermedial experimentation, has become a key vehicle for the exploration of what Chiara De Cesari and Ann Rigney refer to as the 'non-linear trajectories and complex temporalities' of transnationalism.[11] In his discussion of photographic essays such as *Let Us Now Praise Famous Men* (1939) by writer James Agee and photographer Walker Evans, commissioned for *Fortune* magazine to document the conditions of farm workers in the 'dustbowl' of the American South, W. J. T. Mitchell argues that the form is characterized by a 'resistance' between word and image.[12] In Agee and Evans's book, for example, there exists a 'blockage' or 'mutual independence' between word and image.[13] Captions fail to fully explain or contain the explosion of potential meanings and connotations set in motion by the images, and vice versa. This blockage undermines the usefulness of the form as part of a state 'surveillance and propaganda apparatus'.[14] In their study of the political uses of photographic texts in Latin America, Marcy Schwartz and Mary Beth Tierney Tello argue that the 'resistance' between word and image identified by Mitchell has a denaturalizing effect and draws the reader and viewer's attention to the ethical and political uses to which each mode has been subjected.[15] As with other hybrid textual practices such as the graphic novel, the lack of consensus on fundamental aspects of the structure of photobooks, on the part of authors, photographers and critics, has been a motivating force behind the creativity and continual reinvention of the form.

Thanks to the growth of the self-publishing movement and the flourishing of independent publishers in the country, the last decade or so has seen an upsurge in the publication of formally and conceptually innovative photobooks in Brazil. One of the dominant tendencies in these texts is the return to the preoccupations that surrounded the form during the nineteenth and early twentieth centuries. For example, the collaboratively produced *Projeto*

[10] Crary, 'Techniques of the Observer', p. 14.

[11] Chiara De Cesari and Ann Rigney, 'Introduction', in *Transnational Memory: Circulation, Articulation, Scales*, eds Chiara De Cesari and Ann Rigney (Boston, MA: De Gruyer, 2014), pp. 1–25 (p. 6).

[12] W. J. T. Mitchell, *Picture Theory: Essays on Verbal and Visual Representation* (Chicago, IL and London: University of Chicago Press, 1994), p. 285.

[13] W. J. T. Mitchell, *Picture Theory*, p. 297.

[14] W. J. T. Mitchell, *Picture Theory*, p. 297.

[15] Marcy E. Schwartz and Mary Beth Tierney-Tello, 'Introduction', in *Photography and Writing in Latin America*, eds Schwartz and Tierney-Tello, pp. 1–18 (p. 12).

Desterro (2014), coordinated by artist Ícaro Lira, is both an account and a textual performance of a 'fictional ethnographic expedition' to the town of Canudos, the site of the war between federal troops and the followers of cult leader Antônio Conselheiro at the end of the nineteenth century, documented by Euclides da Cunha in *Os Sertões* (1902), an epic essay on the war and its causes that is considered by many to be a foundational work of Brazilian literature.[16] Through combinations of photographs, historical and fictional accounts of the town in which the past traumatically infects the present, the book undermines the temporalities of national progress reinforced by the journalistic photographs taken by Flávio de Barros at the time of the war. While the form of the photobook is historically bound up with positivistic attempts to visualize time and render it knowable and controllable, they can also function as temporal 'events' in the sense that Elizabeth Grosz uses the term: 'Events are ruptures, nicks, which flow from causal connections in the past but which, in their unique combinations and consequences, generate unpredictability and effect sometimes subtle but wide-ranging, unforeseeable transformations in the present and future.'[17] Photobooks such as *Desterro*, and the focus of analysis for the rest of this chapter, *Tcharafna* (2014) by Gui Mohallem, use the form to intervene into hegemonic strategies of producing conceptions of time that legitimize nationalistic and imperial projects in order to create the conditions of an encounter between reader and text that produces an openness to the future, an unstable temporality of becoming.[18]

The photobook *Tcharafna*, which was published in São Paulo with a print run of 400 copies, is an account and phototextual enactment of a journey undertaken by artist Gui Mohallem to the town of Fakiha in eastern Lebanon, the home of his parents before they migrated to Brazil in the 1950s in search of better economic prospects. The book consists of fragmentary photographic documentation of the trip to Lebanon and a meditation on his family's history of migration, particularly through an intervention into an archive of photographs given to him by his father. In many ways, *Tcharafna* is part of a broadening trend in Brazilian narrative that centres on second- or third-generation immigrants exploring the experiences of transnational movement and migration that structure their family histories. Although novelistic and cinematic versions of these immigrant narratives are numerous – including *Diário da queda* (2011) by Michel Laub and *O sol se põe em São Paulo* (2008)

---

[16] Ícaro Lira, *Projeto Desterro: Expedição etnográfica de ficção* (São Paulo: Vibrant, 2014); Euclides da Cunha, *Os Sertões* (São Paulo: Martin Claret, 2002).

[17] Elizabeth Grosz, *The Nick of Time: Politics, Evolution, and the Untimely* (Durham, NC and London: Duke University Press, 2004), p. 10.

[18] Gui Mohallem, *Tcharafna* (São Paulo: Pingado-Prés, 2014).

by Bernardo Carvalho – the most relevant examples are the novel *A chave de casa* (2007) by Tatiana Salem Levy and the documentary film *Um passaporte Húngaro* (2001) by Sandra Kogut.[19] Both narratives intertwine and meditate upon the connections between the forced migration of their grandparents to Brazil and the privileged transnational mobility that allows them to travel to Turkey (in the case of Salem Levy) and Hungary (in the case of Kogut) in search of their family roots.

As we will see, Mohallem's incursion into his family's migratory past is an attempt to construct a vision and a temporality of a transnational future. A uniting feature of these narratives of immigration is an attempt to expose the hidden histories of movement within monumental Brazilian national narratives and the temporalities that these entail. In his study of narratives constructed from the perspective of Syrian–Lebanese communities in Brazil, Ramón J. Stern argues that novels such as *Lavoura Arcaica* (1989) by Raduan Nassar and *Relato de um certo Oriente* (1989) by Milton Hatoum explore the 'glaring invisibility' of these immigrant experiences within dominant national discourses and their emphasis on the absorption of immigrant experience within the 'cordial' embrace of Brazilian national life.[20] *Tcharafna* lends visibility to these histories through Mohallem's exploration of his family's photographic archives. Mohallem is more archivist than auteur. His creative intervention into his own family is an active generation of collective memory as a way of tracing a transnational trajectory in the present.

In her study of guidebooks to Portugal from the 1950s, Susana Martins argues that photographic tourist manuals are 'time-structured devices' intended to reassure their users that the territory they are about to visit is mapped, knowable and one coherent, if varied, national entity.[21] However, while these texts 'participate in the consolidation of the national fiction' by giving it a 'visual expression', they are traversed by a complex intersecting network of 'temporal structures'.[22] These include the 'time of actual travel', the 'condensed time' produced by the conflation of numerous trips or an extended trip into one journey, the 'time of reading', the 'retrospective time' of looking back at a trip in the past and the paradoxical sense of 'returning time' that

[19] Michel Laub, *Diário da queda* (São Paulo: Companhia das Letras, 2011); Bernardo Carvalho, *O sol se põe em São Paulo* (São Paulo: Companhia das Letras, 2007); Tatiana Salem Levy, *A chave de casa* (Rio de Janeiro: Editora Record, 2007).

[20] Ramón J. Stern, 'Geographies of Escape: Diasporic Difference and Arab Ethnicity Re-Examined' (unpublished doctoral dissertation, University of Michigan, 2013).

[21] Susana S. Martins, 'Between Present and Past: Photographic Portugal of the 1950s', in *Time and Photography*, eds Jan Baetens, Alexander Streitberger and Hilde Van Gelder (Leuven: Leuven University Press, 2010), pp. 85–102 (p. 92).

[22] Martins, 'Between Present and Past', pp. 88 and 90.

tourists experience when they seem to 'remember' a place they have in fact only known through mass media images.[23] In other words, the form of these books as well as the circuits of production and consumption they are tied into undermine their discursive agenda of reinforcing a stable temporality of the nation. *Tcharafna* harnesses these formal properties to reproduce for the reader the intersecting temporalities of transnationalism. Dissecting this web of temporalities and examining how they combine and overlap will illuminate why the hybrid form of the photobook is becoming such a powerful tool for shaping a transnational future.

One of the dominant temporal structures in *Tcharafna* is the extended ancestral perspective on time proper to diasporic identity. The book contains 32 photographic images, of which 23 were taken during the trip to Lebanon in 2012, five are historical photographs taken from the archive and modified using a number of techniques I will elaborate on below, and five resist easy spatio-temporal placement due to their level of abstraction. By binding together the photographic documentation of Mohallem's journey with the photographs taken from the family archive, *Tcharafna* incorporates the extended temporality of the family into the lived experience of the photographer in the narrative 'present' of the journey. This sense of suture, of binding the time of the family together with lived time, is reinforced by Mohallem's intervention into the archival family images in the process of incorporation. The archival photographs that appear in the book have been mediated by a number of processes. Mohallem first took c-prints of the family photographs found in the family home in Fakiha. He then soaked the resulting prints in heated paraffin to dilute the glue and separate the emulsion from the paper substrate and encased the moderated images, now partly obscured and brittle to the touch, into a series of heavy oval and circular moulds made from red wax and gelatin. The moulds are then backlit by light bulbs so that, to the viewer, the images seem to emerge out of a red mist or slowly surface in a pool of blood. Mohallem then took another photograph of these moulds, which were then printed on low-grade paper and incorporated into the book.[24]

The blood-red tinge of these modified images echoes and reinforces a theme that runs through the photographs of the journey, from the deep red of preserved blackberries and the flesh of a ripe fig, to the photographer's blood-soaked hands held up to the camera (Figure 13.1). The archival photographs are not simply reproduced but worked over in a way that is reminiscent

---

[23] Martins, 'Between Present and Past', pp. 91–92.

[24] The details of this process were described by the artist in private correspondence with the author.

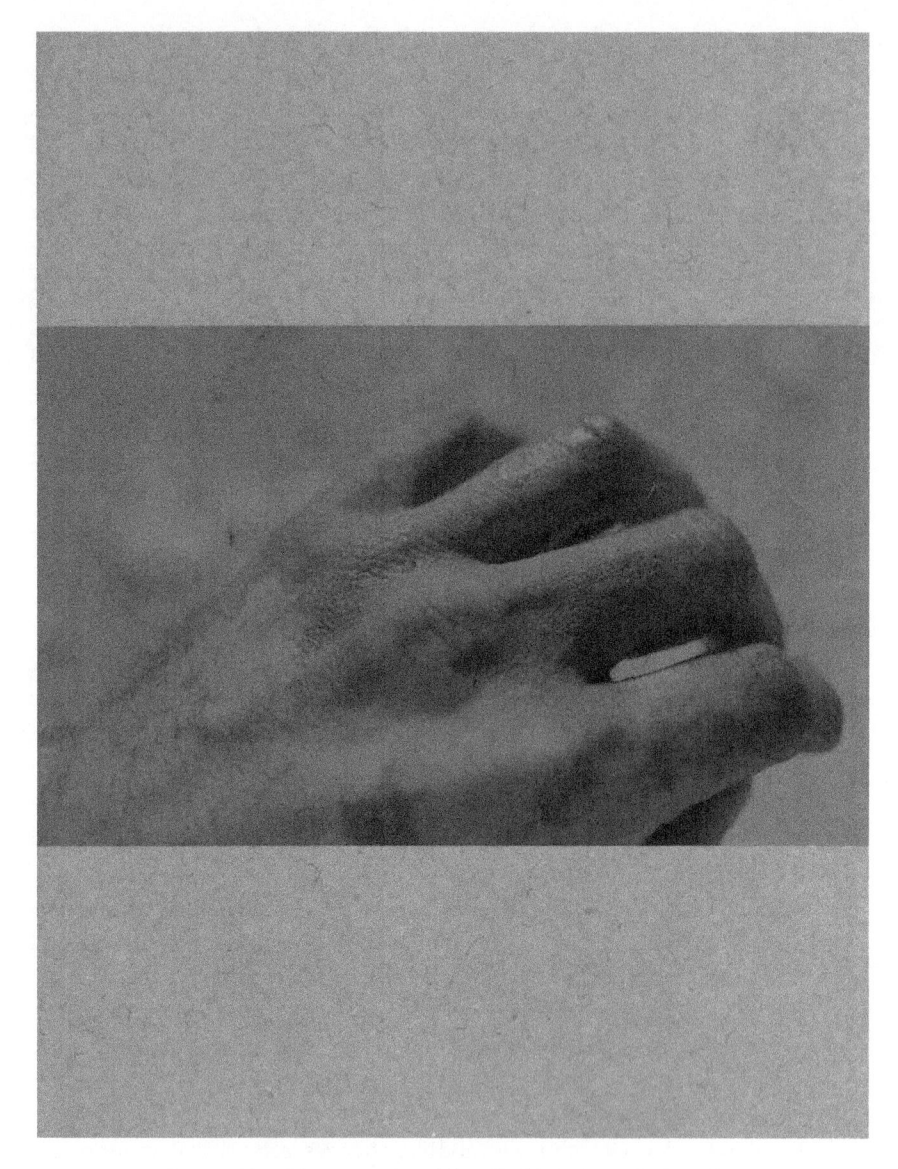

Figure 13.1. Photograph of bloodied hands in *Tcharafna*.

of vernacular photographic processes dating back to the early decades of the medium during the nineteenth century. In *Forget Me Not*, Geoffrey Batchen argues that popular memory practices using photography at the time, including posing for photographs in a position of mourning while holding a photograph of a dead loved one, reveal photography as a powerful temporal device, both an agent of and a response to the 'crisis of memory' of the end of the nineteenth century.[25] If the technological revolution in which photography played a key role sped up the fragmentation of families and communities by migration and travel, photography was also used to heal these fractures. The use of moulds by Mohallem underscores how the *Tcharafna* project is binding together a family temporality. By intertwining the two sequences of images (that of the family and that of the personal journey), Mohallem is incorporating the lives of his ancestors into his own lived experience, the blood-red colour match symbolically soaking them in a common blood.

The images that result from these processes bear a strong resemblance to early photographic practices of using versions of the medium (mostly daguerreotypes) to capture images of the spirit world. The front cover of *Tcharafna*, for instance, holds an image of one of the red circular moulds containing a fragment of an archival photograph. A row of figures is lined up in preparation for a photograph. Their upper bodies are obscured where the red silicone thickens along the wide and uneven rim of the moulded frame. Spiritualist photographers told their clients that this new imaging technology held the promise to reverse the flow of time. Photography could capture images of the dead and, in particular, departed relatives. Louis Kaplan argues that the fantasy to which the spirit photographers catered (the appearance of dead loved ones in family photographs) 'enable[d] consumers to forget their losses by restoring the domestic scene, familiarity, and community in the face of the gruesome and inconvenient fact of mortality'.[26] The resemblance of the moulded images to spiritualist photographic practices underscores a common desire to assert a timeless temporality of the family against the spatio-temporal ruptures of migration and death.

The spirit photographs evoked by *Tcharafna* and the vernacular processes described by Batchen are all partially responses to the idea that the photographic sign is not only 'iconic', to use the terms developed by Charles Sanders Peirce, but also 'indexical'. The idea that analogue photographs contain a material trace of their referent transferred in the moment of exposure when light falls on the light-sensitive material is an appeal that has fascinated critics of photography from André Bazin to Roland Barthes.[27] The photographs of

---

[25] Geoffrey Batchen, *Forget Me Not: Photography & Remembrance* (New York: Princeton Architectural Press, 2004), p. 95.

[26] Louis Kaplan, 'Spooked Time: The Temporal Dimensions of Spirit Photography', in Baetens, Streitberger and Van Gelder, *Time and Photography*, pp. 27–45 (p. 33).

[27] For an overview of debates about the 'indexical' claims of photography, see Tom Gunning, 'What's the Point of the Indexical Sign? Or Faking Photographs', in *Still/Moving: Between Camera and Photography*, eds Karen Beckman and Jean Ma (Durham, NC: Duke University Press, 2008), pp. 23–40.

mourning described by Batchen display a belief in the uncanny temporality of the photographic sign. Due to this belief, photographic texts hold a place of particular importance in practices of mourning. As Alex Hughes and Andrea Noble explain, 'the indexical sign, as relic of past reality, takes us to the scene of memory in ways that are not permitted by other modes of textuality'.[28] However, the metaphotographic textuality of these images (the self-referentiality of having a photograph of a photograph) draws attention to a dimension of photography often occluded in the focus on the index – that is to say, the photograph not as transparent sign, but as a material object that accrues value through being shared (in the case of family photographs), exchanged (in the case of *cartes-de-visites*) and amassed (in the case of national institutional or personal archives).[29] In this sense, the photographs of mourning foreshadow what Batchen in another article has termed the 'ethnographic turn' in photography scholarship.[30] The spirit photographs, meanwhile, both play on customers' faith in the ontology of photographs (since photography is used to provide scientific proof of the afterlife) and draw attention to the instability of the photographic sign, the looseness of the connection between sign and referent, by foreshadowing the manipulable quality of the photograph that will rise to prominence in the digital era.

Tcharafna contains a similar ambivalence towards the uncanny temporality of the indexical sign. On the one hand, as we have seen, the splicing together of the photographs of the journey with the archival photographs of the family constructs the latter as revenants in a way that evokes faith in the ontology of the photograph. As Marianne Hirsch puts it, '[t]he referent haunts the picture like a ghost: it is a revenant, a return of the lost and dead other.'[31] However, on the other hand, the manipulation of images evident throughout the book foregrounds the elasticity of the photographic sign. One of the central photographs in the book is an image of the family summerhouse just outside the town of Fakiha. This house is positioned in the middle ground, with the hills in the background and an unnamed figure with his back to the camera in the foreground (Figure 13.2). The photograph seems to belong to the same temporal sequence as the other images taken during the trip

---

[28] Alex Hughes and Andrea Noble, 'Introduction', in *Phototextualities: Intersections of Photography and Narrative*, eds Alex Hughes and Andrea Noble (Albuquerque: University of New Mexico Press, 2003), pp. 1–16 (p. 5).

[29] See *Photographs Objects Histories: On the Materiality of Images*, eds Elizabeth Edwards and Janice Hart (London and New York: Routledge, 2004).

[30] Geoffrey Batchen, 'Snapshots: Art History and the Ethnographic Turn', *Photographies*, 1.2 (2008), 121–42.

[31] Marianne Hirsch, *Family Frames: Photography, Narrative and Postmemory* (Cambridge, MA and London: Harvard University Press, 1997), p. 5.

Disjunctive Temporalities of Migration in Photobooks from Brazil   243

Figure 13.2. Photograph of family home in Fakiha.

to Lebanon between May and June 2012. Like the others in the series it is a low-res image printed on low-res paper in a way that dulls the contrasts. As such, the reader can place the image within the temporality of the journey.

However, on a closer inspection, the temporal structure of the image is more complex. Mohallem explains that the image has been manipulated using Photoshop software to produce an approximation of what the family house would have looked like when his father left for Brazil in 1950. This process involved taking a photograph of the house in 2012 and reversing the signs of dilapidation and change, in particular evidence of how the building was used as a soldiers' bunker during the civil war in Lebanon between 1975 and 1990, including bullet holes and a sniper's nest appended to the main building. The details of this process of manipulation reveal two things. Firstly, that the construction of the temporality of family is an act of violence, a construction that necessitates the occlusion of other experiences and other temporalities, such as that of the role the family home played in the civil war. Secondly, the incorporation of the archival family images does not serve to buttress a monolithic familial temporality but instead draws out what Jan Baetens et al describe as 'the temporal multilayeredness of the photographic image'.[32] Even when viewed in isolation from its emplacement within the book, the image of the family home is traversed by a number of temporalities, including the time of the journey, the time of photographic development and manipulation, the nostalgic time of the imagined house before the ravages of war, and the projected future time of suture within the process of reading in which the nostalgic image of the house will be read unproblematically as part of the temporality of the journey. If the house is symbolic of the family, it is only made whole again in the projected future time of the reading process.

Eduardo Cadava and Gabriela Nouzeilles argue that photography is a 'transnational cultural practice', a 'multilayered field of technological, aesthetic, social, and critical traditions' that 'resists being fixed in one spacetime'.[33] *Tcharafna* draws attention to the 'itinerancy' of photography at a number of levels. Both of the dominant sources of photographs that make up the book contain traces of movement back and forth between Lebanon and Brazil. The intervention into a cache of family photographs that Mohallem found in Fakiha stages what Nouzeilles describes as the 'paradox' of archives, their 'hesitation between inscription and itinerancy'.[34] Following a similar paradoxical functioning logic to that described by Nouzeilles, the archive in *Tcharafna* is split between 'a centripetal force that painstakingly keeps and arranges records and documents' and a 'centrifugal force that quietly

---

[32] Jan Baetens, Alexander Streitberger and Hilde Van Gelder, 'Introduction', in *Time and Photography*, eds Baetens, Streitberger and Van Gelder, pp. vii–xii (p. viii).

[33] Eduardo Cadava and Gabriela Nouzeilles, 'Introduction', in *The Itinerant Language of Photography*, eds Eduardo Cadava and Gabriela Nouzeilles (New Haven, CT and London: Princeton University Art Museum, 2014), pp. 17–23 (pp. 17 and 18).

[34] Gabriela Nouzeilles, 'The Archival Paradox', in *The Itinerant Language of Photography*, eds Cadava and Nouzeilles, pp. 38–53 (p. 40).

or actively erases, shifts, and expels archival matter'.[35] On the one hand, the archive functions as a cohering force, a centre of gravity that grounds and certifies the extended diasporic temporality of the family. On the other hand, the dynamic set in motion by the project breaks up the archive, rendering it illegible in places (through the manipulation of the images and their encasement in the wax moulds) and exposing the processes of erasure and expulsion that bring the archive into being in the first place (through the visual 'silencing' of the violence committed during the civil war).

The itinerancy of the archive, which is revealed in this way, is echoed at the level of individual images through the foregrounding of process over finished image. In his contribution to *The Itinerant Language of Photography*, Cadava argues that the itinerancy of photography that is clear at the level of circulation, exchange and archivization is inscribed into the materiality and conception of photographic images themselves. Using Michel Foucault's comments on the 'insolent freedom that accompanied the birth of photography', Cadava traces a history of photography's 'capacity to take on different forms' and 'to move away from itself, and often in relation to different forms'.[36] The various intermedial mutations undergone by photography during the digital age (including the explosion of word-image combinations on the internet and the inscription of text in the image through the process of tagging) are extensions of photography's incomplete birth through interaction with a range of other media, including drawing (Henry Fox Talbot's 'pencil of nature'), painting (the traditions of ferrotypes and painted photographs) and engraving (lithographs that take photographs as their base rather than paintings or drawings).

This itinerancy is enacted through the reading performance demanded by the book form of *Tcharafna*. The combinations of images and texts that characterize the unstable entity of the photobook amplify the intermedial itinerancy of the photograph itself. Written text has a restricted presence in the book, but its few appearances place an emphasis on the blurred boundaries between media, emphasizing Mitchell's point that 'all media are mixed media'.[37] Four pages of the 72 contain text. Three of these provide information that contextualizes the journey. The first provides the temporal parameters of the journey ('between May and June 2012') and its motivation ('it was a way of trying to research my father's family'). The last contains a definition of the title 'tcharafna', which can be literally translated as 'estamos honrados'

---

[35] Nouzeilles, 'The Archival Paradox', p. 40.
[36] Eduardo Cadava, 'The Itinerant Languages of Photography', in *The Itinerant Language of Photography*, eds Cadava and Nouzeilles, pp. 24–37 (p. 24). Reference to Michel Foucault, *La Peinture Photogénique* (Paris: Le Point du Jour, 2014 [1975]).
[37] Mitchell, *Picture Theory*, p. 5.

or 'we are honoured' and gestures to an unspoken history of violence within the family. Between these two is a reference to another inspiration behind Mohallem's journey: 'a poem that my father heard before he left the Lebanon, in 1952' and that he repeated to Mohallem himself three times before his own 'return' journey. Another page in the book contains an image of the poem written in Arabic and encased in a lighter, rose-tinged version of the wax moulds. The poem is placed in a precarious intermedial web between aurality (both Mohallem and his father first encountered the poem in spoken form), the written word (the Arabic text is visible in the image albeit partially obscured by the unevenness of its encasement within the wax mould) and the image (the parallels with the way the archival photographs are framed underscore the poem's status as image). The disjointed multilayeredness of *Tcharafna* is staged in its textuality through these multifaceted combinations of image and text.

Di Bello and Zamir argue that the emplacement of photographs in photobooks emphasizes the material dimensions of the medium and demands an embodied mode of reading that engages the full range of sense experiences rather than purely vision. The experience of reading photobooks, they argue, 'must be grasped not just in its mental but also in its sensuous and haptic dimensions'.[38] If the dominant mode of the photobook is visual then its mode of visuality is what Laura U. Marks has described as 'haptic' in her analysis of filmic images that evoke processes of apprehension and meaning-making that involve the whole body.[39] *Tcharafna* is neither bound nor paginated so that the folded pages can be pulled apart and put back together in any order. While underscoring the lack of linear temporality, the lack of binding employed in *Tcharafna*, coupled with the low-grade paper, draws the readers' attention to the tactility of the photobook, the interaction that they enact between senses of vision and touch.

This material quality of *Tcharafna* is reinforced at a referential level within the book through the repeated motif of hands. In two photographs, what seem to be the photographer's hands intrude into the frame (Figure 13.1). A close-up of a left hand shows fingers that are seemingly covered in blood up to the knuckles. There is a theatrical quality to the image that jars with the prevailing tone of the book, which alternates between a documentary mode and the family photograph. The hand seems to be presented to the camera in a gesture of display, the effect of which is threefold. While the image underscores the fact that the book is carrying out a

---

[38] Patrizia Di Bello and Shamoon Zamir, 'Introduction', p. 12.

[39] Laura U. Marks, *The Skin of the Film: Intercultural Cinema, Embodiment, and the Senses* (Durham, NC: Duke University Press, 2000), p. 162.

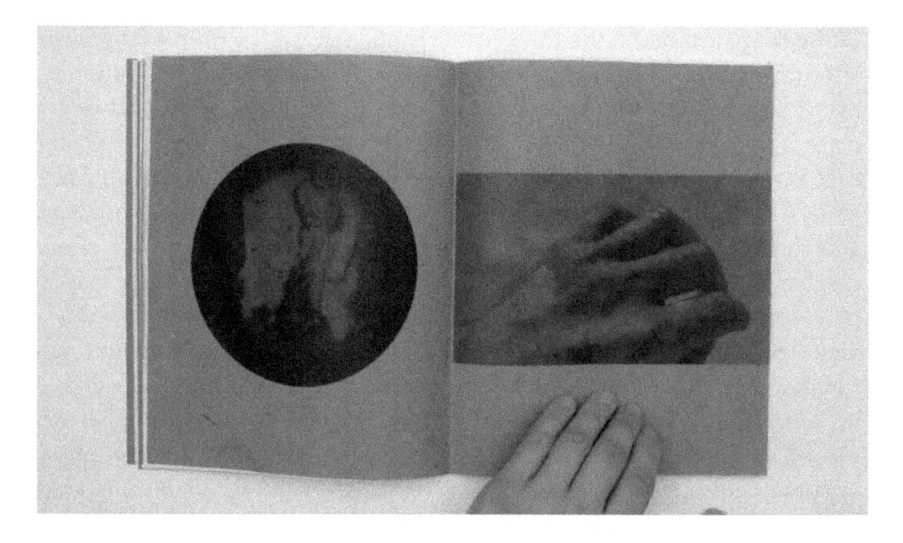

Figure 13.3. Still from 'reading video' embedded in
Gui Mohallem's website.

fusion of the lived time of the photographer with the extended temporality of the family, it also serves the more metatextual aim of underscoring the tactile dimension of reading photobooks. The hand is a *mise-en-abîme* of the reader's hand as she or he turns the pages and announces the fact that, by engaging with the book at an affective or embodied level, the reader is complicit in the extended temporality that it stages. Since the fantasy of familial diasporic time is only completed in the time of reading, the readers also, symbolically, have blood on their hands. This 'meta-photographic textuality', to borrow a term used by Hirsch, is extended in a video embedded in the Tcharafna project's webpage in which the hands of a reader slowly leaf through the pages of the book as it lies flat on a table[40] (Figure 13.3). 'Reading videos' such as these have become a standard way of exhibiting and advertising photobooks and artists' books online. However, the video also performs a wider series of connections, between the hand in the image (indicative of a diasporic temporality) and the transnational community of readers enabled by the internet.

On the one hand, this self-referential gesture points to the role of the body in the genre of autobiographic photography employed by *Tcharafna*. However, it also underscores the centrality of the body in experiences of the transnational produced by Mohallem's book, in particular its function as, in the words of Emma Bond, 'an important hinge of meaning within a mapping

[40] Hirsch, *Family Frames*, p. 8.

of the trans-national'.[41] As theorists of haptic spectatorship in both cinema and graphic fiction have pointed out, the appeal to the range of senses in these media undermines the hierarchical divide between viewing self and viewed object that is often reinforced by visual media. As Marks argues, the 'ocularcentrism' of much visual culture studies is complicit with an 'instrumental' understanding of vision that 'uses the thing seen as an object for knowledge and control'.[42] This is nowhere more obviously the case than in the ethnographic practices that have had such a strong influence in developments of photography in Brazil. Bound up with this hierarchical divide between viewer and viewed is the 'allochronic' temporality that condemns the latter to a timeless pre-modern past. One of the functions of the haptic mode employed in *Tcharafna* is to undermine the boundaries between photographer and viewed and, in the process, bind the reader into its disjunctive assemblage of temporalities. The *mise-en-abîme* carried out in the tactile reading video (which connects the photographed hand to the artist's hand, to the reader's hand) is an invitation to use the book as a portal into the disjunctive temporalities of the transnational. Like the transnational body theorized by Bond, the book functions as an entity 'able to communicate the ramifications and imaginings of movement, in a way that places space and time into a frictional dialectic'.[43] The 'cuts' and 'nicks' in time produced by the photobook's spatialization of time serve the function not of stabilization, in the manner of photographic travel guidebooks, but of an unstable transnational temporal event.

---

[41] Emma Bond, 'Towards a Trans-national Turn in Italian Studies?', *Italian Studies*, 69.3 (2014), 415–24 (p. 416).

[42] Marks, *The Skin of the Film*, p. 162.

[43] Bond, 'Towards a Trans-national Turn in Italian Studies?', p. 422.

14

The National and the Transnational in Brazilian Postdictatorship Cinema

Tatiana Heise

University of Glasgow

On 4 September 1969, two guerrilla groups calling themselves MR-8 (Revolutionary Movement October 8th) and ALN (Action for National Liberation) kidnapped US ambassador to Brazil, Charles Burke Elbrick, in what became known as the most audacious act of resistance against the military dictatorship that had overthrown democratically elected President João Goulart in 1964. In exchange for the ambassador's return the guerrillas demanded the release of 15 political prisoners and dissemination of an anti-government manifesto in the heavily censored media. The demand was accepted and the prisoners were released and flown to Mexico on an aircraft named *Hércules 56*. A decade later, the episode became the subject of a best-selling memoir by Fernando Gabeira, *O que é isso companheiro?* [*What's Up, Comrade?*], subsequently adapted into a political thriller of the same title and released in the USA as *Four Days in September* (Bruno Barreto, 1997).[1] More recently, the kidnapping was addressed in two documentaries: *Hércules 56* (Silvio Da-Rin, 2006) and *Dia que Durou 21 Anos* [*The Day that Lasted 21 Years*] (Camilo Tavares, 2012).

In this chapter I analyse these three films in the context of Brazil's recent phase of reckoning with its dictatorial past. After decades of ignoring or partially acknowledging state crimes, the country underwent a brief post-transitional experience marked by debates about human rights violations and

---

This chapter is part of the project 'Memories of the Dictatorship' which received funding from the Carnegie Trust Research Incentive Grant and the Leverhulme Trust Research Fellowship.

[1] Fernando Gabeira, *O que é Isso, Companheiro?* (São Paulo: Companhia do Bolso, 2009 [1979]).

250 *Tatiana Heise*

the importance of remembering.[2] This shift from a 'culture of forgetting' to a new 'politics of memory' has been conceptualized in predominantly *national* terms.[3] In other words, collective memories of the dictatorship have been construed as national memories, and the renewed interest in Brazil's dictatorial past has been conceived as a national concern by politicians, activists and intellectuals. This prevalence of the national seems to defy recent contributions to the field of memory studies that call for a new, 'transnational' way of understanding how memories are collectively produced and disseminated.[4]

Such an emphasis on the transnational has also been significant in modern film studies, and in this chapter I will employ concepts derived from this body of work to examine the tensions between, on the one hand, the turn towards transnationalism, and, on the other, the emphasis on the national in cinematic reconstructions of collective memories about the Brazilian dictatorship. In so doing, I address two sets of questions. First, what is meant by the national and the transnational in relation to cinema, and how do these categories apply to recent films about the dictatorship? Second, what aspects of the past are more appropriately addressed in films that utilize a distinctively national framework for remembering? Conversely, what new elements are brought to light in films that widen the focus to locate the past within a transnational or global context?

The 'transnational turn' in film studies

Over the past two decades, scholars in film studies have persistently drawn attention to the need to move away from approaches that situate films strictly in relation to the national contexts in which they are produced.[5] These authors

---

[2] This experience began in 1995 with the Lei dos Desaparecidos, a law that recognized the forced disappearance of political opponents as an institutional mechanism utilized by the military authorities. However, Brazil's memory politics has been undermined since Jair Bolsonaro became president in 2019. Bolsonaro has repeatedly praised the military regime and recycled the conservative 1960's discourse according to which the 1964 coup d'état was a 'revolution' that freed the country from impending communism.

[3] Nina Schneider, 'Breaking the "Silence" of the Military Regime: New Politics of Memory in Brazil', *Bulletin of Latin American Research*, 30.2 (2011), 198–212.

[4] For a summary, see David Inglis, 'Globalization and/of Memory: On the Complexification and Contestation of Memory Cultures and Practices', in *Routledge International Handbook of Memory Studies*, eds Anna Lisa Tota and Trevor Hagen (New York: Routledge, 2016), pp. 143–57.

[5] Examples of such debates in relation to Latin American cinema can be found in *Contemporary Hispanic Cinema: Interrogating the Transnational in Spanish and*

suggest that certain changes associated with the latest stage of globalization, including the rise of international funding agreements, intensified circulation of films beyond national borders, and the international trajectory of stars and directors, demand a new way of conceptualizing cinema that transcends national frameworks. One of the most frequently cited examples of cinematic transnationalism is *Diarios de Motocicleta* [*The Motorcycle Diaries*] (2004), directed by Brazilian Walter Salles. This co-production between eight countries has an international cast and crew including a Puerto Rican scriptwriter, a Uruguayan composer and actors from Chile, Mexico and Argentina. The film's subject matter makes it equally impossible to frame it in national terms: based on Ernesto 'Che' Guevara's memoirs, it charts the revolutionary's journey across South America and his political awakening to the injustices and inequalities in the region. *Diarios de Motocicleta*'s global success propelled its director into an international career in Hollywood.

This example serves to illustrate some of the positive effects that globalization can have on Latin American cinemas: for film-makers, it signifies increased economic and creative opportunities beyond their native countries; for audiences, it can mean wider access to Portuguese and Spanish-speaking films on screens around the globe. However, although the increase in international funding agreements has indeed opened new channels for the distribution and exhibition of films abroad, these opportunities apply to only a small proportion of films made in the region. In Brazil, for instance, co-productions account for less than a quarter of the total number of films released each year, and the film industry is heavily dependent on national legislation and government support systems, such as the Lei do Audiovisual [Audiovisual Law] and the Agência Nacional do Cinema [ANCINE] [National Cinema Agency].[6] In terms of distribution, most films produced locally never travel beyond domestic borders, and this is true of all cinemas in Latin America.

Thus, although we do need new theoretical paradigms to account for the growing number of films that defy association with a single nation, we must not disavow the national approach as somehow no longer relevant. In her taxonomy of the different ways in which the term 'transnational cinema' can be interpreted, Shaw includes the category 'national films' to remind us that, even in a globalized world, 'much film production is made for domestic markets, focuses on specific local issues, and relies on modes of narration that

---

Latin American Film, ed. Stephanie Dennison (Woodbridge: Tamesis, 2013) and in *Nuevas Perspectivas sobre la transnacionalidad del cine hispánico*, eds Robin Lefere and Nadia Lie (Leiden, Boston, MA: Brill Rodopi, 2016).

[6] Data obtained from Filme B <www.filmeb.com.br> [accessed 23 May 2017].

may not appeal to international audiences'.[7] Rather than a binary approach that sees films either in terms of the national or transnational, it is more productive to see the two concepts as part of a continuum that can be used to illuminate different aspects of film culture. Such an approach has been taken by Hjort in an influential essay in which she suggests using 'transnational' as a scalar concept that allows for the recognition of strong or weak forms of transnationality. Hjort makes a further distinction between 'marked' and 'unmarked' transnationality, that is, films with deliberately salient evidence of transnational properties, and those whose transnationalism might easily pass unnoticed.[8]

In this chapter I employ the theoretical frameworks proposed by Shaw and Hjort to examine how concepts of the 'national' and the 'transnational' can enrich our understanding of Brazilian postdictatorship cinema. The term 'postdictatorship' itself carries strong transnational connotations. It refers to the art, literature, cinema and other cultural works from South American countries that address the rise and consequences of the military dictatorships that swept the region between the 1960s and 1980s. Despite pertaining to the various countries that share a recent history of political violence, however, postdictatorship cultures are typically framed in national terms in academic scholarship.[9] This framing is problematized in the case of film because of its greater potential to circulate across and beyond national borders. In what follows I examine this issue in relation to the three Brazilian films mentioned in my introduction.

In *Hércules 56*, the use of a distinctively national approach facilitates the representation of sociohistorical developments that had, until recently, been disregarded in state-sanctioned discourses about the dictatorship. By contrast, in the earlier *O que é isso, companheiro?*, the sociohistorical context is downplayed for the sake of making the film more appealing to foreign audiences. The 'commercial transnationalism' of this film is very distinct from

---

[7] Deborah Shaw, 'Deconstructing and Reconstructing "Transnational Cinema"', in *Contemporary Hispanic Cinema*, ed. Dennison, pp. 47–66 (p. 64).

[8] Mette Hjort, 'On the Plurality of Cinematic Transnationalism', in *World Cinemas, Transnational Perspectives*, eds Natasia Durovicová and Kathleen Newman (New York and London: Routledge, 2010), pp. 13–33.

[9] A national approach prevails even in monographs and edited collections focusing on two or more countries. These works tend to dedicate separate chapters or sections to the study of each country, thereby maintaining a national framework. Examples include Ana Ros, *The Post-Dictatorship Generation in Argentina, Chile, and Uruguay: Collective Memory and Cultural Production* (London and New York: Palgrave Macmillan, 2012); and Francesca Lessa and Vincent Druliolle, *The Memory of State Terrorism in the Southern Cone: Argentina, Chile and Uruguay* (London and New York: Palgrave Macmillan, 2011).

the type of transnationalism found in *Dia que Durou 21 Anos*. In the latter, a transnational perspective is employed to make a radical revision of Brazil's past in the light of recent findings about the USA's foreign policy during the Cold War. As we will see, this documentary is an excellent example of how memories of the Brazilian dictatorship, traditionally conceived as *national* memories, can be understood as mnemonic processes unfolding across and beyond national boundaries.

The prevalence of the 'national' in *Hércules 56*

Since the return to democracy in 1985, Brazilian film-makers have been building up an extensive repertoire of narratives about the military regime and its aftermaths. Through their denouncing of human rights violations and other abuses committed by the government, they have helped to construct memories of a period that had, until recently, been obliterated by state-sanctioned discourses. Some of these films celebrate the armed struggle against the military regime and interrogate the labelling of leftist militants as 'terrorists' by shedding light on their ideological convictions and political motivations. Silvio Da-Rin's *Hércules 56* is a good example of this tendency. This documentary brings together six former guerrillas to reminiscence about the events that led to the kidnapping of the American ambassador in 1969. Their collective act of remembering gives us a fascinating overview of the socioeconomic and political developments that culminated in the regime becoming more repressive and resistance becoming more radical. This discussion is intercut with individually-shot interviews with nine of the surviving political prisoners who were released in exchange for Elbrick (Figure 14.1). These interviews centre initially on their political militancy as union leaders, students and politicians; they become more personal in the film's second half as the interviewees remember their time in prison and the flight to Mexico.

Hércules 56 was produced with the support of the Lei do Audovisual, ANCINE and state-controlled oil company Petrobrás, one of the biggest investors in Brazilian cinema. This combination of fiscal incentive support and state-owned investor is one of the most common funding strategies of postdictatorship cinema. In terms of distribution, the film's commercial circulation was limited to national territory but a few screenings at international film festivals gave it some visibility abroad. One of the reasons for the limited international distribution of Brazilian postdictatorship films is that they often require a degree of familiarity with the historical events depicted, which makes them less likely to be picked up by foreign buyers, a feature that was certainly the case with *Hércules 56*.

Figure 14.1. The political prisoners released in exchange for US Ambassador to Brazil Charles Burke Elbrick (1969–70) before boarding the flight to Mexico at the Rio de Janeiro International Airport on 7 September 1969. Nine of the surviving prisoners are interviewed in *Hércules 56*.
Source: Still from *Dia que Durou 21 Anos*. 2012. Directed by Camilo Tavares. © Pequi Filmes and TV Brasil. 2012.

A former militant himself, twice arrested during the dictatorship, Da-Rin made the film to promote remembrance of a period that, in his view, has not been sufficiently discussed in Brazil, particularly among younger generations.[10] Many other directors of postdictatorship cinema reveal a similar interest in communicating, above all, with a *national* audience, for reasons similar to those articulated by Da-Rin. It appears, then, that in terms of production, distribution and reception, and in terms of its subject matter, postdictatorship cinema exemplifies the continuing relevance of the concept of 'national cinema'. Yet, as Shaw reminds us, no cinema is ever 'purely' national. She uses the category 'transnational influences' to point out that 'every film made has been consciously or unconsciously shaped by pre-existing cultural products from all over the world'.[11] Indeed, in *Hércules 56* we can identify 'unmarked' influences of transnationalism in some of its aesthetic choices, such as the

---

[10] Brunna Rosa, 'Hércules 56: luta armada no Brasil revisitada', *Revista Forum* <http://www.revistaforum.com.br/2007/06/06/hercules-56-luta-armada-no-brasil-revisitada/> [accessed 23 May 2017].

[11] Shaw, 'Deconstructing and Reconstructing "Transnational Cinema"', p. 58.

'talking heads' interviews, a staple of documentary film-making all over the world, and the decision to leave the film crew and equipment visible in the frame, a widely used convention in the 'reflexive' tradition of documentary.[12] Another transnational layer is added towards the end of the film as the former prisoners remember their time in Mexico and a visit to Cuba where they met Fidel Castro. These final scenes offer a brief glimpse of the global reach of 1960s leftist movements and of the influence of the Cuban Revolution on Brazilian militants.

However, these transnational elements do not undermine *Hércules 56*'s strong concern with understanding the dictatorship from a predominantly national viewpoint. This will become clearer as I turn to two other films whose textual and extra-textual forms of transnationalism are more evident. What sets these films apart from *Hércules 56*, and from postdictatorship cinema more generally, is the use of narrative features that are markedly 'non-Brazilian' and, partly as a result, their greater success in reaching audiences abroad. What I seek to highlight through this comparison are the different types and degrees of transnationalism and their implications. In *O que é isso, companheiro?*, transnationalism is a commercial strategy designed to make the film appealing to a global audience at the expense of historical specificity. By contrast, in *Dia que Durou 21 Anos*, transnationalism is used to provoke a more critical reflection on aspects of Brazil's past that a strictly 'national' focus would have left hidden.

Commercial transnationalism in *O que é isso, companheiro?*

A resident in the USA when the film was made, director Bruno Barreto's adaptation of Gabeira's memoir was co-produced by Miramax and Columbia and picked up for worldwide distribution by major multinational companies. The budget of R$ 4.5 million, high by Brazilian standards, secured a cast of well-known Brazilian television stars and Hollywood actors, including Alan Arkin in the role of Elbrick. Foreign critics praised the film's skilful use of political thriller conventions such as an event-driven narrative, tension and suspense. This positive international appraisal culminated with an Oscar nomination for Best Foreign-Language film in 1998 and a Golden Bear nomination in 1997. In terms of its mode of narration, production, distribution and reception, then, *O que é isso, companheiro?* is clearly transnational. In terms of its subject matter and historical approach, however, the film is firmly rooted in a national context.

---

[12] Bill Nichols, *Representing Reality* (Bloomington, IN: University of Indiana Press, 1991).

The film opens with a famous *bossa nova* song easily recognizable as Brazilian by audiences anywhere in the world: 'Garota de Ipanema' [The Girl from Ipanema]. This is played over black-and-white images of 1960s Rio de Janeiro filled with national signifiers including Copacabana beach, carnival festivities and a football match at the Maracanã stadium. By means of the film's audio and visual tracks, a clear sense of *brasilidade* is established from the outset. Intertitles with information about the 1964 military coup make the narrative accessible to those unfamiliar with Brazilian history.

The film's dialogue is in Portuguese with a few exchanges in English. When the captive ambassador is interrogated by his kidnappers, he requires the help of an interpreter. These scenes serve to reinforce Elbrick's alienation in relation to the country where he serves as ambassador. He tells the revolutionaries that he has no knowledge of the CIA's workings in Brazil or of the USA's interventionist policies in Latin America. The ambassador's apparent ignorance is used to justify the narrative's move away from this line of enquiry. It privileges instead less politically-charged and more universal themes such as the camaraderie that develops between the ambassador and his abductors, and the conflicts and bonds that emerge among the guerrilla group members.

Any elements that might invite us to establish connections between the Brazilian armed struggle and wider historical processes are simplified, marginalized or excluded altogether. The simplification is achieved by the use of humour in scenes that suggest the revolutionaries' ignorance and idealism about political conflicts elsewhere. In one of these passages the film's protagonist, Fernando 'aka' Paulo (Pedro Cardoso), tells a bemused Elbrick that he believes the Black Panthers are on the verge of overthrowing the US government.

One of the main goals of MR-8 and ALN was to draw the attention of the international press to the loss of civil rights in Brazil. Although this information is discussed in *Hércules 56*, it is omitted in the thriller, which privileges instead aspects that encourage a national reading, such as the group's decision to carry out the operation during the Semana da Pátria (Brazil's national independence week) with a view to deliberately disrupting the government's nationalist propaganda. The film's climax is equally filled with symbols of 'banal nationalism', in this case football: the militants drive towards a packed Maracanã stadium where they release their hostage amidst a crowd of football fans.[13]

Critics at home accused *O que é isso, companheiro?* of excessive fictionalization while deploying documentary devices, such as archive footage, to

---

[13] Michael Billig, *Banal Nationalism* (London: Sage, 1995).

create an illusion of accuracy. Left-wing critics were particularly displeased by the film's characterization of the revolutionary militants as inexperienced students and by the excessive focus on personal relations at the expense of political analysis. While Brazilian critics attacked the film's sanitized version of history, foreign critics applauded what they perceived as its ability to transcend the local context and become 'universal' through a focus on human relationships. These different readings can be understood in the light of Shaw's observation about 'transnational viewing practices' and the different meanings that one film can engender depending on whether it is viewed from a national or transnational perspective.[14]

Robertson's concept of 'glocalization' is also relevant here. Against those who equate globalization with cultural homogenization, Robertson argues that globalization generates renewed interest in local cultures that are in turn adapted for global consumption.[15] With its formatting of national concerns within a global aesthetics and its systematic use of sounds and iconography internationally recognizable for their *brasilidade*, *O que é isso, companheiro?* is a clear case of cinematic 'glocalization'. On a transnational scale, it can be placed alongside numerous films in which a national context or motif is part of a strategy to insert the film into the global market, a practice that Lu has called 'commercial transnationalism'.[16]

Many Brazilian critics perceived *Hércules 56* as a welcome response to *O que é isso, companheiro?*: a more 'serious' film without the 'historical fantasies' of its predecessor.[17] Despite its more sophisticated memory work, however, *Hércules 56* maintains a strictly national approach to recalling the past. The main difference from the thriller is that Da-Rin's film, targeting a Brazilian audience and committed to memory politics, is in some ways 'too Brazilian' for foreign audiences. Barreto's film, in contrast, relies on a simplified, easily digestible version of *brasilidade* that is attractive to Brazilian and non-Brazilian audiences alike: national clichés abound, politics is downplayed and the focus on Brazilian history is made more palatable to a foreign spectator through the presence of American actors and characters.

---

[14] Shaw, 'Deconstructing and Reconstructing "Transnational Cinema"', p. 59.

[15] Roland Robertson, *Globalization, Social Theory and Global Culture* (London: Sage, 1992).

[16] Sheldon H. Lu, *Transnational Chinese Cinemas: Identity, Nationhood, Gender* (Honolulu, HI: University of Hawaii Press, 1997).

[17] Fernando S. Fernandes, 'O monumental e o íntimo: dimensões da memória da resistência no documentário brasileiro recente', *Estudos Históricos*, 26.51 (2013), 55–72, p. 56. All translations from Portuguese are my own unless otherwise indicated.

Dia que Durou 21 Anos and the dark side of globalization

A co-production between Pequi Filmes and state-owned broadcast company TV Brasil, *Dia que Durou 21 Anos* achieved a level of international success that is rare for a Brazilian documentary: it was screened at European and US festivals where it collected three awards and received rave reviews. Most critics praised its well-crafted use of previously unseen archive material and its exhilarating narration in the 'investigative documentary' tradition.

Director Camilo Tavares's father, Flávio Tavares, was one of the prisoners released in exchange for Elbrick in 1969. Flávio lived with his family in Mexico, where Camilo was born, then in Argentina, finally returning to Brazil after the passing of the amnesty law in 1979. Camilo grew up struggling to understand his family history. Exile, torture and political imprisonment were not discussed in Brazilian schools or indeed anywhere in the public sphere. He decided to address these questions by teaming up with his father and making a film. The pair conducted a five-year investigation in the USA where they came across recently declassified documents from the State Department and the CIA. These included audio recordings of presidential meetings and letters and telegrams sent to the White House by Lincoln Gordon, ambassador to Brazil between 1961 and 1966. The relevance of these findings encouraged the director to change his initial focus and instead undertake a political exposé of the ways in which the USA colluded with the military authorities to overthrow President João Goulart and suspend democracy in Brazil.[18]

US support for authoritarian regimes in Latin America is now widely recognized.[19] What is new, as the film demonstrates, is the evidence pointing to the nature and the extent of this complicity. In the film's opening sequence, a CBS newsreel of João Goulart's visit to China in 1961 is used to contextualize President Kennedy's growing uneasiness with the Brazilian president. The following sequences depict Lincoln Gordon's extensive efforts to convince the White House that Goulart's left-leaning tendencies represented a threat to US interests and that, unless they intervened, Brazil would become a communist power (Figure 14.2). Audio recordings and confidential telegrams displayed in the film confirm that both Kennedy and his successor Lyndon Johnson endorsed the regime change.

The film reveals the covert measures taken by the CIA to fuel opposition against Goulart and win domestic support for the coup. These tactics included

---

[18] Post-screening debate with director Camilo Tavares at the Centro Cultural Banco do Brasil in São Paulo on 7 December 2013.

[19] See, for example, John Dinges, *The Condor Years: How Pinochet And His Allies Brought Terrorism to Three Continents* (New York: The New Press, 2004).

Figure 14.2. US Ambassador to Brazil Lincoln Gordon (1961–66) and Brazilian President João Goulart (1961–64).
Source: Still from *Dia que Durou 21 Anos*. Directed by Camilo Tavares.
© Pequi Filmes and TV Brasil. 2012.

the bribery of congressmen, false articles planted in the Brazilian press, anti-communist propaganda, and the financing of conservative corporate alliances and church groups. The kidnapping of Charles Elbrick is introduced as a postscript and in the context of growing popular opposition to the government. These final scenes draw attention to the anti-American sentiment that emerged among the Brazilian Left in response to awareness of US support for the dictators. Archive footage of protesters condemning the 'yankees' and burning an American flag help us to understand that the targeting of Elbrick by revolutionaries was rather more politically significant than we learn from a film such as *O que é isso, companheiro?*. While Barreto's film privileges a view of Elbrick as a hapless victim, aided by a sympathetic performance from Alan Arkin, the documentary invites the spectator to see him as he was perceived by Brazil's left-wing militants, as a representative of US imperialism.

Rather than focusing on the kidnapping itself and its repercussions in the national territory, the documentary turns our attention to how it was perceived abroad, particularly from the moment when the political prisoners arrived in Mexico. Archive footage depicts a crowd of reporters bombarding the group with questions as they make their way across the airport. This event is contextualized by a present-day interview with an American historian who informs us that this was the first time that victims of torture in Brazil were able to express themselves to the international press.

Hence, in contrast to the view of the dictatorship as a national phenomenon, as conveyed in the two previous films, *Dia que Durou 21 Anos* invites us to understand it in terms of the broader political and economic processes associated with the Cold War. The film exemplifies Shaw's 'cinema of globalization', a category she borrows from Zaniello to describe films that 'explicitly address questions of globalization within their narratives, central to which are the ways in which relations of power between nations and peoples are played out on screen'.[20] Shaw's and Zaniello's use of 'globalization' is restricted to its most recent form characterized by free market economies, digitalization and the growing power of multinational corporations. This usage overlaps with what Boaventura de Sousa Santos has called 'hegemonic globalization' and whose most persistent trait is the asymmetry of power in economic, political and cultural relations. Santos's view of globalization encompasses not only recent decades, however, but centuries of capitalist, colonialist and neo-colonialist exploitation by Europe and, more recently, the USA.[21] This more historically aware account of globalization is appropriate for helping us to understand how the geopolitical configuration of the world during the Cold War precipitated the wave of military dictatorships in Latin America, as articulated in *Dia que Durou 21 Anos*.

The film draws our attention to the propagation of a discourse of freedom and democracy whereby the USA accused its left-leaning opponents of endangering these universal values. It charts the spread of this discourse through the media, corporate alliances and conservative groups in Brazil, who, paradoxically, used it to justify the various means – military, cultural, political – that they employed to suspend freedom and democracy in the country, a move that in turn was firmly supported by the USA. The documentary's outward-looking approach continually points out processes that are transnational in nature, such as the efforts of one nation to expand its power over another and the global reach of certain institutions, whether political (the CIA and US State Department), economic (multinational corporations) or cultural (the media). In doing so, it highlights important aspects of the dictatorship that had been largely overlooked in previous cultural productions.

---

[20] Shaw, 'Deconstructing and Reconstructing "Transnational Cinema"', p. 54. See also Tom Zaniello, *The Cinema of Globalization: A Guide to Films about the New Economic Order* (Ithaca, NY: Cornell University Press, 2007).

[21] Luís Gandin and Álvaro Hypolito, 'Dilemas do nosso tempo: globalização, multiculturalismo e conhecimento', *Currículo sem Fronteiras*, 3.2 (2003), 5–23.

Phases of Brazilian postdictatorship cinema

During the 15 years that separate *O que é isso, companheiro?* from *Dia que Durou 21 Anos*, Brazil has undergone a radical change in the way it deals with its dictatorial legacy. Until the early 2000s, the dominant attitude of the authorities and the population was one of wilful oblivion, an attitude best illustrated by the refusal of successive governments to release classified files and by the continued existence of an amnesty law that grants full immunity to military officials involved in human rights violations. A slow shift was initiated with the passing of the Lei dos Desaparecidos [Law of the Disappeared] in 1995 and gained force in the following decade with the launching of two state initiatives aimed at constructing and commemorating memories of the period: 'Direito à memória e à verdade' [The Right to Memory and Truth, 2006] and 'Memórias Reveladas' [Revealed Memories, 2009]. These initiatives paved the way for the establishment in 2012 of a National Truth Commission to investigate the crimes and human rights abuses committed by former military governments. For Schneider, these developments represented a radical shift from a 'culture of silence' to a new 'politics of memory',[22] while Atencio uses the concept of 'memory cycle' to analyse the interplay between these institutional mechanisms and the growing interest in the dictatorship in the cultural sphere.[23]

O que é isso, companheiro? was produced at a time when interest in memory politics was still incipient. Some critics argued that the film in fact contributed to the culture of silence by using the dictatorship simply as a backdrop for an exciting story and for reproducing the conciliatory tone of its source novel.[24] The film's failure to address uncomfortable questions regarding state crimes and accountability is hence in line with the prevailing political sensibilities of the time. It should also be understood in terms of the preference for a particular narrative form that, as Hill has suggested, tends to discourage certain types of political discourse and favour others:

> Hollywood's narrative conventions characteristically encourage explanations of social realities in individual and psychological terms, rather than economic and political ones, while the conventions of realism,

---

[22] Schneider, 'Breaking the "Silence" of the Military Regime', p. 199. As observed earlier, the 'politics of memory' initiated in the mid-1990s has been thwarted by President Jair Bolsonaro (2019–), who has publicly praised the military regime and denied the existence of state crimes during the period.

[23] Rebecca J. Atencio, *Memory's Turn: Reckoning with Dictatorship in Brazil* (Madison, WI: University of Wisconsin Press, 2014).

[24] See collection of essays in 'Encarte Especial', *Revista Adusp*, 10.6 (2010).

with their requirement of a convincing (or 'realistic') dramatic illusion, not only highlight observable, surface realities at the expense of possibly more fundamental underlying ones, but also attach a greater significance to interpersonal relations than to social, economic and political structures.[25]

Employing the cinematic conventions of Hollywood realism and generic formulae were distinctive features of 1990s Brazilian cinema. After a serious economic crisis reduced production down to almost zero, film-makers sought new ways to reach wider audiences and break into the global market, and the strategies they employed were typically the ones used in *O que é isso, companheiro?*: high production values, generic ingredients and an international appeal through the use of foreign actors and characters.[26] Throughout the following decade, greater economic stability encouraged film-makers to experiment with a wider variety of aesthetic codes and to explore niche markets, including the documentary. Coupled with Brazilians' growing interest in the legacy of the dictatorship, this resulted in a veritable explosion of postdictatorship documentaries, of which *Hércules 56* is just one.

It has been argued that the specific conventions of the documentary, such as first-person testimony, interviews and archive material, make it the most appropriate format for a cinema politically committed to reconstructing memories of the dictatorial past.[27] This partly explains the evident preference for the format. The relatively lower cost of documentary production when compared to fiction has also played its part. In contrast to the directors of postdictatorship fiction films, who are typically well-established professionals in the field, many documentarians arrive at film-making by a more personal and politically engaged route. Some of them are former militants like Da-Rin.[28] Others, like Camilo Tavares, have parents who were imprisoned and tortured for their political activities. This personal engagement contributes to their greater commitment to memory politics and their relative independence from the mandates of the entertainment industry.

By the time *Dia que Durou 21 Anos* came out, a few other documentaries

---

[25] John Hill, 'The Political Thriller Debate', in *The Oxford Guide to Film Studies*, eds John Hill and Pamela Gibson (Oxford: Oxford University Press, 1998), pp. 114–16.

[26] For a detailed account, see Stephanie Dennison and Lisa Shaw, *Popular Cinema in Brazil* (Manchester: Manchester University Press, 2004), pp. 205–06.

[27] Cristiane F. Gutfreind and Nathalia S. Rech, 'A Memória em construção: a ditadura militar em documentários contemporâneos', *Em Questão*, 17.2 (2011), 133–46.

[28] Although *Hércules 56* was Da-Rin's first feature-length documentary, he had a previous career as a sound technician and director of short films, including *Fênix* (1980, 12 min), also about the left-wing struggle against the dictatorship.

had been released that approached the dictatorship from a wider range of perspectives, including transnational ones. A notable case here is *Uma operação chamada Condor* [*Condor*] (2007) which details the campaign of state terrorism carried out by an alliance of intelligence agencies from six South American states. A more personal but similarly transnational approach is taken in *Diário de uma busca* [*Diary of a Search*] (2010), which charts director Flávia Castro's peripatetic childhood as her left-wing activist parents fled the military police in Brazil, Chile and Argentina before going into exile in France. The rise of these transnational films can be related to recent developments in film culture described at the beginning of this chapter: film-makers travel more, seek funds from international sources and enjoy more opportunities to circulate their films abroad. But it should also be contextualized in relation to wider changes in the way that memories are constructed and shared in culture, and across cultures, more broadly.

Transnational memories, transnational film?

The so-called 'transnational turn' in film studies has occurred in the context of a wider conceptual orientation in the arts and humanities. This is particularly true in the case of the emerging discipline of memory studies, in which Inglis has noted various calls to shift the terrain 'away from the level of analysing national cultures only or mostly' and towards considering the relations between collective memory formations and globalization.[29] Many of these calls criticize previous analytical frameworks for being too centred on the nation-state and national forms of memory, as exemplified in Assman and Conrad's introduction to *Memory in a Global Age*.[30] The authors argue that while up until recently 'coming to terms with the past was largely a national project', the impact of global mobility and movements has radically changed this situation: 'Global conditions have powerfully impacted on memory debates and, at the same time, memory has entered the global state and global discourse. Today, memory and the global have to be studied together, as it has become impossible to understand the trajectories of memory outside a global frame of reference.'[31] Assman and Conrad draw upon Appadurai in their argument that hegemonic forms of globalization are increasingly cut across by counter-forms of globalization 'from

---

[29] Inglis, 'Globalization and/of Memory', p. 143.

[30] Aleida Assman and Sebastian Conrad, 'Introduction', in *Memory in a Global Age: Discourses, Practices and Trajectories*, eds Aleida Assmann and Sebastian Conrad (Basingstoke: Palgrave Macmillan, 2010), pp. 1–16.

[31] Assman and Conrad, 'Introduction', p. 2.

below'.[32] While Appadurai attributes the emergence of these counter values to 'imagination', they attribute it to memory and its increasing mobility. Human carriers, transnational organizations and the channels of mass media provide memory discourses with a global audience that has 'an important impact on political action and on the interpretation and evaluation of historical events'.[33] Their view echoes those of others for whom the sharing of collective memories in larger, transnational communities has an emancipatory potential because it can destabilize established memory regimes, especially those sanctioned by nation-states. New communication technologies, including the internet and film, are cited as some of the key factors responsible for changes in the way memories are produced and consumed.[34] The greater connectivity provided by these technologies enables 'travelling memories' to circulate more widely and rapidly across the globe, generating new forms of solidarity.[35]

As I have demonstrated in this chapter, however, claims about the enhanced mobility of cultural memories by the mass media need to be qualified. We must be particularly aware of the specific mechanisms that enable some mediated memories to travel, but not others. I have started to address this question in relation to postdictatorship cinema by showing that the mobility of films beyond national territory depends on a number of interconnected factors, including:

- Funding strategies and whether or not these strategies include the participation of major distribution companies that promote the international circulation of the film, as in the case of *O que é isso, companheiro?*
- Visibility at international film festivals, which operate as a showcase for international distributors.
- This visibility, in turn, depends largely on the film's level of historical specificity, which may or may not render it attractive to foreign audiences.
- Visibility is also dependant on the film's mode of narration. As we have seen, the use of generic ingredients can facilitate the circulation of a film outside a local context of production.

---

[32] Appadurai, 'Grassroots Globalization and the Research Imagination', *Public Culture*, 12.1 (2000), 1–19.

[33] Assman and Conrad, 'Introduction', p. 3.

[34] See Chiara De Cesari and Ann Rigney, 'Introduction', in *Transnational Memory: Circulation, Articulation, Scales*, eds Chiara De Cesari and Ann Rigney (Berlin and Boston, MA: De Gruyter, 2014), pp. 1–25; Joanne Garde-Hansen, *Media and Memory* (Edinburgh: Edinburgh University Press, 2011).

[35] Astrid Erll, 'Travelling Memory', *Parallax*, 17.4 (2011), 4–18.

Prizes and award nominations can also enhance a film's visibility. For Erll, awards exemplify the social uses of mediated memory: 'They are a way of steering the economy of attention, by highlighting one topic of memory and not another.'[36] The nomination of *O que é isso, companheiro?* for two of the most prestigious international awards in the film industry suggests how this particular form of 'travelling memory' resonates with the stereotypical expectations that international audiences have in relation to Brazil. Assman reminds us that the prefix 'trans' in 'transnational' stands for transit, implying movement in space across national borders, but that it also stands for translation, 'the cultural work of reconfiguring established national themes, references, representations, images and concepts'.[37] We might then ask what is lost in the process of 'translating' a story about the Brazilian dictatorship for a global audience. The question is answered in an essay in which Almada laments that *O que é isso, companheiro?* reduces the armed struggle to 'um grupo de meninos de classe média carioca que brinca de revolucionário sob o comando de dois mafiosos/terroristas paulistas [...] e sequestram um cândido e inocente embaixador americano' ['a group of middle class kids from Rio who play at being revolutionaries under the command of two mobsters/terrorists from São Paulo and kidnap a sincere and innocent American ambassador']. Lost are the memories of the many Brazilians who were arrested, tortured, humiliated and silenced, he concludes.[38]

What the three cases discussed in this chapter suggest is that the mobility of a Brazilian postdictatorship film beyond national borders is largely *in*dependent of its capacity to contribute to collective memories in a meaningful or relevant way. This view resonates with De Cesari and Rigney's contention that 'memory narratives indeed move with the help of media technologies, but they do so within ultimately limited circuits and along multiple pathways that, while they are sometimes a conduit to something new, may also turn out to be dead ends'.[39]

Hence, at a time when the transnational is being hailed across arts and humanities disciplines, it is important to separate considerations about the success of a cultural work in communicating with global audiences and any judgements about its social, cultural or historical value. Not all 'travelling

---

[36] Astrid Erll, 'From "District Six" to District 9 and Back: The Plurimedial Production of Travelling Schemata', in *Transnational Memory: Circulation, Articulation, Scales*, eds De Cesari and Rigney, pp. 29–49 (p. 39).

[37] Aleida Assmann, 'Transnational Memories', *European Review*, 22.4 (2014), 546–56 (p. 547).

[38] Izaías Almada, 'História: Ficção, Realidade e Hipocrisia', *Revista Adusp*, 10.6 (2010), 24–28 (pp. 27–28).

[39] De Cesari and Rigney, *Transnational Memory*, p. 13.

memories' are conducive to new forms of social or political solidarity. In fact, as demonstrated here, some of them might contribute to collective amnesia by reinforcing certain misconceptions and prejudices.

Conclusion

Rather than imply that transnational forms of mediated memory are inherently superior to, or more complete than, national ones, I have sought to demonstrate that, in the case of Brazilian cinema, these approaches reflect different aspects of reckoning with the past. I argued that a national approach can be a pertinent way to enrich our understanding of certain aspects of the dictatorship that have not been adequately discussed in the public sphere, particularly when this is combined with cinematic techniques that favour sociopolitical analyses in the form of group discussion and first-person testimony, as exemplified in *Hércules 56*. The cost of including such in-depth analyses in a film, however, is its reduced audience appeal, particularly among those unfamiliar with the historical context. Such an approach stands in marked contrast to *O que é isso, companheiro?*, whose commercial transnationalism facilitates communication with audiences anywhere in the world, regardless of their level of familiarity with, or interest in, Brazilian history. As I have demonstrated, such popular acclaim often happens at the expense of historical complexity. In this case, one of the consequences of maximizing entertainment value through generic ingredients is the reification of old state-sanctioned discourses which reduce left-wing resistance to reckless criminality. I further suggested how a politically-committed form of transnationalism such as the one employed in *Dia que Durou 21 Anos* can serve to interrogate such discourses by drawing our attention to elements and processes that cannot be captured by a strictly national perspective. A more extensive study involving a larger number of films would allow us to identify further aspects of the dictatorship era that can only be grasped through a transnational lens, such as the experience of exiles persecuted by the state and the emergence of human rights groups whose work has been crucial for the denunciation of state crimes in the Southern Cone. For now, what this chapter has demonstrated is that by analysing textual elements of films alongside their contexts of production, circulation and reception, and by relating these factors to the different stages of postdictatorship culture, we can better identify those films that do indeed have an 'emancipatory potential' by encouraging new ways of understanding the past and those that, in contrast, simply replicate traditional modes of seeing and remembering.

15

Remembering *New Portuguese Letters* Transnationally

Memory, Emotion, Mobility

Ana Margarida Dias Martins
University of Exeter

Introduction: the Three Marias and *New Portuguese Letters*: what, how, where and who?

My purpose in this chapter is to ask how we can trace memories of *New Portuguese Letters* (*NPL*) that transcend corporeal, national and cultural boundaries. In pursuing this goal, I will draw on the formulation of transnational (between the UK and US borders) and multidirectional (between diverse bodies, places, and times) ways of remembering the impact produced by the publication of this book in the 1970s, and briefly consider how this alternative methodology may shape approaches to transnational/multidirectional enquiry more globally. I will concentrate specifically on the testimonies of two women, Natasha Morgan (NM) and Robin Morgan (RM), who were involved in the international solidarity campaign in support of the authors of *NPL*. Paying close attention to these two accounts, one produced in 1974 in New York and the other in 2015 in Exeter, will lead to a consideration of issues of feminist politics surrounding *NPL* in transpersonal and transnational terms. Before unpacking these considerations, however, it is important to discuss, very briefly, some of the dynamics that have shaped collective perceptions of *NPL* in Portugal and abroad.

In the 'Authors' Afterword' to the 1975 English edition of *NPL*, originally published in Portugal as *Novas Cartas Portuguesas* in 1972, Maria Isabel Barreno, Maria Teresa Horta and Maria Velho da Costa write that 'WHAT is in the book cannot be dissociated from HOW it came to be' (authors' emphasis).[1]

---

[1] Maria Isabel Barreno, Maria Teresa Horta and Maria Velho da Costa, 'Author's Afterword', *The Three Marias: New Portuguese Letters*, trans. Helen R. Lane (London:

Banned in Portugal for exploring sensitive issues such as female eroticism, women's oppression under Catholic patriarchy and Portugal's involvement in the Colonial War, *NPL* was fiercely defended by national and international voices of the so-called second wave feminist movement. Prominent members of the French feminist movement such as Simone de Beauvoir and Marguerite Duras helped publicize the environment of intimidation and repression in Portugal to a wider audience, and soon an international wave of solidarity emerged (1972–73) in support of the book and the Three Marias, as the authors came to be known. The initial lack of available translations from the original Portuguese – the first translations into French, English, German and Italian appeared only in 1974, 1975, 1976 and 1977, respectively – meant that feminists involved in the international protests lacked a real grasp of the book's multifaceted nature. *NPL*'s wide-ranging content was inevitably simplified and coopted as a symbol of sisterhood by feminists of the second wave. This situation reinforced the book's reputation abroad as explicitly feminist and triggered the first internationalist feminist solidarity campaign.[2]

The galvanization of unprecedented transnational solidarity led to the development of a decontextualized memory of *NPL*, which was often read in universalist terms by some of those involved in the campaign. Despite the authors' attempt to break free from both national and universalist categorizations, what functioned as the framework for the reception of the book's model of sisterhood was, more often than not, either the nation-state or territorial/political collectivities, rather than the synergies and transnational and linguistic exchanges that comprise the contents and cultural biography of the book. Consequently, *NPL*, which reached five continents and at least 27 countries,[3] was, for a long time, generally taken primarily as a symbol of sisterhood and feminist unity by white second wave feminists, or inscribed in the anti-fascist struggle and literary feminine tradition in Portugal only.[4] This situation is described in the references to the 'WHAT' and 'HOW' in the 'Authors' Afterword': if the 'WHAT' identifies the Portuguese nation-state as a useful concept, that is as the country where the book was imagined, written

Gollancz, 1975), p. 399; Maria Isabel Barreno, Maria Teresa Horta and Maria Velho da Costa, *Novas Cartas Portuguesas*, ed. Ana Luísa Amaral (Lisbon: Dom Quixote, 2010 [1972]).

[2] For a summary and analysis of the theoretical content and political context of *NPL*, see Ana Margarida Dias Martins, '*Novas Cartas Portuguesas*: The Making of a Reputation', *Journal of Feminist Scholarship*, 2 (2012), 24–39.

[3] *Novas Cartas Portuguesas: Entre Portugal e o Mundo*, eds Ana Luísa Amaral and Marinela Freitas (Lisbon: Dom Quixote, 2014), p. 27.

[4] See Martins, '*Novas Cartas Portuguesas*'.

and published by three women living under the grip of Marcelo Caetano's right-wing dictatorship, and with very different ideas of what feminism and female oppression meant, the 'HOW' describes the manner in which both the contents of the book and its international reception broke away from a strict Portuguese national focus in the early years of the development of the women's liberation movement and the second wave in order to embody a specific notion of feminism.

With their statement in the 'Authors' Afterword', then, the writers attempt to disentangle themselves and their work from national, political, linguistic and ideological containers[5] and to highlight the interpersonal and transnational/translinguistic dynamics that contributed to the making of an object in transit through time (via the appropriation of the letters of the nun Mariana Alcoforado, the protagonist of *Lettres Portugaises*, the seventeenth-century text that supplied the starting point for *NPL*) and space (various nations and linguistic territories).[6]

More sophisticated approaches to the literary and political legacy of *NPL* have surfaced over the years, criticizing competitive attempts to contain the book within the boundaries of either 'international feminism' or 'Portuguese anti-fascism', and challenging the idea of narrating historical memories about it using the nation-state as framework of choice. A recent example of this kind of scholarship may be found in Ana Luísa Amaral, Marinela Freitas and Ana Paula Ferreira's important edited volume *New Portuguese Letters to the World – International Reception* (2015), which charts the reception of the book in Portugal, Brazil, Angola, Mozambique, the UK, Ireland, the USA, France, Germany, Italy, Spain and Scandinavia.[7] Here, the editors use nationalism strategically as a methodology in order to engage with the question of 'WHERE'. Following, at a structural level, a national understanding

---

[5] The notion of 'container culture' may be traced to the eighteenth century German scholar Johann Gottfried Herder, who understood cultures as clearly separate from one another and as ethnically and socially homogeneous, with impermeable boundaries. See Lucy Bond and Jessica Rapson, 'Introduction', *The Transnational Turn: Interrogating Memory Between and Beyond Borders* (Berlin: De Gruyter, 2012), p. 7. I use the term 'container' in this context to refer to attempts, by various readerships, to limit the book's several literary, political and linguistic voices to a single homogeneous culture, geography and/or time.

[6] In the original Portuguese version, *NPL* incorporates a significant amount of material in French, often engaging in linguistic code-switching, particularly in the (fictional) Chevalier's letters. The book also includes several references to other literary and theoretical texts, translated into Portuguese.

[7] *New Portuguese Letters to the World – International Reception*, eds Ana Luísa Amaral, Marinela Freitas and Ana Paula Ferreira (Oxford: Peter Lang, 2015).

of culture, the volume accepts the assumption of uniformity between territories and written archives in order to draw attention to the unprecedented transnational reach and impact of a book whose history exemplifies the interconnectedness of feminist communities globally.

As a source of comprehensive historical knowledge of the events organized to promote solidarity with the writers of *NPL*, Amaral, Freitas and Ferreira's volume goes some way towards challenging the idea that 'nation' is the best container of meanings and relationships. In fact, the national frameworks that govern each of the chapters in *New Portuguese Letters to the World* are often refracted by specific bibliographical references and historical facts that point to transnational archives. Nevertheless, because the book operates, albeit strategically, within the model of national and cultural formations as the chosen paradigm for thinking about the international reception of *NPL*, the memory that it incites – the question of 'WHO' remembers – is arguably still bound to particular nations. In 'Travelling Memory', Astrid Erll notes the flaws of such an approach from a memory studies viewpoint:

> For memory studies, the old-fashioned container-culture approach is not only somewhat ideologically suspect. It is also epistemologically flawed, because there are too many mnemonic phenomena that do not come into our field of vision with the default combination of territorial, ethnic, and national collectivity as the main framework of cultural memory – but which may be seen with the transcultural lens.[8]

Chiara De Cesari and Ann Rigney echo this view, problematizing studies that posit the national frame as the 'natural container, curator and telos of collective memory'.[9] Drawing on Erll's considerations about the travelling of memory, and on De Cesari and Rigney's criticism of methodological nationalism, this chapter suggests that clearing away the mists of total uniqueness and total comparability, which arguably still cover *NPL*, requires dropping the container-culture approach and pursuing what Michael Rothberg has termed as memory's 'multidirectionality'. In his inspiring *Multidirectional Memory: Remembering the Holocaust in the Age of Decolonisation*, a shift is advocated in the conceptualization of memory away from competition/

---

[8] Astrid Erll, 'Travelling Memory', *Parallax*, 17.4 (2011), p. 8. Henceforth, page numbers from this article will be cited in the body of the text.

[9] Chiara De Cesari and Ann Rigney, 'Beyond methodological nationalism', in *Transnational Memory: Circulation, Articulation, Scales*, eds Chiara De Cesari and Ann Rigney (Berlin: De Gruyter, 2014), pp. 1–25 (p. 1).

comparability towards multidirectionality.[10] To Rothberg, ideology is always behind attempts to place memories in hierarchical relationships to one another. Belief in uniqueness, on the one hand, leads to a competitive perception of memory, and to the refusal to pursue analogies with other events, histories and cultures. On the other hand, belief in total comparability is conducive to the loss of specificity. In order to avoid privileging one memory over another, Rothberg provides the more flexible hermeneutical model of multidirectional memory, which holds commonality and difference together by positing collective memory as an ongoing negotiation with other memories and versions of cultural identity: '[P]ursuing memory's multidirectionality encourages us to think of the public sphere as a malleable discursive space in which groups do not simply articulate established positions but actually come into being through their dialogical interactions with others' (5). Owing to its own multidirectionality as a text that traverses a number of interconnected times and spaces, and that comes into being through dialogical interaction between three women writers and several national and transnational audiences, *NPL* is an ideal object to which we can apply Rothberg's model of multidirectional memory.

There is, however, another reason why the debate surrounding *NPL*'s internationalization may benefit from the multidirectional approach. One important consequence of feminist activism in support of the Three Marias and their book was the development of competitive analogies with memories of other anti-fascist and feminist experiences and events in Portugal and the Anglophone/Francophone worlds. As Amaral, Freitas and Ferreira's volume powerfully asserts, these analogies often rendered *NPL* either exceptional, radical, and unique, as 'a literary object of uncommon originality and timeliness in both aesthetic and political terms',[11] or banal by comparison, 'seen as belonging to a "dated order", irredeemably bound to the historical moment of its scandalous emergence'.[12] In this context, adopting a multidirectional viewpoint will demonstrate an alternative way of conceiving of memory of the Three Marias' book beyond the two poles of exceptionality and banality outlined here. As we recognize, with Rothberg, that 'the borders of memory and identity are jagged; [that] what looks at first like my own property often turns out to be a borrowing or an adaptation from a history that initially

---

[10] Michael Rothberg, *Multidirectional Memory: Remembering the Holocaust in the Age of Decolonisation* (Stanford, CA: Stanford University Press, 2009). Henceforth, page numbers from this text will be cited in the body of the text.

[11] *New Portuguese Letters to the World*, eds Amaral, Freitas and Ferreira, p. 7.

[12] Anna Klobucka, '*New Portuguese Letters* in the United States', in *New Portuguese Letters to the World*, eds Amaral, Freitas and Ferreira, pp. 97–120 (p. 112).

might seem foreign or distant' (5), we are better able to grasp the multiplicity and disparity of patterns of remembering, as well as processes of inclusion and exclusion, that have affected the cultural, literary and theoretical afterlife of this important book.

In what follows, I shall focus on the transnational reach of *NPL* by investigating how the memory of the book and the Three Marias themselves have 'travelled' across and beyond these territories.[13] How has memory of them broken the frame of the nation-state? What are the localized ways in which memory of the Three Marias has been put to use? Does memory of the three writers and their book (or lack thereof) pave the way for memories of other writers, books and stories of censorship? Following the transportable logic of mnemonic practices, which, according to Erll, depends on the travelling across space of the 'carriers' of memory, I will attempt to move beyond memories of *NPL* that are bound to particular nation-states (9).[14] This will be done by drawing on two individuals' operations of memory, their intersecting group allegiances, knowledge systems, and remembering and forgetting patterns across nations.[15]

I will focus specifically on the testimony of actress NM, recorded on 10 March 2015 at the University of Exeter, and compare it to that of American poet, author, political theorist and activist RM, detailed in 'International Feminism: A Call for Support of the Three Marias', a text that Anna Klobucka locates under the header 'Memory' in the critical bibliography of her chapter dedicated to '*Novas Cartas Portuguesas* in the United States' in *New Portuguese Letters to the World*.[16] I will suggest, with the help of Rothberg's concept of multidirectional memory, that each of these mnemonic accounts

---

[13] When discussing the travelling of memories, Erll explains that they consist less of movement across and beyond territorial boundaries than the ongoing exchange of information between minds and media (10–11).

[14] While 'memory' is the faculty by which the brain stores information about the past, 'mnemonic practices' are the strategies we use to recall and remember that information. As Erll explains, these practices enable repetition of traces of the past and are often themselves powerful carriers of meaning. Traces of the past may be remembered or forgotten, celebrated or repressed, often due to movement across borders of the carriers of memory and the trajectories of their mnemonic practices (14).

[15] Erll describes 'carriers of memory' as those individuals 'who share in collective images and narratives of the past, who practise mnemonic rituals [...] and can draw on repertoires of explicit and implicit knowledge' (12).

[16] Robin Morgan, 'International Feminism: A Call for Support of the Three Marias', *Going Too Far: The Personal Chronicle of a Feminist* (New York: Random House, 1977), pp. 202–08. Henceforth, page numbers from this article will be cited in the body of the text.

has an impact on how we conceive of memory and the public sphere in the present. NM's transnational memory of her participation in the Three Marias' solidarity campaign events in the UK and USA creates, as we shall see, a narrative that overlaps explicitly with invocations of the Holocaust and imperialism, in order to address women's suffering and solidarity. As such, this account encourages multidirectional memory negotiation across borders rather than exclusive national ownership of memories.

RM's account, on the other hand, while also offering comparisons and analogies as part of her search for justice, provides nevertheless an arguably more competitive mnemonic account that follows the borders of second wave feminism as a political collectivity, since it looks for historical relatedness solely in the history of women's relationship to men, while also investing strongly in the specificities of the Three Marias' case. Whereas RM's account, produced in the heat of the moment, derives its power from the articulation of established positions ('women's memory' *vs* 'men's memory'), and from an understanding of the public sphere as the arena where men and women fight with each other, NM's account, made with the benefit of 41 years' hindsight, offers a view of the public sphere as a space that is more malleable and open to another logic beyond that of winners and losers, thus creating a memory account that is less competitive in relation to Portugal than RM's. NM's engagement with memory in particular challenges preconceived ideas of the public sphere by articulating other histories in multiple national contexts, and has an impact on how we conceive of memory today: less as unique static knowledge and more as dynamic engagement with multiple histories.

From what we know to how we remember it: between NM's reluctant witnessing and RM's celebratory remembering

On 10 March 2015, three actresses (NM, Sue Jones-Davies and Anne Engel), appeared on an Exeter stage to perform excerpts from *NPL*, as they had done some 40 years earlier in London and New York.[17] The performance took place in the context of the event 'Remembering the Translation of *New Portuguese Letters* to the Stage' during which they were also interviewed by Susan Croft,

---

[17] All three were involved in the women's movement and women's theatre in the UK. NM worked for the feminist magazine *Spare Rib* and in different sections of the women's movement; Sue Jones-Davies co-founded the women's theatre company *Raving Beauties*, which was born out of a sense of frustration with domesticity. Anne Engel was a founder member of the Women's Theatre Group, and she formed the company 'Mrs Worthington's Daughters'. See <http://www.unfinishedhistories.com/> [accessed 30 August 2017].

director of the *Unfinished Histories: Recording the History of Alternative Theatre* research project and archive, about their involvement in the 1970s performances of excerpts from *NPL* at solidarity campaign events in Europe and the USA. Holding copies of the original script, they re-enacted, in front of a small audience, the transnational protest tactic of reading in public.[18]

The artistic re-enactment worked as an alternative or complementary form of memory to the oral testimonies they had provided beforehand, in individual and group interviews, about their engagement, in the 1970s, with *NPL*, women's theatre, feminism, and the women's liberation movement more broadly. Throughout the event, verbal and physical movement contributed to triggering the act of remembering. While the interviews demonstrated how memory, in its personal manifestation, may be tainted by absence, unreliability and forgetting, the artistic re-enactment, aided by black and white 1970s video footage of an emotive reading of 'O Pai' ['The Father'] by NM, enabled the actresses to realign their memories as they connected performatively and emotionally with the long-lost script and with each other on stage.[19]

Although failing to remember recurred throughout the actresses' dialogical interactions, something emerged from their forgetting.[20] Something about their forgetting preserved emotion and movement beyond borders – both national and corporeal. What unfolded was a multilayered memory that grew stronger as it travelled back and forth between the three women, in the manner of the readings performed on stage. As they intertwined their personal stories of engagement with the women's liberation movement with their involvement in the *NPL*'s solidarity campaign events, the actresses revealed the extent to which memory of the Three Marias' text should not be perceived as static knowledge, but as the product of back and forth negotiations with other histories and biographies of women's struggles. This in turn shows that it is necessary to consider issues of feminist politics in transpersonal and transnational terms.

NM was present at all of the UK performances of the Three Marias' text, alongside British feminist Faith Gillespie. She was also involved in the organization of the Broadway fundraising event that took place

---

[18] In the 1970s, choreographed public readings became a popular and effective way of making political claims and denouncing abusive conditions in the early years of the women's movement. The three actresses' mnemonic knowledge of the Three Marias attests to the permeability of borders as regards the travelling of this form of protest based on public readings. See Interview by Susan Croft, in Ana Martins, unpublished DVD (2015). References to this interview will appear within the text from now on.

[19] Barreno, Horta and da Costa, *The Three Marias*, pp. 129–30.

[20] In interview the actresses confirm that none of them read the book, only the script that was used as the basis for the solidarity campaign performances.

in New York in January 1974. I read her testimony as exemplifying the weaving of a multidirectional network that brings together other, seemingly unrelated, memories and histories, such as post-memory of the Holocaust and American imperialism, and personal experiences of censorship in the UK. Although her account highlights cosmopolitanism, due to the emphasis on her travels between the UK and the USA, NM's testimony helps us to problematize the narrative of progression, which is characteristic of RM's earlier text, 'International Feminism', by questioning the notion that the international solidarity campaign simply and solely fostered solidarity among women.

Born in Wembley, London, in 1945 in a Jewish community, NM grew up in a highly politicized family influenced by the knowledge of Auschwitz and Holocaust memory. At 16 she played Anne Frank on stage, and later spent most of her time as an undergraduate at the University of Oxford acting. Drama offered her the opportunity to be heard and seen, and experimental theatre allowed her to explore new ways in which the audience could be affected by what was happening on stage: 'The first theatre that I saw that I felt really interested me was Peter Brook's [...] they were doing experimental work with *The Mahabharata*, and there was a big piece [*US*] that was at the Royal Court about Vietnam [...] and I was interested in what happened between the performer and the audience.'

In the late 1960s, NM performed at the Ovalhouse theatre and the Arts Lab in Drury Lane, London. But it was not until she got involved in street theatre, which included political collaborations with nurses, in hospitals, that the actress became aware of, and got involved with, the women's movement. She recalls her participation in Jane Arden's all-female, radical feminist theatre troupe Holocaust, whose work was 'very much to do with the oppression of women'.

NM's testimony about her participation in the solidarity campaign in support of the Three Marias deserves close attention precisely because it starts with memories of her initial encounter with theatre that situate her feminist practice in relation to her Jewishness and to American imperialism, via her early Anne Frank performance, her peripheral involvement in the theatre troupe Holocaust, and her reaction to productions such as Peter Brook's anti-Vietnam war *US* (1966). The various cross-cultural invocations that inform this testimony reveal the extent to which her perspective on the Three Marias' text operates under the sign of multidirectionality. As noted by Rothberg, 'coming to terms with the past always happens in comparative contexts and via the circulation of memories linked to what are only apparently separate histories and national or ethnic constituencies' (272).

NM's post-memory of genocide and imperialism intersects with memories of the Three Marias' text, opening up the possibilities of her testimony to revisit and reformulate sites of memory in a non-competitive mode of remembering. Her understanding of memory as an overlapping of spaces and temporalities draws attention to the historical conjunctions that mark histories of suffering, killing and violence, not only perpetrated by men on women, but also among women, and within the women's movement in particular. During the interview, NM stages memory of the women's movement as troubling, divisive and violent, often leading to the imprisonment and even death of women, as she notes in relation to Jane Arden's film *The Other Side of the Underneath* (1972): 'a number of people died in the making of that film'.

The deaths mentioned here reverberate throughout NM's testimony on *NPL*, and work as an unlikely but effective trigger for her memory of the book. Moving from her experience in Holocaust to her engagement with *NPL*, NM notes that what these early plays shared was a feeling of incarceration, an awareness that there was no way out of the domination and exploitation of patriarchy, which the Three Marias' text attempted to denounce and terminate.

Instead of falling prey to competitive modes of remembering that may render the text and the surrounding solidarity campaign events totally specific or banal, NM uncovers historical relatedness while discarding the possibility of complete comparability and uniqueness. This is emblematic also of the way in which she compares her own personal experience of censorship in the UK to the Three Marias' ordeal in Portugal. Adopting a comparative framework that brings forth the interconnectedness of various victims and perpetrators across borders, NM talks about the censorship threats that she faced with her script, entitled *Room*, which focused on her relationship with Virginia Woolf's *A Room of One's Own* (1929).[21] In a similar way to the Three Marias, NM was engaging with a classic text that had been silenced, and she, like them, experienced threats of court action.

Room, she notes in the interview, was about rediscovering the past and engaging with it. NM read *A Room of One's Own* while working for the iconic feminist magazine *Spare Rib*, writing *Room* as an open homage to the author. However, the Virginia Woolf estate attempted to ban the script, taking her to court just as the play was about to open. Lawyer Oscar Bucelinck was hired to read the book and the script, but, in the end, asked for only two changes to be made (amounting to eight words in total), in order to comply with legal requirements. The changes were made three days before the dress rehearsal

[21] Virginia Woolf, *A Room of One's Own* (London: Penguin, 2000 [1929]).

took place. Due to the publicity it had generated, the play was moved to the Royal Court.[22]

By juxtaposing these two distinct literary experiments in her mnemonic engagement with *NPL*, NM's testimony emerges not from the site of a singular nation-state, but as the result of the approximation of distinct memories of censorship across (fascist authoritarian and democratic) nations. This comparison disturbs the politics of separation between Portugal and Europe as regards feminism, showing that, in the words of Rothberg, 'histories are implicated in each other' (313). Instead of placing one memory of violence above the other, she highlights similar, albeit distinct, structural issues and problems faced by women who were involved in the women's movement across Europe. In doing so, she acknowledges the mutual constitution of the female experiences she is comparing, without falling prey to the logic of competitive memory.

NM's testimony bears witness also to the pitfalls of the idea of sisterhood in the context of the run-up to what Klobucka defines as the third phase of the protest in support of the Three Marias in the USA, which followed the decision by a Portuguese court to postpone the trial of the Three Marias until 31 January 1974.[23] One of the high points of this third phase was the organization of a show, *Women on Trial*, based on excerpts from *NPL*. The show, directed by Brazilian actress and director Gilda Grillo and produced by Lois Sasson, was to open at the Circle in the Square theatre on Broadway in January 1974. In her interview, NM recalls travelling to New York, where she started to attend soirées at Grillo's apartment, performing readings for guests who donated money towards the Three Marias' cause. Slowly, a group of people came together in the development of the production:

[T]here were a band of really quite varied people who became involved in the early evolution of that production, which was to be a musical, because Gilda knew these women... [...] there was a bunch of Brazilian women who had come over, and they became involved [...]. There was a sort of a band, and there was a woman who had been a friend of Faith from London, called Susan, who sort of opted to be stage manager, [...] and the piece took shape.

As the production was about to open, however, a number of incidents happened that crystallized in NM's mind a memory of the event as being

---

[22] The Royal Court Theatre is a renowned venue for innovative and experimental theatre by undiscovered, emerging and unheard thinkers, as well as established writers.

[23] Klobucka, '*New Portuguese Letters* in the United States', p. 189.

tainted by bureaucracy, negligence and a form of unhealthy competition and inequality between the women involved. At the last minute, the lack of an American Equity card prevented her from performing, putting an end to her transnational efforts. To add insult to injury, better-known actors were brought in at the last minute to play the most important parts.[24] This created a sense of unease in NM, which was reinforced when Susan, the stage manager from London, died suddenly:

> Susan died, and that had a profound effect on those of us who were quickly becoming the chorus. [...] Something happened in the company to do with management, to do with who was important, and not to do with the body of the text we were working with, some sort of political mismatch. [...] It had gone sour for me. [...] the piece lost the spirit of the text [...]. It was something to do with an inequality, with a lack of cohesion.

NM's reference to Susan's death is reminiscent of the deaths that took place during the making of Arden's film, mentioned earlier. By articulating both memories in the context of her testimony about the Three Marias' solidarity campaign, NM breaks the frame of the nation state (UK, USA, Portugal) and avoids the pitfalls of the universal (women's liberation movement) *vs* a particular (the Three Marias) viewpoint. Indeed, her testimony does not create a hierarchy of suffering.[25] Instead, it shows how both moments of suffering are intertwined in terms of their legacies, which question dominant visions of sisterhood and community across national borders. NM's mnemonic practice thus helps us move beyond competitive models of memory as regards *NPL*.

The memory of the Broadway event is preceded by a warmer memory of the London solidarity campaign event held at the Institute of Contemporary Arts (ICA) in January of the previous year:

> I remember it was incredibly cold. There was no heating in the ICA theatre [...] I felt really ill, and Nancy gave me a back massage, which I think helped. And we were amazed at how many people came, and it became clear that it was going to be absolutely sold out, and there were people queuing for returns, and so they arranged that, after the

---

[24] The names of these better known actors are not mentioned in Morgan's interview.
[25] I borrow the expression 'hierarchy of suffering' from Rothberg, who writes that 'The dangers of the uniqueness discourse are that it potentially creates a hierarchy of suffering (which is morally offensive) and removes that suffering from the field of historical agency' (9).

first reading, which was normal evening, that we would give another one, and that was full as well.

The bodily sensation registered here, which accompanies remembering, illuminates particularly well the relationship between the body, memory and emotions that is central to NM's testimony. Memory of the massage shows that remembering is both a linguistic and a somatic experience, since it effectively locates NM's multidirectional approach to memory (of the solidarity campaign) in the (ill) female body. In other words, the bodily sensations that accompany remembering in this case are a vital part of her ability to connect with the past. This creates a utopian somatic memory moment that contrasts overtly with the sense of blockage that she had communicated previously in relation to the US event, where competition between women artists, allied to negligence in the run-up to *Women on Trial*, arguably prevented female solidarity and thwarted transnational participation. Memory of the event in London, which pays detailed attention to the local via the female body, therefore conjures up a more enabling vision of transnational solidarity between women. If the back massage in the ICA theatre produces locality, this same locality is then negotiated transnationally in the context of what is to come: the reading of words, 'these fantastic words', written elsewhere, read abroad, remembered now.

RM's text, 'International Feminism: A Call for Support of the Three Marias', picks up where NM's testimony on the US solidarity campaign left off. Written for and delivered as the introduction to the Broadway evening in support of the Three Marias in 1974, the text differs from NM's testimony in that it was produced very soon after the solidarity campaign events. As such, it inevitably incorporates a strong 1970s internationalist feminist bias in favour of dominant visions of sisterhood and community, despite the event's casual backstage violence that NM's account, delivered in 2015, unveils. Contrary to that testimony, which shows (linguistic and somatic) sensitivity to the transnational ripple effects of strong conflicts and disagreements within the women's movement, RM's attention falls exclusively on the historical instances of violent confrontation between men and women, starting with the organization of the event itself: 'I shall never forget, as long as I live, the rehearsal encounters between the arch-conservative male supremacist, the Broadway stagehand, and our female technicians!' (202). This is not surprising, given that the event was meant to galvanize support against the oppression of women by men, described by RM as 'the oldest oppression on the face of the earth, the primary contradiction which entails the subjugation of half the species by the other half' (205). RM's text demands memory and justice for women on the basis of recurrent historical 'murders' of women artists across nations and time who have been driven to suicide and life-long frustration by patriarchy: 'So it has been all along. [...] Another suicide. Call it murder, you see' (206).

In this way, RM's text preserves an image of the women's movement as a united front against one common enemy, according to a dualistic model of self and other that is signalled by the use of the pronoun 'we': 'We will not be ignored. We will not be patronized. We will not accept the institutions which have tried to destroy us' (207). NM's testimony, on the other hand, concerned as it is with the death of women in the build-up to Arden's film in the UK, and later with Grillo's show in the USA, brings out, in a multidirectional manner that is reminiscent of the Three Marias' multivoiced text, the possibility that women can lose their way and yet still be perpetrators: 'What turned sour wasn't to do with the text, it was… it happens in all sorts of companies and political situations, there are differences, people lose their way.' Because her mnemonic labour is haunted by this concern, that is by the responsibilities and complicities of women in their own repression and physical disappearance, it contributes to expanding, in a multidirectional way, the ethical and moral responsibilities of those who participated in the transnational solidarity campaign and, more broadly, in the women's movement, which functioned, at times, as a sort of incubator for female suffering and violence, often pitting women against each other.

Conclusion: from Portugal to the UK and the USA, and back to Portugal

This chapter has paid close attention to the border-crossing itineraries, between the UK and the USA, of NM's flows of memory. Her testimony supplements existing accounts of the women's movement's support of the Three Marias, such as that of RM, which, as we have seen, is also embedded in a transnational perspective. However, while RM's text takes the feminist international second wave community as the ultimate 'home' of the Three Marias' text ('they sing for all of us' [208]), NM's remembering, because it happens 41 years after the solidarity campaign events took place, is arguably more aware of the heterogeneity of the various homes and worlds through which the Three Marias' book has globetrotted, and of the dialogues and tensions that characterized many of the solidarity campaign events. If RM's text strives to retain hegemony by restricting mnemonic echoes to those that confirm a sense of a united feminist home front, NM is able to avoid the pitfalls of competitive memory by applying a multidirectional approach to the act of remembering. Rather than restricting knowledge only to what the Three Marias' text did for 'us' against 'them', she supplements RM's account with memory of the grey areas of complicity of women in their own suffering (the blockages to transnationality and solidarity in the context of the US event), as well as memory of the multidirectional flows of emotion (via the back massage episode in the context of the UK event), and even memory of censorship that problematizes homogeneous conceptions of memory (via the reference to the censoring of *Room*).

The UK/USA comparison of NM's and RM's testimonies developed here must also acknowledge the powerfully competitive memory emanating from Portugal itself as regards *NPL*. Another example of memory travelling along a multidirectional line of transnational communication is the incorporation of the interviews and footage from the Exeter 2015 event into a Portuguese documentary on the Three Marias by directors Luísa Marinho and Luísa Sequeira. The fact that NM's interview was conducted by *Unfinished Histories* director Susan Croft and filmed in Exeter, for possible inclusion in a documentary about *NPL* made in Portugal but filmed in various locations, adds yet another complex layer to the feminist transnational circuit described here, since it brings memory of the book back to a Portuguese space but without casting Portugal or the Portuguese language as the 'true' original birth site of the book. From NM's 'fuzzy edges'[26] of memory, the Three Marias' book or, more accurately, the script based on the book that was used in the solidarity campaign events in both the UK and the USA, emerges as a transportable object/document in transit, enabling transnational mnemonic echoes and innovative routes to justice that mould contemporary conceptions of the public sphere.

---

[26] Erll, 'Travelling Memory', p. 8.

Part IV

Subjectivity

16

'Publish and be Damned'

Memórias da Minha Vida and the Politics of Exclusion in Nineteenth-Century Portugal

Cláudia Pazos Alonso
Wadham College, University of Oxford

Portuguese literary historiography has seldom sought to identify, let alone promote, any nineteenth-century female gems. In fact, as the nineteenth century unfolded, the (re)construction of the Portuguese nation-state following the loss of Brazil in 1822 and ensuing civil wars, together with the rise of imperialism in Africa later in the century, entailed a variety of national(ist) discourses that attempted to pre-empt contamination by the New Woman, as Ana Paula Ferreira perceptively argues.[1] At stake, especially from the 1870s onwards, was the domestication of female otherness present 'within the margins of the nation in the figure of a wild, uncivilised or "naturally" lascivious and, hence, foreign feminine body'.[2] As De Cesari and Rigney postulate in a different context, 'with the help of a transnational lens, however, it is now possible to see retrospectively some of the paths not taken in the formation of dominant national narratives, and so re-open archives and reactivate the potential of certain icons and narratives to become recuperated as new sites of future memory.'[3]

Mindful of the desirability of re-opening cultural archives and activating the potential of previously neglected works, this chapter considers *Memórias da Minha Vida: recordações das minhas viagens* [*Memoirs of My Life: Recollections of My Journeys*] (1864), a rare example of female life-writing

---

[1] Ana Paula Ferreira, 'Nationalism and Feminism at the Turn of the Nineteenth Century: Constructing the "Other" (Woman) of Portugal', *Santa Barbara Portuguese Studies*, 3 (1996), 120–42.

[2] Ferreira, 'Nationalism and Feminism', p. 129.

[3] 'Introduction', in *Transnational Memory. Circulation, Articulation and Scales*, eds Chiara De Cesari and Ann Rigney (Berlin: De Gruyter 2014), pp. 1–25 (p. 7).

writing in nineteenth-century Portugal.[4] Their author was Josephina Neuville, a woman who lived beyond national frontiers during significant parts of her life and who was thus indelibly shaped by other cultures and customs.[5] Her 'kiss and tell' autobiography leads us to revise the long-standing assumption that cosmopolitan cultural experiences were the preserve of a male elite, enjoyed by high profile intellectuals such as Almeida Garrett and Eça de Queirós.[6] Neuville showcases restrictions that mean that pre-1900 women cannot be understood as transnational subjects in the same way as men of letters. Nonetheless, thanks to her French education, Neuville gained cross-cultural literacy and access to some empowering female self-textualizations, including George Sand's autobiography. Her significant acquisition of 'cultural capital'[7] not only equipped her to inhabit a transnational mental space, but also enabled her to articulate and memorialize her own embodied subjectivity.

Changing times

During the 1850s and 1860s a growing contingent of women became active in periodical culture, both as contributors[8] and indeed editors.[9] Two of the

[4] Josephina Neuville, *Memórias da Minha Vida: recordações das minhas viagens*, 2 vols (Lisbon: Tipografia do Panorama, 1864), available at: <http://dbooks.bodleian.ox.ac.uk/books/PDFs/590716508.pdf> and <http://dbooks.bodleian.ox.ac.uk/books/PDFs/555057227.pdf> for vols I and II respectively [accessed 25 September 2018]. For an examination of life-writing in a Hispanic and Latin-American context, see *Feminine Singular: Women Growing up Through Life-Writing in the Luso-Hispanic World*, eds Maria José Blanco and Claire Williams (Oxford: Peter Lang, 2017).

[5] All spellings were modernized for reasons of readability, but 'Josephina' was retained, in preference to 'Josefina', in order to draw attention to a nineteenth-century positionality informed by a French-speaking and Portuguese-speaking hybrid cultural heritage.

[6] For an overview of their cultural interventions, see chapters 9 and 11 in *A Companion to Portuguese Literature*, eds Stephen Parkinson, Cláudia Pazos Alonso and T. F. Earle (Woodbridge: Tamesis, 2009).

[7] The term 'cultural capital' was theorized by Pierre Bourdieu in 'Les Trois états du capital culturel', *Actes de la Recherche en Sciences Sociales*, 30 (1979), 3–6. In the case of Neuville, education and access to French culture can be interpreted as '*incorporated* cultural capital', defined by Bourdieu as 'une propriété faite corps' (p. 4) ['a property made body']. At a time when relatively few women were literate, the prestige of a French education and cosmopolitan sophistication were assets Neuville embodied to her advantage.

[8] Maria de Fátima Outeirinho, 'O Folhetim em Portugal no Século XIX: uma nova janela no mundo das letras' (unpublished doctoral thesis, Universidade do Porto, 2003).

[9] Ana Maria Costa Lopes, *Imagens da mulher na imprensa feminina de oitocentos: percursos de modernidade* (Lisbon: Quimera, 2005).

most prominent journalists were transnational women or *estrangeiradas* [foreignerized]. Antónia Gertrudes Pusich, editor of the pioneer *Assembleia Literária* (1849–51), *A Beneficência* (1852–55) and *A Cruzada* (1858), was born in Cape Verde, where her Croatian-born father had been appointed as Portuguese governor.[10] After spending several decades in Britain, the Portuguese-born Francisca Wood became the dynamic editor of the forward-looking *A Voz Feminina* (1868–69) and its successor *O Progresso* (1869), jointly with her British husband. Her periodicals represented a key instance of dialogue with emerging transnational feminist movements.[11]

Rather depressingly, however, the most memorable transnational nineteenth-century woman – at least after the death of the Marchioness of Alorna in 1844 – remains one of Eça's own fictional characters: Maria Eduarda in *Os Maias* (1888).[12] My contention, though, is that Eça may well have based Maria Eduarda, and her mother Maria de Monforte, on Neuville's colourful life-story. Certainly, when he started living in Lisbon in the summer of 1866, his first texts were for *Gazeta de Portugal*, where a scathing critical review of *Memórias da Minha Vida*, penned by the periodical's editor, Artur de Vasconcelos, had been published a couple of years earlier when the memoirs first came out.[13] It is likely that Eça would have heard about the two tomes published by Tipografia do Panorama in the summer of 1864, because the 'kiss and tell' became an instant *succès de scandale*. *Os Maias* privileges in its very title and narrative thread a male lineage, although Maria Eduarda and her mother, Maria de Monforte, were in fact essential to the plot in symbolic terms. The fact that the fictional Maria Eduarda stood as a vivid figuration of the ultimate disempowerment of women – and moreover displaced Josephina Neuville, the real-life nineteenth-century woman – highlights the gendered economy of the national canon and its neglect of female writers' attempts to articulate their stories in their own terms.[14]

Neuville, not unlike her later fictional counterparts Maria Eduarda and Maria de Monforte, troubled the semblance of a well-organized functioning country and as such became the abject stain that had to be eradicated.

---

[10] See Nikica Talan, *Antónia Pusich: vida e obra* (Zagreb; Dubrovnik: Hrvatska Akademija znanosti i umjetnosti; Zavod za povijesne znanosti u Dubrovniku, 2006).

[11] Cláudia Pazos Alonso, 'Spreading the Word: the "Woman Question" in the Periodicals *A Voz Feminina* and *O Progresso* (1868–9)', *Angelaki. Journal of the Theoretical Humanities*, 22 (2017), 61–75.

[12] José Maria Eça de Queirós, *Os Maias* (Lisbon: Livros do Brasil, 1969 [1888]).

[13] Artur de Vasconcelos, 'Memórias da Minha Vida', *Gazeta de Portugal*, 521, 17 August 1864, n.pag.

[14] The analysis of the multiple ways in which Eça may have drawn on Neuville's memoirs warrants a separate article.

Vasconcelos's critical review indicated that *Memórias da Minha Vida* was the talk of the town and the presence of multiple copies in the Biblioteca Nacional de Portugal attests to its popularity. The book appears to have quickly sold out, according to Inocêncio da Silva's entry: 'a work which, owing to the inclusion of some passages involving rumour and scandal, sold very quickly'.[15] One element stoking the *succès de scandale* derived from her unflattering account of one of her lovers, the MP Jacinto Augusto de Santana e Vasconcelos. Bulhão Pato's memoirs confirm that Santana was known in his youth for his womanizing and quick temper.[16] But while Santana went on to have a respectable career,[17] Neuville became a case of 'publish and be damned', to recall the Duke of Wellington's dismissal of his former lover's memoirs: her taboo-breaking life-writing certainly resulted in a dramatic erasure from cultural memory.

One of the few to break the silence surrounding these memoirs is Cláudia de Campos, in her 1895 study showcasing six women writers.[18] Since Josephina Neuville was the only Portuguese considered – alongside chapters on Charlotte Bronte, Mme de Staël, Mme de Lafayette, Esther [sic] Stanhope and the Romanian Carmen Sylva – this move gestures towards the need to place her in a transnational context. Crucially for our purposes, the digital age brings an unprecedented opportunity to re-open archives, given that the Bodleian Library copy of *Memórias da Minha Vida*, digitalized in 2009, is on open access. The web, then, can grant a belated transnational new lease of life to previously relatively rare and/or unread books. The time is ripe therefore to revisit Neuville's work.

Neuville's formative years

Neuville's formative years were characterized by an itinerant pattern: by the age of 20 she had travelled several times between Brazil, Portugal and France. As merchants, her French-speaking Belgian parents were socially and geographically mobile and transferred from Portugal to Brazil, where she claims she was born, 14 months after her family's departure in 1832. 1833

---

[15] Inocêncio Francisco da Silva, *Dicionário bibliográfico português. Estudos aplicáveis a Portugal e ao Brasil* (Lisbon: Imprensa Nacional, 1858–1923), XIII, p. 247.

[16] Raimundo Antonio Bulhão Pato, *Memórias*, 3 vols (Lisbon: Tip. da Academia Real das Ciências, 1894–1907), II, pp. 271–81 <http://purl.pt/248> [accessed 25 September 2018].

[17] Jacinto Augusto de Santana e Vasconcelos Moniz de Bettencourt (Funchal, 1824–Washington DC, 1888). See *Dicionário Biográfico Parlamentar (1834–1910)*, ed. Maria Filomena Mónica, 3 vols (Lisbon: Assembleia da República, 2004), I, 379–82.

[18] Cláudia de Campos, *Mulheres: ensaios de psicologia feminina* (Lisbon: M. Gomes, 1895), pp. 251–308.

is the birthdate attributed to her by Inocêncio da Silva,[19] but it is very likely that she shaved some years off her age: 30 years later, Cláudia de Campos invoked the testimony of Neuville's contemporary Bulhão Pato to suggest that her true birth date was 1826.[20] Neuville's tendency to be rather liberal with the truth is part of her melodramatic strategy to elicit the sympathy of her readers: if we accept her chronology, some of the more harrowing episodes of her life-story, not least her marriage, would have taken place when she was barely a teenager.[21] Leaving the question of her suspect timeline aside, Josephina's successive tribulations allow us to consider how, in her bid for material and emotional survival, she mobilizes French culture and narrative modes to author(ize) her life experiences. These mediate her frank portrayal of womanhood, sexual scandal and economic hardship in ways previously unheard of in the Portuguese bourgeois context of the period.

After losing her mother when she was barely five, Neuville was sent to Europe by her womanizing father, given the prospect of inheriting from her childless aunt, Clementina Levaillant, a well-known dressmaker to Lisbon high society. During the long transatlantic sea voyage, the loss of her doll, which fell into the water, becomes a poignant symbol of her separation from her alleged motherland; it also foreshadows premature loss of innocence. In Lisbon, Neuville's education included a stint at an English school in Rua da Horta Seca until, deemed to be a handful by Mme Levaillant, she was passed on to other relatives in France to board at the Sacré-Coeur convent-school at Conflans, on the outskirts of Paris. After her education was completed, or cut short (supposedly around the age of 13), Josephina travelled back to Portugal, then Brazil, where she was reunited with her father and siblings. Crucially, as a teenager, a secret which she claimed was not hers to reveal, mentioned again in the penultimate chapter, forced her to leave Brazil and return to Portugal.[22] Suffering at the hands of her now jealous and abusive aunt, she married (supposedly before turning 15).

She tells us that she spent time travelling through countries like France, Germany, Austria, Holland and Hungary with her husband.[23] Indeed, her memoirs morph into a travelog in places, a fact that justifies the subtitle

---

[19] Silva, *Dicionário bibliográfico*, p. 247.
[20] Campos, *Mulheres*, p. 257, n. 1.
[21] Neuville, *Memórias*, I, ch. XXV. There is a marriage certificate in the Portuguese National Archives for a Josephina Neuville in 1846 <http://www.aatt.org/site/index.php?start=260&idx=160&op=TomboSearch&nome=Josephina> [accessed 25 September 2018].
[22] Neuville, *Memórias*, II, 250–51.
[23] Neuville, *Memórias*, I, 118–90.

recordações das minhas viagens. Only the previous year Júlio César Machado had published an account of his travels in Paris and London: *Recordações de Paris e Londres* [*Recollections of Paris and London*] (1863). Neuville was arguably keying into another genre that would enable her to market her text, since the sharing of cultural insights and sightseeing experiences pertaining to relatively little-known lands would likely be another selling-point for her potential readership. It also gave her cultural authority. In the event, her European grand tour occupies less than a quarter of the memoirs as her personal story soon takes over again, leading her to demand a separation from a husband she says she will never love and whose name we never find out.[24] Alone with Clementina, a baby born in Brussels, Neuville returns to Portugal via Britain, having hired a maid for the journey back. Finding a room of her own, both literally and figuratively, never mind 500 a year, would prove a monumental challenge in the years ahead.

Marketing women's writing

Memórias da Minha Vida opens with the transcription of a *folhetim* [commentary], initially published in the liberal daily *Revolução de Setembro*, on 21 January 1859.[25] This paratext seeks to offer an explanation. It recalls that advance notice of the forthcoming publication of her book had been given the previous year (1858) in the same paper, in a *folhetim* titled 'As Memórias de uma Senhora' ['The Memoirs of a Lady']. Although the identity of the lady was initially a mystery, Josephina was eventually tracked down as the author. As a result, she claims to have received threatening anonymous letters to dissuade her from publishing her account in full.[26] This campaign of intimidation, an early version of today's internet trolling, was also experienced by Antónia Pusich in 1848 because of another departure from appropriately feminine behaviour, in her case an interest in politics.[27] This very clearly showcases what a radical move it was for a woman to publish her memoirs in nineteenth-century Portugal.

---

[24] According to Campos, he was a circus owner, *Mulheres*, p. 275. This information throws into question Neuville's carefully curated image as a respectable middle-class lady of leisure.

[25] Josephina Neuville, 'Explicação sobre umas Memórias', *Revolução de Setembro* (21 January 1859), 1–2 <http://purl.pt/14345> [accessed 25 September 2018].

[26] Neuville, *Memórias*, I, p. iv. As the piece published in *Revolução de Setembro* was transcribed at the beginning of *Memórias*, quotations will be from the latter.

[27] Ana Maria Costa Lopes, 'Atitude e documento invulgar – A intervenção de uma prestigiada oitocentista, Antónia Pusich, na Câmara dos Deputados', *Povos&Culturas*, 8 (2003), 207–28.

Neuville's justification for going ahead deploys several arguments. The first was her claim to truth and authenticity: 'I do not portray myself with anything other than truth.'[28] The second is that the writing of these recollections stems from a promise made in childhood, while she was boarding at the Sacré-Coeur convent-school in France. To get readers on her side, she transcribes the relevant episode from the then still unpublished manuscript.[29] She recounts how, excited by the novelty of some newly-published 'memoirs of a lady', the convent girls praised the breakthrough as evidence of suffering, courage and superiority.[30] They then made a pact that 'anyone who experienced in her life extraordinary episodes, worthy of mention' should write them down. Even back then, Josephina was collectively deemed to be the most likely candidate.[31] Crucially, this childhood promise enabled her to deny that she was motivated to commit her recollections to paper by her experience of the previous couple of years (by which she meant 1856–57), and to stress that 'these memoirs do not seek to accuse anyone'.[32] In fact, she claimed that her book was not a spur of the moment decision: the manuscript, completed on 7 November 1857, had been placed 'in the hands of a trustworthy person to ensure it goes to press'.[33] In other words, the wheels were already in motion.

The *Revolução de Setembro* also featured, immediately after the 'Explicação' as part of the same *folhetim*, what would later become the introduction of the published book. There Neuville addressed the 'boldness' of her enterprise on two counts, both of them stemming from the fact that she was a woman writer.[34] The first is generic in that writing is 'a tall order for someone of my sex', showing herself fully aware of the fallout that she was likely to encounter as a result.[35] The second, of a more practical nature, is the audacity of following in the footsteps of the Marchioness of Alorna, even though her intention was 'merely to sketch my intimate life', thereby privileging individual consciousness.[36] For good measure, Neuville framed her introduction by offering two disclaimers that her intention had not been to step into the realm

---

[28] Neuville, *Memórias*, I, p. iv.
[29] Neuville, *Memórias*, I, pp. v–vii.
[30] Neuville, *Memórias*, I, p. v.
[31] Neuville, *Memórias*, I, p. vii.
[32] Neuville, *Memórias*, I, p. ix.
[33] Neuville, *Memórias*, I, p. v.
[34] Neuville, *Memórias*, I, p. x.
[35] Neuville, *Memórias*, I, p. xi–xii.
[36] Neuville, *Memórias*, I, p. xi–xii.

of literature. Yet the intentionality of transgressing and crossing boundaries through writing is undeniable.[37]

While Josephina's autobiography had indeed been announced in 1858,[38] and was ready to come out by January 1859, there was a six-year gap before it was eventually released in 1864. It is of course possible that either she or her publisher, the bookseller António José Fernandes Lopes,[39] had flinched at the likely scandal. If so, what may have been sufficiently different a mere few years later to prompt a change of heart? What might have led an experienced, shrewd bookseller to think that there was a market for the life-story of an unconventional rebellious woman? The answer may lie not simply in the sensational nature of her revelations, but also the timing, hot on the heels of the runaway success of Ana Plácido's *Luz Coada por Ferros* [*Light Filtered Through Bars*] in 1863, which boasted a print-run of 1,000 copies.[40] In other words, by 1864, the boundary between private and public spheres had been significantly eroded, as women's private lives were entering the public domain. Sale expectations must have been high since, unusually enough, on the first page of *Memórias da Minha Vida* readers were faced with the statement that 'the author asserts her right to translate this work into French and English', as well as a threat to sue anyone producing pirate copies 'on account of literary property law'.[41] In short, both publisher and writer were mindful of the possibility of a transnational market. As such, the publication of Neuville's fascinating text may have been a marketing coup, riding on the back of Plácido's notoriety in 1863. Both voiced the changing nature of women's own perception regarding their right to sexual (and textual) self-determination. What marks Neuville's text, though, is her transnational self-presentation.

Neuville's self-portrait is consciously literary and plays on both her European and New World heritage. Her volatile ('exaltada') temperament and whims ('caprichos') are repeatedly attributed to her Brazilian birth both by herself and others, in a manner intended to account for her sensuality, through the figuration of 'a wild, uncivilised or "naturally" lascivious and, hence, foreign feminine body'.[42] By contrast, her French educational background emboldened

---

[37] Neuville, *Memórias*, I, pp. x and xii.

[38] In a favourable *folhetim* by Francisco Serra, 'Sobre as Memórias de uma Senhora', *Revolução de Setembro*, 31 March 1858, p. 1.

[39] His imprint was the well-known Panorama. At the time, Fernandes Lopes was also owner of the immensely popular *A Ilustração luso-brasileira* (1856 and 1858–59).

[40] Plácido's book featured some autobiographical 'meditations', dating from her time in prison, where she was serving a sentence for adultery with the famous novelist Camilo Castelo Branco.

[41] Neuville, *Memórias*, I, n.pag.

[42] Ferreira, 'Nationalism and Feminism', p. 129.

her to aspire to high-minded pursuits: her epigraph, prominently placed on the front cover below the title of her memoirs, was a quotation from George Sand. It smacked of transgression since by then Sand was already a byword for a sexually adventurous woman writer. By recycling the very same epigraph featured in *Histoire de ma vie* [*Story of My Life*] (1854–55) – where Sand spelt out the rules she lived by as 'Charity towards others. Respect towards oneself. Sincerity before God' – Neuville was foregrounding her transnational lineage in order to justify both her rejection of social hypocrisy and a sexually rebellious account.[43] Furthermore, as previously mentioned, her 1859 explanation sought to legitimate her writerly undertaking by stressing that her French convent friends had predicted that she would do it. In the main text, this account comes 20 pages into the narrative, almost verbatim, save for one significant difference: the author of the memoirs that had inspired the girls then, was now named as Mme Lafarge.[44] Marie Lafarge's *Mémoires de Madame Lafarge, née Marie Cappelle: écrits par elle-même* [*Memoirs of Madame Lafarge, née Marie Cappelle: Written by Herself*] (1841) had proclaimed her innocence after a high profile murder trial.[45] Such a controversial backstory may explain why her name was not mentioned in the 1859 *folhetim*, but not why it made an appearance in 1864. It is telling, then, that by inscribing both Sand and Lafarge's names in her own *Memórias*, Neuville was placing the question of transnational female subjectivity at the heart of her narrative.

The chief novelty of Josephina's biographical tribulations does indeed lie in her woman-centred perspective. Her unapologetic subjectivity was mediated through a discernible romantic flavour – other cultural models mentioned include Staël, Hugo, Lamartine and Byron – and it was combined with a skillful deployment of characteristic *roman-feuilleton* traits, which took its cue from bestsellers such as Eugène Sue's *Les Mystères de Paris* [*The Mysteries of Paris*].[46] Neuville also references Alexandre Dumas's *La dame aux camélias* [*The Lady of the Camellias*], implying her similarity with Marguerite Gauthier, a heroine moved by love, not financial gain.[47] While Dumas rehabilitated his sublime character through death, the defiantly alive Josephina brought to Lisbon society an unmistakable whiff of scandal.

---

[43] George Sand, *Histoire de ma Vie*, 20 vols (Paris: Victor Lecou, 1854–55).

[44] Neuville, *Memórias*, I, 19.

[45] See Laure Adler, *L'amour à l'arsenic: histoire de Marie Lafarge* (Paris: Denoël, 1986).

[46] On Staël, see *Memórias*, II, 157, 169; on Hugo, see *Memórias*, II, 176; on Lamartine and Byron, see *Memórias*, II, 257. Eugène Sue, *Les Mystères de Paris* [1842–43], ed. Judith Lyon-Cahen (Paris: Gallimard, 2009).

[47] Neuville, *Memórias*, II, 250.

Emotional and financial survival in Portugal

Josephina's life-story reflects the extent to which she courageously transgressed bourgeois norms. Her raw self-exposure reveals how difficult it was to survive as a middle-class single mother in mid-nineteenth-century Portugal without the protection of marriage or wealth. As she was soon to find out, middle-class female labour such as copying music or embroidery was poorly paid. Josephina dreamt of setting up a school but lacked the funds to do so. Mme Levaillant employed several young French dressmakers, mostly described as women of dubious conduct.[48] Indeed Josephina was quick to dismiss them with the derogatory term *grisettes* (the French word refers to a young coquettish working-class 'lass') in order to demarcate her higher social standing. By contrast, she is at pains to fashion herself as a worthy gentlewoman who has fallen on hard times, not a kept woman. In so doing, her observance of codes of appropriate Portuguese femininity and domesticity included flagging up the maternal function at the outset and close of *Memórias*: she dedicated her memoirs to her two daughters, and in the closing chapter profusely thanked their tutors for helping her to educate them.

Her self-presentation as a lady, not a commoner,[49] required her to embody and perform codes of upper-class femininity predicated upon selflessness and financial detachment. As a teenager in Brazil, she altruistically looked after Emilinha, a toddler struck by scarlet fever, narrowly escaping from death herself.[50] During her European travels, she proved herself a true friend, willing to sacrifice her own reputation to save her friend Frederica's marriage. Instances of Christian behaviour, such as giving alms or proclaiming forgiveness of her enemies, are scattered in her recollections. Moreover, she is not immune to name-dropping: she met the Queen, D. Maria II, in Lisbon as a child; later in Southampton her path crossed with the princess D. Ana Maria de Jesus, wife of the Duke of Loulé; in Belgium, she was helped out in a time of need by the Count of Azinhaga (brother of the Duke of Saldanha). These vignettes enabled her to claim that she had connections in aristocratic circles, in a move designed to impress her contemporary readership.

---

[48] See Maria Antonieta Vaz de Morais, 'Os alfaiates e as modistas em Lisboa (1775–1850): subsídio para a História do traje e da moda', *Revista de Artes Decorativas*, 6 (2012–2014), 197–222 (p. 220) <https://repositorio.ucp.pt/bitstream/10400.14/19587/1/Editorial-%20Revista%20RAD_06–1.pdf> [accessed 25 September 2018].

[49] The distinction between *senhoras* (ladies) and *mulheres* (commoners) is cogently discussed by Vaquinhas. See Irene Vaquinhas, *'Senhoras e mulheres' na sociedade portuguesa do século XIX* (Lisbon: Edições Colibri, 2000), pp. 13–16.

[50] Neuville, *Memórias*, I, ch. X.

By the time that she returned to Portugal as a single mother, Josephina had already undergone several personal traumas. In particular, her memoirs draw attention to early domestic violence. She hints that her uncle, J. L. Lassence, may have been preying on her at night during her first sojourn in Paris, as a child.[51] Later, an explicit account of abuse concerns her aunt beating her.[52] And, to add insult to injury, when the police investigated the incident, Mme Levaillant accused her niece of trying to poison her. This backstory of early trauma aims to win readers' empathy before she embarks on a window courtship.

Her love-story and ensuing relationship with Henrique Pires is at the heart of the narrative. She mobilizes romantic tropes for (melo)dramatic effect, notably: the *buena dicha* predictions of a fortune-teller in Bohemia, which justify her leaving her first husband; a depiction of her 'marriage' to Henrique with God as the only witness, as a way to legitimize her de facto union; the enforced separation of the lovers by his family and their subsequent dramatic reunion; and finally the ominous stopping of a clock foreshadowing Henrique's premature demise. After his untimely death, she would have been a scandalous presence in polite Lisbon society. In fact, although she nursed him, she was prevented by his family from keeping him company in his final moments, and later from tending to his grave. Subsequently, while grieving her partner's loss, she had to survive in a socially hostile milieu, in the full knowledge that, plagued by the stigma of two children by different fathers – the second one outside wedlock, since Henrique never married her – her prospects of remarriage must have been non-existent.

On return to Lisbon as a single mother, a long-standing friend, Emília, had generously given her some money and a ring she could sell, but notwithstanding this display of female solidarity, by and large financial power rested with men. In her bid for autonomy, a fair amount of the second volume of Neuville's memoirs foregrounds her financial difficulties. Picaresque details abound: although entitled to her mother's inheritance, she never received her share of money; later, she appealed to the regent, D. Fernando for intercession in connection with another financial matter.[53] In an unregulated market, unscrupulous *agiotas* (moneylenders) thrived and Neuville kept borrowing money at extortionate rates, pawning her belongings, including jewellery. With so few respectable opportunities to earn money of their own, women were at their mercy and vulnerable to exploitation. After the death of Henrique, Neuville's dependence on a wealthy protector, Manuel Pinto da

---

[51] Neuville, *Memórias*, I, ch. III.
[52] Neuville, *Memórias*, I, ch. XXV.
[53] Neuville, *Memórias*, II, 141–44.

Fonseca, comes to the fore in the second volume. A notorious former slave trader nicknamed Monte Christo, he was the owner of Quinta do Relógio, in Sintra.[54] Their association was implicitly presented as a way for him to expiate his unsavoury past. Certainly, she seems at pains to stress, perhaps improbably, the platonic nature of their friendship and his support of her good behaviour in the form of a monthly allowance.

Neuville, however, was unwilling to forsake her right to sexual fulfilment and embarked on a relationship with the aforementioned MP, Jacinto Santana de Vasconcelos. This second lover, Santana (as she mostly refers to him), is presented as selfish and controlling, as well as verbally abusive. In one scene shortly before she summoned the courage to leave him for good, he helped himself to the money she had gathered by cashing in on some assets in order to pay her creditors, and squandered it. Yet despite his abuses, she indirectly claimed some intellectual equality, by stressing that she mixed with popular men of letters such as Bulhão Pato, Rebelo da Silva, Tomás de Carvalho and Lopes de Mendonça,[55] brought over to her house by Santana. Moreover, although women were not expected to take an interest in politics and the *polis*, Neuville's praise of Minister Fontes Pereira de Melo's modernization is further proof of how her intellectual engagement spilt over into transgressive political discussion.[56] To make matters worse, she declared herself a supporter of the Partido Regenerador – significantly not the Partido Histórico that would elect Santana as MP for the first time soon after.[57] Furthermore, she recounted how she spent a day with Antónia Pusich canvassing influential men for votes, thereby implying she was independently well-connected with the male political elite.[58] Neuville's confident claim of her entitlement to be a thinking woman is here, yet again, mediated by her transnational mindset, as she tells her readers that any objections from Santana could be countered with Staël's famous reply to Napoleon: 'Genius has no sex.'[59]

Although later parts of Neuville's memoirs falter and at times smack of desperation, they foreground her survival skills as she navigates her precarious position. The motivation to write her life-story may have been psychological, a cathartic coping mechanism to bolster her self-esteem. Her

---

[54] See Leonardo Marques, *The United States and the Transatlantic Slave Trade to the Americas, 1776–1867* (New Haven, CT: Yale University Press 2016); and 'Quinta do Relógio' <http://www.historiadeportugal.info/quinta-do-relogio/> [accessed 25 September 2018].

[55] Neuville, *Memórias*, II, 122–25 and 127.

[56] Neuville, *Memórias*, II, 160–62.

[57] Mónica, *Dicionário Biográfico*, I, 380.

[58] Neuville, *Memórias*, II, 152–57.

[59] Neuville, *Memórias*, II, 157.

emotional sufferings ring true, not least her suicidal episode in Paris early on in her marriage.[60] Unable or unwilling to abide by bourgeois social expectations, she experienced difficulties in leaving both her unnamed first husband and later Santana. And, at key moments, prolonged periods of illness point to an untreated mental illness, possibly depression. Simultaneously, the publication of her narrative may have been sparked by financial considerations, since it may have been a way to cash in at a time of need. In so doing, she would have been fully aware of implicating several people and alienating her own relatives further. Yet, following the death of her lover Henrique, that of the controversial Manuel Pinto da Fonseca in 1855, and her break up with Santana in 1857, she must have felt that the alternative was destitution.

Conclusion

Memórias da Minha Vida provides a gripping account that gives a voice to a different subjective perspective, previously overwhelmingly filtered through the male literary gaze: that of the so-called *demi-monde*. Neuville's autobiographical account, which may have helped Eça to engender Maria Eduarda and Maria de Monforte, offers a dissident voice from the margins – one that not only clamoured for recognition, but also damningly exposed prevailing double standards, underpinned by glaring financial inequality and lack of opportunities for women outside marriage. The defiant *Memórias da Minha Vida* elicited moral outrage; it was too greatly in breach of decorum to survive in Portuguese collective memory. But from a twenty-first-century perspective, this symptomatic case-study of exclusion deserves to be re-opened. Neuville's intimate memoirs offer a counterpoint that prompts us to rethink the hegemony occupied to this day by *Os Maias* as representative national saga in the collective Portuguese unconscious, in a nation-building landscape that became, as Ferreira rightly demonstrated, largely dominated by 'a national(ist) alternative to the foreign (mostly English) "women's question"'.[61]

The transnational turn, then, enables us to understand better how Neuville attempted to carve out a space for herself at a time when women had scant cultural legitimacy in the Portuguese literary field. Indeed, the contribution of women in genres other than the novel, and in particular to reputedly minor genres such as life-writing – in this particular instance, a flexible matrix endowed with sociological documentary value, psychological depth and aesthetic value – compels us to interrogate afresh nationally bound cultural and intellectual nineteenth-century history, as well as its

---

[60] Neuville, *Memórias*, I, ch. XXVI.
[61] Ferreira, 'Nationalism and Feminism', p. 132.

economic infrastructure, in relation to women's discursive absences. The case of Neuville was certainly taboo-breaking on an individual level. More broadly speaking, however, any future re-evaluation of the transnational in the emergence of nineteenth-century feminist Portuguese intellectual history will necessarily have to encompass periodical culture, where the combative editorials of the outspoken Francisca Wood in *A Voz Feminina* stood out as a crucial milestone, critiquing the ideological underpinnings of national constructs and pointing ahead towards the strategic mobilization of women's networks across borders.[62]

---

[62] See Alonso, 'Spreading the Word'; and João Esteves, 'Historical Context of Feminism and Women's Rights in Nineteenth-Century Portugal', in *A New History of Iberian Feminisms*, eds Silvia Bermúdez and Roberta Johnson (Toronto: Toronto University Press, 2018), pp. 101–25.

17

Transnational Pessoa

Paulo de Medeiros
University of Warwick

As unrepentant 'moderns', we believe that critique has not ceased to designate philosophy's most characteristic gesture.

Étienne Balibar[1]

For far too long the name of Fernando Pessoa was held as a sort of emblem for Portugal, as if through his artistic greatness the nation could redeem itself from its political failures. 'Minha pátria é a língua portuguesa' ['My fatherland is the Portuguese language'], one of the most frequently cited of his lines, would seem to present him as a fervent nationalist.[2] Yet, the passage of *Livro do Desassossego* [*The Book of Disquiet*] from which it is lifted, when read fully, reveals quite the opposite: 'It wouldn't grieve me if someone invaded and took over Portugal as long as they didn't bother me personally.'[3] More than any other writer in the twentieth century Pessoa has come to

---

[1] Étienne Balibar, 'Critique in the 21st Century: Political Economy Still, and Religion Again', *Radical Philosophy*, 200 (2016) <https://www.radicalphilosophy.com/article/critique-in-the-21st-century>.

[2] Fernando Pessoa, Fragment 333, dated after 18 October 1931, *Livro do Desasocego*. Edição Crítica de Fernando Pessoa, vol. XXII, ed. Jerónimo Pizarro (Lisbon: Imprensa Nacional – Casa da Moeda, 2010), p. 326; Fernando Pessoa, *The Book of Disquiet. The Complete Edition*, ed. Jerónimo Pizarro, trans. Margaret Jull Costa (London: Serpent's Tail, 2017), Fragment 326, p. 302.

[3] Pessoa, *Livro do Desasocego*, p. 326; *The Book of Disquiet*, p. 302. One of the first critics to call attention to the need to take in Pessoa's meaning in full was Onésimo Almeida in 'Da pátria da língua – de Pessoa e de cada qual', *Revista da Faculdade de Letras*, 21–22 (1996–97), pp. 15–21.

embody and represent his nation, in terms of a great culture, genius, verbal virtuosity, a melancholic soul, and proud self-effacement, all of which are clichés for ready internal consumption and easy export. The view of Pessoa as the great national poet, the undisputable heir to the legend of Camões, as appealing as it might be in some quarters or for facile quotation at political rallies, is losing its sway not just because of a decisively transnational inflection to literary studies at present, but also, perhaps more importantly, because Pessoa's literary achievements are increasingly becoming the object of comparative study at the hands of many critics and scholars outside Portugal. At the same time, as the term transnational has become a sort of trendy label, one should also be wary of using it indiscriminately. If Pessoa is to be regarded properly as a transnational writer this does not mean that the specific, local and national context ceases to be relevant. Quite the contrary, I would suggest: Portugal's stale, provincial backwardness at the beginning (and throughout most) of the twentieth century needs to be kept resolutely in mind, in order to understand better not just Pessoa's conditionings but also how he went against them.

The notion advanced by Mads Rosendhal Thomsen of Pessoa, like Borges, being one of those 'lonely canonicals' is highly suggestive but also deeply inadequate.[4] The neat division he proposes between what he regards as the common practice of international canonization – whereby pairs of writers from the various nations would find their way into the pantheon of a (traditionally conceived) World Literature, say Tolstoy and Dostoyevsky – is appealing at first sight but of course based on a strict dualistic view, separating national from international and great from minor, that does not bear much scrutiny. The process of canonization might indeed produce such skewed views that have the benefit of simplifying cultural processes and thus turning the writers in question more readily into convenient commodities. From that perspective one could, perhaps, see a point in the (pseudo) distinction Thomsen proposes. But, as is becoming clearer with a new generation of scholars becoming interested in the modernist archives, other writers and artists surrounding the figure of Pessoa, such as fellow poet Mário Sá-Carneiro or painter Amadeu de Souza Cardoso, must be considered alongside him, in order to provide a more informed view of Modernism in general. This is so, I would suggest, whether one sticks to a traditional view of literary studies based on national demarcations or, as is becoming more common every day, one applies such knowledge to a comparative, transnational study of Modernism. The question, to my mind, is not so much one

---

[4] Mads Rosendhal Thomsen, *Mapping World Literature: International Canonization and Transnational Literatures* (New York: Continuum, 2008), p. 48.

of expanding the repertoire of traditional views of Modernism as centred, almost exclusively, on an Anglo-American axis, to which Paris and Berlin would occasionally have contributed. Rather, the point of viewing Pessoa transnationally would be, on the one hand to contribute to a more inclusive understanding of Modernity as singular – to follow Fredric Jameson's well-known and crucial injunction[5] – and, on the other, to have a less lop-sided view of Pessoa's own achievements.

From the many comparative studies of Pessoa I would just like to mention three as examples: the seminal study *Atlantic Poets: Fernando Pessoa's Turn in Anglo-American Modernism* by Irene Ramalho Santos (2003); several works by George Monteiro, such as *The Presence of Pessoa: English, American, and Southern African Literary Responses* (2000); and the volume of collected essays edited by Anna Klobucka and Mark Sabine, *Embodying Pessoa: Corporeality, Gender, Sexuality* (2007).[6] As important as such studies were when first published, and still remain for anyone interested in Pessoa, for the most part they still follow and accept premises inherent to traditional comparative studies and notions of influence and reception that have strong limitations especially as they often – less so in the case of Santos's work – unwittingly serve to reinforce concepts of culture bounded by nationalism that I consider dubious and problematic.

A first step in bringing about a displacement of Pessoa – mythically held to have never left Lisbon in his adult life – is to consider the fact that to all effects he was brought up, and formally schooled, in another country. It is well known that in January 1896 Pessoa was taken by his mother to Durban, South Africa where she was joining the man she had married, by proxy, after becoming a widow. In March of that year Pessoa was enrolled at St Joseph's Convent School. In 1899 he started at Durban High School, from where he would graduate in 1901. On 1 August of that year he would again set sail, travelling to Lisbon and Madeira before returning to South Africa, taking university examinations, and actually doing his first year of university-level study still at Durban High. In August of 1905 he would then take the *Herzog* and return definitively to Lisbon, aged 17. There are studies of Pessoa's time in

---

[5] Fredric Jameson, *A Singular Modernity: Essay on the Ontology of the Present* (London and New York: Verso, 2002).

[6] Irene Ramalho Santos, *Atlantic Poets: Fernando Pessoa's Turn in Anglo-American Modernism* (Hanover, NH and London: Dartmouth College, University Press of New England, 2003); George Monteiro, *The Presence of Pessoa: English, American, and Southern African Literary Responses* (Louisville, KY: The University Press of Kentucky, 1998); *Embodying Pessoa: Corporeality, Gender, Sexuality*, eds Anna M. Klobucka and Mark Sabine (Toronto: University of Toronto Press, 2007).

South Africa – and he had started writing as a child already of course – such as the above-mentioned one by Monteiro, or, more recently, a special issue of *Pessoa Plural*,[7] guest-edited by Carlos Pittella-Leite and dedicated to the figure of Hubert D. Jennings, a teacher at Durban High who became a dedicated Pessoa scholar specializing in the young poet's relationship to Durban. In that issue, Margaret Jull Costa, while considering Jennings's work, reflects on how Jennings's views went against those of traditional Pessoa scholar and biographer João Gaspar Simões. Whereas the latter saw the sojourn in South Africa as a family trauma, first the loss of the father and then '"losing" his mother to her new husband and new siblings', Jennings emphasized how fond Pessoa was of his siblings.[8]

As nice as that might be, it still leaves totally by the wayside the fact that spending nine years in South Africa was a double displacement for Pessoa, removed from the environment he knew in Lisbon and Europe and placed in the African colony of another country with a language he did not know, yet came to master so well that he beat 899 other candidates, to win the school's Queen Victoria Memorial Prize for best English essay. Even if the imposition of British rule over Zulu sovereignty had been some time beforehand and the second Boer War might not have been of immediate relevance in Durban, independence for South Africa was only five years away when Pessoa left. And in Lisbon, well, stability was nowhere to be found: less than three years after Pessoa's return, both the king and his oldest son, the heir apparent, were murdered on the streets of Lisbon. By 5 October 1910, as the royal family fled to England, the republic was proclaimed.

Irene Ramalho Santos clearly sees the importance of Pessoa's upbringing for his creative process. Drawing a comparison between Pessoa and Hart Crane, particularly Crane's need to deal with America's materialism and rising imperialism, she writes:

> Pessoa, who, as a bilingual poet educated in a British school in South Africa to the age of 17, was heir to not one but two empires, the British and the Portuguese, had to come to terms with the Portuguese empire, practically non-existent at the turn of the century under British

---

[7] *Pessoa Plural*, 8 (2015), Guest Editor, Carlos Pittella-Leite <https://repository.library.brown.edu/studio/item/bdr:698206/> [accessed 20 August, 2018].

[8] Margaret Jull Costa, 'Pessoa in Durban: The Making of a Poet', *Pessoa Plural* 8 (2015) <https://www.brown.edu/Departments/Portuguese_Brazilian_Studies/ejph/pessoaplural/Issue8/PDF/I8A15.pdf> [accessed 20 August 2018]. The book referred to is: João Gaspar Simões, *Vida e Obra de Fernando Pessoa – História duma Geração*, 2 vols (Lisbon: Bertrand, 1951), I, Infância e Adolescência, p. 55.

domination, before he could reinvent Portuguese poetry as cultural imperialism.[9]

This does not mean that one should place all of Pessoa's work and his intense multiplicity, whether in terms of his heteronymic authorship[10] or its generic diversity, under the banner of this dual imperial inheritance, which, as Santos also intimates, was as much a negative inheritance as anything else. But, I would suggest, it should be enough to alert us to the need for constantly displacing Pessoa, to refuse the simplistic national identification for the reductive trap that it is. Certainly, such an upbringing given a different personality, might have yielded precisely the opposite: some sort of avoidance and mistrust of difference. In the case of Pessoa, again, and without forgetting that he remains a highly paradoxical writer, as he could not help but be, one could say that it provided the grounding, or served as the catalyst, for him to flourish, rejecting any form of essential identity and embracing his own rich plurality.

The supreme expression of Pessoa's plurality, of his desire for imagining himself as another, and his actual capacity to take it further than any other writer before or since, was the creation of the heteronyms. The heteronymic quality of Pessoa has long been hailed as one of his outstanding, if not the most idiosyncratic, features. As remarkable as it is, however, this too tends to be exalted along with other clichéd views including the melancholia and the national identification, to the point one could be forgiven for thinking that all three were actually themselves just various facets of the same national genius. Without wanting to contribute to this kind of mythologizing, I would nonetheless like to seize briefly on the heteronyms, and one in particular, as part of reflecting on Pessoa from a transnational perspective. Obviously,

---

[9] Santos, *Atlantic Poets*, p. 110.

[10] Pessoa's creation of heteronyms is one of his most distinguishing and complex traits. Some critics put the number of these 'other' figures of the poet at over a hundred. George Steiner provided a very concise and elegant definition of heteronymy: 'Pseudonymous writing is not rare in literature or philosophy (Kierkegaard provides a celebrated instance). "Heteronyms", as Pessoa called and defined them, are something different and exceedingly strange. For each of his "voices", Pessoa conceived a highly distinctive poetic idiom and technique, a complex biography, a context of literary influence and polemics and, most arrestingly of all, subtle interrelations and reciprocities of awareness', 'A man of many parts', *The Observer* (3 June 2001) <https://www.theguardian.com/books/2001/jun/03/poetry.features1> [accessed 20 August 2018]. For further exploration of the heteronyms, see Fernando Pessoa, *Teoria da Heteronímia*, eds Fernando Cabral Martins and Richard Zenith (Lisbon: Assírio & Alvim, 2012).

the heteronyms in and of themselves do not make Pessoa transnational, just as they do not make him nationalist either. If anything, I would argue that his radical multiplication of the self, far more than that envisioned by other modernists, would imply a rejection of any narrow ideology predicated on sameness. For what binds a nation together, supposedly, is the common ascent of an entire 'people', united in history through a shared language and (traditionally religious) beliefs and cultural norms. Seen in this way, nationalism is basically a form of hyperidentity that would reduce the individual and the unique to a common denominator. My point is simple: by making it imperative to feel for and as another, culminating in the heteronymic project, that irrefutably blurs the borders between self and other, Pessoa aligns himself with transnationalism as a refusal to establish solid borders between nations.

The heteronyms, in and of themselves, can be seen as a kind of rhizomatic machine for desire.[11] A Deleuzian approach to Pessoa has long been a hallmark of the work of Portuguese philosopher José Gil, from the early *Fernando Pessoa ou la Métaphysique des sensations* [*Fernando Pessoa or the Metaphysics of Feelings*] (1984) to *O Devir-Eu de Pessoa* [*The Becoming-I of Pessoa*] (2010).[12] His perspectives generally distinguish themselves from the rest by both their originality and their force. Adam Morris explores this specific angle in his 2014 article 'Fernando Pessoa's Heteronymic Machine'.[13] His extended argument about how Deleuze's notions often seem to be a development of what Pessoa had already done much earlier is well made – even if it is not, of course, new, but has already been explored by Gil, whose work Morris acknowledges, but does not really engage with. Morris's argument has the advantage of drawing out some conclusions that, even if latent in other critics, had not quite been fully formulated. In order to try to

---

[11] See Felicity J. Colman: '"Rhizome" describes the connections that occur between the most disparate and the most similar of objects, places and people; the strange chains of events that link people [The] concept [...] draws from [...] the biological term "rhizome" [that] describes a form of plant that can extend itself through its underground horizontal tuber-like root system and develop new plants. In Deleuze and Guattari's use of the term, the rhizome is a concept that "maps" a process of networked, relational and transversal thought, and a way of being without "tracing" the construction of that map as a fixed entity', in *The Deleuze Dictionary*, ed. Adrian Parr, rev. edn (Edinburgh: Edinburgh University Press, 2010), pp. 232–33.

[12] José Gil, *Fernando Pessoa ou La métaphysique des sensations* (Paris: La Différence, 1998); *O Devir-Eu de Fernando Pessoa* (Lisbon: Relógio d'Água, 2010).

[13] Adam Morris, 'Fernando Pessoa's Heteronymic Machine', *Luso-Brazilian Review* 51.2 (2014), 126–49.

understand Pessoa transnationally, I would focus specifically on the question of 'deterritorialization'.[14]

I would like to seize upon this point about deterritorialization effected by heteronymy and suggest that it opens the way for understanding the transnational in Pessoa. Even if speaking from a very different enunciatory platform and still subscribing to, or rather, fully participating in, the mythologizing of a sort of 'spectral Pessoa' immensely appealing to our imagination – but, as I have tried to show elsewhere,[15] equally pernicious – George Steiner had already adumbrated this. In *Lessons of the Masters* for example, he writes: 'The four poets whom Pessoa conjures into being have their perfectly distinct voice, ideologies, rhetorical manners. [...] They interrelate in a cat's cradle of mutual notice, suspicion or affinity through which Pessoa moves, a "secret sharer" in "exile from himself."'[16]

Even leaving aside the Conradian allusion,[17] itself a hint at transnationality but in the obverse, as it were, as Steiner also states, this game ('alchemy' he calls it), of 'Mastery and discipleship' is marked, but ultimately causes an estrangement of the self from itself that, I would suggest, is the mark of the transnational at the individual level: never 'at home' anywhere, least of all in the space of his Self, too confined, and confining, for the expansiveness of his creative force.[18]

How to render concrete such a suite of abstractions, from the deterritorialization of the self to a transnational condition? Perhaps looking briefly at

---

[14] Of the many concepts introduced by Deleuze and Guattari, 'deterritorialization' is certainly one of the most complex and any one definition risks simply misrepresenting it. What remains fundamental is its connection with how capitalism operates. A reader wanting to explore this further might want to start with the following observations by Alison Ross in 'Psychoanalysis – Family, Freud, and Unconscious': 'Capital operates according to a logic of deterritorialisation in which the flows of capital are no longer extracted from agricultural labour, but, rather than being tied to the produce of the land, are transnational or global. Although capital tends toward a deterritorialisation of geographical, familial and social ties, it defers this limit by reiterating artificial territorialities. In this context psychoanalysis, but particularly its use of the family as an explanatory unit for desire, is criticized as one of the paradigmatic movements by which the family is reiterated and the logic of deterritorialising flows is captured by a function of reterritorialisation', in *The Deleuze Dictionary*, ed. Parr, p. 218.

[15] Paulo de Medeiros, *Pessoa's Geometry of the Abyss: Modernity and the* Book of Disquiet (Oxford: Legenda, 2013).

[16] George Steiner, *Lessons of the Masters. The Charles Eliot Norton lectures* (Cambridge, MA: Harvard University Press, 2015), p. 56.

[17] Steiner is here obviously referring to Joseph Conrad's short story, 'The Secret Sharer', originally published in 1910.

[18] George Steiner, *Lessons of the Masters.*

some of Pessoa's texts might help. Even if all of the heteronyms in a sense provide for the rhizomatic machine of desire – one of the hallmarks of the rhizome is precisely the multiplicity of its points of entry and exit, something which Pessoa took to its logical limit in the *Livro do Desassossego* – Álvaro de Campos could perhaps be singled out, for the moment, as the one who best embodies Pessoa's capacity for such a form of othering. For a start, de Campos, although Portuguese, would be born far from the centre of the country, in Tavira, would be of Jewish extraction, and would have received his university training as a naval engineer in Glasgow. In other words, Pessoa, in creating Campos's biography, is already at pains to maximize the possibilities for personal and cultural deterritorialization of what would be his most profoundly modernist heteronym, not just excessive in his preferences, but a cypher for excess itself. Let us consider for a moment his 'inaugural' poem, 'Opiário' ['Opiary'], published, by chance as it were, in the first issue of the modernist journal *Orpheu* in 1915.[19] In many ways, this poem can be seen as emblematic of Pessoa's deterritorializing strategy in as much as it functions as a sort of 'original' meant to show what Campos was like before he came under the influence of Master Caeiro. Pessoa himself, of course, sets this up in the famous letter to Adolfo Casais Monteiro of 13 January 1935,[20] in which he specifically mentions how *Opiário* came about: 'Of all the poems I've written, this was the one that gave me the most trouble, because of the twofold depersonalization it required. But I don't think it turned out badly, and it does show us Álvaro in the bud.'[21]

That letter to Casais Monteiro is many things and obviously critics should keep a healthy distance from some of its claims as it is also a blatant mythologizing device. Be that as it may, what I would like to focus on is how in this myth of the birth of the heteronyms Pessoa is very lucid as to the intended effect of double Othering. One could argue that the letter is, of course, written two decades after the original poem to which it refers. Yet 'Opiário' is a poem

[19] Fernando Pessoa, 'Opiário', *Orpheu* 1 (1915). Reprinted in Fernando Pessoa, *Álvaro de Campos: Obra Completa*, eds Jerónimo Pizarro and Antonio Cardiello (Lisbon: Tinta da China, 2014), pp. 36–43; Fernando Pessoa, *A Little Larger than the Entire Universe: Selected Poems*, ed. and trans. Richard Zenith (London and New York: Penguin, 2006), pp. 147–52.

[20] This letter sets out one of Pessoa's own versions of how he came to create the various heteronyms. It is obviously in itself a highly charged and poetic fiction. Fernando Cabral Martins and Richard Zenith provide very detailed considerations of Pessoa's heteronymic pronouncements in *Teoria da Heteronímia*. The letter is also reprinted: pp. 273–82.

[21] Pessoa, *Teoria da Heteronímia*, p. 279; Fernando Pessoa, *The Selected Prose of Fernando Pessoa*, ed. Richard Zenith (New York: Grove Press, 2002), p. 257.

of such complexity as to render the account of its creation not only perfectly logical but also, in a sense, modest. One could start with the opening stanza in which, beyond the trappings of decadence and aristocratic abandon to an existential ennui that is only temporarily relieved by opium, we read a sort of programmatic statement that goes far beyond the routine camp posturing that also characterizes many of Campos's provocations, and that is his search for 'Um Oriente ao oriente do Oriente' ['An East to the east of the East'].[22] Needless to say, this elaborate game is a further complication of the depersonalization strategy carried out through the extended heteronymic machine. And yet I cannot help but sense an enormous fragility under that semblance of the jaded world traveller. Pessoa clearly uses Campos to project certain extreme views and yet, in this opening salvo, the excess would still seem to be fairly contained, were it not announced in that beyond of the Orient just mentioned. Campos of course, also announces himself as an inveterate traveller whose journeys, even when derided as futile in comparison to an inner journey, allow him to make explicit comparisons between himself and others whose national attributes apparently differ considerably from his own. For instance, both the Portuguese and the English are directly evoked, and compared, alongside casual references to Germans and Swedes. This comparison is made on a personal register as well as a national and imperial one as Campos not only studied (or pretended to, as he says) in Glasgow, but lived in England as well. And, obviously, it derives from Pessoa's own colonial upbringing. The double move of depersonalization Pessoa evokes here is maintained throughout and, in this regard as well, we get to see how Campos ironically plays down both himself and the Portuguese (conscious of an exhaustion of the imperial dream of the past), while simultaneously ridiculing the supposed mechanical cheerfulness of the English:

> Os ingleses são feitos pra existir.
> Não há gente como esta pra estar feita
> Com a tranquilidade. A gente deita
> Um vintém e sai um deles a sorrir.
>
> Pertenço a um género de portugueses
> Que depois de estar a Índia descoberta
> Ficaram sem trabalho. A morte é certa.
> Tenho pensado nisto muitas vezes.

---

[22] Pessoa, *Álvaro de Campos: Obra Completa*, p. 36; Pessoa, *A Little Larger than the Entire Universe*, p. 147.

> [The English were made for existence
> No people has a closer alliance
> With Tranquillity. Put in a coin
> And out comes an Englishman, all smiles.
>
> I belong to that class of Portuguese
> Who, once India was discovered, were out
> Of work. Death is a sure thing.
> This is something I often think about.][23]

Richard Zenith's translation into English is, as usual, impeccable. And yet, one might quibble with one or two slight changes, made certainly for idiomatic ease. The first is the choice of the term 'class' for the Portuguese 'género', which, perhaps more literally, one might render as 'kind'. Surely the poem depends on notions of class since the speaker certainly enjoys leisure and has the financial means for extended travel and drugs, but Pessoa did not choose to draw this connotation out. 'Kind', I find, in a poem very much concerned with identity and differences among peoples, is both less and more charged. For what is at stake, among other things, in these two paired stanzas, is the difference between the English and the Portuguese. The English are portrayed as a sort of cheerful toy replica of a sentient human being, expected to pop out of some automated coin-operated machine once it is activated. In contrast to this Pessoa has us consider a kind of Portuguese, his kind, who had a historic destiny – the discovery of India – after which it really did not face any task that matched its qualities. Considering that India was then still the 'jewel in the crown' of the British empire, this statement by Campos, which claims the primacy of discovering India but rejects the burden of actually colonizing it, is wonderfully tongue in cheek. Its irony, however, is not intended at all either as a nostalgic longing for the glorious days of the sixteenth century when Portugal, not England, was the hegemonic imperial power alongside Spain, nor as an expression of some national distinction. The ease with which Pessoa undermines both the historical and the then current pretensions towards imperial glory of both Portugal and England is certainly shrewder than the view of many political and historical commentators. Its implicit refusal of any form of national glorification is markedly transnational.

Campos is at pains both to establish himself as a man of the world and to declare that he is not at home anywhere. One might say that all this amounts to nothing more than posturing, with the poem's concluding plea for a return

---

[23] Pessoa, *Álvaro de Campos: Obra Completa*, p. 40; Pessoa, *A Little Larger than the Entire Universe*, p. 150.

to normalcy and faith representing the last pull of the carpet out from under the readers' feet. And yet, his statement about his complete lack of national identification remains significant for it implies that the national is precisely where the self is not, and, by way of logical conclusion, the self is always already an alien, a foreigner: 'Não posso estar em parte alguma. / A minha Pátria é onde não estou' ['I don't belong anywhere. My country / Is wherever I'm not'].[24]

If one is serious about considering Pessoa transnationally, however, it is not enough to identify possible expressions of Pessoa's aversion to nationalism in his literary production. Rather, one should also be looking at the ways in which Pessoa has impacted us across national barriers. Even if much of this material could be the subject of several separate research projects – for instance an attempt to understand Pessoa and Africa, a topic that has received very little attention or even Pessoa and Brazil, an area that has attracted a number of studies already – at the moment I would like to focus on one in particular, from Brazil, as I consider it symptomatic of both the direction one should be looking in to gain a more diversified view of Pessoa, and also of the invisibility that still often accompanies such projects. One way of doing this would be to examine the official reception of Pessoa in Brazil, whether in historical terms (the various important studies and editions of Pessoa that have been influential in shaping the mainstream view of Pessoa, such as the many authored by Cleonice Berardinelli); or works of criticism, by, for example, Leyla Perrone-Moisés; or even, though in a completely different register, the much publicized biography by José Paulo Cavalcanti Filho.[25] Another way, to me more telling in this respect, would be to undertake a mapping of Pessoa's transnational reach into other forms of art and into popular culture.

In that regard, one would do well to differentiate this from the re-mediation effected by high-brow art such as, say, the work of Portuguese artist Júlio Pomar (1926–2018), who has repeatedly turned to Pessoa at different phases of his artistic career and has produced some of the most stunning visual commentaries on the poet. For the concerns at hand, one in particular warrants a mention: the large painting representing Pessoa

---

[24] Pessoa, *Obra Completa: Álvaro de Campos*, p. 39; Pessoa, *A Little Larger than the Entire Universe*, p. 149.

[25] The most recent is Fernando Pessoa, *Antologia Poética*, ed. Cleonice Berardinelli (Rio de Janeiro: Casa da Palavra, 2012); Leyla Perrone-Moisés, *Fernando Pessoa: aquém do eu, além do outro* (São Paulo: Martins Fontes, 2001 [1982]); José Paulo Cavalcanti Filho, *Fernando Pessoa: Uma quase autobiografia* (Rio de Janeiro: Record, 2011).

and the corpse of the lost king Sebastião[26] entitled 'Fernando Pessoa meets D. Sebastião inside his coffin, harnessed to a donkey the Andalusian way' (1985).[27] For anyone even slightly familiar with Portuguese history, the irony behind Pessoa (who is sometimes charged with wanting to revive the myth of Sebastianism as part of a messianic call for a renewed imperial role for Portugal in the realm of culture), actually coming across the body of the king is a powerful and extremely ironic commentary on the follies of nationalism that leads the viewer to reflect on the poet as an enigmatic figure. In my view Pomar does not simply align Pessoa with blind nationalism but, by depicting him with that famous and never found corpse, Pomar also raises all kinds of questions regarding the spectrality and the haunting power of any such claims.

Important as such work is – in addition to Pomar, many other artists from a variety of countries, in a variety of different media, are constantly re-engaging with the figure of Pessoa and of his heteronyms – at present I am much more interested in looking at what I would like to call its counterpart: a recent Brazilian comic book entitled *Eu, Fernando Pessoa em quadrinhos* [*I, Fernando Pessoa in a Comic Strip*] (2013), by Susana Ventura and Eloar Guazzelli (Figure 17.1).[28] This is not the only transposition of the figure and work of Pessoa into the medium of the comic book or graphic novel, labels that fail to encompass the complexity of the work in question. Not excluding others I may have missed (and the relative invisibility of these works cannot be ignored) there are at least two other works that deserve a mention. A comparison of the three will enable me better to draw inferences with regard to the work of Ventura and Guazzelli, which, to my mind, does stand out in its ability to transcend the limitations inherent to the adaptation process. The most easily available one – at least in Portugal where one can find it in a number of bookstores – is *As aventuras de Fernando Pessoa, Escritor Universal* [*The Adventures of Fernando Pessoa, Universal Writer*] (2015), by Miguel Moreira and Catarina Verdier.[29] The other, *A Vida Oculta*

---

[26] Dom Sebastião I (1557–78) vanished during a battle in the north of Africa and his disappearance provoked the loss of Portuguese sovereignty to Castille between 1580 and 1640.

[27] Júlio Pomar, 'Fernando Pessoa encontra D. Sebastião num caixão sobre um burro ajaezado à andaluza', acrylic on canvas, 158.5 x 154 cm, 1985. Caixa Geral de Depósitos Collection, Lisbon.

[28] Susana Ventura and Guazzelli, *Eu, Fernando Pessoa em quadrinhos* (São Paulo: Peirópolis, 2013).

[29] Miguel Moreira and Catarina Verdier, *As aventuras de Fernando Pessoa, Escritor Universal* (Lisbon: Parceria A. M. Pereira, 2015). Parceria A. M. Pereira was Pessoa's original publisher.

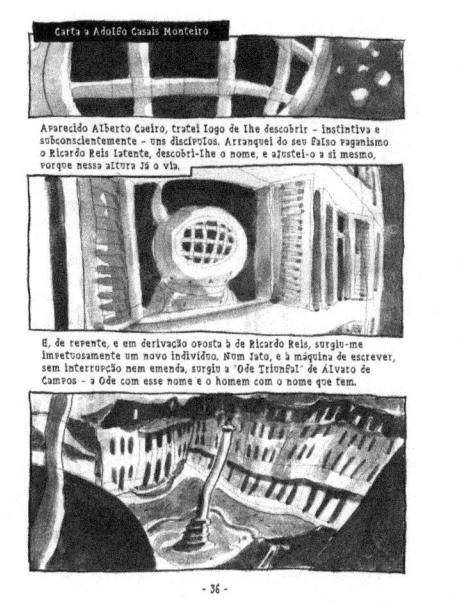

Figure 17.1. Illustration from *Eu, Fernando Pessoa em quadrinhos*,
by Susana Ventura and Eloar Guazzelli.

de Fernando Pessoa [*The Occult Life of Fernando Pessoa*] (2016), by André F. Morgado and Alexandre Leoni,[30] has been published in Brazil (Figure 17.2). It is perhaps more visible online than in actual bookstores but, thanks to social media, perhaps easier to get hold of than the Ventura and Guazzelli book, which has gone almost unnoticed in Portugal in spite of the increasing number of collaborations between publishers on both sides of the Atlantic.

At first sight, *As Aventuras de Fernando Pessoa, Escritor Universal* appears to be the most conventional of the three. This is for a number of reasons, ranging from the title itself, and the notion of the universality of great writers, to the style chosen to draw the figure of Pessoa: fairly conventional in representational terms with a hint of the comic to it, but still largely realistic. Obviously, the question of the dubious quality of universality is by no means limited to this work. It is a rather diffuse view that permeates the critical appreciation of Pessoa and that could easily be

---

[30] André F. Morgado and Alexandre Leoni, *A Vida Oculta de Fernando Pessoa* (Lisbon: Bicho Carpinteiro, 2016). Publishing costs were initially crowdfunded via an internet platform. The authors' original goal was 7,000 reais, but the project was extremely successful and they managed to raise over 24,000 reais.

Figure 17.2. Illustration from *A Vida Oculta de Fernando Pessoa*, written by André F. Morgado and illustrated by Alexandre Leoni.

taken for yet another form of transnationality, which it is not. Whereas transnationality, at its core, refuses to accord any primacy to the concept of the national, and even tries to undo it, the 'universal' more often than not leaves the 'national' intact as a category to which it would be the (greater) counterpart. Another aspect that tends to create the impression of conventionality in this work is the decision to recount Pessoa's life story, which, when coupled with the mostly straightforward and seemingly realistic drawing style, makes for a much easier entry point for a large number of readers than that of the other two works.

Nonetheless, this remains a complex work, with an intricate structure, that took a long time to produce (in an interview in 2011 the authors mentioned that they had been working on it for nine years). Arguably, this book is at its weakest from the point of view of language. By both literally reproducing some of Pessoa's texts and relying on very prosaic and colloquial writing to provide narrative flow and unity, the overall effect is at odds with the beauty and power of Pessoa's own writing so that, in this case, remaining faithful to the original is actually the opposite of what might have been intended. Granted, one key goal of such a publication is to render Pessoa accessible to a wide range of readers who might be expected to be put off by Pessoa's intricate language games and erudition. There is no doubt that this tactic removes any such obstacle. Still, there are moments when the book manages to surpass such an aspiration and, in what could be termed a radical departure from the original, actually by eliding any and all text including Pessoa's, it is most successful when it comes to transforming the seductive strangeness of Pessoa to the medium at hand. Curiously, this section, which goes against the grain of the rest of the book, is a depiction of one day in the life not of Fernando Pessoa, but of his heteronym Bernardo Soares. As Miguel Moreira states, what distinguishes that episode from the rest of the book is the lack of any text.[31] Not only that, but the sequence of images, in their almost complete repetition and banality, go a long way towards actually allowing readers to enter into that special world of 'Pessoa as Soares'. The concluding image of the episode, a duplication in reverse of the opening image, is a good example of a moment when the book transcends the otherwise conventional nature of the images. In the first image, we see Pessoa/Soares standing in a downtown Lisbon street (presumably the Rua dos Douradores, where he worked), not only centre stage but much larger than life, since he dwarfs all the other people walking by. In the last image, it is night time and the street is completely deserted, so that absence, nothing but absence, is what the reader is left with, in a move that,

---

[31] Miguel Moreira, 'As Aventuras de Fernando Pessoa, Escritor Universal', *Pessoa Plural* 2 (2012), 317–31 (p. 319).

in my view, represents much better the theoretical importance of the *Livro do Desassossego* than if Moreira and Verdier had included some 'poetic' or 'paradoxical' fragments from Pessoa's masterpiece.

Interestingly enough, *A Vida Oculta de Fernando Pessoa* also focuses on the biographical even if, as its title also reveals, one of its main concerns is Pessoa's involvement with the esoteric. Written by the Portuguese André F. Morgado and illustrated by the Brazilian Alexandre Leoni, this book demonstrates not only transnational cooperation when it comes to generating innovative work on Pessoa, but also the ever more prominent role played by the internet and social media nowadays. Whereas Moreira and Verdier's book was initially a blog, *A Vida Oculta* went one step further since by using crowdfunding, it (in a sense), gave potential readers a direct stake in the project. The images, in comparison to those in *As Aventuras*, are edgier, definitely drawing on a *noir* aesthetic and casting Pessoa – and his heteronyms – as heroes fighting to help save the Portuguese people. For the purpose at hand, what I want to signal is how this attempt at dislocating Pessoa from the hallowed grounds of Portuguese (and European) high modernism to the realm of popular (and Brazilian?) culture, fits in well between Moreira and Verdier's more conventional approach and the last of the three, which, in my view, goes even further towards radically 'adapting' Pessoa to the present.

Fernando Pessoa em quadrinhos has a much more modest, though direct, title without the pretension of either the 'universal' or the 'adventurous'. Yet, of the three 'adaptations' of Pessoa into the medium of 'quadrinhos' (literally 'little squares') (both this Brazilian term and the Portuguese version, 'banda desenhada' (comic strip), appear more inclusive than the English 'comic' or 'graphic novel'), Ventura and Guazzelli's is the most successful in transposing Pessoa's haunting textuality into a new medium and reaching a new audience. The book appears to have been originally targeted, by the publisher, at children and young adults. However, in its conception and execution, its fusion and contrast between image and text, even the disappearance, or illegibility, of a 'text' that becomes a purely visual representation of what we recognize as 'words', the book erases any supposed border between adult and child audiences. Interestingly enough, the life of Pessoa is yet again the point of departure for the narrative, though here very much concentrated at the beginning and end and actually used as a mere 'pretext' to the narrative, which depends much more on his poetics and heteronymy for its own development.

The Pessoa that surfaces in these pages is haunting but not melancholy. The images make use of text but do not depend on it. By focusing on the account Pessoa provided for the genesis of the heteronyms in the letter to

Adolfo Casais Monteiro, the text directly links with the metanarrativity of Pessoa's texts in a way that evokes them but also transposes them. One of the advantages of this book over the other two lies in the extent to which it reproduces Pessoa's intensity without ever merely copying it. It is as if Ventura and Guazzelli had produced another version of the text rather than an interpretation of it. A version, moreover, that lays bare the dialectical tension between Pessoa's original text and their reworking of it; and which in so doing further deterritorializes Pessoa. Some of the images can be seen as harking back to surrealism as Pessoa is variously portrayed as a familiar silhouette, but also as a deep-sea diver in an old-fashioned diving suit, travelling through what is sometimes space, sometimes Lisbon – and as a caterpillar that turns into a butterfly, and even as an amoeba, and an octopus. At one point he is shown becoming a cat at the window of his room, then in the next image one sees whales flying above Lisbon's streets. Towards the book's conclusion, Pessoa is portrayed as himself, reading his own obituary, before a crow assumes the narrative voice to list a few milestones of the poet's life and then flies off silently in a full-page spread.

In his *Handbook of Inaesthetics* Alain Badiou had reflected on the belated reception of Pessoa in France.[32] One of the most influential Marxist philosophers of our time, Badiou has written extensively on poetry, among other literary forms. Although his views on Pessoa are far from being generally accepted, his commitment to read Pessoa critically and as a thinker, breaching the usual divide between philosophy and literature, merits much attention. Badiou does note how the reception of Pessoa, in France as elsewhere, was belated. Yet Badiou goes further than simply registering a critical failing to declare that Pessoa should be viewed as 'a possible condition for Philosophy' and that '[w]e must therefore conclude that philosophy is not – at least not *yet* – under the condition of Pessoa. Its thought is not yet *worthy of Pessoa*.'[33] One way of understanding such a claim would be to align Pessoa with Friedrich Nietzsche as both authors wrote texts that only received their due attention posthumously. Another might be to recognize that the force of Pessoa's lyrical and critical expression, although still difficult to accept by some, is very pertinent and necessary in the present. Even though some weary cultural critics have sought to decry Modernism and modernity as somehow merely by now historical events or movements, reading Pessoa transnationally might help us recognize that the project of modernity is still an unfinished one. Perhaps, defamiliarizing Pessoa, dislocating him to other media, disciplines,

---

[32] Alain Badiou, *Handbook of Inaesthetics*, trans. Alberto Toscano (Stanford, CA: Stanford University Press, 2004).
[33] Badiou, *Handbook*, p. 36.

fields, audiences and worlds, as Ventura and Guazzelli's *Eu, Fernando Pessoa em quadrinhos* does so seductively, is a way of starting to answer Badiou's injunction. As 'unrepentant moderns', to return to Balibar in my epigraph, perhaps if we can transnationalize Pessoa we can then hope to start becoming his contemporaries.

18

Sound Travel

Fadocore in California

Kimberly DaCosta Holton
Rutgers University, Newark

When I first discovered the California based 'fadocore' band Judith and Holofernes, I asked the band's leader, Chris da Rosa, if the exciting musical hybrid he had invented – a beguiling fusion of Portuguese *fado* and postpunk music – had caught on.

'Are there many other fadocore bands?' I asked, enthusiastically. Amused by the question, Chris said,

'No. I think, for now, we are the only ones.'

What follows in this article is an exploration of a unique musical experiment involving *fado*, an urban ballad form first appearing in Lisbon in the 1820s, and now known as Portugal's 'national song'.[1] The creation of fadocore

---

Excerpts from this article were first presented at the American Portuguese Studies Association (APSA) conference in October 2016 and at Princeton University in November 2016. Thanks to APSA audience members and Nicola Cooney and her students and colleagues for their insightful comments. I would also like to thank Rutgers University, Newark's Global and Urban Studies program for the grant which funded my research trip to California in 2016. And, most of all, thanks to Chris da Rosa, Mark Hobbs, Felicia Viator and Marlene Simas Angeja for their generosity and willingness to share their stories concerning *J&H*, *fado*, art making and life in the Central Valley. Any errors or shortcomings are my own.

[1] *Fado* is the product of varied cultural roots and influences emanating from Africa, Latin America and Europe. Today, there are two main types: Lisbon *fado* and Coimbra *fado*. *Fado de Coimbra* became harnessed to sociability traditions within campus life at the University of Coimbra, while *fado de Lisboa*, initially centred in the capital, witnessed a greater diffusion throughout various Portuguese regions. *Fado*

constitutes an experiment born of the tension between youthful rebellion and a respect for tradition. An experiment born of the desire to express New World grief using an Old World lexicon. It is an experiment that at times parallels other *fado* performances in diaspora, but in many ways is different and singular. This is a story of music and migration and of memory and loss. It is a story of sound travel – sound travel that combines transnational pilgrimages with the nitty gritty of local concerns and sorrows. Finally, it is a story of syncretism, where concerns about cultural orthodoxy, purity and the preservation of tradition become upstaged by the desire to 'rip it up and start again'.[2] By examining the sutured rippings of Judith and Holofernes's sonic oeuvre, we can learn what it is like to be a Portuguese-American child of the 1980s, growing up in a depressed Central Valley, California town, twisting *fado* into postpunk registers for the purpose of finding new ways to lament.

The genesis of fadocore

The fadocore band, Judith and Holofernes (J&H) was created 12 years ago by Chris da Rosa, the son of Portuguese immigrants from the Azorean island of Faial who settled in California's Central Valley. Fadocore is a tantalizingly difficult hybrid music to categorize – a blurring of *fado*, postpunk and goth musics that is so original that critics are stumped as to how to define it. The limitations of genre, in fact, led to the formulation of the term 'fadocore', so the J&H musicians say. At the time that the band was founded

---

de Lisboa first appeared in the capital's popular riverside neighbourhoods and was originally associated with a gritty urban underbelly. Since then, *fado* has experienced a protean evolution as it travelled into the countryside, aristocratic salons, opera houses and along radio airwaves. *Fado de Lisboa*, while composed of many different subgenres, including upbeat and jocular lyrics and melodies, is often thought of as a lament form featuring soulful stories of lost places and people. It is traditionally performed by a vocalist (male or female), accompanied by a Spanish guitar and a 12-string lute-like instrument called a *guitarra portuguesa*. Some people call Lisbon *fado* 'the Portuguese blues'. For more on *fado* history and performance, see Rui Vieira Nery, *Para Uma História do Fado* (Lisbon: Público, Comunicação Social, SA, 2004); Salwa El-Shawan Castelo-Branco, *Voix de Portugal* (Paris: Actes Sud, 1997) and 'Vozes e Guitarras na Prática Interpretativa do Fado', in *Fado: Vozes e Sombra*, ed. Joaquim Pais de Brito (Lisbon: Museu Nacional de Etnologia. Electa, 1994), pp. 125–40; and Lila Ellen Gray, *Fado Resounding: Affective Politics and Urban Life* (Durham, NC and London: Duke University Press, 2013).

[2] 'Rip It Up and Start Again' is the well-known title of Simon Reynolds's exploration of what he calls a 'neglected genre'; his book and its title are referenced as a type of postpunk doctrine. See Simon Reynolds, *Rip It Up and Start Again: Postpunk 1978–84* (New York: Penguin Books, 2006).

in 2003, Chris da Rosa said, there were so many 'cores' being thrown around, hardcore, metalcore, screamcore, emocore – it was within the proliferation of subgenres – and the muddiness and increasing meaninglessness of this runaway typology – that fadocore was coined. 'It started as a joke', Chris said.[3]

Chris da Rosa and his two best friends – brothers Mark and Mitch Hobbs – had been in numerous rock and indie bands, together and separately, by the time they started the fadocore band Judith and Holofernes in 2003. Chris had grown up listening to *fado* on the radio in the Central Valley town of Manteca where he was born and raised. He states:

I spent a lot of time at my grandparents' house while my mother and father were working. My grandmother used to turn the radio on in the morning and let it play all day. She loved this station out of Los Banos called KLBS. Some days the reception was terrible but that thing stayed on so we could catch every bit of *fado* the DJ would play.[4]

Chris showed an early talent for music and his parents bought him a trumpet in hopes that he would join the Escalon Portuguese Marching Band, following in his older brother's footsteps.[5] However, according to Chris, when he was a teen in the 1980s and 1990s, he began rejecting his parents' Portuguese culture. He drew his friend group from outside the Luso-American community, stopped attending *festas*,[6] quit playing the trumpet, and began to listen to postpunk bands such as the Cure, Sonic Youth

---

[3] Chris da Rosa, Interview with Author, email correspondence, July 2016.

[4] da Rosa, Interview 2016.

[5] *Bandas filarmónicas* – 'marching bands', made up mostly of wind instruments and percussion – are 'omnipresent' in Portugal, Castelo-Branco, *Voix de Portugal*, p. 63, and very common in Portuguese-American communities as well. For a case-study, see Katherine Brucher, 'Viva Rhode Island, Viva Portugal! Performance and Tourism in Portuguese-American Band', in *Community, Culture and the Makings of Identity: Portuguese-Americans along the Eastern Seaboard*, eds Kimberly Holton and Andrea Klimt (Amherst, MA: University of Massachusetts Press, 2009), pp. 203–26.

[6] *Festa* is the general term used for outdoor summer festivals, modelled after the Portuguese tradition, and often comprising religious processions, live music, civic display of heraldry and outdoor feasting on Portuguese cuisine. For a comprehensive discussion of Azorean *festas* in diaspora, see João Leal, *Açores, EUA, Brasil: Imigração, e Etnicidade* (Açores: Direcção Regional das Comunidades, 2007) and *Azorean Identity in Brazil and the United States: Arguments about History, Culture and Transnational Connections* (Dartmouth, MA: Tagus Press, 2011); and in California, see Tony Goulart, *The Holy Ghost Festas: A Historic Perspective of the Portuguese in California* (San Jose, CA: Portuguese Chamber of Commerce, 2002). The relevance of *festas* to *J&H* iconography will be discussed later in the article.

and Depeche Mode. The darker sounds and the corresponding subculture seemed a better fit for Chris and his friends at the time, who were experiencing loss and hopelessness born of a rash of suicides among friends and bandmates – tragedies that occurred against the backdrop of a local youth culture grappling with addiction, restlessness and a lack of economic opportunity. In addition, the suicides took place during a time when Manteca and the surrounding towns were experiencing dramatic demographic changes, as a large influx of bay-area urbanites, priced out of city neighbourhoods, traded manageable commute times for cheaper housing. And although Manteca was not considered an idyllic location – Mark Hobbs described it as a blue-collar town where rows of tract housing punctuated acres of dairy farms and a patchwork of 'beat-up fruit trees' – the influx of outsiders was perceived as an invasion and added to feelings of alienation and disconnect among local youth in the late 1990s.[7]

Following two suicides – one by a close friend and bass player named Ray – Mark, Mitch, Chris and Chris's best friend, Charles Bennet, continued playing rock music together. Composing and performing music offered belonging, purposefulness and a creative outlet for the experience of grief and turmoil. However, during this period, Charles, the drummer, began experiencing severe health problems, and his slow decline, addiction to pain medication and eventual suicide in the same location where Ray had killed himself three years before, shook the remaining band members to the core. It was during the downward spiral leading to Charles's death that Chris da Rosa turned back towards Portuguese culture and ultimately to *fado*.

Musical pilgrimage

So what specifically did *fado* offer Chris and his friends? What was it about this music, played in the background full of static on the radio at Chris's grandmother's, a component of his parents' heritage that he had rejected, that warranted a new listen? In turning to *fado*, Chris da Rosa seemed unlike other second-generation Portuguese-American *fadistas* on the east coast, who describe ethnic pride and identity as being important features of their attraction to the music.[8] Instead, members of J&H sought out *fado* as an

---

[7] Mark Hobbs, Interview with Author, 2 August 2016.

[8] For more on second-generation *fadistas* in New Jersey, see Kimberly DaCosta Holton, 'Fado in Diaspora: Online Internships and Self-Display Among YouTube Generation Performers in the US', *Luso-Brazilian Review*, 53 (2016), 210–32. For a discussion of the relationship between *fado* and ethnic identity and prestige among first-generation *fadistas* in New Jersey/New York, see Maria de São José Corte-Real,

expressive outlet for grief, a salve to a wound, a means toward probing a dark mystery. Independent of issues of heritage or identity, J&H turned toward *fado* in an effort to express loss in ways that playing in rock bands had not allowed.

Having lost one close friend, Ray, to suicide, and fearing that bandmate Charles Bennet might be headed in the same direction as he battled drug addiction and depression, Chris da Rosa felt helpless. He and J&H bassist Mark Hobbs describe the pain of witnessing Charles's decline, as if in 'slow motion'. 'He kept losing weight because of a health problem. The doctors didn't know what was wrong with him. He kept taking pain pills, getting weaker and skinnier. He couldn't really eat. He would promise and try, but after a while he wouldn't show up for rehearsals; after a while he just stayed in his house, wasting away.'[9] Feeling helpless and unable to reverse his friend's course, Chris searched for a different musical idiom to try to grapple with his bandmate's slow-motion tragedy. It was during the year of Charles's downward spiral that Chris da Rosa travelled to Lisbon for the first time. Chris thought that perhaps *fado* held the key to unlocking his experience of grief at home in the Central Valley.

When he arrived in Lisbon, Chris located all the *fado* venues he had heard and read about. He frequented out-of-the-way *fado* venues in Alfama and Bairro Alto. He visited Lisbon's Museu do Fado and examined historical displays. He combed guitar shops and sampled instruments. On this same trip Chris also acquired his first *guitarra portuguesa*. Chris's first experience of *fado* as a young adult interested in learning the music is, again, somewhat different from his second-generation counterparts in the northeastern USA. Many young New Jersey *fadistas*, for example, also report hearing *fado* on their parents' or grandparents' radios, like Chris did, or on record players or in local clubs – almost as a background music growing up. But in New Jersey the reacquaintance with *fado* as young adults who were interested in performing music often happened online, and sometimes by chance while searching for other musics.[10] Chris, on the other hand, travelled to Lisbon in a concerted effort to hear and research live *fado* at its source.[11] He had an

---

'Revising Citizenship: Music and Migration in the Play of Identities in the United States', *Migrações Journal*, 7, *Special Issue on Music and Migration* (October 2010), 73–96.

[9] Mark Hobbs, Interview.

[10] Holton, 'Fado in Diaspora'.

[11] In using the word 'source', I mean the source of Lisbon *fado* as we know it today, as a vocal ballad music traditionally accompanied by a *guitarra portuguesa* and a Spanish guitar, first appearing in Lisbon around 1820 (distinct from the *fado de Coimbra*). Although space does not allow a lengthy treatment of *fado*'s 'origins debate', there is general consensus that *fado* first appeared in late eighteenth-century

inkling that *fado* held answers for him during a difficult period of his life. He willfully sought to connect the dots between his experience of loss at home, and the aesthetic and emotional possibilities that Lisbon's *fado* scene held for an expression of this loss. Chris used religious terminology to describe his journey, calling it a 'pilgrimage'.[12] Chris wanted to experience the birthplace of *fado* for himself – and, more specifically, 'the mixture of wine, tragedy and Catholic guilt that the time-honored *fadistas* had perfected'.[13]

Like other young second-generation *fadistas* in the USA, Chris sought to relate *fado* to his own life experience, but along darker lines of connection. While Kimberly Gomes in New Jersey, for example, was attracted to the love stories recounted in *fado* lyrics, connecting them to her 20-something life stage,[14] Chris showed more interest in the edgier features of *fado*'s early history. His visit to the Museu do Fado seemed pivotal in making a connection to the darker underbelly of Lisbon's early *fado* scene. The curatorial vision of the Museu do Fado was influenced by an important exhibit at the Museu Nacional de Etnologia during the Lisbon 94 Festival called 'Fado: Vozes e Sombras'.[15] The section of that exhibit called 'Marginalidade' (marginality) displayed the connection between violent street life, wine, promiscuity and *fado* in Lisbon's early twentieth-century riverside neighbourhoods, exhibiting drawings of scars, knives, tattoos and *fadista* prostitutes. The Museu do Fado later included similar displays of iconography and historical exposition, among many other objects, documents and audio/video clips relating to *fado*. The curatorial angle celebrating *fado*'s early relationship to an urban underclass related, curiously, to the conditions Chris had experienced in rural California. The image of two friends who had hanged themselves, the tattoos their high school friends had got in their honour, the drowning of sorrows and substance abuse, the desire to escape tragedy through music, all seemed to resonate with the sights and sounds of Lisbon *fado* that Chris had encountered during his pilgrimage.

Brazil, primarily as a danced form. Several important scholarly works discuss *fado*'s relationship to other musical traditions and its history of evolution. See, for example, Rui Vieira Nery, *Para Uma História do Fado* and José Ramos Tinhorão, *Fado, Dança do Brasil, Cantar de Lisboa* (Lisbon: Editorial Caminho, 1994).

[12] Felica Angeja Viator, '"Abraça a Tristeza": Fado and Fadocore in the California Central Valley', in *Untamed Dreams: Faces of America*, eds F. Dinis and J. Rodrigues (San José, CA: Portuguese Heritage Publications of California, 2016), pp. 213–18.

[13] Viator, '"Abraça a Tristeza"', p. 214.

[14] Holton, 'Fado in Diaspora', p. 219.

[15] *Fado: Vozes e Sombras*, ed. Joaquim Pais de Brito. For an analysis of this exhibit, see Kimberly DaCosta Holton, 'Bearing Material Witness to Musical Sound: Fado's L94 Museum Debut', *Luso-Brazilian Review*, 39 (2002), 107–23.

Points of departure

When Chris returned to Manteca, he began teaching himself to play the *guitarra portuguesa*, a 12-string guitar akin to the lute and an essential component of traditional *fado* instrumentation. Chris played in an unorthodox manner, with a pick instead of the traditional *unhas* (nails), as if playing an electric guitar. While experimenting with his new instrument, Chris laid down some tracks, which he sent to Mark and Mitch Hobbs, asking if they would like to start a band that sounded something like this. That early demo came to be the single 'When Drones Leave the Hive'. And with that single, the band Judith and Holofernes was born. J&H would go on to record five CDs, all but one of them self-released under their own 'Fadocore' label, and all but one of them featuring CD titles in Portuguese.[16]

This first fadocore song is an intriguing hybrid of almost raucous postpunk sound combined with certain elements of traditional *fado*. First, there is the dominance of *fado*'s signature instrument, the 12-string *guitarra portuguesa*; it anchors J&H's first song and seems to be mixed at a higher volume than even the vocal tracks. In the introduction a series of single notes plucked up and down the scale, arpeggios as opposed to strummed chords, resemble a slowed-down version of a *fado guitarrada*.[17] Typical *fado* chord progressions also drive the instrumental introduction. Ultimately, though, a distorted electric guitar track joins the *guitarra*, lending the song a darker ragged sound. The male and female voices, mixed with an echoey effect, sing repetitive lyrics in unison – a feature atypical of traditional Lisbon *fado*, which features singular voices sometimes alternating verses with other vocalists, but often singing the *fado* alone in its entirety.

Similar to the hybrid elements in the instrumentation and melody, the lyrics for 'When Drones Leave the Hive' strike an original path, while making reference to thematic features of traditional *fado* poems. The narrator's experience of loss due to the departure of another, 'a drone leaving the hive', serves as the song's central metaphor. Longing for an absent someone, of course, constitutes the emotional infrastructure for the feeling of *saudade* ('longing, nostalgia or homesickness') – the affective fuel or inspiration

---

[16] The CDs, in order of release, are: *Dairymen and Festa Queens* (2003), *Mantança* (2005), *Abraça a Tristeza* (2006), *Enterramos Estas Almas Miseráveis na Terra* (2011) and *Canções de Ninar para o Apocalipse* (2016).

[17] A *guitarrada* is 'a purely instrumental composition of a virtuosic nature for the *guitarra portuguesa* in the context of Lisbon *fado* and Coimbra *fado*', Salwa El-Shawan Castelo-Branco, 'Guitarrada', in *Encyclopédia da Música em Portugal no Século XX*, C-L, ed. S. Castelo-Branco (Lisbon: Círculo de Leitores, 2010), p. 603.

behind many *fados*. Many *fado* laments explore the feeling of *saudade* by musing about loss and absence, regretting loss, mourning loss, and through the extended consideration of the impact of leave-taking on those left behind. Sometimes *fado's saudade*-filled consideration of absence and loss produces visible signs of sadness. As *fado* scholar Ellen Gray argues, the tear is an essential icon of *fado*, influencing the way the voice and guitar are stylized. In *fado*, she states, tears 'index both a private emotional and aesthetic experience and a moment of shared sociality'.[18]

This condition of shared sadness over the loss of a loved one characterized J&H's situation at the time of its initial turn toward *fado*. Witnessing the painful demise of their friend Charles influenced Chris's first pilgrimage to Lisbon's *fado* scene. However, the particularities of Manteca and its string of suicides, turbulent and fatal losses, may account for the marked differences in tone, language and narrative arc among J&H songs when compared to traditional *fados*. These songs are not so much inflected by tears and *saudade*, as they are by aggression and anger.

The first two verses of 'When Drones Leave the Hive' describe an oppressive situation where people are physically proximate but 'divided' and 'shackled':

> Divided into hives
> Divide into departments
> Divide worthwhile from worthless
> Expendable from ruthless
>
> Decided to leave the hive
> Decide to lose your shackles
> Decide to turn your blank stare
> From the hypnotic glow of hardware

Given the negative environment sketched out in the first verses, one might expect the narrator to approve of an escape, especially the escape of a loved one. However, the narrator tells us that the drone who attempted an 'inspired flight from drudgery', ultimately 'failed to prove a point'. Whereas the first part of the song considers the drone's impending leave-taking, the second half of the song deals with the impact of the departure – and that departure inspires anger and harsh judgement.

'When Drones Leave the Hive' portrays the absence of a loved one according to a markedly different emotional register than many *fado* poems

[18] Gray, *Fado Resounding*, pp. 41–42.

describing similar situations. In *fados* about absent people or places these longed-for figures, in addition, are often given proper names (Chico, Maria, Severa, Lisboa, Alfama, Mouraria, the Mariquinhas) or a repeated referent (meu amor, etc). These names or references serve to distinguish and identify the leave-taker and to show the connective emotional tissue between narrator and lost one. 'When Drones Leave' does no such connective work. By nature, a drone is one of many, and the drone at the centre of this song is never identified by name. This anonymous figure is critiqued for trying to distinguish him or herself, through leaving the hive. The narrator admits that there is potential freedom and distinction in leave-taking. But in the end, we are told, the drone's departure 'failed to stake a claim', and ultimately came to 'Well, I'll tell you', says the narrator in the last line, 'Nothing'.

Perhaps the most immediate, micro reading of 'When the Drones Leave the Hive' is that the song tracks the ultimate departure – through Ray and Charles's suicides – from a place that offers no other way out. And perhaps it is the finality of death and the elective nature of suicide that shake up the passivity and sometimes even pleasure intrinsic to the feeling of *saudade*. In addition, the harshness of the tone in this first J&H song – less longing and sadness and more anger and menace – comments on and differentiates between various modes of departure. Drones leaving the hive for healthier situations who have maintained their connection to one another are not subject to the narrator's harsh critique. However, those drones whose disappearance is more final, violent and solitary amount to 'nothing' – their departures ultimately deemed 'failures'.

In 'When Drones Leave the Hive', the person who has been abandoned is left not so much in a passive state of longing and *saudade* as would typically be the case in *fado*, but in an active state of anger and judgement. The hopeless conditions in the song's 'hive' connect to the way Chris, Mark and the artist Marlene Angeja, a native of Manteca who created a J&H music video, describe their hometown and the kind of daily lives it produced – lives of hard and monotonous labour in the company of other workers on farms, vineyards or in factories 'seven days a week'.[19] Lives, particularly for young people, of hopelessness and, sometimes, self-harm. Lives that, for immigrants, reveal the illusive nature and perhaps unattainability of the American Dream. And within Manteca's social context, one dominated by immigrants and their children, the topic of coming and going, staying together or leaving alone,

---

[19] Marlene Simas Angeja, born in Manteca, California to parents who emigrated in 1953 from the island of Pico, describes her father's first job working at a 'large farm, miles of property, a dairy farm and my father worked 7 days a week. He was out.' Interview with Author, Audio Recording, 12 June 2017.

is charged territory, especially for those whose migratory plan had been predicated on a 'diaspora of hope'.[20] In this way the narrator's 'sour grapes' attitude toward the one drone who had the courage to leave parallels a history of antagonism between those who left twentieth-century Portugal in search of greener pastures and those who stayed. Scholar of Portuguese migration Caroline Brettell argues that returning Portuguese emigrants often endured a stigma, viewed as 'traitors' to their nation.[21]

In response to the conditions in their hometown hive, Chris da Rosa and Mitch Hobbs ended up leaving Manteca for San Francisco several years after recording 'When Drones Leave the Hive'. In San Francisco they found a fanbase, a fertile outlet for J&H music and a fresh start. Mark Hobbs ended up moving there as well, as had Marlene many years earlier. So, in a very real sense 'When Drones Leave the Hive' portrays the tension surrounding plans for leaving a troubled hometown, a hometown comprising an older generation who had already experienced a major migratory leave-taking in search of better lives for future generations. The song alludes to fraught decision-making and its aftermath along vectors of transnational as well as local migrations and, in the case of Charles, the fatal decision to leave life among the living.

Postpunk and *fado*: a *sombre simpatico*

The fact that J&H consistently portray loss as death, and specifically violent death and suicide, pushing past the traditional borders of melancholic longing characteristic of *fado*, not only reflects the band's own experiential trajectory, but also the other musical genres the band engages, namely postpunk and goth musics. Postpunk, a period generally thought to span from 1978 to 1984, is understood as a distinctly Cold War phenomenon that focused on a sense of social and geopolitical hopelessness and a feeling that there was no future. In his book *Bomb Culture*, Jeff Nuttal argues that much of post-war youth culture owes its disaffection and anxiety to having grown up in the shadow of the bomb.[22] Mark Fisher writes that postpunk engages 'apocalyptic terror'

---

[20] Arjun Appadurai, *Modernity at Large: Cultural Dimensions of Globalization* (Minneapolis, MN: University of Minnesota Press, 1996).

[21] Caroline Brettell, *Anthropology and Migration: Essays on Transnationalism, Ethnicity and Identity* (Walnut Creek, CA: AltaMira Press, 2003). For an examination of jealousy ('inveja') towards Portuguese emigrants who left a coastal town, see Sally Cole, *Women of the Praia: Work and Lives in a Portuguese Coastal Community* (Princeton, NJ: Princeton University Press, 1991).

[22] Jeff Nuttall, *Bomb Culture* (London: Harper Collins, 1970).

in its creation of both a focus on death and an urgency geared toward living intensely in the present.[23] Chris da Rosa describes a similar environment growing up in California's Central Valley, where both the Portuguese brand of Catholicism and Cold War fears created a sense of 'doom and gloom.' He states:

> To be Portuguese means to be Catholic usually and growing up not only do you have this bleak attitude of the Portuguese, you also have Catholicism on top of it. So it's like doubling down on this ever present feeling of doom and judgement [...]. Growing up in the eighties it's like, cool, the Cold War is still happening, the bombs could drop at any moment.[24]

The focus on doom, death and its iconography that Chris and Cold War scholars describe is also central to the goth subgenre of postpunk, a movement with which the fadocore band also directly engages.

The goth movement started in the UK in the 1980s and has continued into the 2010s, drawing its inspiration from disparate sources, such as horror films, eighteenth- and nineteenth-century gothic literature, mythology, philosophers such as Nietzsche and Sartre, and iconography from Salvador Dalí to Pre-Raphaelite painting. Fan and performer costumes reminiscent of the grim reaper and Frankenstein's bride reveal a goth ethos, where 'every day is Halloween'.[25] It is a movement that favours bricolage and self-study and operates according to a DIY circuitry independent of and in opposition to mainstream commercial infrastructure for recording, distributing, selling, performing and writing about music.[26] The self-study element of goth, and the importance not only of sound, but also of image and thought, precisely reflects the way Chris da Rosa approached his research on *fado*. It is no coincidence that he visited the Museu do Fado in search of imagery and iconography, in addition to auditory experiences of *fado* performed live. He went in search of sounds *and* sights. The postpunk focus on Christian mythology and macabre iconography also parallel Chris's attraction to the 'Marginalidade' portions of

---

[23] Gavin Butt, Kodwo Eshun and Mark Fisher, 'Introduction', in *Post Punk, Then and Now*, eds Gavin Butt, Kodwo Eshun and Mark Fisher (London: Repeater Books, 2016), pp. 21–22.

[24] Chris da Rosa, Interview with Author, Audio Recording, 13 June 2017.

[25] Andi Harriman and Marloes Bontje, *Some Wear Leather Some Wear Lace: The Worldwide Compendium of Postpunk and Goth in the 1980* (Bristol: Intellect, 2014), p. 34.

[26] Harriman and Bontje, *Some Wear Leather*.

fado exhibits where pocket knives hang ominously in glass cases and tattoos of stabbings and scars sit alongside images of *fadista* virgins and whores.

The postpunk/goth bricolage of dark Christian imagery and horror film narratives are front and centre in J&H CD covers art (Figures 18.1, 18.2 and 18.3) as well as in the gory biblical tale that inspired the band's name.[27] These CD covers not only draw on postpunk iconography, they are also in keeping with early *fado* history and Portuguese-American traditions. The covers for *Abraça a Tristeza* and *Matança*, for example, feature two female icons in the foreground: a woman dressed in flowing robes and surrounded by rays of light, and a menacing hooded figure holding a scythe in one hand and a man's decapitated head in the other. Taken together, these figures display a range of religious archetypes along the virgin/whore continuum, from the fierce temptress who uses sex to entrap her enemy to the benign virgin bathed in light and virtue. These two figures play into multiple systems of signification for both goth and *fado* genres. The hooded figure with a scythe, a recognizable horror film archetype, also resembles many fifteenth-century Judith and Holofernes sculptures – eponymous imagery for J&H in keeping with the postpunk grab bag of references combining female sexuality and gore.

Powerful temptresses also appear, however, in *fado* history and iconography. The early nineteenth-century figure of Severa, widely hailed as *fado*'s first diva, was a prostitute from a poor Lisbon neighbourhood who used her feminine charms to corrupt an aristocratic lover, luring him to the 'dark side' of her urban underclass with all its moral degradation and danger. Severa's life has been dramatized in well-known paintings, plays and operas and

---

[27] According to the Bible, King Nebuchadnezzar sends General Holofernes to subdue his enemies, the Jews. Judith, a daring and beautiful Jewish widow, takes matters into her own hands, ingratiating herself with General Holofernes. Finding him alone and drunk one night, Judith decapitates Holofernes with a scythe and carries his head back to her countrymen. Her act becomes the catalyst for the retreat of Nebuchadnezzar's army and the victory of the Jews. Well-known painters, sculptors and writers have used this tale as the inspiration for their works over the centuries. Chris said that he first learned about the story in an art history class. He makes a comparison between sexual baiting, desperation and drunkenness in both the Judith and Holofernes paintings he learned about in class and early *fado* iconography he discovered in Lisbon. He states, '[the Judith and Holofernes painting by Artemisia Gentileschi (1614–20)] seemed like a story of desperation and triumph and without apology [...] I feel like a lot of *fado* songs are loaded with the same kind of sentiment of desperation and sorrow [...] the further back you go with the really old stuff [...] a man and woman arguing back and forth in *fado* and it was the epitome of that, that struggle and the debauchery and drunkenness of Holofernes. It seemed applicable at the time I was thinking of starting the band based on these themes. I had a dark attraction to it I suppose.' See da Rosa, Interview, 2017.

Figure 18.1. *Judith and Holofernes* cover art, 2003.
Chris da Rosa.

constitutes a major nucleus in the compendium of early *fado* iconography.[28] Images of erotic *fadistas* from the mean streets of early twentieth-century Lisbon – where *fado*, violence and eroticism are all intertwined – appear in body art and theatrical posters of the period. Along these same lines, José Malhoa's legendary painting *O Fado* features a fallen woman, drinking, smoking, and scantily clad, sitting alongside a more innocent-looking man playing the *guitarra portuguesa*. Malhoa's ubiquitous painting constitutes

---

[28] For a critical analysis of the historical *fado* figure Severa as related to changes in her Lisbon neighbourhood of Mouraria, see Michael Colvin, *The Reconstruction of Lisbon: Severa's Legacy and the Fado's Rewriting of Urban History* (Lewisburg, PA: Bucknell University Press, 2008).

Judith and Holofernes
Matança

Figure 18.2. *Judith and Holofernes* cover art, 2005. Chris da Rosa.

an almost formulaic visual element on the walls of amateur *fado* clubs throughout both Portugal and the USA. The powerful temptress, therefore, a woman who uses sex, song and/or violence to lure and ensnare, constitutes an important figure in both goth and *fado* genres; this archetype is widely featured in J&H iconography and song lyrics while also providing the inspiration for the band's name.

At the other end of the virgin/whore dichotomy, J&H cover art also taps into Marian iconography on *Matança* and *Dairymen and Festa Queens*, once again combining both specifically Portuguese and goth references. Goth fans and performers are known for dressing up as both vampire-like vixens and virginal brides in white gowns. These opposing archetypal costumes have been worn indiscriminately by both male and female goth fans. Critics analyse this

Figure 18.3. *Judith and Holofernes* cover art, 2006.
Chris da Rosa.

gender-bending flexibility as a reaction to the oppressively masculinist rock scene that came before.[29] Once again, while the virginal bride imagery taps into goth sartorial habits and progressive conceptions of gender identity, it also resonates within important Portuguese-American traditions. The Virgin Mary, a powerful Portuguese-American symbol, lent her name and image to countless Our Lady of Fátima ethnic parishes throughout the USA.[30] Statues,

---

[29] Harriman and Bontje, *Some Wear Leather*; and Butt, Eshun and Fisher, *Postpunk*.
[30] For more on the importance of Marian iconography within Portuguese-American immigrant communities, see Lori Barcliff Baptista, 'Images of the Virgin in Portuguese Art at the Newark Museum', in *Community, Culture and the Makings of Identity*, eds Holton and Klimt, pp. 175–202.

medallions and paintings of Our Lady of Fátima abound in Portuguese-American homes on both coasts. Marianesque costumes also find themselves in the Central Valley's tradition of *festa* parades – where Luso-American communities designate young girls as *festa* queens, often dressed in lavish white gowns with veils and shawls.[31] One Portuguese-American seamstress who makes particularly sought-after California *festa* gowns, 'draws a picture of the Virgin Mary [...] on heavy satin material from a picture on a Holy Card [...]. Her goal is to make the mother of Jesus look beautiful.'[32] Once again, Portuguese and goth traditions come together in J&H iconography in an oddly symbiotic way, despite their differing ideological purposes. Goth bridal wear, worn by both men and women, pushes a gender-bending agenda protesting against the masculinist characteristics of rock, while Portuguese-American *festa* queens, resembling young brides or first holy communicants with the Virgin Mary in sequins on their backs, promote conservative values such as female purity, chastity, modesty and charity.[33] Sanguine about the opposing values that co-exist within J&H's musical and visual syncretism, Chris da Rosa explains that Portuguese-American Catholicism was part of his daily life growing up and the cacophonous mashup of ideologies present in fadocore reflects his experience and the collision of differing worlds and value systems.

Although at first glance, the title of the Marian-clad CD *Matança* ['Killing' or 'Massacre'] would appear more in dialogue with the goth interest in blood and gore, it does double duty as a powerful Portuguese-American trope as well. In a Portuguese-American context 'matança' is shorthand for 'matança do porco', rituals of conviviality and male bonding so often referenced in Luso-American and Luso-Canadian literature, where lessons on becoming a (Portuguese) man intensify within the fragile context of diaspora.[34] So the bricolage present in this goth/*fado*/Portuguese-American mashup is both transnational and local, both traditional and cutting edge, both familiar and strange, both conservative and rebellious, paying homage to disparate

---

[31] Goulart, *The Holy Ghost*.

[32] Teresa Douglass, 'Tulare Woman Creates Capes for Portuguese Festas', *Visalia Times-Delta*, 16 January 2015, 1–16.

[33] *Festa* queens in the Azorean Holy Ghost celebrations prevalent throughout California are modeled after the Portuguese Queen Isabella (1261–1325), famous for feeding the poor.

[34] Luso-Canadian author Anthony de Sá's *Barnacle Love*, for example, features an extended scene of a *matança do porco* [pig killing] gone wrong, which leaves the novel's young male protagonist effeminized, for having failed to learn the loaded lessons of how to become a Portuguese man in diaspora. See Anthony de Sá, *Barnacle Love* (Chapel Hill, NC: Algonquin Books, 2010), pp. 148–52.

musical genres and spheres of meaning and reference. J&H's array of album cover art and titles accomplishes complex signifying work, finding common iconographic ground between two disparate musical genres while connecting them to locally entrenched ethnic symbols.

Conclusion

Fado acts as a conduit for the sharing of sentiment and, especially in diaspora, to the collective remembering of absent people and places. As ethnomusicologist Salwa Castelo-Branco states: 'The words are the essence of *fado*, sculpted by the voice, transformed into melodies that are in dialogue with the guitars, submerging the musicians and audience members into intense emotions, evoking places or lives, pasts or presents, lives marked by *fado*.'[35] And although some purists questioned the degree to which J&H engaged with traditional *fado*, the band managed to convince many listeners to 'submerge' themselves into the 'intense emotions' required by the experience of lament and the goals of 'evoking' the absent. The first fadocore website emphasized the importance of this shared experience, explaining, '*fado* provides hope for the listener. It's the knowledge that others are with you at the bottom of the well.'[36]

In order to find both kindred spirits – others at the bottom of the well – and a musical vocabulary for grief, Chris da Rosa had to cross the ocean, a pilgrimage that took him to his parents' home country for the first time. This transatlantic crossing engages an important concept of memory studies, particularly with regards to trauma. Ruth Leys identifies trauma studies' core concern with 'the constitutive failure of linguistic representation' related, post-Holocaust, to a 'crisis of witnessing, a crisis at the level of language itself'.[37] Transposing literary expression to musical, this linguistic failure brought about by a crisis of witnessing, relates to Chris's overseas journey in search of new modalities of lament. Left a witness to the traumatic deaths of multiple friends in the prime of youth, and finding other musical genres insufficient to express what he and his bandmates had experienced, Chris crossed the ocean to expand his lexicon, to address something akin to a 'linguistic failure'. He found expressive solutions in the music, lyrics, history and iconography of *fado*, a genre he brought home and combined with the postpunk sights and sounds of his youth. It was only in this surprising syncretism that Charles's

---

[35] Castelo-Branco, *Voix du Portugal*, p. 75.

[36] Bambouche, 'Judith and Holofernes', Vanguard Squad <http://vanguardsquad.com/comrades/judith.php> [accessed 13 September 2011].

[37] Ruth Leys, *Trauma: A Genealogy* (Chicago, IL: University of Chicago Press, 2000), pp. 267–68.

demise, suicide and memory could be fully explored. And ultimately, it was the transatlantic pilgrimage to explore the sonic memories of his parents and grandparents – 'prosthetic memories'[38] – that opened up the possibility of more local journeys away from a dead-end hometown. A full investigation of J&H's music, pilgrimages and memory work is only possible through an understanding of the cultural trafficking between Portugal and the USA that undergirds fadocore's creation. And this transatlantic lens parallels new academic directions as, 'memory studies has begun to turn away from its prevailing methodological nationalism and become interested in forms of remembering *across* nations and cultures'.[39]

Within this transnational musical composite, where does postpunk goth music end and *fado* begin? How do their aesthetics and politics support one another or diverge? The core similarity seems to be in the common focus on loss, not only at the level of lyrics and musical sound, but also present in their overlapping iconographies. While J&H more explicitly depicts loss as death with skulls, skeletons and tombstones favoured in the goth scene, *fado* also traffics in symbols of death. *Fadistas* typically wear black, female vocalists are shrouded in black shawls, all, of course, the uniform of mourning, visual tropes communicating a service to the dead. Further, across discipline and expressive form many critics have pointed to 'an underlying necrophilia in Portuguese society'.[40] And perhaps the fadocore band sought out the musical expression of this Portuguese love of death by focusing on the shady, morally 'dead' cast of characters who often sang and listened to *fado* in its early days. But I think what *fado* offers J&H that perhaps postpunk does not, is a move from the incantation of death itself and the raging and railing against loss, to a focus on the act of mourning – and, more specifically, the collective act of mourning. Rather than crossbones and skeletons, scythes and swords, one of *fado*'s central motifs is the tear. And the tear is the lachrymal product of mulling over loss, a half step from moving beyond its grip. On their first website, the fadocore band seems to support this reading:

> [T]he music of Judith and Holofernes is not for the faint-hearted. This music is about getting it all out – all of it, no matter how painful. The

---

[38] Alison Landsberg, *Prosthetic Memory: The Transformation of American Remembrance in the Age of Mass Culture* (New York: Columbia University Press, 2004).

[39] Astrid Erll, 'Traumatic Pasts, Literary Afterlives and Transcultural Memory: New Directions of Literary and Media Memory Studies', *Journal of Aesthetics and Culture*, 3 (2011), 1–12 (p. 3).

[40] Alfredo Margarido, 'Necrophilia in Portuguese Poetry: From the Eighteenth Century to the Present', *Portuguese Studies*, 4 (1988), 100–16 (p. 100).

narrative, then, is a messy one, not unlike the deliberations of those of us who've survived farm life. To survive is to stay afloat day after day. Enduring the doldrums of everyday life, we find the same thoughts swirling around our heads over and over. Charles, Brian, Ray – regret, love, loss. It's in the reliving that we learn more about ourselves.[41]

J&H was born out of the moody, edgy music of the band's teenage years and the melancholy nourishment of *fado*. *Fado* and postpunk – two bedfellows that were far from strange – gave the musicians a musical and lyrical vocabulary to express the loss and pain unique to their experience of the Central Valley, imbricated as it was in sometimes tragic comings and goings.

---

[41] Bambouche, 'Judith and Holofernes'.

19

'Can't We All Just Be Queer?'

On Imagining Shared Translational Space

Christopher Larkosh
University of Massachusetts Dartmouth

> Where there is an 'I' who utters or speaks and thereby produces an effect in discourse, there is first a discourse which precedes and enables that 'I' and forms in language the constraining trajectory of its will. Thus there is no 'I' who stands *behind* discourse and executes its will through discourse. [...] The 'I' is thus a citation of the place of the 'I' in speech, where that place has a certain priority and anonymity to the life it animates; it is the historically revisable possibility of a name that precedes and exceeds me, but without which I cannot speak.[1]
>
> Judith Butler, *Bodies That Matter*

For those who have been paying attention to its ebbs, flows and permutations over the past three decades, it often appears that what we have come to call queer theory has frequently posited its approach to literary, film and cultural studies alongside a recurrent, if alternating, discursive mode of self-referential, first-person narrative, which serves to stress the importance of the author's continuing existence, presence and lived experience in the form of anecdotes or other forms of autobiographical examples, as well as to emphasize an enduring connectedness and ethical commitment to the questions being posed.

Knowing queer theory more than just in passing might mean a familiarity with specific examples from scholars in the field who have employed this mode of discourse: Sedgwick's consideration in her book *Touching Feeling* of her role

---

[1] Judith Butler, *Bodies That Matter* (London and New York: Routledge, 1995), pp. 225–26.

at a 1991 Act Up demonstration to protest the censorship of black gay filmmaker Marlon Riggs's groundbreaking film *Tongues Untied*, chanting slogans and waving signs, until she unexpectedly passes out and has to be taken to the hospital, with the requisite cross-identificatory 'die-in' of such events cutting too close this time to the real thing; or J. Halberstam's descriptions and interpretations after viewing a drag king show in the 2005 book *In a Queer Time and Place*; or work that highlights the lived experience of people of colour: of these, E. Patrick Johnson's account of understanding Black 'quare' studies through conversations with his grandmother is no doubt the one example that remains most immediately emblematic for me.[2] In fact, one might find so much evidence of first-person discourse as an integral part of queer theoretical discourse that one might even consider it more of a challenge to find texts that do not exhibit this mode of address, at least to some extent, and even begin to question whether those texts, if not the scholars themselves, can even be considered representative of queer theory at all, at least in the personally engaged and explicitly implicated way that many have come to understand it.

So how did we get to this by now firmly established queer space, which many scholars still bound to more conventional norms of academic discourse might consider an uncomfortable level of unabashed self-referentiality, indulgence or disclosure? What, if anything, might even be considered queer about it? And what should my approach to it be as I gauge its relevance to current and future directions in the field of Lusophone Studies, an indisputably transnational discipline that already both consolidates and complicates understandings of linguistic and cultural identity within an ever-shifting set of intersectional frameworks of self and other, be it those of national or linguistic identity, gender and sexuality, race and ethnicity, socioeconomic class, and other forms of social marginality, physical disability or illness, professional precarity, intersecting forms of subalternity (whether Gramscian, postcolonial, or otherwise), or varying degrees of societal (in)visibility?

For this reason, my contribution to this volume on the possible dynamism, vibrancy and increased inclusivity in the field of Lusophone Studies as it is taught, researched and studied today within both a transnational and

---

[2] Eve Kosofsky Sedgwick, *Epistemology of the Closet* (Berkeley and Los Angeles, CA: University of California Press, 1990); *Tongues Untied*, dir. Marlon Riggs (Signifyin' Works, 1989); E. Patrick Johnson, '"Quare" Studies, or "(Almost) Everything I Know About Queer Studies I Learned From My Grandmother"', in *The Routledge Queer Studies Reader*, eds Donald E. Hall and Annamaria Jagose et al (London and New York: Routledge, 2013), pp. 96–118; Judith (Jack) Halberstam, *In a Queer Time and Place: Transgender Bodies, Subcultural Lives* (New York: New York University Press, 2006).

translational framework, may well have to chart a different course. I may even have to go so far as to reiterate that queer theory, or any literary theory for that matter, can only be considered such when it takes on these uncommonly personal ways of thinking and imagining literary texts, whether those firmly centred within the Portuguese language or, as is perhaps more common, in translational dialogue with an ever-expanding set of texts, lived experiences and cultural materialities in other languages, whether those of other former European colonial powers (English, French, Spanish etc.), those indigenous native languages already present in colonized spaces long before the arrival of Portuguese in the tri-continental context of South America, Africa and Asia, or those of global transmigrations, south to north, east to west, that continue to characterize our globalized interactive cultural landscape.[3]

Studying Portuguese language and nominally Lusophone cultures in a mainly Anglophone academic context, i.e. both as a linguistic system and as a semantic vehicle for a specific set of representational signs and symbols, has always been to some extent one in which officialized registers of writing, speech and thought, which all too often succeed in maintaining hegemony over less powerful forms of being in language, must invariably give way at some point to other paradigms of languaging or seeing, not to mention understandings of self (gender identity, linguistic or cultural identity) gained through linguistic, spatial or even sexual interaction with others. It is precisely in these uncertain moments that what we call queer translational space can be said to emerge alongside and overlapping with others upon this inherently unstable and often fiercely contested planetary landscape.

Moving across the variegated and often violent cultural terrain, one both Lusophone and translational, transcontinental and personal, of the by now irreversibly queer planet that I and others cohabit, I am reminded not only of

---

[3] One example of the ways that such acts of literary translation can create shifts, not only in target, but also in source language cultures, not to mention in the ever-evolving understanding of self and others, can be found in the foundational work of Brazilian queer history, João Silvério Trevisan's *Devassos no paraíso*, one that was itself actually first published in English under the title *Perverts in Paradise*, and only later in Portuguese for a Brazilian audience. See João Silvério Trevisan, *Devassos no paraíso* (São Paulo: Max Limonad Editora, 1986), pp. 203–04. See also his original *Perverts in Paradise* (London: Gay Man's Press, 1986). In his narrative, we see the sequence of events that begins with a simple request of texts for translation into another language, which sets off a whole set of political initiatives, as well as a series of important questions about language and meaning, not only words once used only to hurt and kill, like *viado* and *bicha*, but more fundamental words that made it possible for gay men and others to speak openly about themselves as such, as we see here, in the first person.

the well-worn slogan of by now faraway Queer Nation activism of the early 1990s – 'We're here, we're queer, get used to it' – words that would, in slightly modified (perhaps misquoted?) form act as a theoretical point of departure for European philosopher Alexander García Duttmann's book *Between Cultures: Tensions in the Struggle for Recognition*.[4] Those who took part in these Queer Nation demonstrations will no doubt recall that this continually repeated slogan was often subject to any number of creative, and overtly self-ironizing, reiterations: for instance, in consumer spaces like malls or busy commercial areas, it became 'we're here, we're queer, we're not going shopping'. The slogan thus becomes a critical response not only to the main idea of one's own protest, i.e. that it is essential to be visibly and identifiably queer in places most commonly identified as common to all, but also to the very possibility of 'being out in public' at a moment when the notion of public space itself appears to be at risk of shrinking or disappearing entirely into an admittedly common, but still privately owned and securitized, consumer space.

This confrontational act of protest as a form of discursive displacement may appear to run counter to that of another important contemporary voice of the early 1990s: the by now iconic Californian, African-American, Los Angeles resident, and motorist Rodney King, whose words can be summarized much more succinctly: 'Can't we all just get along?' The ethical generosity of such an utterance, offered as it was from a hospital bed shortly after being brutally beaten by the police on the edge of a highway, has always astounded and awed me. The all-too-obvious ironies and contradictions of even attempting to reconcile and reimagine the idea of a 'we' in light of such violent and unequal circumstances forced me to reconsider the way I thought of my relatively secure place in the putative public spaces we inhabited. Whether a single street, or a patchwork of neighbourhoods bordered by freeways and natural barriers with all their attendant and corresponding socioeconomic distinctions, policed by increasingly militarized local and state forces and private security concerns; whether a gay neighbourhood in San Francisco, or a predominantly black one in the USA, Brazil, southern Africa or elsewhere, with even more extreme levels of socioeconomic inequality, juxtaposed within the seemingly permeable but often quite limited confines of an interconnected, yet still unmistakably segregated, world.

It is with these inherent inequalities of visibility when attempting acts of political cultural contestation that I must admit I am not too fond of the idea of the transnational or the bi- or multilingual as a singular, monolithic or univocal '-ism', any more than one might understand any single instance

---

[4] Alexander García Duttmann, *Between Cultures: Tensions in the Struggle for Recognition* (London and New York: Verso, 2000).

of queer sexuality or gender as one. It seems to imply that there may be a single, comprehensive ideology, movement or methodology equally accessible to all who have at least some stake in translational solutions through which one might approach the transnational in all of its varied thematic focal points and schematic connections, or a single established, to say nothing of an institutionally preferred theoretical framework, however useful and broadly accepted it may appear to be. In fact, I would argue that it is only by disputing the all-too-commonly unquestioned status of such recurrent theoretical approaches, especially in light of the all-too-visible power differentials in which we are clearly and inextricably implicated, that our field can gauge the potential for future practical incorporations and engagements, and not only in the context of by-now institutionalized and, yes, politically instrumentalized theories. That applies not only to what we might call queer theory, but any number of theoretical currents that circulate in Lusophone Studies and other humanistic disciplines, whether successive waves of feminisms, variants of poststructuralism, postmodernism and deconstruction, reworkings of Lacanian psychoanalysis, ethnic studies, critical race theory, post- and decolonial critiques, and the intersticial spaces they point to.

It is here in this nominally shared, yet still openly contested critical and institutional, space that I wish to posit not only queer theory *per se*, but also the palpable, and recurrent, presence of a living, and yes, identifiably queer first person, operating both in the singular and the plural:

We're here. We're queer. (Or perhaps not.) Can't we all just get along?

'It's all about "me"': or is it?

So let us follow the lead of these queer theorists and talk about this 'I' in personal terms: Over the course of my own circuitous, 20-odd-year-long professional transition in and out of Lusophone Studies, I have often focused on queer male authors from Brazil: in particular, the novels and short stories of Caio Fernando Abreu, Wilson Bueno and João Gilberto Noll.[5] I have

---

[5] On Abreu, see Christopher Larkosh, 'Two in Translation: The Multilingual Cartographies of Néstor Perlongher and Caio Fernando Abreu', in *Re-Engendering Translation: Gender/Sexuality, Transcultural Practice and the Politics of Alterity*, ed. Christopher Larkosh (London and New York: Routledge, 2011). On Bueno, see Christopher Larkosh, 'Forms of A-Dress', *Social Dynamics*, 33.2 (2007), 164–83; and Christopher Larkosh, 'Flows of Trans-Language: "Translating Transgender in the Paraguayan Sea"', *Transgender Studies Quarterly*, 3.3–4 (2016), 552–68. On Noll, see Christopher Larkosh, 'Submarine: Germany Resurfacing in the Contemporary

completed translations of some of their short works, and plan to do more, in the wake of the deaths of all three of these authors. Abreu died of AIDS in 1994, along with so many gay men of his generation and others who did not live to see the combination treatments that would save so many just a year or two later. Bueno was murdered in 2010 (like countless gay, female, trans and genderqueer individuals in Brazil and elsewhere, with his identified and self-confessed killer, as is frequent in these cases, eventually acquitted and set free). As for Noll, he died in 2017 of what the obituary in *O Globo* called 'undisclosed causes', through most probably of sudden cardiac arrest.[6]

And while I value and would expect inclusion of all three within any historiography of Brazilian literature, let alone its queer iterations, the writing of Wilson Bueno is of special significance to me, and not only because of the way that he befriended me personally and attempted to involve me as part of his own transnational and interlingual literary journey by way of translation. Once again, this is why the personal matters: in order to even attempt to tell the whole story, I must, at least to some extent, tell my own story. It might mean going back through personal correspondence between Wilson and me to which few others if anyone has direct access, and I must divulge my queerness, not obliquely or discreetly, but explicitly as the only way that queerness can matter: not just in words that say, 'I', 'I am', but go one step further, back into the lived circumstances and queer time and space that made our cross-cultural interaction possible.

'I' was the one who originally initiated contact between us during my stay in Brazil in early 1998. While I had spent the year researching to present at a number of academic conferences,[7] when I set off to Curitiba after a conference

---

Brazilian Novel', in *KulturConfusão: German-Brazilian Interculturalities*, eds Anke Finger, Gabi Kathöfer and C. Larkosh (Berlin: DeGruyter, 2015), pp. 247–66.

[6] *O Globo*, 29 March 2017 <https://oglobo.globo.com/cultura/livros/morre-escritor-joao-gilberto-noll-vencedor-de-cinco-jabutis-aos-70-1-21128194> [accessed 11 February 2019].

[7] A description of one of the apparently more 'historic' panels that I and other queer academics took part in 1998 (the 6th International Conference of Comparative Literature of Abralic, the Brazilian comparative literature association, held at the Universidade Federal de Santa Catarina in Florianópolis) is included in the introduction to the 2002 collection of gay and lesbian studies, *A escrita de Adé: Perspectivas teóricas dos estudos gays e lésbic@s no Brasil*, eds Rick Santos and Wilton Garcia (São Paulo: Xamã: NCC/SUNY, 2002), p. 9. As in aforementioned examples of gay and lesbian activism in Brazil, participation by foreign (in this case, mainly US) scholars allows for an external perspective, and this is what I mean when I call Lusophone Studies a translational field, one always both taking and shifting place, not only in Portuguese, but simultaneously in other languages.

in São Paulo I really had no professional agenda other than wanting to relax, and only then contact the author of what I considered to be one of Brazilian literature's more original and inventive short novels, *Mar paraguayo*, his 1992 story of love and loss, uses what he called 'Portuñol brasiguayo', adding Guarani to destandardized Spanish and Portuguese. The Paraguayan Sea I came looking for remains one that cannot exist, at the same time that it cannot *but* exist; while Paraguay is a landlocked country, it is bordered by rivers and other bodies of water, much like the ones that Wilson created with words, as that oft-disputed space beyond nations where multiple languages meet: 'yo desearia alcançar todo que vibre e tine abaixo, mucho abaixo de la línea del silêncio. No hay idiomas aí. Solo la vertigen de la linguagem. Deja-me que exista.'[8]

One possible translation might be: 'I would like to reach everything that vibrates and rings below, far below the line of silence. There are no languages there. Only the vertigo of language. Let it exist for me.' But is that an adequate response to the call for translation? What translation could I possibly provide for a language that was not one, but many languages and no language at the same time? To expect a simple and presumably straightforward translation of meaning into standard English of a linguistically multilayered creative work, after all, may well be to miss the point entirely. The question might also be: do the waters of this multilingual sea extend to those found in a gay sauna in Curitiba, presumably so far from the recognized zones of academic activity, and yet so close? And do these waters extend so far as to reach 'me', or 'my language'? This was, after all, where Wilson suggested that we meet when we talked over the phone, and while it was never an explicitly sexual proposition, one has to recognize that my accepting his invitation to meet in this undeniably sexualized queer space did seal our friendship in some way. And while we did speak of literature that day, I have no written record of it (it was not as if I could have brought a notebook along – put it that way).

This contact, followed by years of rereading, would result in a 2007 article I wrote that discussed Bueno's work up to that point, published in the well-known South African social science journal *Social Dynamics*;[9] the very idea of his literary work being discussed in Africa brought him such pleasure that he sent me his latest book in appreciation: the 2005 literary menagerie *Cachorros do céu*, and later, the 2007 novel *A copista de Kafka*, in the hope that I would translate them after *Mar paraguayo*.[10] While I was translating *Mar paraguayo*, however, Wilson was brutally murdered in Curitiba by a

---

[8] Wilson Bueno, *Mar Paraguayo* (São Paulo: Iluminuras, 1992), p. 1.
[9] See Larkosh, 'Forms of A-Dress'.
[10] Wilson Bueno, *Cachorros do céu* (São Paulo: Editora Planeta do Brasil, 2005) and *A copista de Kafka* (São Paulo: Editora Planeta do Brasil, 2007).

sexual acquaintance of his, interrupting my work on the translations we were planning via email correspondence. This completed fragment of this work was eventually published, however, more or less in the same state that it was at the moment I learned of his death, along with a brief discussion of the circumstances of his murder, and the public travesty of justice that followed.[11] In the end, it was not the completed work, but an interrupted text that gave the text an unforeseen capacity to speak to 'the line of silence' that still guards the tragic and unjust circumstances surrounding his murder. Then again, there is still so much left unfinished and left in fragments here, and not just for a translator.

Another more current example: in returning to one of the works from what was to be the end of Wilson's life, the 2007 novel *A copista de Kafka*, I now find that I cannot read or interpret this new project of translation as anything but one promised years ago to a dead author and friend and not yet delivered. In this way, I begin to make good on a debt that I have perhaps temporarily neglected, yet never forgotten.

For the purposes of this particular discussion, what are the ways in which this novel can be considered a work of queer fiction? At first glance, it may only appear to be a retelling of the relationship between the by-now emblematic twentieth-century author Franz Kafka and his fiancée, the stenographer Felice Bauer. At the same time, the novel assumes a set of additional layers of signification and interpretation; the central Europe of place names and characters Wilson creates seems at times intentionally inauthentic, more like a German town in southern Brazil or the multiethnic pseudo-central European Curitiba that Wilson himself inhabited, or perhaps even the imaginary Austria-Hungary of his Argentine counterpart (counterpoet?) Néstor Perlongher, whose early work also explored an imaginary Austria-Hungary superimposed upon Brazil and Argentina.[12]

But that is what I find so fascinating about this novel, as it allows me to escape the commonplaces of the actual, historical central Europe, whether articulated in German or any other language of the former Habsburg empire (if not Wilson's own Curitiba), to thereby make way for a parallel queer space, both a sort of fictional translation from Kafka's German as well as an unmistakable linguistic invention in Brazilian Portuguese. Perhaps in this way, much as in *Mar paraguayo*, this literary work is always somewhere on the border with another version of itself.

In *A copista de Kafka*, there are numerous passages that attempt to capture the pervasive hopelessness of Felice as she observes a world war unfolding

---

[11] Larkosh, 'Flows of Trans-Language'.
[12] Larkosh, 'Two in Translation'.

before her: 'the war takes proportions of a universal catastrophe, I would say. Millions dead, Europe shaken by a hatred so corrosive as it is general. Life seems so to have become so banal to me, as if the death of thousands of young people on the front were the changing of a lamp on a post.'[13] But consider also the short stories interspersed as chapters in between the fragments that comprise the main narrative, much in the style of a classical frame tale; one in particular, 'Lindonéia a Bailarina', about a dance teacher who teaches ducks, herons and vultures to dance on the banks of a lake named Ehness.[14] While these thematically varied pieces interspersed throughout the novel do not seem like an attempt to create, say, short stories that could have been written by Kafka; the camp sensibility and humour might well be that of some other Kafka still unknown to me. It is more identifiably the fruit of a literary imagination that finds its voice through transgender identification, that is to say that of the same man I met in a gay sauna in Curitiba some 20 years ago.

So, who is performing the transgender literary role of Felice Bauer now? After all, Wilson made it clear in our email correspondence that he wanted me to be his translator, both of this book and the one preceding it, *Cachorros do céu* (or, as I playfully renamed it, *Sky Pups*): if not right away, then at some point in the future. I reread the words of Wilson as he interprets Felice: 'Independently of the geographical separation that signals our love, if I can call love this literary fever that sets our days in motion, we are physically more than separated, what we are is out of touch – in every sense of the word.'[15] Maybe this is not love in the conventional or sexual sense, but who is still dictating, and who is still here reading, copying down, translating and typing into the night to make deadline on yet another article, in the perhaps vain attempt to do my part to preserve and extend the literary soul of another? And what in the world does this act of transgender identification and translational longing all add up to?

From this vantage point, it becomes all the more clear that the ways that 'I' map this academic and referential field are unavoidably conditioned by questions of recognition and access: the languages and literary works you or I know, the messages and aesthetic and ideological biases that I wish to convey to others as a scholar and critic, not to mention a set of interpersonal relationships, often tied to one's own cultural capital and professional success as an academic – but, as I have tried to show here, not always. Every scholar will naturally find points of convergence and divergence with others researching and publishing in the field; for instance, two foundational compilations, both

---

[13] Bueno, *A copista de Kafka*, p. 76. All translations are mine.
[14] Bueno, *A copista de Kafka*, pp. 122–27.
[15] Bueno, *A copista de Kafka*, p. 129.

published in 2002. For Lusophone scholars, there is Susan Canty Quinlan and Fernando Arenas's suggestively titled *Lusosex* (Fernando once confided to me that the name was taken from the sign of a now defunct sex shop close to Rossio railway station in Lisbon, again underscoring how the mundane, often ignored spaces we transit and the apparently random signs we reinterpret there, can become a significant and inseparable part of our work).[16] For Brazilianists, there is the collection edited by Brazilian-American academic and activist Rick Santos and his colleague Wilton Garcia named *A escrita de adé*, which takes as part of its title the Yoruba word for male homosexual, *adé*, 'to announce a hybrid discursivity', one presumably between 'African cultures' and contemporary 'Brazilian gay culture' and its ever-emergent, if ever-precarious, modes of academic production.[17] When these two collections are considered together, it becomes even more possible to envision a clearly delineated Brazilian and Lusophone queer literary canon, in which a number of the central topics, recurrent themes and foci still hold in many respects today.

As each of us attempts to continue our so often interrupted discussions or incomplete compilations of transnational research by perhaps first addressing the more serious omissions, such as, say, an Argentine exile in Brazil like the aforementioned urban anthropologist, poet and queer theorist Néstor Perlongher, any sign of dissonance, if not intentional neglect, should remind any or all of us not only of the enormous task that inclusivity represents in academic terms: at times chronicling histories and documenting activities of others, but also an accompanying reflection on the precarious nature of the imagined inclusion of any one of us in that ever-expanding network of recognition and citation.

Each of these dialogic critical contexts provides us with just one more set of examples of why we research, develop and share knowledge concurrently with others in academic, and perhaps queer, community, ideally both in practice and in theory: so that our own work is never simply a self-indulgent, stand-alone monologue or part of some insider conversation, but actually becomes part of a more broad-based social encounter based on mutual recognition, not only of those authors we read in common or theories we are all familiar with, each with a set of divergent thematic emphases, interpretations and methodological approaches, but also with a set of specific people, pedagogies and practical strategies for transcultural work that extend beyond the lines of

---

[16] *Lusosex: Gender and Sexuality in the Portuguese Speaking World*, eds Susan Canty Quinlan and Fernando Arenas (Minneapolis, MN: University of Minnesota Press, 2002).

[17] Santos and Garcia, *A escrita de Adé*, p. 12.

textual, stylistic and cultural analysis, in which we can ask questions about ourselves and others in an immediate and critical sociopolitical context, one in which actual human, and quite often identifiably queer lives, are at stake.

At the same time, one must be careful, especially over time, not to confuse one's reduced academic group with a representative community, to allow chance encounters, whether in presumably queer spaces or other uncommon places, to inform the current linguistic community model of *Lusofonia* still dominated by deep-rooted elite cultural hegemonies, as well as lingering prejudices from different geographical, political, cultural, and, yes, academic and linguistic differences over where exactly our epistemological 'centre' (or perhaps 'center'?) is. And as each of us continues to research and communicate in connection to others, it is often the case that we to some extent become inextricable from those disciplinary and discursive entanglements with other scholars, especially in a discipline smaller than a small town, often not sure where the ideas of one end and those of another begin. It may well be the queers in any village, whether they are living both comfortably and visibly within it or barely hanging onto its jagged edges, that give some indication of whether we all can, in fact, get along there.

(Not) for queers only

Perhaps this queerness of translation, especially the ways in which it encourages us to think of language in transnational terms, might also allow for a certain kind of cross-identificatory thinking that may not be just another potentially dominant theoretical paradigm that can be somehow instrumentalized not just to critique, or even attempt to bring down, an already compromised international nation-state system, but might be instead a continuing theoretical and praxis-based engagement that does not even allow for a reconsolidation of the mechanisms that the system in question currently deploys as part of its systematically oppressive institutional structure, ones that have all too often been deployed against lgbtq+ people, particularly those of colour and from the Global South, to render them all the more invisible and without a suitable language to speak in the first person.

So while we may all be able, at least to some extent, to 'get along' in this cramped and shrinking academic enclosure (even as we can hear police sirens in the distance and may walk over the broken glass left behind as evidence of both normalized violence and social unrest), there will be no vague invitations for generalized recognition, much less 'use' or 'application', of queer theory by students and scholars. I refer in particular to those which adopt the vague and quite frankly often dismissive, if not blatantly appropriating and ultimately invisibilizing rhetoric of the statement 'maybe we are all a bit queer', one that might be identified in Sedgwick's *Epistemology of the Closet* as a 'universalizing' discursive move, one that Tim Dean discusses in *Beyond Sexuality* as one that also extends to HIV/Aids when he contends, perhaps provocatively, perhaps as a recognition of a shared social responsibility or pathology, that 'in a psychotic society we are all PWA's [people with Aids]'.[18] However chronic, manageable, or presumably destigmatized HIV/Aids may be seen to be today, anyone who is actually still being treated for this illness should at least reserve the right to disagree, if not protest out loud, its presumption that a shared societal psychosis might be some form of equivalent status with someone who is subject to the direct consequences of living with the virus: drug regimens, stigmatization, discrimination or outright violence.

Another example that comes to mind: the once common t-shirt from the early 1990s that my boyfriend John[19] has kept as part of his impressive queer t-shirt collection, which reads 'Nobody Knows I'm a Lesbian'. As a queer cultural object, it reminds us how a single written statement of identity can be read, interpreted, ironized, or even rejected by those who view it, depending on who in particular chooses to wear the shirt (most telling is that the t-shirt was, as I recall, most often seen on young, white, presumably straight males – and, as such, can it really be considered seriously as one of solidarity or sharing space?) Recent well-publicized cases of white people attempting to pass as African-American, going often so far as to assume positions of power and authority in community organizations, should also remind us (regardless of whether we think we need reminding) that while Black Lives Matter should matter, we still cannot all be black, and if any of us were to believe that we could be it certainly would not help us 'all get along'.

So while it might be construed at first glance to some as an act of solidarity, alliance or imagined common ground, this and other statements

---

[18] Sedgwick, *Epistemology of the Closet*, p. 40; Tim Dean, *Beyond Sexuality* (Chicago, IL and London: University of Chicago Press, 2000), p. 132.

[19] While some may take issue with this reference to my own boyfriend and his queer t-shirt collection as too 'self-indulgent' for an academic article, for most queer folks, being queer today usually means being out, quite often by being openly in a romantic and/or sexual relationship with at least one other self-identified queer person. In contrast, it does not necessarily mean having read, discussed and referenced queer theory for the instrumentalized benefit of one's academic career, especially when accompanied by an all too often glaring absence of said out self-identification or any explicit mention of direct personal relationship to other queer people. That to my mind is what I would consider a truly self-indulgent use of queer theory, not my making a case here or elsewhere for the crucial relevance of queer people's often marginalized lived experience to contemporary academic discourse.

might even be viewed as a political tactic deployed in the shared space by those already entitled to claim or appropriate more of it than others and, for this reason, working more to determine and shape the ways that claims on discursive and, by extension, institutional space are made than to actually create more space for others. What has often been considered simply a well-intentioned gesture to generalize, if not completely normativize, queerness or other forms of marginality, has also all too often served merely to invalidate attempts by lgbtq+ groups to name themselves, to say 'I' and perhaps even 'we', and in so doing define certain community boundaries and/or de-emphasize others, and create alternative models of (dis-)connectedness and safety in the face of persistent and all-too-real violence, even if it is seldom if ever crystal clear who those gatekeepers should ideally be.

Far be it from me to say. But what I will venture here is that, at the very least, we may need to rethink entirely the ways that we cross-identify with others. Much as the policing of space and property has often been outsourced to private security firms, one has to wonder to what degree we have now become crowdsourced to police our own identities and even those of others: i.e. pressured to be more actively involved and personally invested in policing the imagined boundaries of our own identities than any particular institution, public or private. What might serve as an alternative?

To answer, permit me a final personal anecdote. During Pride Month this year in New York City, my boyfriend and I had the chance to view two artistic happenings: first, that of an all-female Brazilian-style drum group called Fogo Azul NYC; and the opening of a public installation on the outside of the Leslie-Lohman Museum by the by-now legendary artistic collective fierce pussy. The photographic images displayed were those of the artists as children, superimposed with words often considered offensive, like 'dyke' or even 'bulldagger'. And yet this was a celebration. First I was entertained by a Brazilian drum beat, then asked to come closer and, finally, to clap and dance alongside a group of mostly white lesbians clearly displaying their love of what remains an identifiable element of Brazilian culture, even if it is one usually performed mainly by men in its cultural context of origin, and here it was given a clearly intentional re-engendering. Second, I was invited by the members of a mostly lesbian artists collective to take on and share the names that most oppressed them as they grew up and eventually came out, taking pictures in front of the portraits, speaking to and personally thanking the women depicted for including me in the act of saying: 'I AM A queer androgyne feminist trannie pervert stone butch tomgirl dyke AND SO ARE YOU.'

So, I ask again: when is it truly appropriate to appropriate? When are we entitled to involve ourselves in, and translate ourselves into, the life, identity and culture of another, in contrast to when we ourselves consider ourselves to be? One time might be when we are explicitly asked to do so, all the while recognizing that at other times it might not mean that such an invitation will be extended unconditionally, much less in perpetuity, especially in those times and places where separate space for queer people or for people of colour is still clearly needed

So, it is on these fine, often blurred lines between welcome cross-identification and undue appropriation that we might begin to map out the uncertain and varied terrain of cross-cultural engagement. Such crossings into queerness can at times be so necessary as to constitute a matter of life or death, such as in the by-now classic aforementioned example of Eve Kosofsky Sedgwick at the Act Up demonstration: she might even be considered the honorary queer *par excellence*, that is if she is not actually the one who was indispensable in creating the theoretical space on which anyone would make or dispute such determinations. At other times, however, such gestures can also end up manifesting themselves more as a perceptible erasure of the specific historical struggles of queer/trans/gender activists to leverage these marginal spaces they occupy at their own risk to enact a measure, however modest, of concrete social change, struggles from which many were and still are either all too noticeably absent or still closeted away in the recurrent fiction of 'no one knows I'm gay' (even when they were not actually fooling anyone else who was).

For some of us, our queer political activism and the theories that often emerged from it were never intended to be merely a discursive adornment for professional advancement, or yet another maker of cultural capital in front of a depoliticized classroom in an increasingly globalized yet also undeniably neoliberal university, in which modes of knowledge are also bought and sold as just another late-capitalist commodity. Because, as I recall, we were fighting for something much more basic: our lives, our losses and mourning, and the right, however dubious it may appear to some, to be 'out of the closet': open, vocal and visible in 'public space', however that uncertain term is to be understood, to say nothing of an academic space increasingly subject to forces of commodification. As we do so, we become all the more aware of what is at stake in reasserting one's identity and presence alongside others, and the indisputable value (and price) of that lived human experience, even if it may only matter to others as just another traded commodity in the vast global exchange of information that continues to be interpreted, translated and otherwise set in transit over time.

There will always remain those for whom this word 'queer' remains, like gender, race, socioeconomic class or other categories of identity and/or institutional marginalization, a sort of less commonly taught foreign language (perhaps much like Portuguese?) to be researched, mastered, perhaps translated or taught, simply to be added to one's own professionalized credentials and persona like so many other already academically entrenched ideologies, theoretical stances and subject positions that come into play in academic discourse, often without ever even having to say 'I', much less to present that personalized narrative of embodied familiarity or lived experience that hopefully we can begin to identify as the *sine qua non* of queer theory as we know it.

The 'bottom line'? Well, as we have seen over the last 30-odd years, these realities and palpable degrees of gendered difference still subject some of us who identify as queer to greater systemic or institutional violence than others. Other will choose not to identify as such, whether that means not openly and publicly or not at all, even when increasingly aware of the indistinct boundaries of (dis)identification and alliance that even non-normative subject positions can make manifest. With this in mind, how can those who do not identify as queer engage and dialogue with queerness in a symbolically and practically non-violent way, perhaps even translate it while reimagining it utopically, as if into an impossibly common idiom, but with a uncommon degree of care? And, in so doing, how might this work, alongside queer people in the academy, benefit, hopefully not just oneself first and foremost, but above all those undeniably present ones who we claim to share space with, those who often have no choice but to occupy the vulnerable jagged edge of shared space that the marginality of queerness still implies, whether as theoretical concept or as concrete and institutionalized subject position?

That said, if only in caution, how can theorizing on the queerness of shared translational space, especially between Lusophone and even 'less commonly taught' languages, also be a part of activist projects for actual cultural, political and social change? Can there even be a queer transnational theory, Lusophone or otherwise, that does not call for, or extend into, a set of political, social or discursive practices and their inescapable ethical implications? But those are questions that I hope to have already answered here, at least for myself. Whatever else, I leave for others.

20

International Departures and Transnational Texts in Contemporary Brazilian Literature

The 'Amores Expressos' Series

Claire Williams
St Peter's College, Oxford

Brazilian literature has always reflected a deep concern with national identity, in a concerted effort to differentiate Brazilians from (1) their former colonial masters, the Portuguese, (2) challenges to their territory from surrounding countries in South America, and (3) the cultural imperialism of Europe, and, more recently, the USA. In an article published in New York in 1873, the great Brazilian novelist and journalist Machado de Assis (1839–1908) famously detected a 'national instinct' in the literary production of his fellow countrymen, centred on what he called a 'certain intimate feeling that renders him a man of his time and country, even when he addresses topics that are remote in time or space', for a writer could 'be a good Scot without ever mentioning the thistle' if they possessed 'a certain inner Scottishness, which was distinct and superior for not being merely superficial'.[1] He argued that writers should not feel impelled to linger on descriptions of local colour, and vocabulary, to the detriment of exercising their intuition and imagination, inspired by wider philosophical and moral questions. This, he felt, would lead to the independence of Brazilian literature.

The ingredients of Brazilianness may have changed since the nineteenth century but the assertion of a unique cultural identity has not, according to recent surveys of trends in contemporary Brazilian literature,[2] even as initiatives

---

[1] 'Reflections on Brazilian Literature at the Present Moment: The National Instinct', trans. Robert Patrick Newcomb, *Brasil/Brazil*, 26.47 (2013), 85–101 (p. 89).

[2] See Beatriz Resende, *Contemporâneos: Expressões da literatura brasileira no*

are developed to increase the visibility of Brazilian literature abroad.[3] After a period at the end of the twentieth century in which there was a sustained focus inwards, in the form of neo-realist fiction highlighting social issues, the best-known example being Paulo Lins's *Cidade de Deus* [*City of God*] (1997) (and its hugely successful film adaptation),[4] there has been a distinct growth in more transnational Brazilian literature.[5] Writers with experience of living abroad (diplomats, students, writers in residence at foreign institutions, first or second-generation migrants) have incorporated their impressions into their fiction to the apparent avoidance of 'Brazilian' subjects and settings, and produced popular, prize-winning works.[6] In their introduction to issue 121 of *Granta* (2012), which grandly presents 'The Best of Young Brazilian Novelists', the editors go as far as to claim that this generation of writers is 'not especially concerned with parsing what derives from within and what comes from outside. Sons and daughters of a nation that is more prosperous and open, they are citizens of the world, as well as Brazilians.'[7]

The notion of a particularly Brazilian way of doing global citizenship, underpinned by a twenty-first-century cosmopolitanism, was manifested in a project initiated in 2007, known as 'Amores Expressos' (AE),[8] which

século XXI (Rio de Janeiro: Casa da Palavra, 2008); Karl Erik Schøllhammer, *Ficção brasileira contemporânea*, 2nd edn (Rio de Janeiro: Civilização Brasileira, 2011).

[3] See Regina Zilberman, 'Desafios da literatura brasileira na primeira década do séc. XXI', *Nonada: Letras em Revista*, 13.15 (2010), 183–200; Carmen Villarino Pardo, 'Literatura brasileira atual e desafios do contemporâneo', *Abriu*, 6 (2017), 9–14.

[4] Paulo Lins, *Cidade de Deus* (São Paulo: Companhia das Letras, 1997); *City of God*, trans. Alison Entrekin (London: Bloomsbury, 2006); *Cidade de Deus*, dir. Fernando Meirelles (2002). See Tânia Pellegrini, 'No fio da navalha: literatura e violência no Brasil de hoje', *Estudos em Literatura Brasileira Contemporânea* 24 (2004), 15–34.

[5] See, for example, Leonardo Tonus, 'Alteridades expressas no romance brasileiro contemporâneo', in *Das Luzes Às Soleiras: Perspectivas Críticas na Literatura Brasileira Contemporânea*, eds Ricardo Barberena and Vinícius Carneiro (Porto Alegre: Luminara, 2014), pp. 107–28; *Transnacionalidades: Arte e Cultura no Brasil Contemporâneo*, ed. Cimara Valim de Melo (Porto Alegre: Metamorfose, 2017).

[6] I am thinking of writers like Adriana Lisboa, Paloma Vidal, Bernardo Carvalho, Tatiana Salem Levy and Fernando Bonassi, whose book of fragments of travel narrative, *Passaporte* (São Paulo: Cosac Naify, 2013), is the size and shape of a passport.

[7] Roberto Feith and Marcelo Ferroni, 'Foreword: The Best of Young Brazilian Novelists', trans. Nick Caistor, *Granta*, 121 (2012), 7–11 (p. 7). Here, 'young' means under the age of 40.

[8] The title is difficult to translate into English. 'Amores' (loves) is straightforward, but 'expressos', an adjective derived from the past participle of the verb 'expressar' (to express, explain, present) has several interpretations, including 'rapid', 'urgent'

sought to showcase the versatility and creativity of Brazilian authors. A collaboration between film producer Rodrigo Teixeira, prestigious publishing house Companhia das Letras and up-and-coming writer João Paulo Cuenca, the project took the form of a series of novels.[9] Seventeen Brazilian writers were sent to destinations around the world, for one month, to write a love story inspired by the setting, which would then be published as a novel and also turned into a film.[10] During their time abroad, the authors had to write a blog. At some point a film crew would accompany them for three days, and turn the resulting footage into a television series.[11]

The writers and their destinations were Amilcar Bettega (Istanbul), Bernardo Carvalho (St Petersburg), João Paulo Cuenca (Tokyo), Daniel Galera (Buenos Aires), Cecília Giannetti (Berlin), André de Leonés (São Paulo), Adriana Lisboa (Paris), Chico Mattoso (Havana), Reinaldo Morães (Mexico City), Lourenço Mutarelli (New York), Antonia Pellegrino (Mumbai), Daniel Pellizzari (Dublin), Antonio Prata (Shanghai), Luiz Ruffato (Lisbon), Sérgio Sant'Anna (Prague), Paulo Scott (Sydney) and Joca Reiners Terron (Cairo).[12]

---

and 'obvious'. In relation to coffee, 'expresso' is an import to Brazil, which is ironic considering that for centuries coffee was used stereotypically as synonymous with the country. All translations from Portuguese are mine, unless otherwise attributed. All references to these novels appear parenthetically within the text.

[9] The project was announced in daily newspaper *Folha de São Paulo*: Cadão Volpato, 'Bonde das Letras', *Folha de São Paulo*, 17 March 2007 <http://www1.folha.uol.com.br/fsp/ilustrad/fq1703200707.htm> [accessed 8 August 2017].

[10] In 2003, Teixeira masterminded the volume *Parati Para Mim* (Rio de Janeiro: Agir, 2003), for which Cuenca, Mattoso and Santiago Nazarian wrote a short story about Paraty, in order to commemorate the first year of Brazil's most important Literary Festival, FLIP. Cecily Raynor describes a similar project called 'Año Zero' involving Latin American writers being sent abroad, 'The Digital Ruins of *Amores Expressos*', *Revista Brasileira de Literatura Comparada*, 31 (2017), 139–51. I am aware of only one other comparable literary project involving travel: *The Weekenders: Travels in the Heart of Africa* (London: Ebury, 2001). For this collection, established writers from various genres were commissioned by the *Daily Telegraph* to visit 'one of the most extraordinary and inaccessible places on the planet', now South Sudan, to 'engage with a previously unreachable war' and produce texts, the royalties going towards aid. Susan Ryan, 'Introduction', pp. 1–3 (p. 2).

[11] The television series was directed by Tadeu Jungle and Estela Renner and first broadcast in 2011. The blogs were first posted in April 2007 and most are still available, such as Adriana Lisboa's: <http://blogdaadrianalisboa.blogspot.com/> [accessed 10 September 2019]. See also Raynor, 'The Digital Ruins of *Amores Expressos*', on the blogs.

[12] The contributors ranged widely in age and experience: veterans Sant'Anna (b. 1941) and Morães (b. 1950) were the oldest, Pellegrino (b. 1979), a scriptwriter and columnist, the youngest. In 2007, all had published short stories, some had a

At the outset, Cuenca and Teixeira expressed the intention that in their interpretations of their new environments the writers would 'make some noise'.[13] The immediate reaction in the press and on social media to the announcement of the project was shock at the fact that it might be partly funded by public money, under the Lei Rouanet (a law that enables companies to offset income tax by investing in cultural projects), although, in the end, this did not happen. There was also criticism of the choice of writers (lack of experience, rumours of nepotism), questioning of the destinations (too glamorous?), the length of time spent away (insufficient) and debate about the potential effects that writing on commission may have on the quality of the work produced.[14] Critics were surprised at the choice of the love story theme, calling it old-fashioned, but the organizers promised that they had selected writers who were talented and creative enough to avoid clichés. Whether or not they succeeded is debatable, but what is certain is that this experiment provides us with a set of very different novels that do, nonetheless, illustrate how Brazilians abroad, both authors and their characters, engage with cultures different from their own and repackage them in a literary form for the Brazilian reader.[15]

By the end of 2017, ten years after the project was first announced, ten novels had been published and one adapted for cinema.[16] Companhia das Letras rejected two authors (Giannetti and de Leonés).[17] Lisboa abandoned

few novels under their belts, several had won national prizes. Carvalho, Ruffato and Lisboa already had an international reputation. Cuenca, Galera, Mattoso and Prata were among *Granta*'s 'Best Young Brazilian Novelists'.

[13] See Volpato, 'Bonde das Letras'.

[14] Rosane Correa Lobo has analysed the media reaction to the announcement in Volpato's article: firstly, an outraged letter published in *Folha de São Paulo* the next day by author Marcelo Mirisola, then, a week later, an article summarizing accumulated criticism from assorted writers and bloggers. 'Amores Expressos: Narrativas de Não-Pertencimento' (unpublished master's thesis, PUC Rio de Janeiro, 2010), pp. 36–39.

[15] For more on the AE novels as 'literary tourism', see Humberto Fois-Braga, 'Tourism of Literary Writing: The Brazilian Author as an International Tourist in the Amores Expressos Collection', in *Literary Tourism: Theories, Practice and Case Studies*, eds Ian Jenkins and Katrín Anna Lund (Wallingford and Boston, MA: CABI, 2019), pp. 149–62.

[16] *Estive em Lisboa e Lembrei de Você* [*I Went to Lisbon and Remembered You*] directed by José Barahona (2015). There were rumours, as yet unsubstantiated, of a film version of Carvalho's novel *O Filho da Mãe* [*The Mother's Son/Son of a Bitch*] (2009), to be directed by Karim Aïnouz, with a screenplay by *Downton Abbey* creator Julian Fellowes, and starring Wagner Moura.

[17] De Leonés published *Como Desaparecer Completamente* [*How to Disappear Completely*] with Rocco in 2010.

the project for 'structural' reasons. Pellegrino's was still due.[18] Mutarelli, Morães and Prata stated publicly that they felt hampered by the restrictions of the commission but might rework their notes at a later, unspecified date.[19]

The AE project seemed to tick a lot of boxes in terms of catering to national tastes, as well as potentially international ones: they are at once travel narratives, tourist guides, adventure stories and romances.[20] The 'authenticity' of the authors' experiences, attested to in the blogs and documentaries (which prove that they really went), bolstered by background reading and research (as evidenced in the blogs and acknowledgements in the texts) reassures the reader that their encounter with a foreign city will be genuine.

Although it is an unashamedly commercial venture, the resulting texts provide interesting representations of the ways different cultures interact and how Brazil sees its place on the world literary stage. If read as ten composite interlocking parts of a literary project, they try to assert a cosmopolitan outlook that broadens the horizons of the Brazilian reader, celebrates the apparent global intercultural competence of Brazilian citizens (both authors and their characters), and as Berthold Schoene puts it, 'imagin[es] the world instead of the nation.'[21] When considered as cosmopolitan novels, they can be seen to counter the potentially flattening effect of globalization, dismantle borders and invite interaction between Brazil and other cultures. This 'forced

---

[18] In her *Cem Ideias que Deram em Nada* [*A Hundred Ideas that Came to Nothing*] (Rio de Janeiro: Foz, 2014), two sections or 'ideas that came to nothing' refer to a trip to India, one of which '52: Ideia para livro de amor' ['Idea for a love story'], pitches a book or film combining a love letter and impressions of visiting India, p. 86.

[19] Marco Rodrigo Almeida, 'Encomenda travou escritores da coleção Amores Expressos', *Folha de São Paulo* (27 July 2013) <https://www1.folha.uol.com.br/ilustrada/2013/07/1317373-encomenda-travou-escritores-da-colecao-amores-expressos.shtml> [accessed 29 March 2017].

[20] To date, Ruffato's *Estive em Lisboa e Lembrei de Você* (2009) has been translated and published in France, Germany, Argentina and Italy, as well as in Portugal, where a slightly different title reflects a grammatical divergence between the European and Brazilian variants of Portuguese: *Estive em Lisboa e Lembrei-me de ti* (Lisbon: Quetzal, 2010). Translations of Carvalho's novel were published in France and Argentina in 2010 and 2014 respectively. Of the other ten, Cuenca's *O Único Final Feliz para uma História de Amor é um Acidente* [*The Only Happy Ending for a Love Story is an Accident*] (2010) is the only one to have been translated into English, by Elizabeth Lowe (Dartmouth, MA: Tagus Press, 2013), but also Spanish, German, French, Finnish and Romanian, the last perhaps because the female protagonist hails from the city of Constanța.

[21] Berthold Schoene, *The Cosmopolitan Novel* (Edinburgh: Edinburgh University Press, 2009), p. 12.

internationalization' is a lot to ask of a series of novels and not all of them live up to the challenge.[22]

Schoene identifies central traits of the cosmopolitan novel as follows: 'its representation of worldwide human living and global community'; 'opening oneself up to a radical unlearning of all definitive modes of identification', and the aim 'to reveal the anachronism of [...] hegemonic distinctions between self and other'.[23] The Brazilian archetype of the 'cordial man', a concept created by Sérgio Buarque de Holanda in 1936, is worth mentioning briefly here.[24] Holanda suggests that Brazilians are particularly gifted at establishing smooth social interactions, though his definition of cordiality 'does not refer to politeness or civility, but rather to an abhorrence of distant – even formal, or ritualistic – relationships'.[25] This is largely borne out by the behaviour of the Brazilian characters in the novels, who avoid confrontation and seek to establish intimate relationships with local people as soon as possible, though their attitudes towards others are sometimes less than cordial.

The authors of the AE novels negotiate Machado de Assis's version of Brazilianness in different ways: by overasserting it or by hiding it. In the novels by Bettega, Galera, Mattoso, Ruffato, Sant'Anna and Terron the narrators or protagonists are Brazilian citizens abroad, representing their nation and channelling the new culture for Brazilian readers. In contrast, Carvalho, Cuenca, Pellizzari and Scott eliminate almost every reference to Brazil except the language of their prose. For example: while Sant'Anna's protagonist Antônio is a thinly-veiled portrait of himself (a Brazilian writer commissioned to portray Prague),[26] Scott's Narelle is a truly global citizen, a woman of Maori and British descent, who is constantly travelling, for business and pleasure, and interacting with people around the world via Skype and mobile phone.[27]

When the backdrop is not so exotic, or more familiar, the distancing effect is achieved in different ways. Male authors write female protagonists (or transgender in Terron's case).[28] Carvalho and Ruffato set the action in the past.

---

[22] Raynor, 'The Digital Ruins of *Amores Expressos*', p. 141.

[23] Schoene, *The Cosmopolitan Novel*, pp. 17–18, 21, 28.

[24] Sérgio Buarque de Holanda, *Raízes do Brasil* (São Paulo: Companhia das Letras, 2014 [1936]).

[25] Rachel Randall, 'Cordiality and Intimacy in Contemporary Brazilian Culture', *Journal of Iberian and Latin American Studies*, 24.3 (2018), 295–310 (p. 299).

[26] Sant'Anna, *O Livro de Praga: Narrativas de Amor e Arte* [*The Book of Prague: Tales of Love and Art*] (2011).

[27] Scott, *Ithaca Road* (2013).

[28] Terron, *Do Fundo do Poço se vê a Lua* [*From the Bottom of the Well you can see the Moon*] (2010).

Pellizzari employs multiple narrators and parallel plots.[29] Scott creates characters with mental health issues or medical conditions. Sant'Anna narrates a surreal, almost psychedelic fantasy. There is a strong feeling of irony in most of the novels that seems to be a reaction by the authors against producing cosmopolitan texts to order. Machado de Assis's injunction to Brazilian novelists not to linger on local colour is taken to extremes in these novels set beyond the country's borders, and yet nods and winks to the readers (jokes about Argentinians, slang, comparisons in which the Brazilian element is superior) ensure that the fellow-country reader does not feel too far out of their depth.

The voracious, curious novelist's gaze is not that different from that of an eager tourist, always on the lookout for the odd and quirky as well as the outrageous or shocking, in order to convey the extra-ordinary difference of the alternate, temporary world of the holiday or the text. Patrick Holland and Graham Huggan try to explain the success of travel writing as the creation of what they term 'a new *exotic*':

> The travel literature industry [...] has been quick to cash in on Westerners' growing fears of homogenization, promoting its products as thrilling alternatives to the sanitized spectacles of mass tourism; as evidence that the world is still heterogeneous, unfathomable, bewildering; as proof that the spirit of adventure can hold off the threat of exhaustion. In this sense, the travel (literature) business has capitalized on, while contributing to, a new *exotic*.[30]

The AE project is an excellent example of this assertion of global heterogeneity and the use of the 'wow factor' of the exotic to draw in readers/visitors. The writers describe wonders, natural and man-made, the breathtaking and the repulsive, emphasizing differences in customs and behaviour, to the readers' horror and delight. Such literature, when discussing everyday routines and 'normal life' in a foreign setting, tends to involve a certain ethnographic dimension. This always runs the risk of becoming reductive, and even exploitative, when an author persists in presenting a culture negatively in relation to their (and their readers') own, or 'purports to [...] report on other peoples and cultures while using them as a backdrop for the author's own personal quest'.[31]

---

[29] Pellizzari, *Digam a Satã que o Recado foi Entendido* [*You Can Tell Satan we got the Message*] (2013).

[30] Holland and Huggan, *Travellers with Typewriters: Critical Reflections on Contemporary Travel Writing* (Ann Arbor, MI: University of Michigan Press, 1998), p. 2. Original emphasis.

[31] Holland and Huggan, *Travellers with Typewriters*, p. 12.

360 Claire Williams

Paloma Vidal identifies three strategies used to convey the narrators' approach to the host culture in the original AE blogs: introspection, rejection and indifference, none of which seems conducive to a return trip, or a productive long-term relationship.[32] She goes on to note that Antonia Pellegrino's blog at times appeared to project a prejudiced view of Indians as 'dirty, macho, thieves'.[33] This comment seems to express a cosmopolitan legacy of colonial prejudices, with international intellectual elites determining what is civilized and what is savage. Indeed, in the novels, the visiting Brazilian characters' appreciation and treatment of the locals can be patronizing and reductive.[34] They never feel completely comfortable, nor do they contemplate staying, never mind 'going native'. Even in the novels without Brazilian characters, outsiders and foreigners in the 'host' culture are subject to racist, sexist and transphobic aggression, which does not uphold the cosmopolitan ethos of learning from each others' differences, nor does it promote 'cordiality'.

Mattoso's protagonist Renato undergoes a kind of rebirth (as his name suggests) in Havana when his girlfriend leaves him and he starts a new relationship with the city. On arrival he had never felt so foreign but, once he is alone, he sees things for the first time and can explore systematically and scientifically: 'Equipped with guidebook and map, I set out to explore Havana methodically, neighbourhood by neighbourhood, block by block. I drew up itineraries. I turned myself into an obsessed tourist, able to time walks, calculate distances, organize the day so as to do as much as possible in the least possible amount of time.'[35]

Abandonment gives Renato a new sense of purpose and the determination to know the city and somehow tame it by walking its streets. In *Barreira* [*Barrier*], Bettega's characters are scathing towards tourists because of their tendency to consume the world through a series of clichéd phrases, sites and images.[36] The initial narrator, Ibrahim, feels like a stranger in Istanbul, but emphatically not a tourist:

> [You] can't help feeling a certain pleasure at blending in with all those people like one more of the thousands of tourists who come to see the

---

[32] Paloma Vidal, 'Viagem e experiência comum: *O filho da mãe* de Bernardo Carvalho', in *Fora do retrato: estudos de literatura brasileira contemporânea*, eds Regina Dalcastagnè and Anderson Luís Nunes da Mata (Vinhedo: Horizonte, 2012), pp. 81–92 (pp. 82, 83).

[33] Vidal, 'Viagem e experiência comum', p. 83.

[34] We could read this as an echo of Freyre's lusotropicalism (see Klobucka, ch. 2 in this volume).

[35] Mattoso, *Nunca vai Embora* [*It Never Goes Away*] (2011), p. 48.

[36] Bettega, *Barreira* (2013).

show of this 'pulsating city', 'true bridge between West and East', a city that is 'mysterious', 'mythical', 'magical' and however many adjectives you want to add which effectively say nothing, [...] you are different, there is nobody more foreign than you in this city not because you bring no reference or preconceived idea, but because what you bring with you cannot be verified here or anywhere else. (28)

Bettega's narrators tell stories from multiple perspectives and act out alternative dénouements, losing the reader in a maze of back streets and views of the city. He also explores the limits and possibilities of images both static (such as the photographs of Turkish life by Ara Güler and Fátima's tourist photos of locations that her father revisits during his search for her) and moving, such as Marc's installation of small screens, each showing videos of views of Istanbul taken by tourists and sourced from YouTube, re-creating the effect of Google Earth to construct a 'truly ever-changing mosaic [...], an image of what the city is metaphorically [...], a living thing which never repeats itself' (197).

The ten authors' month-long stay was intended to give them more than a tourist's experience of the cities they visited. Most of those who decided against creating a Brazilian tourist protagonist did achieve convincing portrayals of a new *exotic*, immersing the reader in non-Brazilian cultures as the norm, although they needed to provide assistance with linguistic, historical and culinary specificities. The most disconcerting aspect of arriving in a new place is, according to Ibrahim in Bettega's novel, being greeted and overwhelmed by a foreign language: 'the disconcerting spelling that assaults your eyes and instead of awakening dormant reminiscences in your subconscious prepares you for what it won't take you long to realize, you are a complete stranger in this city, the most complete stranger there could be in Istanbul' (24). Indeed, Pellizzari's novel opens with an Irish curse[37] and Cuenca's with Japanese ideograms.[38] Carvalho helps the reader unfamiliar with Russian terms or cultural concepts by explaining them in footnotes or asides, as do Terron and Bettega when describing untranslatable Egyptian and Turkish customs. Pellizzari's novel is full of untranslated Gaelic or Irish sayings and slang, emphasizing the reader's 'tourist' status.

Even the languages closest to Brazilian Portuguese become strange,

---

[37] The Gaelic reads '*Go n-ithe an cat thú is go n-ithe an diabhal an cat*' ['May the cat eat you and the devil eat the cat'] (5).

[38] The Japanese characters are a literal translation of the Portuguese title according to Marcel Vejmelka, 'O Japão na literatura brasileira atual', *Estudos em Literatura Brasileira Contemporânea*, 43 (2014), 213–34 (p. 224).

especially when spoken with the 'wrong' accent. Anita started her visit to Buenos Aires believing that she could get by 'speaking Portuguese and hearing Spanish' (31) but soon discovers otherwise.[39] At the end of the novel, much to her humiliation, Argentinians still comment on her poor pronunciation. Ruffato's Serginho discovers, to his surprise, that the people he encounters in Lisbon speak a different Portuguese to the variant he grew up with in Minas Gerais. Not only do they not understand his accent, they laugh at it with undisguised vestigial colonial superiority. Working illegally as a waiter, he makes use of his schoolboy English, pronounced the Brazilian way (60): 'Rei ser, Rei mádam, Ria chípe fude, gude fude, uaine, fiche, mite, têm-quíu (obrigado, dona Gilda, minha professora no curso noturno [...], onde a gente repetia as lições achando que nunca iam servir pra nada)' ['Hey sir, hey madam, Here cheap food, good food, wine, fish, meat, thank you (thank you Miss Gilda, my teacher at night school [...], where we repeated our lessons thinking they'd never be of any use')].[40]

Interestingly, and in line with the underlying proposition behind the whole series that Brazilians are not provincial and inward-looking but experienced and capable global citizens, the lingua franca in most of the novels (if not the official language of the city involved) seems to be the last resort of the tourist: badly and loudly-pronounced English (Sant'Anna, Pellizzari, Mattoso, Barreira, Terron, Cuenca). Terron's William speaks 'Fisk' English in Cairo.[41] It is the language of communication between the Japanese and Romanian lovers in Cuenca's novel and Mattoso's Renato, who speaks perfect Spanish, is frustrated when a Havana taxi driver insists on addressing him in English.

In the tourist hotspots visited by many different nationalities, the guides, hotel employees, waiters and local shopkeepers have to be able to converse in several languages if they want a continuous flow of customers. In the Grand Bazaar in Istanbul, in *Barreira*, tourists are subjected to a 'barrage of hellos, good mornings, bonjours, buenos díases and persistent invitations to come in, sit down, have a cup of tea' (61), and those who deal continually with international visitors end up speaking 'a little bit of everything, not everything, just a bit [...], and it's that bit of each [...] which means that all the languages blend together inside you in a kind of personal Esperanto, a language with only one speaker, but which enables you to communicate with others' (64).

---

[39] *Cordilheira* [*Cordillera/Mountain Range*] (2008), p. 31.

[40] By the end of the novel, Serginho has absorbed European Portuguese terminology into his daily vocabulary ('autocarros [...] elétricos, metro e comboio' rather than 'ônibus', 'bondes', 'metrô' and 'trem' ['buses, trams, the underground and trains']), p. 82.

[41] Fisk is an American language-learning methodology specifically targeted at Brazilians, set up by Richard S. Fisk in 1958.

Even though the tone of all ten novels is often heavily ironic, the objectification and sexualization of most female characters, including, rather worryingly, pubescent girls, echoes classic patriarchal and imperialist travel writing where the male protagonists are 'drawn to surfaces – more particularly, to bodies – onto which they project their fears and fantasies of the ethnicized cultural "other"'.[42] The narrators' gaze consistently objectifies women, whether they are wearing *burkas* or bikinis. Any independent female character who travels alone is a target for sexual harassment, aggression or abduction, or symbolically punished with rape (Terron, Galera, Cuenca). Female foreigners, like Romanian Iulana in Tokyo (Cuenca) or Slovakian Stefanija in Dublin (Pellizzari), are physically and culturally different from the locals, which adds to their exotic allure. There are certainly echoes here of Gilberto Freyre's Lusotropicalism, which, to use Anna M. Klobucka's words in this volume, celebrates 'the male [Brazilian] subject of the colonial conquest and settlement, whose affective engagement with the welcoming woman/land of the tropics defines and distinguishes the Lusophone imperial and post-imperial experience'.[43]

It is disappointing that twenty-first century Brazilian authors are still formulating intercultural encounters between men and women in this way, no matter how ironic and performative. Women writers are noticeably absent from the list of publications, despite the fact that three were part of the original project. There are two female protagonists (Galera, Scott), and one trans woman (Terron), but, like the secondary characters, they are distorted portrayals.[44] Male consumption and desire are the driving forces behind much of the action in these novels, whether quests, missions, practical struggles to survive on a daily basis, or a more metaphysical search for knowledge of self and other. Concurrently, female characters are often conflated with food and drink.[45]

From the nightclubs of Havana to the pubs of Dublin, from the El Horreyya Bar in Cairo to cybercafés in Prague, from a (poor) imitation Dunkin' Donuts near Shinjuku Station in Tokyo to the McDonald's on Tsverskaya Street in Moscow, all these settings function as backdrops to some of the most

---

[42] Holland and Huggan, *Travellers with Typewriters*, p. 20; see also Anne McClintock, *Imperial Leather: Race, Gender and Sexuality in the Colonial Conquest* (New York: Routledge, 1994).

[43] Anna M. Klobucka, 'Translational Travails of Lusotropicalism', p. 46, in this volume.

[44] See Leonardo Tonus, 'Alteridades expressas no romance brasileiro contemporâneo'.

[45] Pellizzari's Marcus, in Dublin, describes second-generation Chinese schoolgirls in uniform as 'a paradox as delicious as Welsh lamb with *hoisin* sauce' (30).

interesting scenes of multicultural bricolage in the novels. The staff at the restaurant where Serginho (a proud mixture of 'Coropo Indian, Portuguese and slave' (28)) works replicates the colonial hierarchy: a white Portuguese manager bosses around the Ukrainian and Brazilian waiters, an elderly, white, female cook and a Guinean dogsbody (58). Pellizzari's novel begins in the 'Bleu Note', where Marcus reflects on the irony of 'a Frenchified name for an Irish pub where they play American music and the clientele is Slav' (10).[46] In Istanbul Robert is able to purchase a cappuccino that tastes exactly the same as the coffee from his local café back in Paris (129).

Love, the theme that appeared in the original brief to all the authors, takes many different forms in the AE novels, which feature heterosexual and homosexual romances, but also parent–child and sibling relationships, as well as intense friendship, and fleeting, erotic encounters, unrequited and imaginary love, nostalgia, jealousy and sexual fantasy. However, despite the variety of formulations, there is not one conventional happy ending among them, and many storylines are left without resolution.

The novels paint a world characterized by disenchantment and frustration. Cities are chaotic and impenetrable. Quests are fruitless. The object of desire escapes and the attempt to 'capture' the experience of being in a place is thwarted.[47] Bettega puts this best when his characters discuss the human need for logical sequences of events, answers, solutions, closure: 'trying to understand, searching for meaning, ends up distancing you from what really matters, what could finally give the thing meaning. Meaning doesn't exist until we reach it' (235). His character Robert, who writes tour guides, sees his job as trying to help people to 'read the unknown' (137) and find 'a solid base for them to stand on' (101), but the certainty this implies evaporates progressively as the narrative proceeds. The chaos, alienation and fragmenting of identity in the AE novels are signs, according to Rosana Correa Lobo, of 'panic generated by new kinds of migration' and they reveal the 'fractures caused by globalization'.[48]

The four novels whose authors eschewed obvious references to Brazilianness fit Schoene's definition of cosmopolitanism much better than the other six,

---

[46] The action also passes through an American-style diner with 'orgasmic' milkshakes, traditional Irish pubs on the search for the secret pint, and a picnic involving Ribena (whose taste of 'defeated blackcurrant [...] is the most appalling thing in the universe of non-alcoholic drinks'), Lucozade ('radioactive urine with sugar') and a '"wild" Jamaican chicken wrap', pp. 13, 48, 54, 55.

[47] According to John Frow, disappointment is an integral and inevitable part of the tourist experience, 'Tourism and the Semiotics of Nostalgia', *October*, 57 (1991), 123–51 (p. 125).

[48] Lobo, 'Amores Expressos: Narrativas de Não-Pertencimento', p. 35.

because they embrace the host culture as the norm and make few concessions to readers' ignorance of local customs. On the other hand, the reader who accompanies all ten writers to their destination is left with the feeling that the novels in which Brazilians are tourists are still infused with Machado's 'national instinct', asserted through comparisons in which abroad is always a poor version of home. Anita, Renato, Ibrahim, Serginho, Antônio and William and Wilson end up by rejecting the host culture, or being rejected by it, forced to admit that cultural integration is not possible. They are incapable of what Schoene calls the 'radical unlearning of all definitive modes of identification' in order to 'reveal the anachronism of [...] hegemonic distinctions between self and other'[49] because they are too set in their ways, too Brazilian to change, too 'self' to really see or know the 'other', particularly the foreign female other.

So, if we take these ten novels as representative of contemporary Brazilian literature, we might also conclude that cosmopolitanness is not something quintessentially Brazilian. From Holanda's concept of the cordial man to Freyre's lusotropicalism, cultural mixing lies at the heart of the nation's identity. But, in their essentially male, often colonially prejudiced gazes the novelists and characters fail (to a large extent) to address the perspective of the Other. Rather than challenging stereotypes of national literature, they replicate them, often in very entertaining, but sometimes in uncomfortable ways. Machado de Assis's hopes for the 'independence' of Brazilian literature are not fully realized in the AE novels. When it comes to transnational projects, Machado's exhortations continue to define, haunt and confront today's writers, and from the evidence of these ten texts only a few are able to live up to the challenge.

[49] Schoene, *The Cosmopolitan Novel*, p. 28.

Index

1940 Exposição do Mundo Português [Exposition of the Portuguese World] 228

Abreu, Caio Fernando 341
AE *see* Amores Expressos (AE) project
Africa 27, 133
　European colonization 104
　Portuguese empire 129
　travel accounts 34
African slaves 154
Agência Nacional do Cinema [National Cinema Agency] (ANCINE) *see* ANCINE
Alcoforado, Mariana *see* nun Mariana Alcoforado
allochronism 234–35, 248
ALN, Action for National Liberation 249, 256
Amaral, Ana Luísa, *New Portuguese Letters to the World – International Reception* (2015) 269–70
American hegemony 260
American imperialism 275
Amores Expressos (AE) project 354
　authors and destinations 355
　cosmopolitan cultural experiences 358
　global heterogeneity 359
　intercultural encounters 363
　outcome 356–57
ANCINE 251, 253
　see also Agência Nacional do Cinema [National Cinema Agency] (ANCINE)
Anglophone/Francophone worlds 271
Angola 3, 47, 54–55, 72, 130, 136
　civil war 4
　colonization 130
　indigenous languages 3, 72, 130, 136, 139
　oilacracy 86
　political disempowerment 86
　post-independence 85
　socioeconomic inequality 72, 86
　urban popular music 71
　war of independence (1961–75) 4
anti-austerity protests 206
anticolonial imagination 54
anti-European European cinema 113
Appadurai, Arjun 263–64
Appiah, Kwame Anthony 133

367

368   Index

Arabian Nights trilogy (2013–14) by Miguel Gomes 109, 114
  O Desolado [*The Desolate One*] 110
  O Encantado [*The Enchanted One*] 110
  O Inquieto [*The Restless One*] 110
  music 116
  see also Gomes, Miguel
Araújo, Terezinha, 'N na nega bedju' 81–82
archive 223, 232, 269, 288
  cultural archives 285
  modernist archives 300
  official archive of national experience 227
  personal memory 227
  photographic archive 238
  written archive 270
archive of memories 221, 223
  embodied knowledge 226
Arden, Jane
  feminist theatre group Holocaust 275
  The Other Side of the Underneath (1972) 276
Armada see Spanish Armada
Asia, travel accounts 34
assimilados 163
Assis, Machado de 353, 359
Assmann, Aleida 263, 265
Atlantic 30, 59–60, 76, 85, 144, 149
  entrepôt 77
  islands 27
  Lusophone 129
  Lusotopian 129
  migrations 76
Atlantic slave trade 72, 77, 88, 130, 132, 136, 146
  Rio de Janeiro 207
austerity 115, 118, 123, 126
  see also Portugal
Auto de Fama see Vicente, Gil

autobiography 286, 292, 337
Aventura e Rotina [*Adventure and Routine*] by Gilberto Freyre (1953) 45, 50, 52–54, 56
  see also Freyre, Gilberto

Badiou, Alain, *Handbook of Inaesthetics* 315
Balibar, Étienne 125, 299
Barreno, Maria Isabel see *New Portuguese Letters*
Barreto, Bruno, *O que é isso companheiro?* [*Four Days in September*] (1997) 249, 252, 255, 261–62, 265–66
Barros, João de 24, 168
  account of Great Wall 38
  Décadas da Ásia 25
Barthes, Roland 115, 241
Bastos, Cristiana 45, 54
Bazin, André 241
Belas-Artes [Fine Arts School], Lisbon 98
Benin 137
Blaufuks, Daniel 224, 227–28, 230, 232
  Sob céus estranhos [*Under Strange Skies*] 224, 226–27
Book of Francisco Rodrigues 36
bossa nova, 'Garota de Ipanema' ['The Girl from Ipanema'] 256
Brasileiro em Terras Portuguesas, Um [*A Brazilian in Portuguese Lands*] by Gilberto Freyre (1953) 45
Brazil 3, 27, 54
  Africans 152, 154
  American Ambassador to Brazil 249, 253, 258
  American support for regime change 258
  civil rights 256
  communist threat 258
  Creole languages 154
  Creoles (Brazilian-born) 155

film industry 251
guerrilla groups 249, 257, 259
human rights violations 249, 253, 259, 261
independent publishers 236
indigenous languages 3, 63
intellectuals 43
international press coverage 256, 259
Lei do Audiovisual [Audiovisual Law] 251
Lei dos Desaparecidos [Law of the Disappeared] 261
Lei Rouanet 356
literary culture 183, 197
Maranhão 130
migration 233
military dictatorship 189, 249–50, 253, 263
Ministério das Relações Exteriores 6
miscegenation ideology 47
national flag 8
National Truth Commission 261
nationalist propaganda 256
Palmares 131, 141
pardos (mixed-race, Brazilian-born) 154
Petrobrás 253
Portuguese language 142
post-dictatorship cinema Chapter 14 (249–66), 252, 255, 265
post-dictatorship culture 266
queer authors 341
slaves 155
socioeconomic inequality 340
Standard Brazilian Portuguese (SBP) 154
state crimes 261
street protests in June 2013 203
Vernacular Brazilian Portuguese (VBP) 154, 156

Brazilian Football Federation (CBF) 209
Brazilian literature
 citizens of the world 354
 cosmopolitanism 365
 national identity 353, 365
 transnational literature 354
BRIC (Brazil, Russia, India and China) block 56
British empire 302, 308
 decolonization 96
Bueno, Wilson 341
 Cachorros do céu (2005) 343, 345
 A copista de Kafka (2007) 343–44
 Mar paraguayo (1992) 343
 translation 343–45
Butler, Judith, *Bodies That Matter* 337

Cabot, Sebastian 58
Cabral, Amílcar 77, 80, 148
 Cape Verde 77
 Guinea-Bissau 77
 utopian vision 77
Camões, Luís Vaz de 2–3, 49, 67–68, 91, 93, 100, 300
 Os Lusíadas [*The Lusiads*] 2, 49, 67–68, 93
 Lusotropicalism 50
Campos, Álvaro de (heteronym) 91, 93, 103–04, 306, 308
 'Ode Marítima' 93, 103
 'Opiário' ['Opiary'] 306
 see also Pessoa, Fernando
Canijo, João 224, 227, 230, 232
 Fantasia Lusitana [*Lusitanian Fantasy*] 224
Cannes Film Festival 109
 see also Gomes, Miguel
Cape Verde 47, 50, 52, 130, 132, 287
 African influences 144–45
 Atlantic Slave trade 72
 Claridade 50
 Cobiana Djazz 78

colonialism 72
Creole languages 51, 157
Cuba 79
Évora, Cesária 74
first Creole society 74
and Guinea-Bissau (union) 77
intellectuals 50
islands 66
Kriolu 143–45
Lúcio, Mário 73
poetry 91
São Tiago 132
socialist internationalism 79
urban popular music 71
Cardoso, Luís 1–3
The Crossing 1–2
see also Cardoso, Luís
cartographers Chapter 1 (23–41), 24–25
background 24–25
Carvalho, Bernardo, *O sol se põe em São Paulo* (2008) 237–38
Casa-Grande & Senzala [*The Masters and the Slaves*] (1933) by Gilberto Freyre 43
see also Freyre, Gilberto
Casais Monteiro, Adolfo 306, 315
Castilian 167, 169
Castro, Fidel 255
Cavendish, Thomas 58, 60, 64
attack on Santos 58, 60–62
censorship 193, 276, 281, 338
Central Intelligence Agency (CIA) (United States) 256
interventions in Brazil 258
China, Great Wall 38
CIA see Central Intelligence Agency (CIA) (United States)
cinema, Brazilian post-dictatorship cinema Chapter 14 (249–66)
cities
Allada 135–38
Bissau 80

Curitiba 342, 344
Durban 301–02
Lisbon see Lisbon
London 64, 95, 191
Luanda 84–85, 87, 141–42
Manteca, California 319, 323–24, 326
New York 209
Panaji (Pangim) 56
Paris 289
Praia (Santiago Island, Cape Verde) 73–77
Recife 63, 66
Rio de Janeiro see Rio de Janeiro
Salvador da Bahia 59, 140–41
San Francisco, California 326, 340
Santos 58, 60–62
São Paulo 82, 206, 237, 342
Tarrafal (Santiago Island, Cape Verde) 73
urban transformations 201, 208
see also Macau
Claridade 50
see also Cape Verde, intellectuals
Clavin, Patricia 19
'Defining Transnationalism' 15
Cobiana Djazz 78, 83
Coelho, Pedro Passos 110, 125
Cold War 253, 260, 326–27
collective memories 229, 263–64, 270–71
fado 333
colonial conquest 46
colonial enterprise 149, 159
colonial settlement 46
colonialism 137
colonization of language 136–37
colony 2
as settlements of groups of people originally from Portugal 26
see also Angola; Cape Verde; East Timor; Guinea-Bissau; Macau; Mozambique

Columbus, Christopher 57
commercial transnationalism 255, 266
Companhia des Letras 355
   see also Amores Expressos (AE) project
Comunidade dos Países de Língua Portuguesa (CPLP) 8–9, 147
conquest 24
continent 24
cosmopolitan cultural experiences 286
cosmopolitan novel 358
cosmopolitanism 39, 275, 365
Costa, António 125
Costa, Maria Velho da
   Novas Cartas Portuguesas (1972) 267
   see also New Portuguese Letters
Council of Europe, Eurimages 113
CPLP see Comunidade dos Países de Língua Portuguesa (CPLP)
Creole languages 135, 143–44, 147
   Bidau Creole 161
   Cape Verde 51, 72, 89, 150, 157
   creolization 161
   East Timor 160–61
   Guinea-Bissau 72, 89, 150
   hybridity 165
   Indo-Portuguese Creole 160
   Makista 161
   pidginization 161
   Portuguese-based 72
   post-Creole 154
   São Tomé 150, 157
   Vernacular Brazilian Portuguese (VBP) 154
   see also Portuguese
Creolophone sphere 71
   see also Creole languages; Lusophone sphere; urban popular music
Croft, Susan, interview for 'Remembering the Translation of *New Portuguese Letters* to the Stage' 273
cross-cultural engagement 349
Crossing, The see Cardoso, Luís
Cuba, socialist internationalism 79
Cuenca, João Paulo 355–56
   see also Amores Expressos (AE) project
cultural anthropology 46
   literary turn 47
cultural hybridity 47, 84
   musical hybridization 84
cultural imperialism 303, 353
cultural memory 107
cultural revolution, 1960s 96
cultural translation 48
   see also translation
culture of memory 231
Cunho, Euclides da, *Os Sertões* (1902) 237

Dahomey 137
Dali, Salvador 327
Da-Rin, Silvio, *Hércules 56* (2006) Figure 14.1 (254), 249, 252–57, 262, 266
de Cesari, Chiara 236, 265, 270, 285
debt crisis see EU debt crisis
Décadas da Ásia by João de Barros 25
   see also Barros, João de
'Defining Transnationalism' by Patricia Clavin 15
Deleuze, Gilles 88, 304
deterritorialization 108, 305
Di Bello, Patrizia 233, 235, 246
dia que durou 21 anos, O [*The Day that Lasted 21 Years*] (2012) see Tavares, Camilo
dialects 191
   powerful literary resource 185
   social context 185
   socioeconomic inequality 185
   translation 197

Index

Dias, Pedro 140–41
diasporas 149, 318, 332
dictatorship 4
    Brazil (1964–85) 4
    Portugal (1926–74) 4
discovery 24, 167, 308
    of the New World 57
documentary Chapter 12 (221–32), 223, 262, 266
    archive footage 259
    declassified documents 258
    Diário de uma busca [*Diary of a Search*] (2010) by Flávia Castro 263
    documentary movement 235
    embodied knowledge 226
    Fantasia Lusitana [*Lusitanian Fantasy*] by João Canijo (2010) 224
    first person testimony 253, 262
    Hércules 56 (2006) 253, 262, 266
    interviews 255
    post-dictatorship cinema 262
    Proxy Reverso (Guilherme Peters and Roberto Winter, 2015) 214
    Sob céus estranhos [*Under Strange Skies*] by Daniel Blaufuks (2002) 224, 226
    transnational documentary 218
    Um passaporte Húngaro (2001) 238
    Uma operação chamada Condor [*Condor*] (2007) 263
    see also *Domínio Público* [Public Domain] project; witness accounts
Domínio Público [Public Domain] project 202–03, 205, 217–18
    activist graffiti Figure 11.1 (213)
    crowdfunding campaign 210, 216
    decisions about translations 214
    Facebook 211
    interviews 205
    local visual environment 210–14
    partial translation 210–14
    press coverage 208, 217
    street protests in June 2013 214
    transnational documentary 204, 218
    use of subtitles 210–14
    see also RioOnWatch
dos Santos, Bartolomeu Cid see Santos, Bartolomeu Cid dos
Drake, Francis 64
    circumnavigation 60
Dutch East India Company (VOC) 27

East India Company 65
East Timor 2–3, 54
    Creole languages 150, 161–62
    independence (2002) 4
    indigenous languages 3
    Indonesian occupation 4
    Macanese 152
    Portuguese presence 162
EC see European Commission
Eça de Queirós see Queirós, José Maria Eça de
ECB see European Central Bank
economic hegemony 57
    see also hegemony
Elbrick, Charles Burke Figure 14.1 (254), 249, 253, 258–59
    foreign policy in the Cold War 256
emancipation of women 194
empire see Portuguese empire
empire-building 23
Entrecampos metro station 91
    stone panels by Bartolomeu Cid dos Santos Figure 5.1 (92), Figure 5.2 (94), Figure 5.3 (101), 100, 103
Erll, Astrid 107, 224, 265, 270, 272
    transcultural memory 107
    travelling memory 224

Estado Novo [New State] 8, 44, 53, 96, 99, 134, 143, 148, 232
  anti-communism Figure 12.2 (229)
  ideology 53
  Jewish refugees in Portugal 227
  official archive of national experience 227
  Polícia da Vigilância e Defesa do Estado (PVDE) [Police for the Vigilance and Defence of the State] 225
  socioeconomic inequality 228
  state violence Figure 12.2 (229), 228
  see also dictatorship; Portugal
ethnographic encounters *see* narrativization of ethnographic encounters
ethnographic practices 248
EU debt crisis 111, 124
Eurimages 113
Euro Zone 125
European Central Bank (ECB) 110
  see also Troika
European cinema 113
European colonization 52, 57, 106
  Africa 104
  Stanley, Henry Morton 104
European Commission (EC) 110
  see also Troika
European co-production of films 112
European integration 19
European powers 57
European Union (EU) 19, 110, 125
  2011 memorandum of understanding with Portugal 110
'Euro-pudding' film 113–14
  see also European cinema
Évora, Cesária 74
expansion 24, 40
exploration 106

fado 317, 328
  collective memories 333
  guitarra portuguesa 321, 329
  iconography 328–29, 333
  Judith and Holofernes (J&H) 326
  melancholy 334
  saudade 323
fadocore Chapter 18 (317–35), 318, 332
  see also Judith and Holofernes (J&H)
Fanon, Frantz, *Black Skin, White Mask* (1952) 136
Fantasia Lusitana [*Lusitanian Fantasy*] by João Canijo (2010) Figure 12.2 (229), 224, 227–28, 230–31
  act of forgetting 231
favelas 205
  Complexo do Alemão 207
  Favela Não Se Cala (*Favelas Won't Keep Quiet*) social movement 216
  military occupation 207
  pacification scheme 209
  police violence 209
  see also UPP
feminist politics
  interconnectness 270
  international solidarity campaign 268, 273, 275, 278–80
  second-wave feminist movement 268
  transnational 267, 274
  women's oppression 277
feminist theatre group Holocaust 275
Ferreira, Ana Paula 8, 285, 297
  New Portuguese Letters to the World – International Reception (2015) 269–70
  'Specificity Without Exceptionalism' 8–9
film festivals 258, 264–65
  Berlin 255

film funding 251, 253, 263–64
film industry, Brazil 251
Film Studies
    cinema of globalization 251, 260
    transnational turn 250, 263
first person testimony 253, 262, 266, 273, 276, 337–38
Fon 137–38
Fonseca, Manuel Pinto da 296–97
Foucault, Michel 115, 121, 245
Frazão, Aline 71
    'Tanto' 71, 84–88
freedom and democracy, American foreign policy in the Cold War 260
Freitas, Marinela, *New Portuguese Letters to the World – International Reception* (2015) 269–70
Freyre, Gilberto Chapter 2 (43–56), 43–46, 48–50, 52, 55
    Aventura e Rotina [*Adventure and Routine*] (1953) 45
    as cartographer 55
    Casa-Grande & Senzala [*The Masters and the Slaves*] (1933) 43
    gender ideology 52
    intellectual transition 46
    Lusotropicalism 363, 365
    O Mundo que o Português Criou [*The World the Portuguese Created*] (1940) 45
    Um Brasileiro em Terras Portuguesas [*A Brazilian in Portuguese Lands*] (1953) 45

Gabeira, Fernando, *O que é isso campanheiro?* [*What's up, Comrade?*] (1979) 249
Garrett, Almeida 190, 286
Glick Schiller, Nina 6
    'Methodological Nationalism and Beyond: Nation-State Building,
    Migration and the Social Sciences' 6
global economy 34
global heterogeneity 359
global histories 39
global movement against inequality and capitalism 205
Global Navigations Chapter 1 (23–41)
global Portugueseness 53
globalism 8
globalization 8, 19, 251, 257
    collective memories 263
    cultural harmonization 257
    cultural production 72
    early globalization 39
    film funding 251
    global movement against inequality and capitalism 205
    Latin American cinema 251
    mobility 263, 364
    solidarity 264
    world music market 72
globe 24, 38
Goa 25–26, 48, 51, 55–56, 167
    Palace of Idalcão 35
    Portuguese influences 159
    union with India (1961) 4, 56
Gomes, Karyna 82–84
    'N na nega bedju' 83
Gomes, Miguel 109, 111, 115, 117
    Mil e Uma Noites trilogy [*Arabian Nights*] (2013–14) see Arabian Nights trilogy (2013–14) by Miguel Gomes
    Tabu (2012) 110
Gordon, Lincoln, American Ambassador to Brazil Figure 14.2 (259), 258
Goulart, João Figure 14.2 (259), 249, 258
Guazzelli, Eloar 310
    Eu, Fernando Pessoa em quadrinhos [*I, Fernando*

Pessoa in a Comic Strip]
(2013) Figure 17.1 (311), 310,
314, 316
Guevara, Ernesto 'Che' 251
Guinea-Bissau 47, 52, 55, 143
    anticolonial independence struggle 79
    Atlantic Slave trade 72
    and Cape Verde (union) 77
    colonialism 72
    Cuba 79
    socialist internationalism 79
    urban popular music 71
    utopian vision 80
Gujarat 26, 159

Hakluyt, Richard 58
    The Principal Navigations (3 volumes, 1598–1600) 58, 64
hegemonic globalization 260, 263
hegemony 24, 57, 114, 260, 280, 308, 339, 347
Hércules 56 (2006) *see* Da-Rin, Silvio
heteronym 304–05
heterotopia 115, 118, 123–25
Hill, John 261–62
Hirsch, Marianne 226, 230, 242, 247
    familial post-memory 230
    post-memory 225
Hispanic Studies 6–7
historical categories 23–25
HIV/AIDS *see* queer activism and protests
Hollywood 251, 255, 261
    Hollywood realism 262
Holocaust 225, 227, 231, 273, 275, 333
    Auschwitz-Bucharest 231, 275
Horta, Maria Teresa *see New Portuguese Letters*
human rights groups 266
human rights violations, Brazil 253
hybridity 48, 163, 236
    see also cultural hybridity

ICA *see* Institute of Contemporary Arts (ICA)
identity construction 149, 152, 163, 167
    social networks 156
IMF *see* International Monetary Fund
immigrant experiences 238
imperialism *see* Portuguese empire
India 167
Indian Ocean 30
Indo-Portuguese Creole 160
Institute of Contemporary Arts (ICA) 278–79
Instituto Camões (Portugal) 6
intellectuals
    African 54
    Cape Verde 50
    Marxist 56
    Portuguese-speaking world 43
inter-cultural encounter 234
intercultural translation 48–49, 52
    see also translation
International Monetary Fund (IMF) 110
    see also Troika

J&H *see* Judith and Holofernes (J&H)
Japan 26
    travel accounts 34
Jews
    early modern 181
    Jewish refugees in Portugal 227
Judith and Holofernes (J&H) 317, 323, 326, 334
    CD cover art Figure 18.1 (329), Figure 18.2 (330), Figure 18.3 (331), 328, 333
    Dairymen and Festa Queens 330
    fado 320–21
    Matança 330, 332
    'When Drones Leave the Hive' 324–25

Kafka, Franz 344
Kikongo 154, 156–57
Kimbundu 130, 136, 139–42, 147, 154, 156
  see also Angola indigenous languages
King, Rodney 340
Klobucka, Anna 277, 301, 363
Kogut, Sandra, *Um passaporte Húngaro* (2001) 238
'Kreol' 73–77
  see also Lúcio, Mário
Kriolu 145

Lancaster, James 63–64
  attack on Recife 63, 66–68
language Part II (127–218), 168
  of colonization 137, 146
  concept of language 151
  European 129
  knowledge and culture 129
  lack of territorial stability 38
  language practices 151
  marker of identity 170
  need to use language skills 168
  porosity 38
  Portuguese empire 24
  'vehicle not of nations, but of empires' 24
  see also Barros, João de
Lebanon see Mohallem, Gui
Lei do Audiovisual [Audiovisual Law] 251, 253
Leoni, Alexandre 311
  A Vida Oculta de Fernando Pessoa [*The Occult Life of Fernando Pessoa*] (2016)
    Figure 17.2 (312), 310–11, 314
Lerner, Alan Jay, *My Fair Lady* 183
Lettres Portugaises 269
Levy, Tatiana Salem, *A chave de casa* (2007) 238
life writing 285–86

cosmopolitan cultural experiences 286
linguistic exchange 168
linguists 10
Lins, Paulo, *Cidade de Deus* [*City of God*] (1997) 354
'liquid modernity' 95
Lira, Ícaro, *Projeto Desterro* (2014) 236–37
Lisbon 1, 40, 65, 82, 84, 89, 91, 103, 119, 121, 294–95, 301, 313, 317
  Alfama 321
  Bairro Alto 321
  fado 317, 322
  graveyard 225
  Museu do Fado 321–22
  Pessoa, Fernando 302, 315
  place of transit 222
  Rossio 346
  wartime naval visits 227
  World War II 222, 230
literary turn 47
  cultural anthropology 47
Liz, Mariana 113, 115
Lúcio, Mário 71, 73–77
  'Kreol' 71, 73–77
  Kreol (album) 74–75
  Minister of Culture 73–77
  'Planet' 75
Lusíadas, Os [*The Lusiads*] 2–3, 49, 67–68
  see also Camões, Luís Vaz de
Luso-American community
  Catholicism 327, 332
  festa 332
  migrant identity 319
  second-generation fadistas 320, 322
  Virgin Mary/Our Lady of Fátima 331–32
Luso-Brazilian Studies (University of Wisconsin-Madison) 7

Lusofonia 8, 129–34, 136, 347
Lusophone 71
 spaces 6–7
Lusophone archive 38
Lusophone cultures 11
Lusophone space 148
 theorizing 45
Lusophone sphere 71, 129
 see also Creolophone sphere
Lusophone Studies 341
 transnational discipline 339
Lusophone transnationalism 150
Lusotopia 129
Lusotropical transculturation 51
Lusotropicalism Chapter 2 (43–56), 8, 11, 51, 129, 363
 see also Estado Novo [New State]

Macau Figure 1.2 (31), 27, 159
 Cantonese 3
 Creole languages 150, 160–61
 gateway to other places 39
 handover to People's Republic of China (1999) 4, 152
Machado, Júlio César 365
 Recordaçõs de Paris and Londres [*Recollections of Paris and London*] (1863) 290
Madeira 26, 301
Malhoa, José, *O Fado* 329
mapping 25, 27, 55
 latitude and longtitude 30
 metageography 35
 'portolan' style maps 27–30
maps Chapter 1 (23–41), 24–25, 33
Marchioness of Alorna 287, 291
Mediterranean 27
mega-events 201–02
 international press coverage 208
 Olympic Games 2016 201–02
 opposition to 202
 transnational dimension 206

 transnationalization of local/localization of the transnational 204, 206
 World Cup 2014 201–02
memory 221, 224, 267, 318
 censorship 281
 collective memories 229–30, 232, 250, 263–64, 270
 culture of memory 231
 decontextualized 268
 Holocaust 275
 life writing 285
 memory politics 261
 Memory Studies 263, 333–34
 migration 318
 mnemonic practices 272, 280
 multidirectional memory 270–73, 279
 New Portuguese Letters 272
 post-memory 225, 275
 remembering 250, 267, 272
 transnational memories 265–66, 273
 travelling memory 272
memory's archive 221
 see also archive of memories
Mendonça, Henrique Lopes 8, 296
 'A Portuguesa' 2
merchants, finance of privateers 64
metaphotographic textuality 241, 247
methodological nationalism 7–8, 19
'Methodological Nationalism and Beyond: Nation-State Building, Migration and the Social Sciences' 6
 see also Glick Schiller, Nina; Wimmer, Andreas
Mignolo, Walter 135–36
migrant identity 107, 149
 immigrant experiences 238
 invisibility 238
migration 149
Mil e Uma Noites [*Arabian Nights*]

trilogy (2013–14) *see Arabian Nights* trilogy (2013–14) by Miguel Gomes
Miller Atlas Figure 1.1 (28–29), 30
Ministério das Relações Exteriores, Brazil 6
miscegenation 48
   Brazilian miscegenation ideology 47
   cultural 52
   racial 48
Mme de Staël 296
mnemonics 225, 272, 278
Modern Languages 5
   as a discipline 5
   see also transnational turn
Modernism 300–01, 315
Mohallem, Gui
   Fakiha Figure 13.2 (243), 242, 244
   family's migratory past 238
   journey to Lebanon 237, 239, 243, 246
   photographic archive 238–39, 244
   Tcharafna (2014) Figure 13.1 (240), 237, 239, 241–42, 245–48
   use of Photoshop software 243
   website Figure 13.3 (247)
monarchs, Portugal
   assassination of the king in 1910 302
   D. Ana Maria de Jesus 294
   D. Catarina 177–78
   D. Maria II 294
   Dom Afonso III 169
   Dom João III 38, 177
   Dom João IV 130
   Dom Manuel I 170
   Dom Pedro II 131
   House of Bragança 139
Moreira, Miguel 310, 313
   As aventuras de Fernando Pessoa, Escritor Universal [*The Adventures of Fernando Pessoa, Universal Writer*] (2015) 310–11, 314
Morgado, André F. 311
   A Vida Oculta de Fernando Pessoa [*The Occult Life of Fernando Pessoa*] (2016) Figure 17.2 (312), 310–11, 314
Morgan, Natasha (NM) 267, 272–73
   censorship 276–77
   feminist politics 275
   feminist theatre group Holocaust 275
   Holocaust 275
   international solidarity campaign 278–79
   interview for 'Remembering the Translation of *New Portuguese Letters* to the Stage' 273
   mnemonic practices 280
   New Portuguese Letters 274
   The Other Side of the Underneath (1972) 276
   post-memory of genocide and imperialism 275
   Room 276
   US (1966) 275
   Women on Trial play 277, 279
Morgan, Robin (RM) 267
   'International Feminism: A Call for Support of the Three Marias' 272, 279–80
Mozambican Portuguese (MP) 163
Mozambique 3, 47
   civil war 4
   Goans 152
   indigenous languages 3
   Portuguese as second language 162
   Vernacular Mozambican Portuguese 163
   war of independence (1964–75) 4
MP *see* Mozambican Portuguese (MP)
MPLA 85–86

MR-8, Revolutionary Movement
 October 8th 249, 256
multidirectional memory 270–73, 277, 279
multilingualism 152
Mundo que o Português Criou, O [*The World the Portuguese Created*] by Gilberto Freyre (1940) 45
 see also Freyre, Gilberto
My Fair Lady Chapter 10 (183–99)

'N na nega bedju' 77–84
 see also Schwarz, José Carlos
narrativization of ethnographic encounters 234
nation state 6, 19, 24
 beyond the borders 19
 boundaries 6
national and transnational see transnational
national identity 57, 96
nationalist propaganda 222, 256
Neuville, Josephina 286, 289, 297
 Memórias da Minha Vida: recordações das minhas viagens [Memoirs of My Life: Recollections of My Journeys] (1864) Chapter 16 (285–98), 292, 294
 Memórias da Minha Vida: recordações das minhas viagens [Memoirs of My Life: Recollections of My Journeys] (1864) 285
New Portuguese Letters Chapter 15 (267–81), 267, 277
 banning 268
 censorship 276
 collective perceptions 267
 international solidarity campaign 267
Nietzsche, Friedrich 315, 327
NM see Morgan, Natasha (NM)

Noll, João Gilberto 341
Novas Cartas Portuguesas (1972) see New Portuguese Letters
NPL see New Portuguese Letters
nun Mariana Alcoforado
 Lettres Portugaises 269
 see also New Portuguese Letters

O que é isso campanheiro? [*Four Days in September*] (1997) see Barreto, Bruno
official language 11, 151
Olympic Games 2016 201–02, 215

Pacific 60
PAIGC 78, 81
Palmares 131, 141
pardos 154
Partido Social Democrata (PSD) 110
Pato, Bulhão 288, 296
Pessoa, Fernando Chapter 17 (299–316), 91, 313
 Campos, Álvaro de (heteronym) 91, 306–08
 great national poet 300
 heteronymic authorship 303
 literary reception in Brazil 308
 literary reception in France 315
 Livro do Desassossego [*The Book of Disquiet*] 299, 306, 314
 metanarrativity of his texts 315
 'Minha pátria é a língua portuguesa' ['My fatherland is the Portuguese language'] 299
 Soares, Bernardo (heteronym) 313
 transnational 316
 see also Campos, Álvaro de
Petrobrás, Brazilian state-controlled oil company 253
photobooks Chapter 13 (233–48)
 allochronism 234
 colonial enterprise 233
 family photo album 233

    hybrid textual practices 236
    mobility 234
    narrativization of ethnographic encounters 234
    photographic practices 233
    relationship between texts and images 235–36
    visuality 237, 246
photographic archive 238
photography
    autobiographic 247
    ethnographic turn 242
    powerful temporal device 240
    spirit photography 241
pidginization 161
    see also Creole languages
Pinto, Fernão Mendes 38, 40, 168
    Peregrinação [*Peregrination*] 40
pirates 57–69
Police Pacifying Unit *see* UPP
popular music *see* urban popular music
Portugal
    1940 Exposição do Mundo Português [Exposition of the Portuguese World] 228
    Africans 152
    Anglo-Portuguese relations in the early modern period 57–69
    anti-austerity protests 111
    assassination of the king in 1910 302
    austerity 115, 118, 121, 123, 126
    borders 169, 223
    Carnation Revolution (1974) 99, 120, 123, 189, 194
    censorship 193, 222, 268, 276, 281
    colonial war 268
    debt crisis 124
    Defesa Civil 222
    dictatorship 188, 269
    empire *see* Portuguese empire

Estado Novo [New State] 8, 96, 99, 134, 143, 188, 227–28, 232
fado 317
film industry 112
Gazeta de Portugal 287
Holocaust 225, 227
Instituto Camões 6
literary culture/history 183, 197, 268, 285, 288, 297, 300
mapping 25
Minho 49, 54
nation state 4, 111, 268, 285
national anthem 2
national flag 8
nationalist propaganda 222, 224, 228
Polícia da Vigilância e Defesa do Estado (PVDE) [Police for the Vigilance and Defence of the State] 225
PSD coalition 111, 125
refugees, exiles, and spies 222
reinós (people born in Portugal) 25
retornados 134
Salazarism 148, 224, 227, 229
Sebastianism 309
'small nation' 112
status of women 194, 285
    see also women in Portuguese society
territory 25–26, 169
theatre 183, 190
Trás-os-Montes 49
twentieth-century emigration 326
women's oppression 268
World War II 221, 223
see also Portuguese empire
'Portuguesa, A' 2
    see also Mendonça, Henrique Lopes
Portuguese 3
    academic discipline 6
    as colonizers 43, 47

Creole languages 3
empire *see* Portuguese empire
as a language 3–4
Portuguese artists in Britain
Cutileiro, João 96
Rego, Paula 96–97
Vieira, João 96
see also Santos, Bartolomeu Cid dos
Portuguese empire Chapter 1 (23–41), 4, 8, 129, 159, 167
1940 Exposição do Mundo Português [Exposition of the Portuguese World] 228
in Africa 135–36, 143, 145, 147, 285
in Africa and Asia 47, 167
anticolonial imagination 54
anticolonial independence struggle 72, 88, 268
assimilados 163
colonial enterprise 149, 152, 285
colonial hierarchy 364
colonial ideology 48, 143
compared to other Western empires 44
diasporas 149
'Discoveries' 167
expansion 40, 150
global Portugueseness 53
harmonious colonial rule 134
hegemonic imperial power 308
hybrid identities 165
hybrid languages 165
imperial aspirations 44
imperial past 23, 44
imperialism 129
independence (2002) 129
intra-Asian commercial network 159
language of colonization 137
Lusotropicalism 43, 363
migration 149, 160

miscegenation 44
settlements 141, 159
social networks 153, 165
Sociedade de Geografia 143
in South America 167
trade 159
transfer of Portuguese court to Rio de Janeiro 1808 207
Portuguese expansion 40
Portuguese Guinea 47, 52, 55
see also Guinea-Bissau
Portuguese language 7, 148, 167, 169, 177, 339
Africa 150
Brazil 142
Comunidade dos Países de Língua Portuguesa (CPLP) 8–9, 147
East Timor 150
language of colonization 146
Macau 150
official language status 11, 72
Ponto de Encontro. Portuguese as a World Language 10
social networks 156
social status 182
sounding Jewish 181
speakers 150
teaching 10
trade 167
as transnational language Chapter 8 (149–65)
vernacular/national languages 73
post-dictatorship cinema 252, 255, 262, 265
post-dictatorship culture 266
post-memory 225, 230, 275
Holocaust 275
prazos 163
privateering expeditions 59, 64
PSD *see* Partido Social Democrata
Pusich, Antónia Gertrudes 287, 290, 296
PVDE *see* Polícia da Vigilância e

382 *Index*

Defesa do Estado (PVDE) [Police for the Vigilance and Defence of the State]
Pygmalion Chapter 10 (183–99)
  dialects 186
  non-standard language 187

'Que se Lixe a Troika' ['Screw the Troika'] 111, 117
queer activism and protests 337–38, 340, 350
  HIV/AIDS 342, 348
Queer theory Chapter 19 (337–51), 337–38, 350
  queer transnational theory 351
  transnational 341
Queirós, José Maria Eça de 286
  Os Maias (1888) 287, 297

refugees, Lisbon, World War II 222
reinós (people born in Portugal) 25
retornados 134
Riggs, Marlon, *Tongues Untied* (1989) 338
Rigney, Ann 236, 270, 285
Rio de Janeiro 140, 191, 201, 205, 207–08
  capital of Portuguese Empire (1808–21) 207
  Copacabana beach 256
  favelas 207
  'Garota de Ipanema' ['The Girl from Ipanema'] 256
  Maracanã stadium 256
  military occupation 207
  Olympic Games 2016 216
  urban transformations 208
  World Cup 2014 216
  see also RioOnWatch
RioOnWatch 215–17
RM *see* Morgan, Robin (RM)
Roberts, Henry, ballads 67–69
Rosa, Chris da 319

guitarra portuguesa 323
  trip to Lisbon 321
  see also Judith and Holofernes (J&H)
Rothberg, Michael 272, 275, 277
  Multidirectional Memory: Remembering the Holocaust in the Age of Decolonization (2009) 270

Salazar, António de Oliveira, speeches 228
Sand, George 286, 293
  Histoire de ma vie [*Story of My Life*] (1854–55) 293
Santana e Vasconcelos, Jacinto Augusto de 288, 297
Santos, Bartolomeu Cid dos Chapter 5 (91–108), 100–03
  Africa Discovered (1981) Figure 5.5 (105), 104, 107
  Aleph (1978) 99
  The Confession (1963) 99
  Homenagem [*Tribute*] (1975) 99
  Homenagem a Cesário [*Homage to Cesário*] (1985) Figure 5.4 (102), 103
  Para Que Não Voltem É Presciso Não Esquecer [*It must Not Be Forgotten So That They Don't Return*] (1976) 99
  Stanley (1980) 104, 106–07
  stone panels at Entrecampos metro station Figure 5.1 (92), Figure 5.2 (94), Figure 5.3 (101), 103
Santos, Irene Ramalho 302–03
  Atlantic Poets: Fernando Pessoa' Turn in Anglo-American Modernism (2003) 301
Santos, José Eduardo dos 85
São Paulo, street protests in June 2013 206

São Tomé 47, 142
    Creole languages 157
saudade 323–24
SBP *see* Standard Brazilian Portuguese (SBP)
Schiller, Nina Glick *see* Glick Schiller, Nina
Schleiermacher, Friedrich 48–49
    'On the Different Methods of Translating' 48
Schoene, Berthold 357–58
Schwarz, José Carlos 71, 77–81
    imprisonment 78
    'N na nega bedju' 71, 77–81
Sebastianism 309
Shakespeare, William 190, 195
    As You Like It 62
Shaw, George Bernard 190–91
    Estado Novo [New State] 188
    Pygmalion Chapter 10 (183–99)
Shaw, Lisa 251–52, 254
    cinema of globalization 260
Silva, Inocêncio da 288–89
Slade School of Fine Art, London 95, 97–98
slave 139, 154
    African slaves 160
    Chinese slaves 160
slave diasporas 150
slave trade 130, 296
slavery, photobooks 234
Soares, Bernardo (heteronym) *see* Pessoa, Fernando
Sob céus estranhos [*Under Strange Skies*] by Daniel Blaufuks (2002) Figure 12.1 (226), 224, 227–28, 230–31
social networks 151–53, 156, 163, 165
socioeconomic inequality 72, 86, 205, 221, 340
Sousa Santos, Boaventura de 260
space 24
    city 32

early modern Lusophone writing 38
    empire 32
    Lusophone 6–7
    navigating 36
    place 30
    spatial political forms 32
    translational space Chapter 19 (337–51)
Spanish Armada 60, 65
spatial political forms
    cities 32
    empire 32
spatial turn 41
spatiality Part I (23–126)
    European 35
spatialization of time 235
Sri Lanka 26, 35, 39, 159
    first Portuguese map 30
Standard Brazilian Portuguese (SBP) 154
    see also Vernacular Brazilian Portuguese (VBP)
street protests in June 2013
    activist graffiti Figure 11.1 (213)
    Brazil 203
    Domínio Público [Public Domain] project 214
    international press coverage 208
    São Paulo 206
    transnationalization of local/localization of the transnational 208
    Turkey 205
subjectivity Part IV (283–385)

Tabu (2012) 110
    see also Gomes, Miguel
'Tanto' 86–88
    see also Frazão, Aline
Tavares, Camilo, *Dia que Durou 21 Anos* [*The Day that Lasted*

21 Years] (2012) Figure 14.1 (254), Figure 14.2 (259), 249, 258, 262, 266
Tcharafna (2014) see Mohallem, Gui
Teixeira, Rodrigo 355–56
   see also Amores Expressos (AE) project
temporality Part III (219–81), 235–36, 242, 244
   disjunctive temporalities of the transnational 248
   intersecting temporalities of transnationalism 239
theatre Chapter 9 (167–82)
   see also Vicente, Gil
Three Marias 267, 272, 276, 281
   censorship 276, 281
   interaction between authors and international audiences 271
   international solidarity campaign 267, 279
   trial 277
   Women on Trial play 277
trade 35
   Indian Ocean 159
   trans-Sahara trade 138
   see also Atlantic slave trade
transcultural 7–8
transcultural memory 107
transcultural methodology 96
   see also transnational methodology
transcultural practices 96
transculturation 47, 51
   Brazil 51
   linguistic 52
translation Chapter 10 (183–99), 55, 183, 185, 190, 192–93, 195, 198–99, 212, 214, 342, 347
   censorship 193
   concept in cultural anthropology 46
   culturally mediated activity 184

dialects 184, 191, 197–98 *see also* dialects
discourse standardization 192, 197
intercultural 46, 48
linguistic hierarchies 199
My Fair Lady Chapter 10 (183–99)
partial translation 210–14
Pygmalion Chapter 10 (183–99)
retranslation 185
symbolic capital 191, 197
translating Lusophone space 45
see also Schleiermacher, Friedrich; Venuti, Lawrence
Translation Studies, discipline 184
transnational 5–6, Figure 17.2 (312), 45, 52, 57, 71, 88, 100, 103, 108, 112, 126, 167, 169–70, 177, 198, 201–04, 229, 249, 252, 254, 265, 268, 305, 316, 351
   border-crossing Figure 12.2 (229)
   cinema 250
   circulation of American cultural products 203
   commercial transnationalism 266
   culture of memory 250
   digital culture 203
   disjunctive temporalities 248
   documentary 204
   feminist politics 274
   flows of influence 184, 199
   forced migration 238
   mapping of 248
   methodology 7, 96, 198
   mobility 177, 234, 237–38
   transnational documentary 204
   transnational networks 88
   transnational turn 5, 41, 263
   universal 313
   women 287 *see also* women in Portuguese society
   see also transnational dialogue; transnational turn
transnational communication 183

transnational communities 165, 264
transnational diasporas 150
transnational documentary 218
  Domínio Público [Public Domain] project 204
transnational individuals, language practices 151
transnational influences 133, 137, 229
transnational lens 17, 266, 285
transnational memories 265–66
Transnational Modern Languages. A Handbook, edited by Jenny Burns and Derek Duncan 5–6
transnational organizations 264
transnational social networks 153, 164
Transnational Spanish Studies, edited by Catherine Davies and Rory O'Bryen 6
transnational turn 5, 41, 263, 297
transnational writer 300
transnationalism 11, 114, 133, 149, 266, 304
  commercial transnationalism 255
  as a historical concept 19
  intersecting temporalities 239
  Lusophone transnationalism 150
  Portuguese Studies 9–10
trans-Sahara trade 138
travelling memory 224, 264–66, 270, 272
  see also Erll, Astrid
travelogues 33
Troika 110–11, 116–17, 119
Twitter 215–17

United States of America
  American Ambassador to Brazil 249, 253, 258
  American imperialism 275
  American neo-imperialism 260
  Black Panthers 256
  CIA in Latin America 256
  declassified documents 258
  foreign policy in the Cold War 253, 256, 258, 260
  Luso-American community 319
  support for regime change in Brazil 258
  see also Central Intelligence Agency (CIA) (United States)
universal values of freedom and democracy 260
UPP 202
  pacification scheme 209
urban popular music 71
  Angola 71
  Brazil 85
  Cape Verde 71
  Guinea-Bissau 71
urban transformations 201
  reliance of textual information 212

VAP *see* Vernacular Angolan Portuguese (VAP)
VBP *see* Vernacular Brazilian Portuguese (VBP)
Ventura, Susana 310
  Eu, Fernando Pessoa em quadrinhos [*I, Fernando Pessoa in a Comic Strip*] (2013) Figure 17.1 (311), 310, 314, 316
Venuti, Lawrence *see* translation
Verde, Cesário 91, 100
  'O Sentimento dum Occidental' ['The Feeling of a Westerner'] 100
Verdier, Catarina 310
  As aventuras de Fernando Pessoa, Escritor Universal [*The Adventures of Fernando Pessoa, Universal Writer*] (2015) 310–11, 314
Vernacular Angolan Portuguese (VAP) 158, 162–63

Vernacular Brazilian Portuguese (VBP) 154, 156, 158, 162–63
Vernacular Mozambican Portuguese 162
vernacular/national languages 163
Vicente, Gil 131, 133, 167, 169, 174, 182, 190
    Auto das fadas [*The Farce of the Fairies*] 170–72, 179, 181
    Auto de Fama 169
    Frágoa de amor [*The Forge of Love*] 177, 181
Vieira, António 130–32, 135
voyages 57–58, 106
    Cabot, Sebastian 58
    Drake, Francis 59
    East India Company 65
Voz Feminina, A (1868–69) 287

'When Drones Leave the Hive' see Judith and Holofernes (J&H)
Wimmer, Andreas 6
    'Methodological Nationalism and Beyond: Nation-State Building, Migration and the Social Sciences' 6
Wolof 144–45
women *see* feminist politics
women in Portuguese society 285, 294
    domestic violence 295
    domesticity 294
    female otherness 285
    foreign feminine body 292
    intellectual history 298
    life writing 285
    politics of exclusion Chapter 16 (285–98)
    O Progresso (1869) 287
    sexual abuse 295
    transnational women 287
    A Voz Feminina (1868–69) 287, 298
women's oppression, politics of exclusion 285
Wood, Francisca 287, 298
Woolf, Virginia, *A Room of One's Own* (1929) 276
working class 87
world, cross-cultural image of the world 34
World Cup 2014 201–02, 216
    ticket prices 217
world music 72, 74, 88
    role of postcolonial Lisbon 89
    traditional West African music 83
    see also Évora, Cesária; Gomes, Karyna; Schwarz, José Carlos
World War II, Portugal 223
written archive 270

Yoruba 154
YouTube 209

Zamir, Shamoon 233, 235, 246